MONASTERIES
OF WESTERN EUROPE

WOLFGANG BRAUNFELS

MONASTERIES OF WESTERN EUROPE

THE ARCHITECTURE OF THE ORDERS

PRINCETON UNIVERSITY PRESS

TRANSLATED BY ALASTAIR LAING

Frontispiece: the cloister of Fontenay

THIS EDITION © 1972 THAMES AND HUDSON LTD, LONDON

PUBLISHED IN THE USA BY PRINCETON UNIVERSITY PRESS
PRINCETON, NEW JERSEY

FILMSET IN GREAT BRITAIN BY FILMTYPE SERVICES LIMITED, SCARBOROUG

LCC 73-2472   ISBN 0-691-03896-1   ISBN 0-691-00313-0 pbk.

First Princeton Paperback Printing, 1980

Contents

Foreword

This book has grown out of a lecture that I gave in 1964 in the Department of Architecture of Aachen Technical College. I have carried about with me scattered thoughts on the subject for more than thirty years. They go back to the time when I was a student. The material was supplemented by papers read in a seminar of the Art Historical Faculty of Munich University in 1966. I was able to draw on a whole series of contributions by my student helpers for ideas, arguments and evidence. I would especially like to thank my junior colleagues, Dr Rudolf Kuhn and Dr Albrecht Haenlein, and even more especially Frau Dagmar Kierzkowski, who went through, and supplemented, parts of the manuscript. In addition to this, Frau Kierzkowski saw to the mass of transcriptions of monastery plans. The transcriptions of the plans of Cluny are due to Anja Bühring, the plan of Ottobeuren to Dieter Schneider. The English edition has been considerably expanded in comparison with the German one. I am most grateful to Mr Alastair Laing, the translator, who checked innumerable details and suggested alterations, and to Mr Ian Sutton and Mrs Vanessa Whinney, who attended with great care to the choice of illustrations and their captions.

The question of the choice of material was one of the central considerations in composing the text. It was governed by the need, which I overstepped, to keep this book within the limits of the series in which it originally appeared, and by the urge to make a vast, unwieldy whole graspable. For there were in the West between the fifth and the eighteenth century altogether around 40,000 monasteries. According to my reckoning we can form a picture of the structural shape of at least 5,000 of these. Any choice from such profusion cannot avoid being to some extent arbitrary. Such prodigality is inimical to a history which aims at tidy classification. One must also accept the risk of provoking criticism by short descriptions of groups of buildings on which there are already thorough, but often contradictory, works – I am thinking of monasteries like Cluny, Mont-Saint-Michel, San Francesco in Assisi or the Escorial. It has been particularly hard for me to omit isolated findings which I believe to be original, in favour of more important, yet familiar, accounts. Some of these I hope to be able to publish in other contexts.

The starting-point of this investigation is the question of the correlation of Order and Organization. The Rule of an Order prescribes a way of life and worship, to which in all artistically vigorous periods the architectural organization of the monastery must correspond. Inward discipline is manifested externally as planning. In this, in the course of the centuries, the various Orders, like styles in art, successively took the lead. The foundation of a new Order was not only a creative response to an educational mission, but an avowal of a new way of life and a new style of worship. This style of worship also imprinted itself upon works of art and architecture. For every worthy monastery represented a body by which life according to a Rule was first made possible, then rationalized, and finally symbolized. That monasteries were themselves works of art derives partly from the belief that any earthly happiness and all heavenly bliss could only flourish in an ordered world built on the principles of the Kingdom of Heaven. Every good monastery strives to embody the *Civitas Dei*. This persists as the reason behind the extravagance of the princely abbeys of the Baroque.

Monasteries in all periods devoted their greatest efforts to the construction of their churches. This book's title is misleading, inasmuch as these are not described, or at least only insofar as they influenced the disposition of monastic buildings as a whole. If great monasteries can be compared to towns – as they are expressly in Chapter 9 – then in this book churches are only dealt with for their significance in town-planning. The kernel of this account is monastic architecture in the restricted sense of the buildings and sequence of rooms in which monks, nuns and friars lived. I have pursued the formative forces on the physical framework fostering the *vita communis*, to which all Orders in their different ways aspired.

The choice of the documents in the appendix and their reproduction in both Latin and English needs a special word. Not one religious Rule nor any medieval author expressly prescribed how monasteries should be built. There are only hints and isolated prohibitions, and sometimes the description of some organism seen as a prototype (Document No. VI). Attention was meant to be drawn to life in the buildings, not to the buildings themselves. The extracts we present obscure the fact that monastic architecture did not lay claim to the importance ascribed to it in a literary description – however much it may have been appreciated. Architectural feats or constructional specifications mostly receive only casual and incidental mention. In the last analysis most of our information derives from works of edification and education. We may indeed allow that the creators of monasteries were just as clearly aware of their architectural beauty as ourselves. The monks loved their home. But they never spoke of it. Neither projects, new building nor rebuilding were supposed to distract the monk from his true vocation. When Clairvaux had to be built afresh, some of the brethren begged St Bernard to come down to earth at least for a moment to attend to their want of room (Document No. XII). This was when the classic Cistercian monastery arose. In each case the supreme achievements were those, like Odilo's Cluny, Bernard's Clairvaux or Guigo's Chartreuse, that were only undertaken as a means to a vocational end.

W.B.

I

Planning and the Rules

Whoever sets foot in some peaceful haven of the Cistercians, whoever comes upon a scene of ruins in the snow, a church choir forgotten in the woods, a monastery perched on the Pyrenean cliffs, is moved by them. Solemnity, calm and dignity speak from the stones. Some part of everyone knows the longing for unconditional self-commitment, which gave these works birth; renouncing the world, living in an isolated community, in which each day is to be imbued with special meaning by that ultimate Truth of daring ideal, that through unceasing meditation upon God and his incessant praise one's self may be forgotten and yet found. The monastic impulse is common to many religions – Islam, Buddhism, and both the Greek and Latin Churches. The monastic ideal represents one of humanity's truly imposing designs for living. Strong natures have repeatedly striven to vest this idea with a form suited to their time and culture. The spiritual attitude of the West is distinguished from that of the East in that here new Orders arose each century, taking over from one another like artistic styles. For those fleeing the world could still not escape their time. Thus the buildings of the Cistercians and the Cluniacs were Romanesque, which could embody both the dignity of the Abbots of Cluny and the austerity of St Bernard. The Franciscans and Dominicans, each in their own way, imparted lyricism and logicality to the Gothic style. Mannerism found new formulations in Jesuit architecture; Baroque worldliness, in the princely abbeys of the seventeenth and eighteenth centuries. Monasteries became interpretations of the Rule according to the changing spirit of the times.

Innumerable such Rules have been transmitted, just as there are and have been countless Orders. Monks become leaders of their fellows by composing or revising rules of conduct for their brethren. The Rules are the summit of pedagogic effort in the Middle Ages. Five of these collections of precepts have a special status: the Rule of St Basil the Great, which governs the life of almost all monks of the Orthodox Church; the Rules of SS. Augustine, Benedict and Francis, which were to be the models for most others in the West; and finally the Constitutions of the Society of Jesus, constantly revised by Ignatius Loyola until at his death in 1556 he could regard them as final. The Carthusian Statutes were a special development. These Rules underwent manifold interpretation and supplementation. In certain monasteries customs were established – *consuetudines*, as they were called – that became binding as interpretations of the Rule for later generations. Relaxations alternate with greater strictness – and ultimately it is the strict Orders that show a greater capacity for survival. The Trappists are an example. Without a Rule no monastery can endure. Its spirit governs the attitude of the monks; it also defines the characteristics of their art. We shall frequently have occasion to speak of the conflict inherent in the contradiction between a vow of poverty and the desire to give visible and hence artistic expression to the means by which it was practised. This book could scarcely have been written had not that will to form in many monasteries proved the stronger.

The Greek monks, who lived according to St Basil's Rule, built magnificent monastery complexes. There were, and still are, monastic villages and monastic towns. Whole monastic provinces are known, like the Egyptian Thebaid, and monastic states, like Mount Athos. Yet the East developed no norms for its monasteries. The visitor to Athos senses that the monks were challenged by its remoteness and apartness, by its idyllically sheltered situation and virtual inaccessibility on rocky heights, to the creative mastery of these situations. The Greeks manifested their individuality in ever fresh combinations of ever similar architectural and decorative forms. It was left to the Latin sense of order to evolve really programmatic monasteries. From the tail-end of the seventh century Benedictine abbots attempted to shape their monasteries into perfect instruments for the realization of the Rule. Firmly articulated traditions grew up. Down the centuries the intention was always to meet the same old requirements and at the same time to take the particular features of the site into account; whether it was a sheltered plain like the Reichenau peninsula in Lake Constance, or a conical protrusion from the sea like Mont-Saint-Michel.

The stipulations of the 66th chapter of the *Regula Sancti Benedicti*, that are always taken to be the point of departure for the Western monastic system, are equally valid for a Basilian monastery in the East: 'Whenever possible the monastery should be so laid out that everything essential, that is to say water, mills, garden and workshops for the plying of the various crafts, is found within the monastery walls' (Document No. 1, Ch. 66). Athos too aspires to self-sufficiency. The demand for silence applies similarly to all monasteries. Basil counsels his monks to practise handicrafts, but discourages those that make a noise. However, in a comparison of an early Basilian with a Benedictine monastery it is conspicuous that in the former each monk or nun lives alone in some hut, cave or arbour. The same is true of the early monasteries in Egypt, Syria, Spain or Ireland. At the common meal- or service-times they hurry together to a central point from all corners of their town or monastery. A centripetal coming-together is succeeded by a centrifugal drawing apart again. In contrast to this, everything in a Benedictine monastery is done communally. The monks sleep, pray, read and eat together, and wherever possible they work together. In place of single monks streaming together or apart, one sees the measured tread of processions through the monastery, according to a precisely fixed daily routine. The Benedictine layout grew out of the desire to keep the course of these processions as short as possible. When we come to defend the thesis that the Benedictine cloister, the heart of the monastery, found its definitive position in Northern Europe, it will be supported by the observation that there alone was it necessary to protect these paths from the inclemency of the weather. We shall also discuss the fact that in some monasteries, like the Carolingian St Riquier or Centula, the processional paths were deliberately long, since special prayers and litanies were prescribed for each of them.

None of the Rules explicitly refers to works of art or architecture, though the Benedictine Rule does name a great number of the essential monastery buildings (Document No. 1). They talk of the life of the monks, of the course of their day, their prayers, their work, their meals and clothes, of their attitude to one another, to their superiors, to the world and women, to possessions, money and honour. But whoever reflects upon their spirit – and many conventual precepts are devoted to meditation on the spirit of the Rule – is forced to consider the optimum framework for the daily round to be realized as exactly as the Rule demands. Numerous scattered instructions on this survive from later monks' synods. The perfect life called for the perfect monastery. Fresh attempts were constantly made by large communities to achieve this functional perfection. In no other sphere of non-ecclesiastical architecture in the Middle Ages, except the military, was the problem of the relation of form to function so resolutely tackled. The monastery, independently of its church, emerged as the one branch of secular art to combine the purest idealism with the strictest functionalism.

I must again refer to the difference between the Latin and the Greek or even the Irish-Celtic constitutions. The Rules of St Basil or St Columba are monks' Rules. They contain instructions and admonitions for the single monk. Columba could thus put his ideas in the form of a Penitential, a table of punishment for every imaginable offence, as a monument to the Irish yearning for asceticism. St Benedict's Rule is by contrast centred on the abbot. It concerns itself with the conduct of the *Abbas*, or father, toward the monks, and instructs him in his role as guide. Whereas in the East we are enchanted by the idyllic picture of each monk separately working on the stone- or woodwork of his hut, or tending his garden, in the West everything depends on the abbot, who organizes down to the last detail. At no other point in the history of architecture does the client so overshadow the builder, and we often find abbots themselves active as builders. The St Gall Utopia (see p. 43) even specifies the simples in the herb-garden. Whoever actually designed the Benedictine monasteries of St Michael at Hildesheim or St Denis outside Paris, Bishop Bernward and Abbot Suger regarded themselves as the architects in charge: building was one of their duties. Their imaginative grasp of planning was challenged by the task. The monastery as a whole was their work, their *Abbey*. There was even a provision in the Rule directed against the self-assurance of the artist-monk: 'If there are craftsmen in the monastery, they should exercise their craft – if the abbot allows it – with all modesty. If one of them is overweening on account of his skill in his craft, believing in his usefulness to the monastery, let him be removed from this activity. He shall not apply himself to it again unless he has humbled himself, and the abbot given him leave'. (Document No. 1, Ch. 57.)

Basil the Great ordained repeated intervals of prayer. St Augustine's Rule allocated definite prayers to the prescribed offices. Benedict went a step further. The whole course of the day was divided into hours of prayer, reading, work, eating, meditation and sleep. In his Rule many of these activities were allotted distinct buildings. To the organization of the day in time corresponded its organization by place, and the perfect monastery could only emerge from their complete agreement. Each activity was to take place in its appointed room, which was to be used for no other purpose, whether this was sleeping, eating, working, meditating, washing, or even speaking.

Reflection on the spirit of the Rule led to the attempt to make each building's appearance commensurate with its functional status. The church – the House of God and the place where the Gospel was read – had to be the largest, richest, and indeed the dominant building in the composition of the monastery. If the monastery is seen as a well thought-out workshop (Document No. 1, Ch. 4), then the church is the place where the 'end-product', God's praise, is delivered. The section of the Rule prescribing the punishments for any error, failure, or false note in singing the psalms or the lesson (Document No. 1, Ch. 45) reveals the intense concern in a monastery for the absolute perfection of the end-product. There is also a concern that every activity throughout the long progression of the day through the monastery should occur with the same dignity and perfection; particularly as eating, washing, and working were all invested with a higher meaning – a symbolic importance in the Divine Order of things. Buildings and works of art were to manifest this symbolism.

The Rule was the most important object of monastic meditation after Holy Scripture. It was incumbent on the monks to read it 'diligently', day in, day out; always the same sentences. Their simplicity, clarity and order were to govern the conduct and style of monastic existence. Once the abbey churches had been ever more richly and artistically decorated for worship and for the lessons from Holy Scripture, the need was soon felt for a secondary place devoted to the Book of the Rule, and readings from it to the assembled monks. After the eleventh century most Benedictine monasteries had a chapter-house. It takes its name from the chapters of the Rule that were read there. Until the Franciscan and Dominican houses of the fifteenth century, it was second only to the church in artistic display. Those among the monks and patrons of the monastery who did not have the right to be buried in the church sought their grave in the chapter-house. In its costliness and decoration the building stood midway between profane and sacred architecture; and in the course of its development it became more and more of a chapel. Even Brunelleschi's Pazzi Chapel is a chapter-house.

St Augustine had ordained: 'When ye go to table, so hearken till ye rise up from it to the wonted lessons without noise or disputation; for not merely with the mouth shall ye take your nourishment, but with your ears also shall ye hunger after the Word of God.' Through these admonitions, taken over by the Benedictines, eating itself became a symbol of spiritual processes. It was early associated with the sacramental event of the Lord's Supper. This association must have suggested that the third place in the hierarchy of monastery buildings should go to the refectory, initiating a development that finally culminated in Leonardo's *Last Supper*, which through the use of perspective so dissolves the end wall of the Dominican refectory of Sta Maria delle Grazie in Milan, that Christ and the Twelve seem actually present. But even the fountain at which the monks washed, the cloister in which they meditated and read, and the dormitory, were buildings that could catch the eye with a holy message, whether through their form or their decoration – through capitals, windows, paintings, or even patterns on the floor. Whoever reflects on the importance that was attributed in a good monastery to hospitality and care of the sick, will also comprehend why in the St Gall plan or in Cluny the hostel and infirmary were exceptionally richly decorated.

In the 31st Chapter of his Rule Benedict speaks of the duties of the cellarer, the steward of the monastery: 'Let him handle all implements and goods of the monastery like sacred altar-vessels. Let him regard nothing as indifferent' (Document No. 1, Ch. 31). This precept was the origin of the efforts devoted in good monasteries to having the finest possible furniture and utensils. Here, monks are charged to see something hallowed in the everyday, because it belongs to the monastery. An ethical approach to things is demanded, inspired partly by aesthetic considerations.

As in St Augustine's Rule of almost a century earlier, the insistence on daily prayer stands at the heart of the Benedictine Rule. 'Seven times a day will I praise thee' read the monks in Psalm 119. Seven times they assembled for prayer, from before daybreak until dusk. Benedict specified exactly what prayers should be said hour by hour on workdays and Sundays, what in winter and what in the summer months, and what in Lent (Bibl. No. 12, pp. 168-173). And for a millennium and more this was adhered to. The psalms of David are the core of all the Offices from Matins to Compline. They are among the oldest songs of humanity. Many of them were already sung as royal hymns before the Pharaohs. According to Benedict's indications all 150 should be sung at least once in a week; many of them were uttered daily in the community – at least fourteen at Matins immediately after awakening, and two or three when it was already dark. Next to the solemn simplicity, humility and clarity of the Rule, it was the passionate, often obscure images of this continuous conversation of the psalmist with his God, his entreaties and his complaints, that set the tone for the spiritual life of a monastery. There are dirges and songs of joy. From the depths of abject remorse they mount to the heights of presumption – to the feeling of being chosen, safe-guarded, rescued, marked out even, from all others.

Rule and Psalter are the two poles of the forces moulding Western monasti-cism, its thoughts, feelings, and imaginative world. They are also the taproot for extensive areas of monastic art. The liturgy, which alone might resound through the silence of a monastery, fused the intensity of the divine soliloquy from the Orient with the rigorous discipline of the Rule from Rome. The Rule sets out the why and where, the Psalter the what and how. Builders were confronted with the task of creating places fit for both together.

2

The Beginnings

In 529, Benedict (*c.* 480–before 553), an anchorite from the Umbrian Nursia, founded an abbey on the old military way from Rome to Naples, on Monte Cassino, where the monks lived according to a precisely fixed Rule. In that same year Justinian suppressed the School of Wisdom in Athens. A page was turned in the spiritual history of mankind. Monastery succeeded Academy; and monasteries soon saw themselves compelled to take over its functions. They became the schools of the Middle Ages. Monte Cassino was a beginning; but it also stood at the culmination of a development that was more than three centuries old.

EGYPTIAN MONKS AND ANCHORITES
There have been anchorites since the earliest days of Christianity – hermits who have withdrawn from any human contact for their own sanctification. Many non-Christian religions have known this, the greatest temptation for monachism, as did Old Testament Judaism. The yearning to forsake everything, to surrender up to limitless meditation upon God, and thereby to accept living conditions whose audacious asceticism barely ensured mere existence, to flee into the desert, to take refuge in ravines, to experience utter solitude on rocky islands in the sea, to withstand burning sun and nocturnal chill atop the capital of a Roman column for decades on end, to shut oneself away in dark, dank cachettes – such were the forms of existence through which, throughout the Middle Ages and sporadically right into the nineteenth century (and in India to this day) the longed-for hereafter, an undisturbed dialogue with God, was to be forced down into the here and now, at once dissipating and affirming the sense of self. There were retreats of exquisite exclusiveness. Columns, for instance. Up there one could be quite alone, nearer to and more surrounded by heaven than in any other place. For Simon the Syrian, who came to Trier in the eleventh century, the indestructible stonework of the Roman Porta Nigra was an irresistible invitation to have himself walled up in it for the rest of his life. The huge blocks, piled on top of one another as a show of might against the thrusting Germanic tribes, were given by the anchorites an interpretation more comprehensible to the Middle Ages. They were intended as a conspicuous and effective shield against the distractions of the world for the saint's unbroken communion with God. The recluse who had built herself a cell on the Ponte alle Grazie, in which she could exist wrapped in meditation on the edge of the throng, was one of the sights of medieval Florence. In the thirteenth and fourteenth centuries there was no lack of applicants for this position, whose activity the city envisaged as a guarantee of God's constant involvement in the fate of the common weal.

Eremitism, and with it retreat, is one of the roots of monasticism. Retreat could turn into an epidemic. St Anthony set off such a movement around 305, after he had lived totally withdrawn for about twenty years in the desert on the east bank of the Nile. By the end of the fourth century about 5,000 of his followers are supposed to have lived with rigorous asceticism, partly alone and partly in small groups, beside Mount Nitria in Egypt (now Wadi Natron). We have moving accounts, legends and pictures of their everyday life; both monuments to an archaic faith in God and record feats of self-mortification. The hermit idyll was to become an ideal of the old world. In later times too the appeal of the sanctity of an anchorite repeatedly drew numerous disciples into colonies round his cell, out of which monasteries often evolved. For the desire grew to impose a greater degree of regulation upon communal living. Such regulations for the *vita communis* are the second root of monasticism. Organization produced Orders.

The Egyptian Pachomius seems to have been the first to have founded a monastery, around 320. This was near Tabernisi, opposite Denderah on the right bank of the Nile: the monks prayed, worked and ate together; each was to learn to read and write. By Pachomius's death in 346 there were already nine large monasteries and two nunneries in Egypt. They were like villages, in which each monk or nun lived in his own house, whilst a common dining-hall and one or more chapels for common worship were erected in the middle of the settlement. A reliable source states that Egyptian monks founded similar monastic settlements in Rome in Pachomius's lifetime. Ambrosius and his sister Marcellina founded comparable monastic villages on their estates outside Milan.

BASIL THE GREAT

Through Basil the Great (*c.* 330-379) Eastern monasticism took coherent shape. In company with his brothers Gregory of Nyssa, and Peter of Sebaste, his sister Macrina, and his friend Gregory of Nazianzus, he initiated the renewal of the Church of Asia Minor. The roots of Orthodox monasticism are also Basilian. He was the first to set down detailed rules, which reveal many of the salient characteristics of later Benedictine monasticism. All later Rules derive from the two Rules, one long and one short, of this remarkable pedagogue. He speaks of the relative importance of the commandments, of the long periods of prayer, silence, temperance, humility and obedience, of work and the advantages of life in communities; he speaks of the love of God, but also of love of one's neighbour. Basil was the first to divide the day up into periods of prayer, work and reading the Scriptures. Where monachism had always seen the world one fled, with its greed, lust and pride, as the enemy of the perfect life, Basil insisted emphatically on the work of monks both in the world and for the world. The Basilians maintained orphanages, hospitals and lazarets, and workshops in which the poor could earn their bread. The monks assumed a social role. Giant monasteries arose, and their large-scale architecture prefigures later Western monastic architecture in many of its elements, notably in the walls that set the monastery apart from the world outside. But we cannot go so far as to speak of an Order. Basil deals always with the single monastery, and in it with the single monk. Under the influence of St Saba of Cappadocia (439-532) new forms of existence sprang up, notably in Palestine, within the context of this Rule, which once more allowed the monks hermitages – the *lavra*. Saba's *typikon* was later to provide the basis for the Rules of Studion and Athos, after which most Byzantine monasteries live.

Two general plans of Basilian monasteries are given here, less on their own account than with the intention of presenting a basis of comparison with later Benedictine layouts. Both monasteries belong to the monastic republic of Mount Athos, and both, in the form we see them, stem from the later Middle Ages (the depictions are archaeologically not quite accurate). Plate 1 shows a schematic representation of the plan of the Great Lavra monastery. In the middle of the site stands the cloister, in whose centre in turn stands the small church. Around it are disposed the monastic buildings. The fountain is in front of the church. The church is exceeded in size by the refectory, a very original T-shaped building, its portico facing the narthex of the church. It is the largest structure there. It was, next to the church, the sole common meeting-place, in which the monks regularly assembled for meals. In the East as in the West the common meal stood at the

1 The Great Lavra monastery, Mount Athos, dating in its present form from the later Middle Ages but preserving the original Basilian plan

1 Portico	*7 Refectory*
2 Chapel	*8 Kitchen*
3 Guests' lodging	*9 Cells*
4 Church	*10 Outbuildings*
5 Cloister	*11 Postern*
6 Fountain	*12 Tower*

2 *The Watopedi Monastery, Mount Athos: a nineteenth-century engraving after a seventeenth- or eighteenth-century original*

beginning of the trend to a *vita communis*: the Basilian monasteries rarely got beyond this stage.

Plate 2 also shows a monastery on Mount Athos at the height of its development. It is a nineteenth-century engraving after a Greek original of the seventeenth or eighteenth century. It is laid out, like most monasteries of the Orthodox Church, as a rectangle bounded at either end by the monks' dwellings, and along the sides by high walls. It was intended to be defensible. The function of particular buildings is not apparent from their shape. The whole area is all but filled by the two monastery churches. There are other complexes, with yet greater numbers of churches contained within the walls. The West too was to adopt the custom of several churches, referred to as 'families' of churches. It is significant in these Greek monasteries that each building stands on its own. They are not subordinated to a schema from which one could for example deduce the processional paths traced by the community on the way to their churches. There were such processions here anyway only on special occasions.

SYRIAN MONASTIC CULTURE

Out of the multiplicity of buildings created by Eastern monachism as appropriate housing for its ideals, those in the cradle of Christianity deserve special mention. Not because they were older than other establishments in the Eastern Empire. They too originated in the fourth century, i.e. after the recognition of Christianity as the state religion. Nor were they probably either the largest or the most advanced of their kind, but they do survive in their original form.

From the fourth to the sixth century Syria was a flourishing country (Bibl. No. 30). The spread of Christianity was not, as in Italy and Greece, disrupted by the invasions of the Goths and Vandals. For almost three hundred years the monasteries were able to evolve their own tradition in building, until at the beginning of the seventh century they were first threatened by the Persian conqueror (610–

3 Qal'at Sim'ân, Syria. The monastery arose round the column of St Simeon Stylites, the ruined base of which still survives

612), and then destroyed by the Arabian (633–638). Unlike the monasteries of the Greek lands, the buildings of the early period could not be replaced by successors. They remained deserted, as did the whole area, once their culture was destroyed. The land dried up. The ruins of the Syrian monasteries of the fourth to sixth centuries are in regions remote both from the thickly settled coastal areas, and from the large towns with their fertile hinterland – Damascus, Aleppo and Jerusalem. South, North, and North-East Syria – these were regions whose history and architecture knew no continuity.

We must renounce a glance at the highly interesting development of ecclesiastical architecture, to concentrate on one question: what did a Syrian monastery look like? How much do the plans of a few giant monasteries reflect the joint existence of the monks?

We know first of all that in Palestine there were both Basilian monasteries, in which the common life prevailed, and *lavra*, in which the followers of St Saba sought ways of combining communal with eremitical existence.

Analysis of the native Syrian monasteries must start from the realization that they were to an increasing extent the goal of, or stations on, pilgrimages. In North Syria most monasteries lay on the way to the country's chief shrine, the monastery Qal'at Sim'ân. There Simeon Stylites the Elder (b. 390) had perched for thirty years atop his last, roughly sixty foot high, column. It was probably still in his lifetime that the singular church arose, composed of four basilicas centred like processional ways on the great octagon, in which the saint persisted on his feet in the open, only inclining for prayer, and addressing the bystanders twice a day. His *Vita* relates that in his earlier years he had himself walled up during Lent without any nourishment, later preferring to be chained to a rock, and finally taking up permanent abode upon a block of stone and then on a column, that grew ever higher as protection against his admirers. On Sundays and holidays he is reputed to have raised his arms unremittingly to heaven. He died on his column in

4 Qal'at Sim'ân, Syria. The monastery today from the north-west

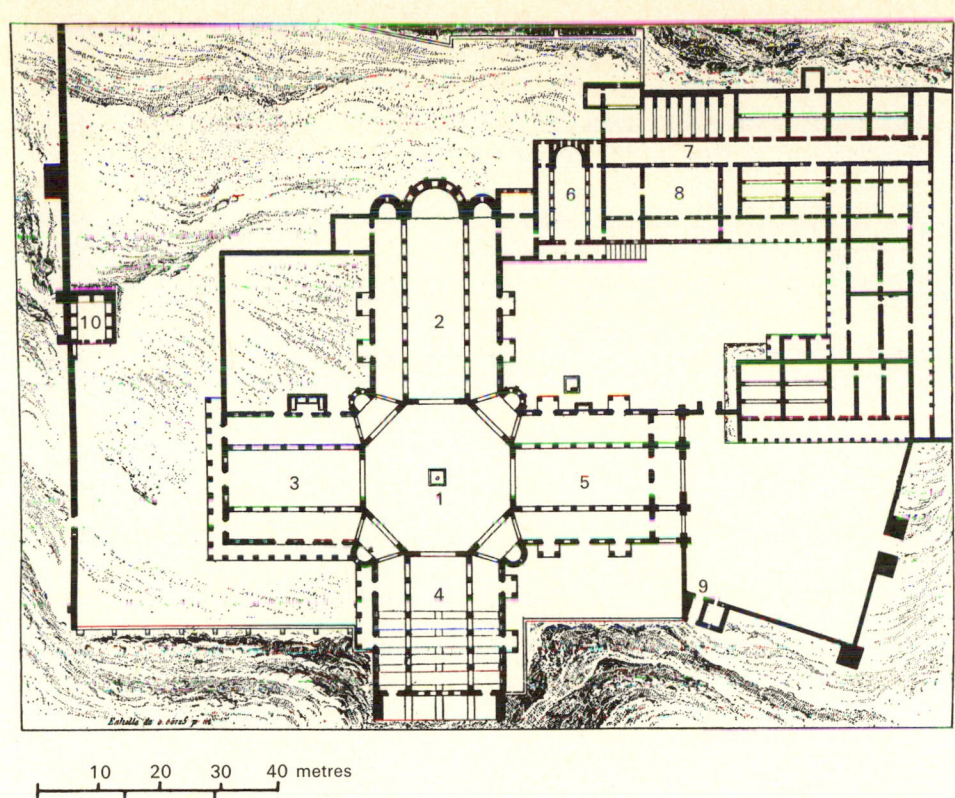

5 *Qal'at Sim'ân, Syria. Plan*
 1 *Base of St Simeon's pillar,*
    surrounded by an open court
 2 *Eastern basilica, with apse*
 3 *Northern basilica, with entrance*
 4 *Western basilica*
 5 *Southern basilica, with narthex*
    leading to monastery courtyard
 6 *Small church, probably fifth century*
 7 *Corridor*
 8 *Residential buildings*
 9 *Gate*
10 *Mortuary chapel*

| 10 | 20 | 30 | 40 metres |
| 50 | | 100 | feet |

6 *Qal'at Sim'ân, Syria. View of the monastery as it was in the nineteenth century,*
from the north

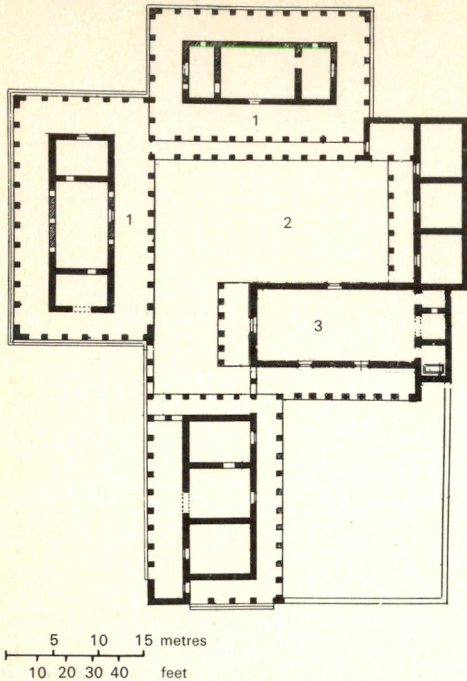

5   10   15 metres
10 20 30 40   feet

7 Der Sim'ân, Syria. A monastery whose layout was largely conditioned by the tourist traffic

1 Pilgrims' hostels
2 Courtyard
3 Church

September 459. There he now stood, whilst round about him rose the most important work of architecture in the eastern half of the Empire between the Temple of Baalbec in the second century and Hagia Sophia in the sixth. Butler (Bibl. 30) assumes that in the main this church was built between 450 and 470. No dates are transmitted; the estimate derives from its influence on later, datable works. Round the saint, first of all in the open, then amongst the early buildings, and finally in the completed colonnaded halls, there was never any lack of gaping pilgrims gazing toward the centre, where he stayed resolutely upright. It is known that the large monastery to the south of the church was already in existence. But it is hard to distinguish the monastic buildings from the pilgrims' hostels. Not one of the numerous visitors to or investigators of the site, starting with its rediscoverer the Marquis de Vogüé, who published it in his work, *Syrie Centrale*, in 1865–97 (Bibl. 26), informs us about the uses of the individual rooms. We have a court onto which colonnades opened, and there was a passage along which rooms of differing size were grouped. No cells, no dormitory and no dining-hall are distinguishable.

The plan does not show the whole site. The course of the defensive wall shows that the monastery occupied a still more extensive area to the east and south. One can also assume that there were innumerable wooden buildings of which no trace remains. But what we have is enough to prove that we are faced with an institution in which the common life of the monks was quite secondary to the service of the saint. The focal point was this solitary and his austerities. In his own lifetime he not only stood out visually from the community, but both ecclesiastical and monastic architecture were centred on him. We have here a columnar monument with its auxiliary buildings.

In other Syrian monasteries too the general plan was, along with the church, governed by the buildings serving the pilgrim traffic. The Southern Monastery in Dêr Sim'ân may serve as a further example. The town lies at the foot of the hill of Qal'at Sim'ân. It had three large monasteries. One of them was a stop in the ascetic peregrinations of St Simeon. The Southern Monastery possessed but a relatively small church. Four two-storey buildings with superimposed arcades surrounded a court through which one entered the church. The building with the three large rooms adjoining the church to the north and probably also the building to the left of the church in the south are likely to have met the needs of the monastery. The larger two stone buildings to the north and west were pilgrims' hostels, great caravanserais, in which one could doss down in the huge halls and in their porticoes. The architectural conception was ambitious yet practical. It left little room for a retired monastic existence.

It should cause no surprise that a soil which for centuries had borne Hellenistic structures, should display quite regular layouts alongside highly individual improvizations. It is true that H. C. Butler found only one important example on his expeditions – id-Dêr ('the monastery'), in South Syria. The name itself asserts its special renown. Antique fragments, re-used, demonstrate that it was built on the site of a Hellenistic temple. A square court in the form of an atrium bordered by stone buildings precedes the church. Again neither the shape nor the size of the rooms betray their purpose. The entrance was exactly opposite the church portal. Traversing a tunnel vault, the court and the portico, one was confronted in the church by an apse pierced by the three east windows at regular intervals. Once again a secluded precinct for monastic life is wanting. Whoever did not choose solitude or a cell outside the institution felt, as ever in the Orient, no compulsion to withdraw from the hurly-burly of a pilgrimage-station.

It has frequently been remarked that individual features of Western Benedictine monasteries are foreshadowed in the East, above all the cloister. All these features were long familiar to Mediterranean builders, even in the secular sphere. A Benedictine of the eighth or ninth century would have seen nothing to emulate in Qal'at Sim'ân or id-Dêr. For the Orient's whole conception of a monastery, with its polarization around extreme eremitical asceticism and public service to pilgrims and travellers, was rooted in fundamentally different habits.

ST AUGUSTINE'S RULES

The Rules of St Augustine (354-430) are held to be the oldest in the West. Their early origin has been doubted, and they have been described as a later compilation from the saint's writings. But this has been refuted both by general historical arguments and by recent textual criticism. Augustine came to know monasticism in Milan. After his return to Africa in 387, but before his ordination, he founded with his friends his first monastery in Tagaste. He must have written down the routine of the young community as his first Rule straight after founding it. This document, breathing a new spirit of monasticism, contains the earliest known prescription of the Hours. A few years later he supplemented this text with a second Rule in which he set out the moral and theological basis of the duties of the monks. He refers to the texts of the Rules in several later writings. At his death there are supposed to have been more than twenty monasteries in Africa. We do not know how one of them looked.

Ever increasing numbers of monks found themselves forced to flee Africa by the Vandal conquest. They brought their Rule with them to South Italy, Spain and France. Alongside the Hours and choral singing, they were bound to work. Many characteristics of St Benedict's subsequent Rule were adumbrated in this, which long continued to be accepted as an independent authority. When Chrodegang forced the common life on the canons of Metz cathedral in 755, the thirty-four chapters of his Rule appropriated elements from those of both Augustine and Benedict. The Synod of Aachen in 816 made these articles binding on all cathedral chapters. At the same time the pure Augustinian Rule survived in many of the older monasteries. It was adopted by Orders of priests – the Premonstratensians in the twelfth century, and the Dominicans in the thirteenth. And by most knightly Orders too. A little later a number of eremitical communities joined in adopting it. Alexander IV's Bull *Licet ecclesiae catholicae* sanctioned this federation in 1256, and thus there arose as a new Order the Friars Hermit of St Augustine. There were thus, aside from many lesser offshoots, four large organizations that had in the course of time subjected themselves to the precepts of the greatest of the Church Fathers: the Augustinian canons and canonesses as well as all the other canonical foundations, to the number of 4,500 for men alone around 1600 in the West; then later the Premonstratensians and Dominicans; and finally the Austin friars. New Orders were always being added. In 1514 a Benedictine could enumerate thirty-four varieties of religious living after St Augustine's Rule. In 1623 there were forty-three Orders and twenty-eight Congregations, among them the Trinitarians, Servites, Ursulines and Visitandines. Were one to add up all their Houses, they would outnumber those of any other group, including the Benedictines and their reformed branches.

Despite this, they did not formulate a specific monastic architecture of their own at any point in their history. There is no schema whose features enable us to recognize all, or even some of the most important communities which shaped their life according to this one Rule. The question whether the characteristic arrangement of having the cloister next to the church and the other buildings grouped schematically round it was first developed amongst the cathedral foundations living after the Augustinian Rule or amongst the Benedictines must be resolved in favour of the latter. I shall return to this. In other respects too the Augustinians, whose Rules must have been before St Benedict when specifying the offices, were able in turn to draw on the more thoroughgoing development of the Benedictines. The architectural history of the canonical foundations is outside this survey. It has still to be researched. It will clearly be possible to introduce numerous buildings of individual importance for the history of monastic architecture, but I cannot detect in them novel or pioneering ideas.

TOURS AND LÉRINS IN GAUL

Monasticism reached Gaul shortly after the middle of the fourth century. The first outstanding monastic leader in France was St Martin of Tours (*c.* 316-397). This Roman soldier's son, whose father's regiment had accepted Christianity in

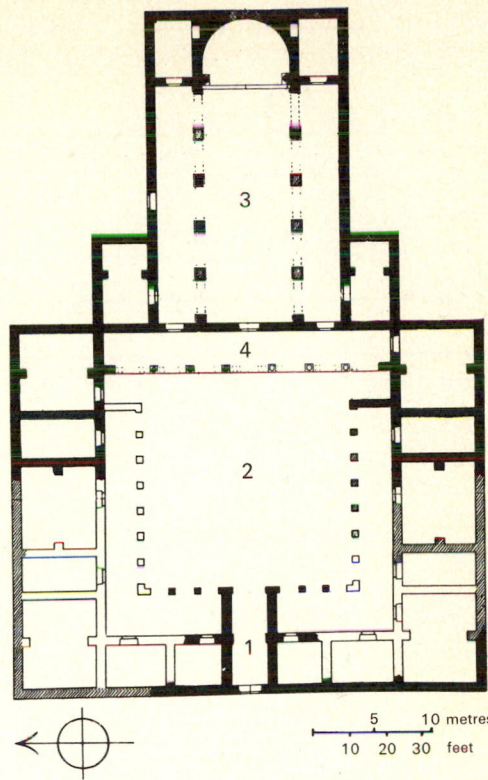

5   10 metres
10 20 30 feet

8 *id-Dêr ('the monastery'), Syria*
1 *Gateway*
2 *Atrium*
3 *Church*
4 *Portico*

316 in Hungary, was to become the national saint of the Franks. Between 360 and 370 the first full-scale monastery grew up round his cell by the Loire. As history and legend soon gathered round its imposing form, numerous daughter houses were founded in emulation during the fifth and sixth centuries. Western France became a land of monasteries. The large new monastery at Tours was already described by Sulpicius Severus in his *Life of St Martin* of about 400. The monks lived in huts against a wall protecting an area in whose centre stood a two-storey house, with the cells of Martin and some of the brethren beneath and a common dining-hall above. A small church, and soon several others, lay nearby. There were funerary chapels, that became reliquary crypts. The ensemble gave more the impression of a village or settlement than of a monastery; or rather, the monastic idea had not resulted in any characteristic architectural innovation. Furthermore, these centuries of the decline of the Roman Empire, the Germanic invasions and the emergence of the barbarian kingdoms, were hostile to monumental architecture. All the buildings of the period of tribal migrations are small – e.g. the Baptistery in Poitiers or the Crypt chapel of Jouarre – and take effect more through ornamentally conceived walls, columns and sarcophagi than through their construction. The artistic history of these centuries is that of the lesser arts. Even the churches whose foundations have been revealed were all small. Where surviving Roman buildings did not still provide the framework, large monasteries must have been more like nomadic encampments with people living in scattered tents, than like a classical town. Only the wall marked the area off as hallowed ground. The Tours of St Martin was a monastic 'kraal' with a Roman stone-built house in the centre.

As important as Tours was the island monastery of Lérins, that was founded between 400 and 410 opposite Cannes off the southern French coast by St Honoratius, believed to have been a refugee Roman from Britain. The rule of Macarius, which they observed, did not prevent the monks from living in

9 Crypt chapel of Jouarre, a unique Merovingian survival. The coffin in the foreground is that of the first abbess, Theodochilde, died 662

hermitages scattered successively over all four isles of Lérins and the coast. At the beginning of the seventh century 3,700 monks are reputed to have lived in this monastic polity. In 732, 500 of them, together with the abbot, were hewn down in a Saracen raid. An attempt to introduce the Benedictine Rule failed. In 677 the monks slew an abbot who had dared to require of them this disciplined life, in which limits were set even to asceticism. In the early period there was even less adherence to any plan of construction for the monastery. Today only seven crumbling little churches of great antiquity bear witness that for centuries men lived in this island paradise, exposed to God and the sun. Yet this monastery was the seed-bed of southern French theology. It produced over seventy saints, and innumerable bishops and archbishops. After the tenth century Benedictine customs took over here as well.

Friedrich Prinz has shown, through an impressive map, the three stages of the diffusion of monasticism from its fountain-heads in Tours and Lérins from the south and west towards the north and east (Bibl. 33). Albrecht Mann has compiled another map incorporating all the known major buildings, that is to say cathedral and monastery churches, up to the middle of the ninth century, to the Emperor Lothar's death, in order to show the expansion of Carolingian culture.[1] In the Frankish Empire there were no less than 1,695, 1,254 of them monasteries. It also emerges that in this early period the size of a town can be computed from the number of monasteries in or around it. According to this calculation the chief places of the West would range from Rome with 54 monasteries, Paris with 17, and Ravenna with 16, to Le Mans (15), Vienna (13), Lyons (10), through Tours, Cologne and Milan with 8 apiece, to Metz, Orleans, Trier, Pavia and Lucca all with 7. We owe to Jean Hubert the demonstration that in the seventh century alone eight monasteries were built between 200 and 1,000 yards from the town walls on the main roads out of Le Mans.[2] The protection of the Roman walls was needed in case of emergency; but the furthest possible withdrawal from the bishop's jurisdiction was also sought. Several powerful nobles, moreover, evidently preferred founding their own monastery to entering someone else's. But these urban monasteries were only a fraction of the whole. The majority were in lesser places or in the open country. Most of them were founded between the fifth and seventh centuries. One must remember that the astonishing

10 Lérins consisted of four islands, one of which is shown here. During the fifth century it was occupied by monks living in hermitages and following the Rule of Macarius

11　*A page from the earliest monastic manuscript in the Merovingian empire, written in the monastery of Luxeuil in 669*

12　*St Columba, a pen drawing from the ninth-century 'Vita Sancti Columbae'*

successes attained by Lérins at the beginning of the fifth century were connected with the flight of the Roman élite from northern Gaul and the Rhine and Moselle regions, caused by Stilicho's withdrawal of his army and the administration of the Empire to Milan and Arles in 401. Refuge from the barbarians was transformed into monastic retreat. This urge to renunciation may account for the astonishingly slight achievements of Merovingian monasteries in the fields of culture, art and architecture. Apart from a few late examples to be discussed in a moment, we have no idea of the plan of a single one of these innumerable monasteries. The beautiful crypt of Jouarre, with its tombs and Aquitanian chapel, is constantly brought up simply because it is about the only surviving monastic interior that we have. It is dated to the end of the seventh century. This period lacked the energy for great undertakings even within monastery walls. There was no concept of the dignity of labour, to stimulate ambitious building. There was no urge to build something up, to found some new Order. Saving a few famous scholars and historiographers, the early ascetics of both East and West did little or nothing for centuries. The Benedictine ideal of work had still not found any concrete application. It is certainly not accidental that we possess not a single book produced in any of the early monasteries of the three Germanic kingdoms in Italy, Spain or France. The earliest existing volume was written in the monastery of Luxeuil in 669 (New York, Pierpont Morgan Library 334). There certainly were earlier ones, but hardly such as to seem worthy of preservation thereafter.

Eastern monastic rules thrust northward, as we saw, from Lérins up the Rhône. Still in the fifth century, St Patrick transmitted certain traits to Ireland from Auxerre, a daughter-foundation of Lérins.

IRISH MONACHISM

In the Italy of the fourth and fifth centuries, in France and the British Isles the start of the monastic movement was wholly under the influence of the East. In this the unrelenting ascetic urge of Africa played a greater role than the moderate spirituality of the Greek provinces in Asia. Celtic monachism which, from the last years of the fifth century in Ireland, blossomed out into a monastic Church, was based on Egyptian anchoritism. We need not concern ourselves here with its growth from British roots, probably under Burgundian influence – St Patrick (385/86-461), himself a Briton who came to Ireland as a prisoner and slave of the Irish, became after his escape a monk in Lérins and a priest in Auxerre. By his death in 461 Ireland was a Christian country. A few monasteries prided themselves on their foundation by St Patrick himself, Downpatrick and Armagh amongst them. But the monastic ideal only reached its full unfolding in the sixth century. St Finian (549) transformed (around 513) St Patrick's episcopal see of Clonard into a monastery, and soon the Christian life of the whole island was transmuted by numerous foundations from having been Roman and hierarchical to being ascetic and monastic. Great sections of the population appear to have entered monasteries. From generation to generation the abbot came from the family that had made over the land and dominated the region. Clonard itself is supposed to have sheltered thousands of brethren, teachers and pupils. It is said that St Brendan (577) presided a little later over a settlement of over 3,000 monks, living after a fearsomely strict Rule. Ascetic endurance seems to have increased from decade to decade. Columba (521-597) required his brethren to keep going on a minimum of sleep and food, and to accustom themselves to appalling scourgings and interminable masses. Fintan of Clouenagh even forbade his monks to use beasts of burden on their stony fields. They were to harness themselves to the plough. Asceticism covered both life as a hermit and vows of eternal wandering, a distinctive feature of Irish renunciation. This was the first time that even the monastic refuge was felt to endanger self-abnegation.

The most important Irish monastic authority, St Columban (*c.* 530/40-615) had most influence on monastic development through his penitential – a table of punishments for even the vaguest stirrings of carnal thought. It was appended as the tenth to a Rule of only nine chapters, which was to be followed in many Frankish monasteries along with that of St Benedict. It is not for us to belittle this extreme rigorism in the light of modern medical and moral-theological ideas. The precautions taken in monastic regulations through the centuries against the stirrings of sensuality, especially against the dangers of sodomy and masturbation, would, like the punishments carried out whenever they proved ineffectual, fill a volume in the history of civilization. It is a memorable picture, that of the solitary monk standing up to his neck in water from dawn to dusk in the rough seas off the Irish coast, singing psalms to purge some frailty of the flesh. It was realized that the monks should never be left unobserved alone or in small groups; that the proper observation of the Rule demanded a minimum number of monks; fewer generally led to corruption. What is more, in Luxeuil, Columban's most important foundation on the Continent after Bobbio, he introduced continuous worship, one monks' choir relieving another. The nocturnal choir-service in winter was enlarged to seventy-five psalms (in summer twenty-four). Just four hours remained for sleep.

Whoever considers the monasteries of the West in the fifth and sixth centuries – the places sheltering individual despairers of the world amongst the debris of the Roman Empire in decline, the first monasteries of Spain, the southern French coast, Ireland and Scotland – is not confronted by buildings. Nor is it relevant to speak here of the legacy of culture saved from destruction by individuals like the great Cassiodorus (c. 490–583) in his monastery of Vivarium. Ireland and the Scottish coast are signal demonstrations that the places and rare monuments of the early monastic settlements must be themselves sought out if we are to understand their spirit. Islands and crags, ravines, and wilderness – the uninhabited and the uninhabitable appeared to them as so many invitations to asceticism. They were drawn to the inadequate and what might be reached only with great hardship. Cliffs with a thundering backdrop of the constantly raging sea, monasteries in caves and cave-like monasteries, surrounded by barren marshland, such was the scenario of their ascetic vocation. A hidden gully, a jutting mass of rock, these were invitations to conceal themselves throughout their life. Buildings arose too. I mentioned monuments – an almost lightless church of packed, unshapen stone, a tower, a cross, and high walls. Where a monastery flourished into the Romanesque period, like San Juan de la Peña, it adopted that vocabulary. Pl. 13 shows the church and the little monastery buildings round the Romanesque cloister nestling in the protection of the massive overhang of the

13 The monastery of San Juan de Peña, in the Pyrenees, its tiny church and cloister clinging to the steep cliff

14 Air view of Iona. Nothing of the sixth-century buildings remains, but the site is still remote and lonely

15 *Stone beehive cells of the monastery at Inishmurray in Ireland, probably early seventh century*

cliff. It is not the architecture, but Nature, the situation and the sojourn amongst the grandiose and barren, that denote the spirit of the monastery.

If there are but few traces of the once numerous Irish monasteries, the reason lies above all in the small scale of their architecture. The monks inhabited separate huts of loose stones, vaulted and mortarless like the *trulli* of Apulia, only simpler. Often they were content, like the monks in the Orient, with wattle. For St Columba's most successful foundation, the monastery on the island of Hy or Iona, we possess a description, according to which the monks lived in small cells of wood and earth, whilst a rather larger cell, called *tuguriolum*, was set aside for the abbot. The layout is reminiscent of Tours. Such beehive-like cells survive at Inishmurray in Ireland. The churches too were small dim-vaulted rooms, none longer than a bare ten yards. They resembled stonework baskets. There were detached towers. The walls enclosing the extensive area of the monastery were like those of the vine-slopes of the Mediterranean. The splendid ornamental art created by these monks is well-known – the books and goldsmith's work, carrying on the ornamental vocabulary of Germanic and Celtic prehistory. Together with Anglo-Saxon art, Irish illumination asserted its influence on the Carolingian *Renovatio* on the Continent. The importance of the missionary Irish monks in the Frankish Empire is well-known. From at least the eleventh century onwards the 'Scots monks' built worthy monasteries, even if only seldom after their own formulae. Their actual architecture radiated no influences across the Channel capable of attracting attention. Wherever it was found in an occasional new foundation, the Irish plan would be displaced by one more spectacular. Irish monastic architecture thus lays no claim to treatment in the history of Western art. It seems to have been that urge to wander which prevented the emergence of monumental buildings in Ireland. The Irish loved improvization, distrusted the lasting or anything presumptively suited to eternity. Not until the *stabilitas loci* required by Benedict was there a basis for monumental construction, for a stable architecture.

BENEDICT OF NURSIA
The richness and fantasy of the Celtic imagination, its impassioned fervour and developed taste for the extreme, found telling expression in Irish monastic culture, resembling therein the Egyptian and the Syrian. It is noteworthy that it

was not these, but rather the sober and moderate spirit of Benedict of Nursia (*c.* 480-pre-553), largely mediated through the English Church, that was to prevail in the West. The Benedictines laid the foundations of the Latin Middle Ages. Theirs can be described as the first Latin monastery after the numerous Greek, Celtic and Gallic experiments.

At the outset stood a small book containing the seventy-three chapters of the *Regula Sancti Benedicti* (Bibl. 12) – guidance for the rule of the abbot, or father, over the monks put under him (Document I). It is no longer generally agreed that St Benedict was the author. It has been discovered that in the short text two different Rules are superimposed, one for the abbot and one for the monks. In any event the chapters were not all written down at once, but bit by bit. The book of the Rule is disorganized, without composition or subdivision, just stuck together. Its author does not employ classical Latin, but the directness of vulgar Latin. He was not amongst those who had studied rhetoric in Rome. Many ideas and sentences from earlier monastic Rules were inserted in the text. Its simplicity and Roman clarity assured it worldwide success. For after the Gospels, this little volume was the second work of the new religion of the Word that the missionaries carried with them everywhere. Charlemagne had a transcription made, that was then transmitted without any embellishment to every monastery. The St Gall copy is held to be the only text we possess of a work of classical literature at no more than one remove. The two monks who produced it state specifically that they kept word for word, even letter for letter, to their model. Contemporaneously the Synod of Aachen of 816 stipulated that every monk in a position to do so was to learn to recite its chapters by heart.[3] At least once a week, and in many monasteries daily, the Abbot assembled his monks for the reading and exposition of the Rule. Its simple paragraphs became the object of creative meditation.

We know virtually nothing of the Monastic Father of the West. The very first account of his life, from the pen of Pope Gregory the Great (pre-540-604), transfigures it into legend. Nonetheless we can be certain of the following. He was a Roman from the township of Nursia (Norcia), thirty miles east of Spoleto in the Sabine Hills, who withdrew to the solitude of Subiaco when he was about twenty. He spent three years as a hermit in a cave. Miracles were soon ascribed to him. He attracted disciples, and the idea arose of creating an organization consisting of twelve monasteries of twelve monks each, living round a central monastery. However, this first organization went awry. Benedict saw himself compelled to retreat south with a few disciples to the mountainous ridge of Monte Cassino. In view of his experiences, firstly with the organization of hermits, then of communities in huts, he now undertook that of joint life in one great House. The reputed date is 529.

From whatever sources this great pedagogue may have drawn for the separate sections of his Rule, their choice and sequence exactly convey his temper; distinguished by moderation, lucidity and simplicity. He was averse to all extremes. He was intent on reconciling the diurnal fluctuations of the year, the Church's Calendar, the needs of the community and provision for them, and even duty toward God, with the diversity of human nature. No thought was however as yet given to providing housing perfectly tailored to this precise, clock-like mechanism. There is no mention of architecture in St Benedict's Rule.

To understand the Rule one must be aware that the Roman day was subdivided into twelve intervals of equal length from sunrise to sunset, and similarly to sunrise again. These intervals only corresponded to our hours at the two equinoxes, at the beginning of Spring and of Autumn. On the latitude of Monte Cassino each hour of Midsummer Day was of seventy-five minutes, and of Midsummer night forty-five minutes. Winter was exactly the other way round. The monks worked, prayed, studied and slept the same number of 'hours' the whole year through, but not the same amount of time. On the shortest night of summer they rose at one in the morning and only went to bed at eight at night, according to our reckoning. That meant just five hours sleep. The midday rest had to make

16 *The oldest existing copy of the Rule of St Benedict, copied at Aachen in 816. This page shows the end of Chapter X and beginning of Chapter XI*

17 A page from St Gregory's life of St Benedict, eleventh century. Six scenes are shown, reading from left to right: writing the Rule, his death, his burial, the path by which he ascended to Heaven, a madwoman cured by sleeping in his cave, and St Gregory finishing his 'Life'

it up. In winter they rose at 2.30 a.m. and were in bed by 5 p.m., i.e. had nine and a half hours sleep. According to the season the monks did six to eight hours bodily work, prayed about three and a half hours a day, and devoted the same amount of time to study, meditation or reading. This last activity could be adjusted for the differing duration of physical work. In summer they worked more, and in winter read more. As well as regulating prayer, work and sleep, the Rule also specified the exact times and quantities of meals and drinks. Allowances were made for the young, the sick, the old and the infirm. Prayer and work were done together, sleep taken at the same time. Benedict even appreciated that not everybody was able to get up equally suddenly, and therefore permitted the slow singing of the first psalms in the morning to enable the latecomers to catch up. He foreswore the harsh rigorism of earlier Orders. The Benedictines preferred taciturnity to perpetual silence, and treasured frugality above total poverty. Even wine was allowed. Correction and not penance was the chief object of punishment.

In the first chapter of his Rule Benedict refers to four kinds of monks, but inverts the order of their appearance. He calls the 'coenobites' the first, living together in a monastery under a father, the abbot, and fighting in the strength of a set rule of life. It is typical of this late Roman that he compares the monks to soldiers, and the monastery to a camp or fortress. He characterizes the anchorites as champions who 'trained by long trials in the monastery, have learnt through the help of their brethren to combat the Devil alone'. Benedict's own career, like that of most outstanding monks, happened the other way round. It led from the hermitage to the monastery, and only in exceptional instances back from the community to the hermit's cell. His real rage was directed against the 'Sarabaites' who recognized no Rule: 'What they say and choose, that they call holy; what does not suit them, they regard as forbidden.' They embody an attitude responsible for some of the most original personalities ever found, including artists and sages of all descriptions. To Benedict the *gyrovagi* were yet worse – wandering monks who spent their whole life going from country to country, staying in some monk's cell for three or four days at a time, always on the move and never staying put, slaves to self-will. In his own youth he had suffered from them most. He would certainly have condemned several Irish monks for being footloose. One of the basic tenets of his Rule is the *stabilitas loci*. It was part of the discipline to spend one's whole life in one monastery in the same spot.

Benedict wanted the monks in each monastery to be kept down to a controllable number. They are estimated at about 150 in the last years of his activity in Monte Cassino. He repudiated the monster monasteries of the East with up to 3,000 monks. The Latin concept of the family was also to apply to the monastery. The abbot as father was to know each member intimately and guide him. The monastic family was at the same time a school, the *scola dominici servitii, scola* meaning school, a platoon in the military sense, a workshop or even a guild. Benedict also wanted to leave room for development. His Rule was only to be a beginning, and for the beginners on monastic life. He allowed himself no illusions about its potential outside his own community.

Nonetheless, by his death twelve establishments had already affiliated themselves to Monte Cassino. His fame had spread far. Even King Totila sought him out in 543. But between 580 and 590 Monte Cassino was taken by the Lombards and the monastery destroyed. The venture seemed finished.

Yet success followed destruction. A handful of monks had fled to Rome. Gregory the Great, if not a member of the order at least a friend of the Rule, became Pope. It is owing to him that the Benedictine ideal prevailed in the West. His *Life of Benedict* now stood alongside the slim book of the Rule and gave posterity the paradigm of a perfect abbot. Under his auspices the English Benedictine, Augustine, took the decision to return to England with books and missionaries. From Canterbury he founded the English Church, which was a monastic church in which the chief sees were reserved for Benedictines. From England the eastern kingdom of the Franks was proselytized and given an ecclesiastical structure by Willibrord, Boniface and others. The courts of the Carolingians fell under increasing Benedictine and Roman influence. This culminated in Charlemagne's command to all the monasteries in his Empire to adopt Benedict's Rule. The founder's achievements became, through the efforts of Pope Gregory and Charlemagne, the basis of Western civilization.

THE ORIGIN OF THE BENEDICTINE MONASTIC SCHEMA
The ideal plan of St Gall of about 820 – the impossibly perfect monastery that I shall deal with in the next chapter – confronts us with the Benedictine schema almost fully realized. It was to remain predominant throughout the Middle Ages. The church, with the cloister to the south surrounded by monastic buildings – dorter, refectory, kitchens and cellars –, then outside this core the abbot's house,

buildings for the sick and novices, lodging for pilgrims and guests, housing for the schools and doctors, workshops and farm-buildings – everything has been provided for and suitably disposed. The only thing not envisaged was the chapter-house, sited under the dorter not long after. The chapter was held in the arm of the cloister adjacent to the church. Whence and when came this scheme? What features mark the phases of its development?

This question has provoked much research (Bibl. 27-31). It emerged that each component was known to earlier monasticism. There was no need to invent categories of building. The material was already to hand, it only remained to organize it functionally.

Archaeology was of no help to research into this. In the East there were large-scale layouts but no Benedictine Rule. In the West the period of barbarian migrations was notable for the lack of any sense of the monumental. Its buildings are irregular and small. Where it was not possible to squat in deserted Roman ruins, the scale was modest. Single elements of the later scheme can be pointed out on many sites. The question, 'Rome or the Orient?' was variously answered, and the solution, 'Rome and the Orient', just begs the question.

No rules, at any rate no more than rudimentary ones, for the classic schema were to be found. The search for preliminary stages of the classic Benedictine monastery of the West was inevitably conducive to error, for what was sought could never have existed. The St Gall plan is a work of the Middle Ages, not of late antiquity. It was shaped by the special role conferred on the monasteries by the Frankish kingdom. The monks who had fled this world were given duties in it by the Germanic rulers. They saw themselves compelled to evolve new sets of buildings facilitating the fulfilment of their novel civilising mission. Monasteries became centres of agriculture, links in the chain of defence, hosts to the progress of the peripatetic court; they became schools, chanceries, centres of research and missionary bases. In many monasteries the abbacy was a political office, sometimes more high-ranking than that of bishop or count. The entire monastery emerged as a political institution. It is only possible to resolve the question of the origin of the Benedictine schema in conjunction with that of the origin of this political institution.

Everything suggests that Monte Cassino was not the starting-point. The settlement was destroyed and deserted at the end of the sixth century. At the beginning of the eighth century a few hermits were again living on the mountain, whom a certain Petronax from Brescia tried to merge into a new community around 720. In 729 a small monastic body was found by St Willibald on his way back from Jerusalem. It is attributable to the work of this Englishman, who remained there ten years, that the mother house regained her influence, though her former importance only returned with endowments from the Carolingian kings.

A better start was made by certain Frankish monasteries, of which we have good descriptions, notably two large monasteries of the early period: Jumièges in a bend of the Seine, and Fontenelle not far from Rouen. The description of Jumièges is in the eighth and ninth chapters of the *Vita* of St Philibert, its founder around 655. We have reproduced the crucial portions of the mid-eighth century text in the Appendix (Document 11). Philibert was a reformer who, starting out from Columban's Rule, made important features of the Benedictine Rule mandatory upon his monastery. The same text tells us that the new buildings of his monastery aroused great admiration and were imitated. It was a huge monastery, sheltering 900 monks under the abbot. One should picture a large, square site fortified with walls and towers, with a cruciform church in the middle. Next to the church was the cloister, with stone-hewn arcades, and admired for its rich decoration. Here then we find mention for the first time in the West of this grandiose motif with such an inexhaustible potential for variation. Abutting the eastern transept of the church rose a dorter 290 feet long and 50 feet wide, lit by great glazed windows; a room never surpassed in size, if the figures are reliable. It is obscure in the text whether there was a second such room to the west of the cloister, or whether a two-storeyed section faced the writer. Even scrutiny of the St Gall plan yields no answer to the question of the purpose of the room underneath the dorter in the upper storey. Later the chapter-house and a room for the monks would be placed there. So it was not taken up by anything else. The author of the *Vita* expressly names only two buildings, the cellar and the refectory 'where those assemble that serve Christ worthily, own nothing and ask for no reward but, trusting in God, are nevertheless furnished with everything'. It seems probable that the cellar and refectory enclosed the court of the monastery, just as seen in later layouts.

The chronicler of Fontenelle includes the story of its Abbot Ansegis (822–33) in his account and so informs us not only about the buildings but also about the order of their construction. Fontenelle and Jumièges belonged and still do belong to the same diocese, so the builder of the former naturally knew the earlier building. We are now at the zenith of the Carolingian *Renovatio*, its final phase under Louis the Pious, just a few years before the Norse invasions cast everything into the melting-pot. The kernel was an earlier church that Ansegis wanted to have enlarged and embellished, but not to replace (Document IV). The chronicler singles out the three buildings of equal height round the cloister; in order of building: the dorter, the cellar and refectory opposite it, and on the north side a third house referred to as *camera* and *caminata*. This can only have contained study-rooms for the monks, and perhaps the wardrobe. These three buildings were about 70 feet high, and must therefore have had two storeys. Whilst the dorter is precisely described – again a very large room, 280 feet long though only 30 feet wide – we learn nothing of the function of the ground floor. We learn of the refectory-building that served half as storeroom and half as dining-hall, the division being more probably crosswise than between storeys. The third building served a purpose that claimed no structure of comparable importance in any subsequent monastery. It is interesting that in the cloister, in front of the dorter or refectory, a special room was set aside for use as an archive or library. The southern arm of the cloister was built out like a portico alongside the church as the particular meeting-place of the chapter. The chapter was held here in many early monasteries. The idea of choosing this place for the grave and memorial tablet of the founder-abbot was also taken up on many later occasions. One is inclined to believe that Ansegis was not the first to select this spot. The chapter-house was always the focal point of the abbot's activity.

This description of Fontenelle shows that the classic Benedictine schema was not fully evolved even in the Late Carolingian period. It is true that the dorter, as in Jumièges, had achieved its final position, but it had not yet been realized that it was better to split the refectory and storeroom between two buildings on the south and west in order to insert the kitchen where it belonged. It also emerged subsequently that there was no need for a separate building for the monks' common-rooms, since there was enough room under the dorter. The cultural level attained by the monastery is indicated by the fact that special rooms were used for library and archive. The scale of building and the wealth of artistic decoration are impressive. The monastery takes its place next to the imperial palace and the cathedral amongst the key architectural challenges of the age.

There was still much to be done to tailor the three large uniform buildings on the cloister to one another functionally. The description of Ansegis' own monastery is itself an indication that up to now no monastery plan was generally accepted as binding. The St Gall project was to be an important step in this direction. The Synod of Aachen seems to have been the first occasion when the relationship of the plan to the Rule was thoroughly discussed. But that no conclusion was then reached is clear from the fact that the chapter-house is not demonstrable as the chief room under the dorter till the beginning of the eleventh century. It is probable that a chapter-house was first built in Cluny at the end of the tenth century. Nonetheless, what proofs we have permit us to say that the classic monastic layout of the Middle Ages was in its essentials a work of the Carolingian renaissance.

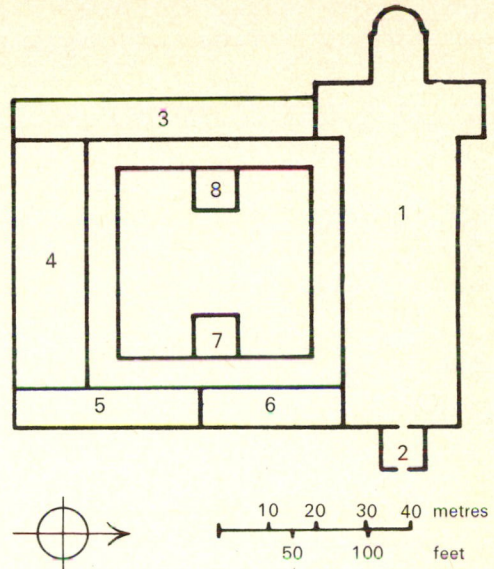

18 *Fontenelle, as reconstructed from a Carolingian description*
1 *Church*
2 *Narthex*
3 *Dorter, with chapter-house below*
4 *Camera and caminata*
5 *Refectory*
6 *Cellar*
7 *Archive*
8 *Library*

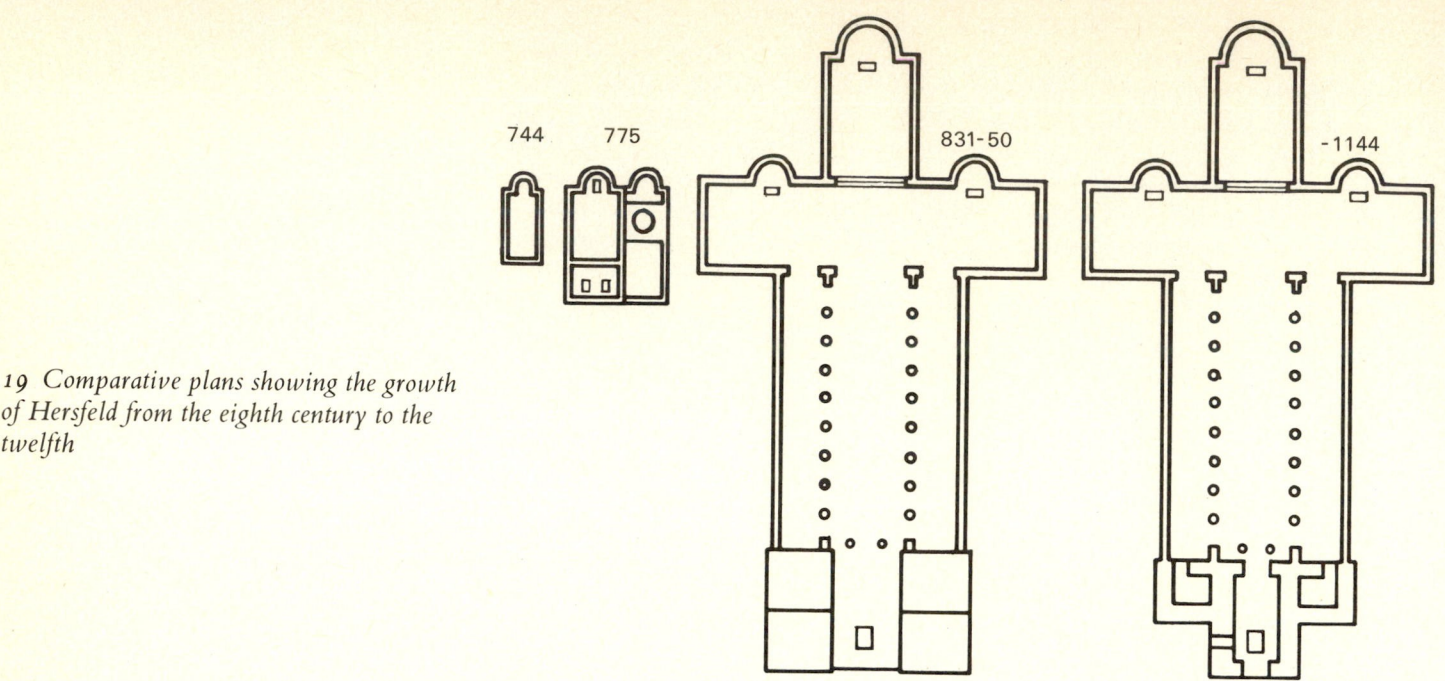

19 *Comparative plans showing the growth of Hersfeld from the eighth century to the twelfth*

744   775   831-50   -1144

20 *Hersfeld. View from the nave looking east. Most of the actual structure is eleventh century, but built on the original foundations*

CAROLINGIAN GIANT MONASTERIES

The multiple roles conferred increasingly on the monasteries by the Frankish kings caused them to mushroom in a way of which Jumièges in the seventh century is an early example. The monasteries became larger, richer, and more powerful. Charlemagne, in making over the national shrine of the Franks in Tours to Alcuin, the most learned man in his realm, was transferring a monastic state in which 20,000 people lived. This huge monastery in no way obeyed Benedict's injunctions. The consequences of this were drawn shortly after Alcuin's death, and the freer way of life of canons introduced. Never before on the continent, and rarely thereafter, did so many monks live in Benedictine monasteries. Few of them came out of personal inclination; most were compelled by their lords; very many also were imprisoned opponents of the king, like Tassilo of Bavaria or the Lombard king Desiderius. Monks were recruited like soldiers, and bought like slaves and serfs; wherever it seemed useful, one could be condemned to monkhood. The state, insofar as one can speak of such a thing, took the monastery in hand. Angilbert required 300 monks and 100 pupils for the functioning of his monastery of Centula near Abbeville; Adalhard, Charlemagne's cousin, 300 monks and 150 menials for Corbie. These are huge numbers, if we compare them with those of the inhabitants of the far from populous towns. And the buildings were in keeping with these numbers, some of them grossly inflated. Art history is familiar with this tendency to the outsize in many archaic cultures, just as it is with the contrary movement to reduce the colossal and often shapeless to manageable and delicate proportions. Parallels are supplied by the comparison of archaic Greek *kouroi* with classical sculptures of youths, or of Trecento Florentine buildings with the early works of Brunelleschi. In the Carolingian era this shrinkage stemmed from Benedict of Aniane (*c.* 750–821); his new monastery of Inden near Aachen, the later Cornelismünster, is astonishingly small (Bibl. 35).

The thrust of Carolingian civilization from west to east in the course of the eighth century is reflected not only by the map of new foundations. Giant monasteries were also built first in the west – examples are Jumièges, Corbie and Tours – and only later near the missionary frontiers in the east. Their swift rise indicates the interest taken in them by Charlemagne. After only a few decades the risk was taken of replacing the first two little churches in Hersfeld and Fulda by new buildings that are among the very largest of the Middle Ages. A comparison of the plans of Hersfeld reveals the process. The motives inclining the dominant abbatial figures to burden their monks with such huge piles were two: on the one hand a passion for building inspired by the desire for a *renovatio* of Roman grandeur, and on the other the demand for almost impossibly sumptuous religious pomp. Fulda is an example of the first, Centula of the second. The two rebuildings rose contemporaneously, the monastery of Centula from 789 onwards, the new church of Fulda from 791.

Under Abbot Baugulf, Radger had designed a building in Fulda that was to be comparable in size and shape to St Peter's. It was begun in the east. In 802 Radger was elected Baugulf's successor – the builder turned abbot. Only then does he seem to have revealed the full extent of his plans; the whole abbey was to bear the marks of his passion for building. The monks constantly complained to Charlemagne that they had entered the monastery for prayer and study, and not as builder's mates. Louis the Pious yielded to these plaints in 817 and had Radger, called in the later abbatial roll a *sapiens architectus*, replaced. In the *Vita* of his successor Eigilis (817–822) he is stigmatized as *Monoceros*, the rampant unicorn. We possess an engraving made after a Carolingian miniature from this Life which shows Radger penned in his new church, whilst a unicorn harries a herd of sheep, i.e. the monks.[4] The monastery was built from 819 onward behind the mighty western transept of the church. We know neither the allocation of the buildings nor their shape. The site alone proves that the schema contemporaneously developed on Reichenau and transmitted to us by the St Gall plan (*vide* next chapter) was not adhered to; the date shows that it must however

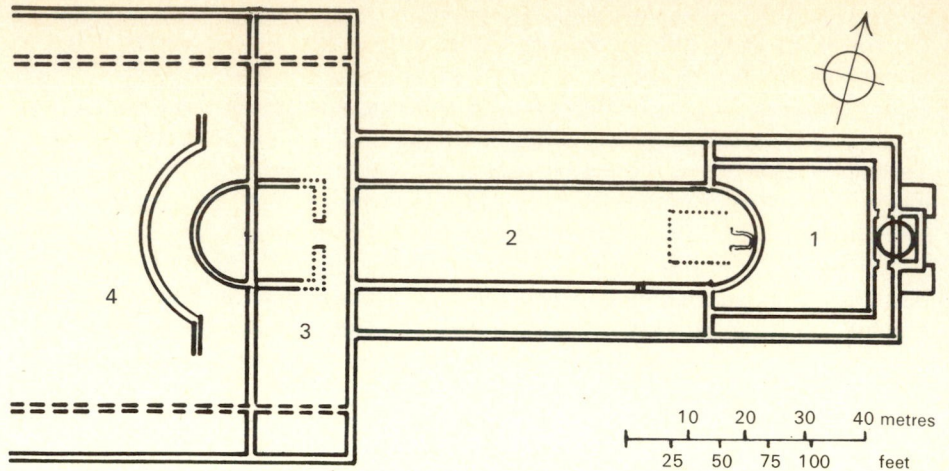

*21, 22 Fulda. Right: conjectural
reconstruction of the Carolingian plan.*
1 Atrium
2 Nave of church
3 Western transept
4 Monastic buildings
*Below: woodcut of 1550, showing the
church from the east; most of the monastery
lay behind the large western transept*

have derived from a similar approach. Eigilis, and even more his successor Hrabanus Maurus (822-42), undoubtedly required and built a complete monastery. In keeping with the church it was monumental.

We know nothing either of the conventual buildings of Centula. Like most giant monasteries of the time it had several churches – a 'family of churches' as Edgar Lehmann called it. Effmann reconstructed the appearance of the most important church, whose altar layout we know.[5] Recent excavations have also revealed that one of the three churches, the little chapel of Our Lady, was centrally-built like the Palatine Chapel at Aachen (Bibl. 46, pp. 369ff.). It is a novel idea to give the cloister the job of connecting these churches by a covered processional way. It did not, that is, just have the role of an atrium surrounded by the conventual buildings, but beyond this the more important role of passage to the churches. This involved making it not small, but as large as possible, not least because the songs prescribed for the processions from church to church were to be long.

A detailed Order of Worship of Abbot Angilbert's survives (Bibl. 43, pp. 296–306). Monastery and church were the means of realizing it. The fundamental idea was unceasing praise of God throughout the day and night. This *laus perennis* was developed in Eastern monasteries and first adopted by the mountain monastery of St Maurice in the Valais. Angilbert organized 'shiftwork to the glory of God' for his monastery down to the last detail. The monks split into three choirs of a hundred voices each, plus thirty boys apiece. It was exactly laid down what each of the three choirs was to sing at the chief festivals at specific places in the main church, whilst processing, and in the ancillary churches, and where they were to combine, and what they were to sing in unison. Reading these texts evokes the picture of a monastery grouping traversed by singing monks the whole year through, sometimes meeting, then parting again, singing sometimes singly, then in unison, then answering each other antiphonally.

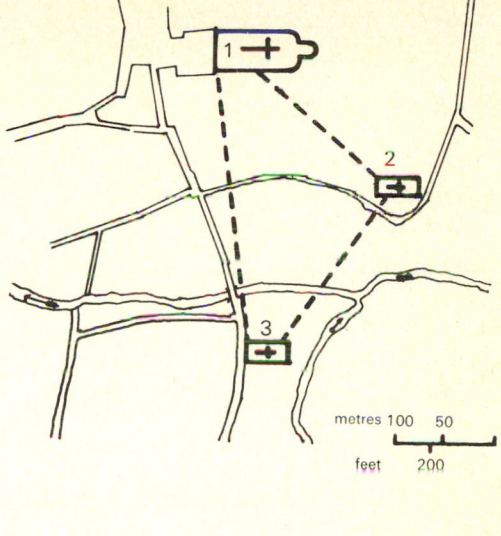

metres 100 50

feet 200

23, 24 *Centula (Saint-Riquier). Above: plan showing the relationship of the three churches and the processional path between them.*
1 *Church of St Richarius (Riquier)*
2 *Church of St Benedict*
3 *Chapel of Our Lady*
Left: a print of 1612, based on a much earlier manuscript illustration which showed the monastery's three churches before the rebuilding of 1071–97

25, 26 Monte Cassino, as it probably
looked under Abbot Desiderius, 1058–87.
Opposite: a bird's-eye view reconstructed by
Professor Kenneth Conant. Right: plan,
after J. von Schlosser, made in 1889.
Conant's version represents more recent
research.

1 Church
2 Chapter-house
3 Dorter
4 Refectory
5 Kitchen
6 Cellar
7 Novices' cells
8 Vestry
9 Old infirmary
10 New infirmary
11 Abbot's lodgings

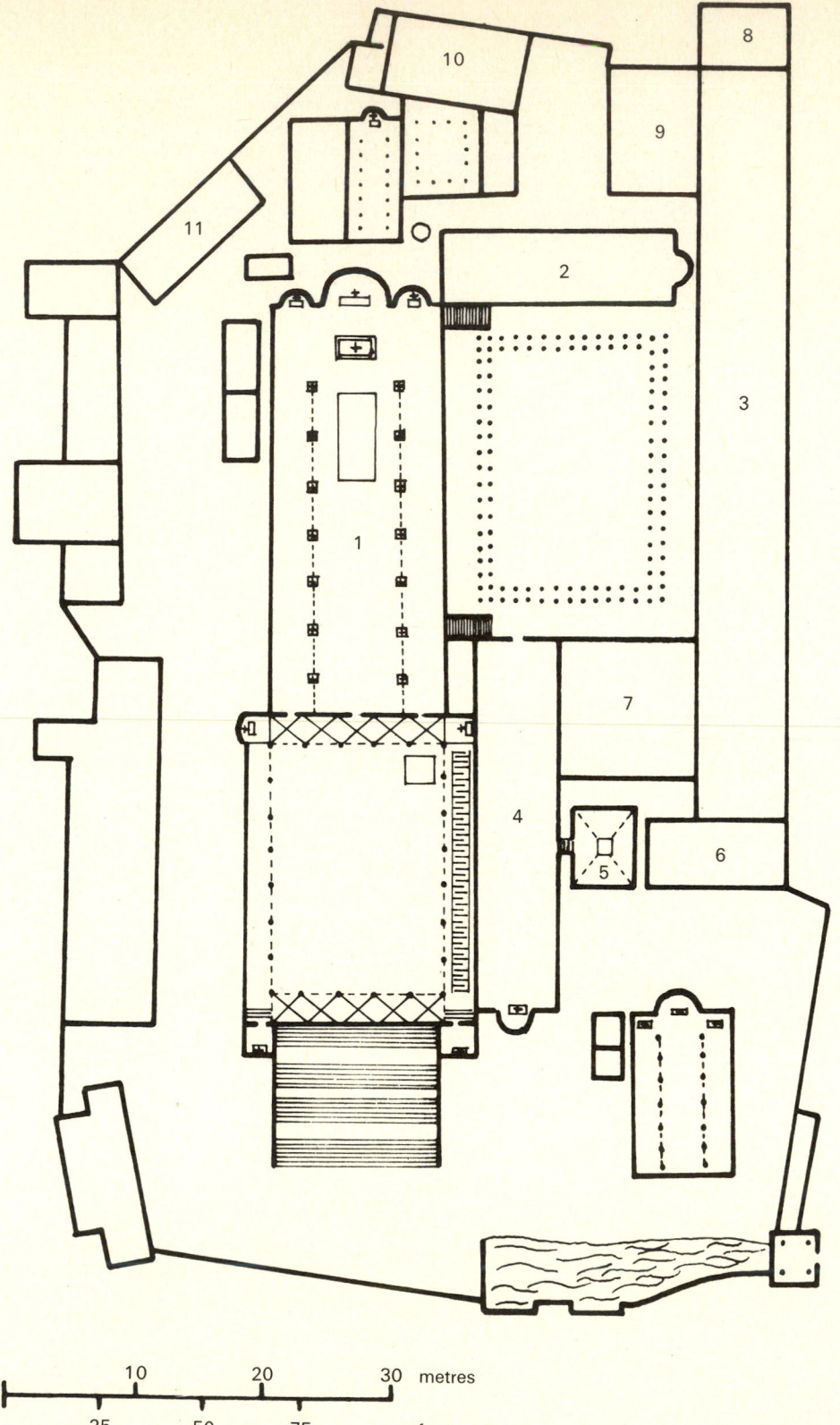

10   20   30   metres

25   50   75   feet

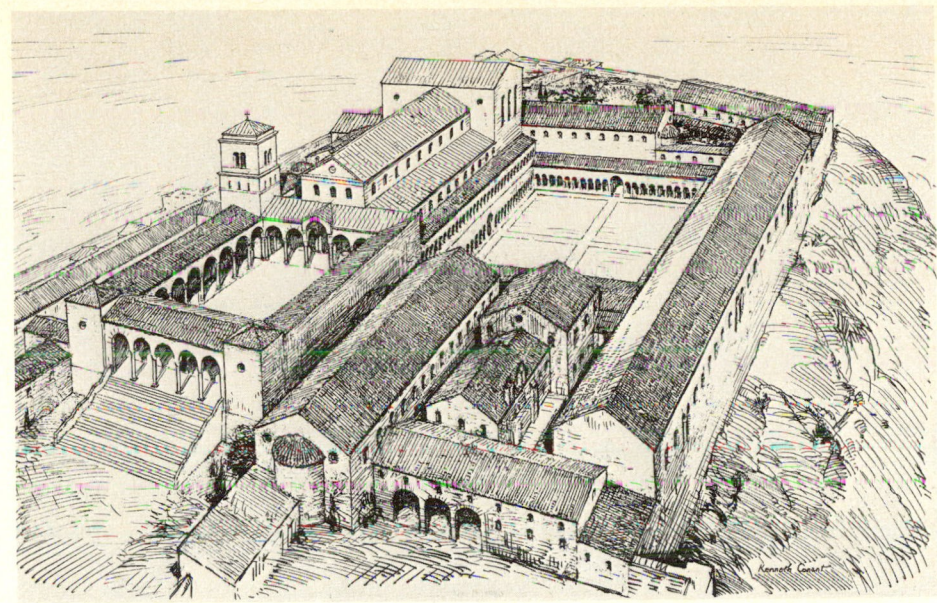

There is a famous seventeenth-century engraving after a miniature or drawing
of the eleventh century showing as the monastery's three churches and its
cloister prior to the total rebuilding of 1071-97. Jean Hubert had the inspiration
of extracting its measurements from the cadastral survey of Abbeville (Bibl. 45,
pp. 293ff.). This produced a total length for the cloister of about 2,350 feet, the
stretch from the main church to the Lady Chapel alone measuring 975 feet. We
can people these arcades in the light of the *Institutio Angilberti Centulensis* (Bibl.
43, 70-75). They were traversed several times a day by the various monks'
choirs. At great festivals they were drawn into the liturgy of the church. The
three churches, and in the main church the various altars, were the points at
which the choirs assembled. The machinery of the monastery as a unit thus not
merely sprang into action for the needs of daily life, but also proved essential to
the conduct of the liturgy.

Saint-Riquier was a monastery that began to flourish when Angilbert took it
over and continued to do so after his death during the incumbency of his son
Nithart, the great historian and a grandchild of the Emperor, but never really
recovered from its destruction by the Norsemen. Corbie had both a more
distinguished past and a greater future, even if its greatest expansion took place
during the abbacy of Adalhard, a statesman and cousin of Charlemagne, who
held sway for almost half a century, from 781 to 826. In the Merovingian period
this foundation of around 660, by Queen Bathilde, wife of Clovis II, had housed
the most important scriptorium in the Frankish Empire. It was there that Abbot
Maurdramnus sometime before 781 evolved the purest form of the Carolingian
minuscule, the basis of our alphabet today. Corbie – so it is thought – was
appointed by Charlemagne as the Lombard king Desiderius' prison in 774. In
Adalhard's statues of 822 the number of monks was fixed at 300, and that of the
menial brethren at 150. The same document's enumeration of the monastery
buildings conjures up the picture of a giant monastery.[6]

It had no less than five, perhaps even seven, places of worship, three churches
and two to four chapels. The list of the secular buildings falls clearly into three
groups: the monastic buildings round the cloister, the rest inside the monastery
walls, and those buildings outside these walls. Round the cloister lay as usual the
dorter, refectory, kitchens and cellar. There was also a *calefactorium* (warming-
house), but as yet no chapter-house. The abbot's palace and the sick-bay are
mentioned, but with no indication of their position. Within the walls were
numerous domestic buildings such as the bakery, brewery, laundry, and several

workshops. There were as well pilgrims' hostels and guest-houses, and a building for two doctors. Beyond the walls lay the stables, the mill, sheds and even a school for the laity. We learn nothing of the size of the individual buildings. If we apply the relative measurements of the St Gall plan, which reckoned on only seventy-two beds for the monks in the dorter, the site must have been vast. Once again there is doubt as to the function of the rooms below the dorter. Mention of a centre portal indicates a certain regularity in the layout. A 'St Albin's Gate' is singled out as a second entry, which must have led to the church of the same name before the monastery walls.

Giant monasteries, as we saw, stemmed from a Frankish tradition. The first men of the court competed in innovations in organization, like Charlemagne's friend Angilbert at Centula, and his cousin Adalhard at Corbie. These men loved to manœuvre their monks in choral worship like Frankish warriors in knightly exercises. A final example is supplied by the regulations of Adalbert's half-brother Wala. Louis the Pious had banished him, as head of the imperial party seeking to defend the unity of the imperial inheritance against the Emperor's plans for partition, to Bobbio, Columban's famous foundation, the Monte Cassino of North Italy. We do not know whether he was able to concern himself there with building schemes, but a regulation dealing with the distribution of administrative functions in the monastery, showing how thoroughly he had scrutinized the institution, fell within his brief abbacy (834-36). He instituted no less than twenty-four posts in this abbey. The general administration was entrusted to the *praepositus primus*, discipline to the *decanus*, church services to the *custos ecclesiae*; there was a librarian, an archivist, a cellarer, with his subordinates the *cellarius familiae* for the wine, the *cellarius junior* for the table utensils, and the *cellarius panis* for the bread. Alongside the *portarius hospitum*, the porter of the guest-block, stood the *hospitalarius religiosorum* and the *hospitalarius pauperum*. The various spheres of stewardship, building and handicrafts were entrusted to divers officers who were probably all monks. There is no need to enumerate them here.[7] The striving for perfect order, for provision for the slightest minutiae, characterizes the organization of this former commander. Everything was to be subordinate to the plan. The principles of a princely household were taken over by a monastic republic. The body of monks was scoured for the personalities best equipped for each of the twenty-four posts. Compared with what was available in the way of vigour and ability, such over-organization neared a Utopia in which the play of ideas outran the essential. The St Gall plan showed similar forces at work in the architectural sphere.

Monte Cassino itself, the mother house, can only with reservation be called one of the institutions affecting the structural appearance of the monastic schema. Up till now archaeological investigations have not succeeded in revealing a master-plan either for the first monastery, destroyed by the Lombards in 581, or for the second, Carolingian, monastery, destroyed by the Saracens in 883. The Carolingian monastery, started with the help of Willibald in 717, whose church Pope Zacharias consecrated in 748, to which Pepin's brother Carlmann withdrew, and which was visited by Charlemagne himself in 787, was undoubtedly an important ensemble. However, the first monastery we can reconstruct with any certainty, that of the Abbot Desiderius (1058-87), was built under the influence of Odilo's Cluny. French ideas of construction influenced the Italian site. Divergences from the adopted schema were chiefly induced by topographical considerations, such as the situation on a narrow ridge. The sketch shows that the whole area to the east of the cloister was kept for the chapter-house, that the elongated dorter occupied the whole south side, whilst the refectory abutted on both the cloister and the atrium. The siting of the kitchen, infirmary, and cellar manifests the rational thinking behind Monte Cassino too. But I am anticipating. I am however inclined to assume that even the eighth-century monastery was more likely to have been influenced by those in France than the other way round. To repeat my thesis: the Benedictine monastic schema is a distinctive product of the Carolingian renaissance.

3

The St Gall Utopia

The most astonishing document of early medieval Benedictine monastic architecture is the plan of an ideal Carolingian monastery preserved in the library of St Gall. It represents the only architectural drawing antedating the thirteenth century in Europe to reveal the exercise of powers of planning. It owes its preservation to its obverse having been re-used for a transcription of a Life of St Martin in the twelfth century, so that the folded sheet enjoyed the protection of a library. Seventeenth-century scholars were already aware of its value, the great historian of the Benedictine Order, Mabillon (1632-1707), being the first to discuss it. Its elucidation reaches a high point in Walter Horn's model, associated with a comprehensive monograph.

The plan is 44 Carolingian inches long, by 30 inches wide. It was drawn with red lead on the carefully smoothed faces of five calfskins. Scrutiny of the technique reveals that it is a copy of a slightly older original. The drawing contains more than forty buildings in plan on a scale of 1:192. Walter Horn has explained how $\frac{1}{16}$ of a Carolingian inch was appropriate for representing each Carolingian foot on the ground ($16 \times 12 = 192$). The English-speaking world still uses scales that are multiples of twelve. Everything is entered on this plan, from the purposes of the buildings, the names of the titular saints of the altars, and details of some of the furnishings and their scale, down to the names of trees in the orchard. Wherever a designation is complemented by reference to its spiritual significance, prose yields to verse to express the participation of the client in his work. These lines are for instance legible round the Cross in the centre of the cemetery:

> *Inter ligna soli haec scissima crux –*
> *In qua ppûae poma salutis olent.*
> The holiest of the trees of the field is the Cross,
> Fragrant with the fruits of eternal salvation.

The conceit is extended by two lines above and below the Cross:

> *Hanc circum iaceant defuncta cadaura frmm*
> *Qua radiante Iterum Regna polj accipiant.*
> Let the bodies of the departed brothers lie round this Cross
> And through its radiance attain the Kingdom of Heaven.

We have entered an ideal world. Its inspirer wanted to create an ideal model. He was aware that a monastery of such perfection could never be built. Therefore he did not attempt to submit a plan fit for use. The preamble makes this plain: 'I have sent you, Gozbert my dearest son, this modest example of the disposition of a monastery, that you may dwell upon it in spirit. . . .' Gozbert was Abbot of St Gall from 816-36, and had occupied himself with plans for rebuilding the

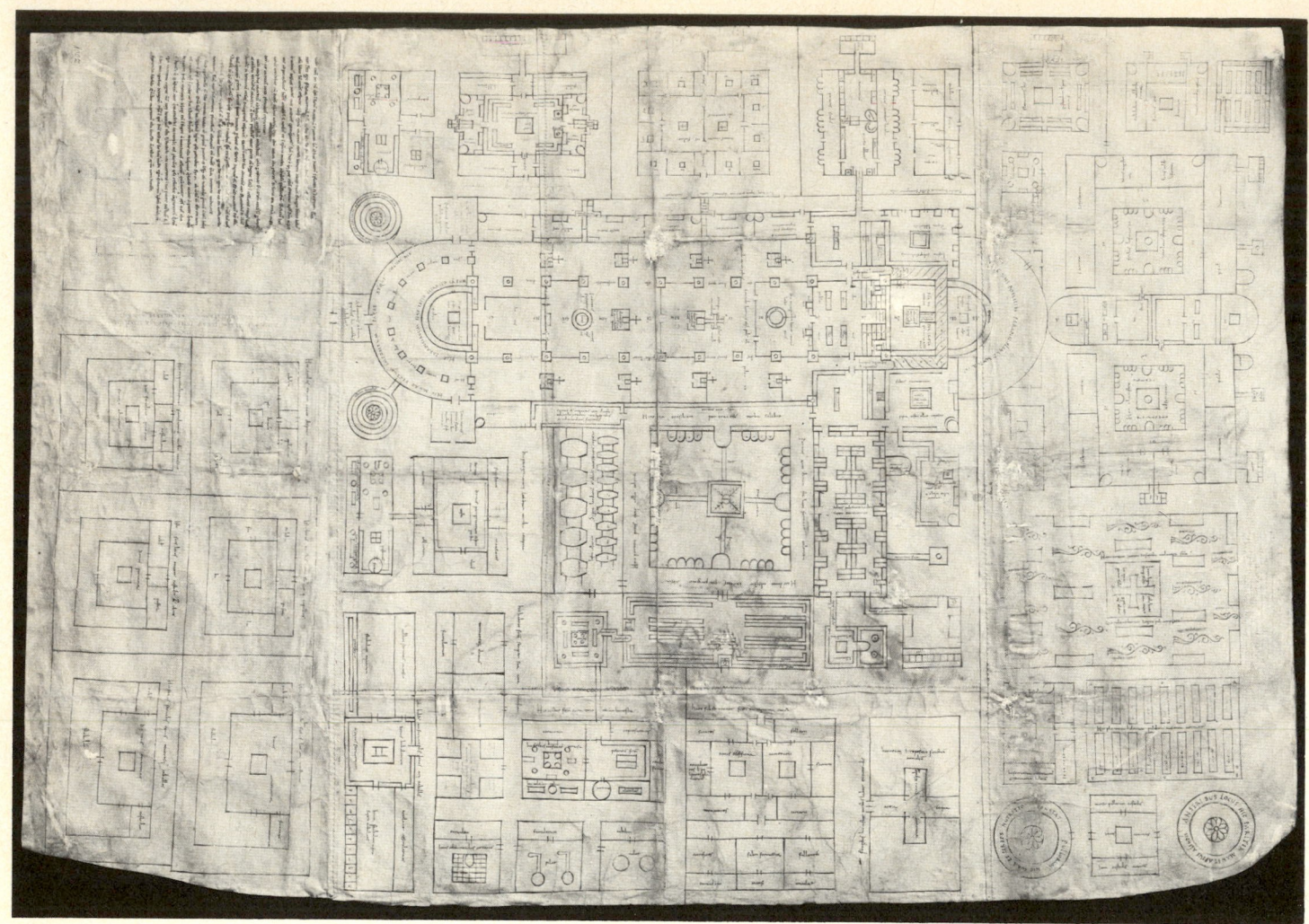

27 *The St Gall plan, this copy made between 816 and 836*

abbey from at least 830, possibly even years beforehand. A monk from Reichenau emerges as the scribe of 265 out of 341 of the entries on the plan. Gozbert's copy was meant to be the basis and inspiration for fresh plans. The original in Reichenau, which it will have agreed with in all purely architectural details, was not immediately related to any rebuilding, for, as far as we know, no giant monastery was at that time intended to replace the existing one. The copyist only allowed for the données of the situation in St Gall in the disposition of the altars and choice of their titular saints. Nonetheless there are numerous indications that Haito (763-836), Abbot of Reichenau from 806-23, and from 802-23 also Bishop of Basle and one of the leading men at Charlemagne's court, designed the plan. For we know what prompted him mentally.

Once the earlier Frankish kings had appointed the monasteries with new tasks in the world and for the state, Charlemagne recognized that the Benedictine Rule was best suited to provide the objective framework for them. It was essential that the monastery as a school, mission centre, agricultural concern and administrative base, should be a tightly disciplined unit. He looked with approval on the reforming zeal of Benedict of Aniane (*c.* 750-821), the son of a count and comrade-in-arms of his youth, in the south of France. Benedict was Frankish. Yet he remained in thrall to the urge toward boundless asceticism, that had condemned both Eastern and Irish monasticism to an attitude basically hostile to refinement, and to which really only the chief church of his southern French monastery formed an exception. It is described to us as decorated with great splendour. He must early

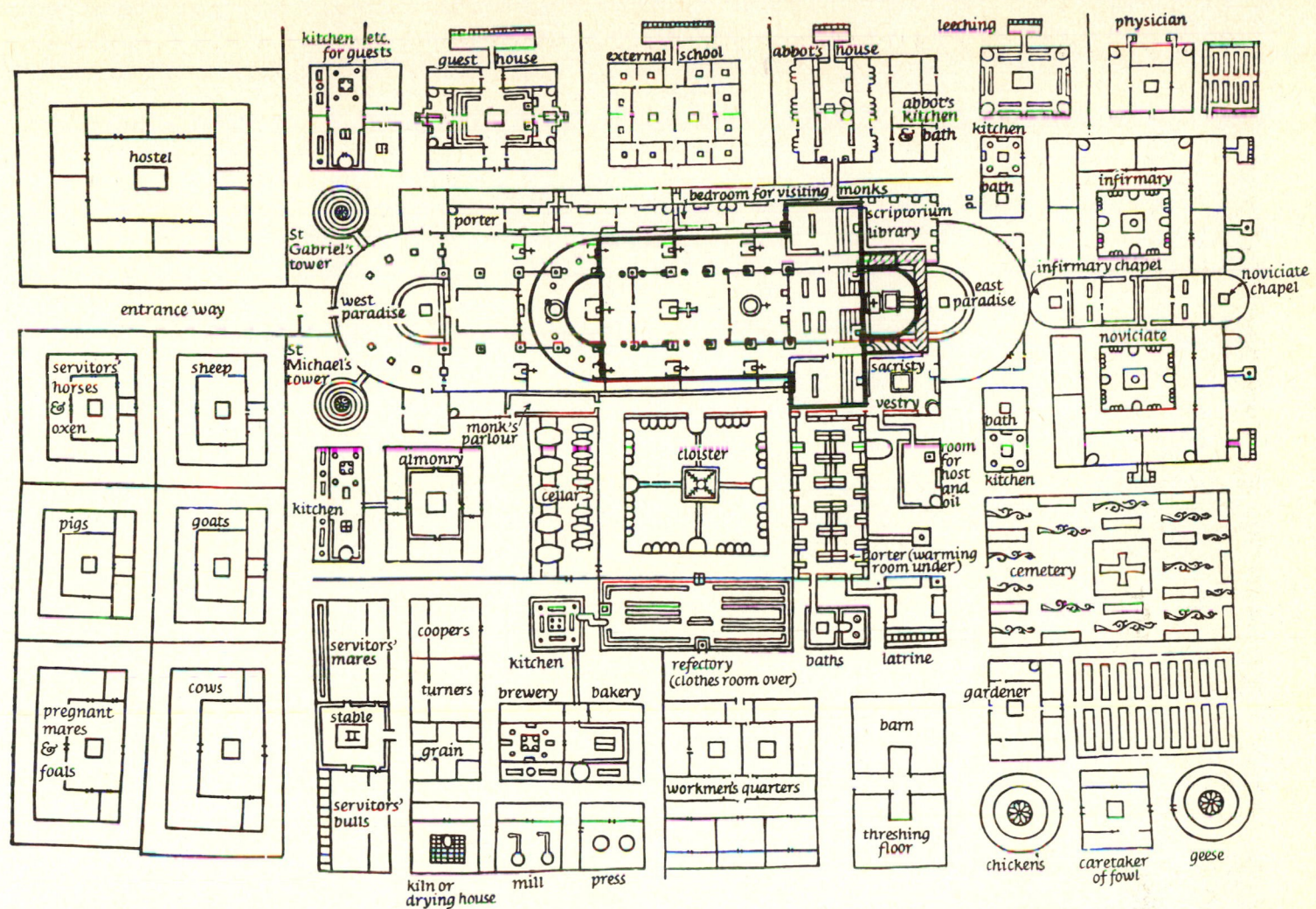

28 The St Gall plan redrawn, with identifications translated

on have gained an influence over Louis the Pious, who spent his youth in the royal residences of Aquitaine. He bears the chief responsibility for having made this Frankish prince into the 'Pious', a waverer consumed by agonies of conscience, whose doubt in his own mission, his 'divinity', led to the breakup of the Empire. If Charlemagne was intent on creating a monastic hierarchy, then Louis found the one man in his century with the stature to head it. Louis summoned Benedict to Aachen and gave him the opportunity of building a new, model monastery at Inden, the later Cornelismünster. As 'Abbot of the Empire', Benedict of Aniane presided over both synods, of 816 and 817 *in domo Aquis palatii qua ad Lateranis dicitur*. Their conclusions survive in the edicts of 23 August 816 and 10 July 817 (q.v. extracts, Document 111). The resistance of many abbots – of those, one would like to assume, from monasteries in the north of the realm – may have compelled the watering down of the stiff resolutions of 816 into the milder ones of 817. Benedict must here not only have been influenced by allusions to the Rule itself, but also by others to old and venerable customs in monasteries close to the ruling house. The St Gall plan can be described as a visible demonstration of monastic life according to the mild resolutions of 817. Taking up a much-discussed suggestion of A. Dobsch's in 1916, Walter Horn has demonstrated this in his great book on St Gall.[8]

Abbot Haito seems to have been one of the leading figures in the fight against southern French ideas of asceticism. In the so-called *Murbach Statutes* we have a collection of the 816 resolutions written, according to a suggestion of B.

Bischoff's, in his see of Basel, the commentary to which partly prefigures or argues for the milder decisions of 817. The political role conferred by the Frankish leaders on the monasteries is not reconcilable with the extreme asceticism of a community of monks turning their backs on the world. It is again Walter Horn who has drawn attention to five key points, of which three retreat from the severe conclusions of 816, but follow the milder ones of 817, whilst of the remaining two the first was subjoined in 816 itself, and the other in 817. The first three points concern themselves with the questions of whether an abbot could lay claim to his own palace as on the plan; whether the monks themselves, and not merely the novices and the sick, were entitled to at least a few baths; and whether the monastery besides an inner school for the noviciate, should have an external one for laymen and strangers. This last point especially had long been a cause of contention in Frankish monasteries. Was one to align oneself with the educational projects of the ruling house, or with the idea of retreat from which monasticism stemmed, and which Irish monks were trying to uphold everywhere on the continent? The two schools on the plan are so situated that they are roughly equidistant from the room over the scriptorium next to the north side of the choir, where the library was to be housed. (The first is at the top of the plan; the second, labelled 'noviciate', is on the right below the infirmary.) Our fourth point, that already insisted on in 816, involves the decision that working-space for the craftsmen who produced shoes and clothes for the monks should be supplied inside the walls. In this way the autonomy of the monastery was enhanced, and traffic with neighbouring settlements was reduced to a minimum. A fifth conclusion makes the connection with the edict of 817 particularly apparent. It embodies the stipulation that monks passing through should be shown to a bed-chamber near to the church. *Ut dormitorium iuxte oratorium constituatur, ubi supervenientes monachi dormiant* (Document III, Cap. XXIV). The position of this chamber (to the left of the church) shows that the abbot wanted to exercise the tact of any true host. It allowed the transient monks the choice between the strict life of the monks singing the offices, and the free life of lay visitors. This is a detail also prescribed by Hildemar in his commentary on the Rule (Document v, pp. 611ff.). In this document of about 850 the reasons are found for Benedict's Rule having already lodged visiting monks right by the church, and laymen separately in a third place.

The fact that for the church itself the St Gall plan reproduces fairly accurately the plan of Cologne cathedral, then in course of construction, may be taken as further evidence of the link with the Synod of Aachen. In the nature of things, the Imperial Chaplain and Archbishop of Cologne, Hildebald, must have been associated with Benedict of Aniane in presiding over the synods. He was also the builder of the new cathedral. That we nonetheless prefer to assume that the St Gall plan was commissioned by Haito, is because it is not the sole document in his life incorporating the urge for a perfectly ordered Utopia. Haito must have stood out amongst his peers as a strong and many-sided, but also as a head-strong character. He is the builder of the great new monastery church of Reichenau and of the new Basle Cathedral. Charlemagne sent him as ambassador to the imperial court in Constantinople in 811, and his vanished dispatch is reputed to have been both thorough and impressive. He attempted to arrest the decline of the diocesan clergy in Basle by sensible and severe statutes that won some renown as the *Capitulare Hettonis*. Following the first Synod of Aachen he wrote the *Murbach Statutes* we mentioned, containing his glosses on the edicts in the light of the Rule of St Benedict. Their rediscovery in 1950 by J. Semmler in an original version in Wolfenbüttel removed all doubts as to the identity of their author. It is also likely that it was he that commissioned the two monks of Reichenau, Grinald and Tatto, to travel to Aachen, where they made an exact copy of the transcription of the Rule that Charlemagne had got from Monte Cassino. 'In our transcript not a sentence, not a syllable, yea not a letter of the original is wanting', they comment on their text, which also survives in St Gall. The 816 Synod of Aachen laid down as its first and most important article, which Haito expanded upon in his *Murbach Statutes*, that every last word of the Rule was to be discussed in the monasteries, and secondly, that wherever possible every single monk should learn to recite it by heart. Here we are faced by the same determined desire for unattainable perfection as in the Plan. *Primo enim capitula denuntiandum est, ut cum abbates ad propria loca remeassent, regulam per singula verba discutientes relegerent et adimplerent. . . . Secundo, ut qui possent regulam memoriter discerent. . . . Uni iungendum putavimus ut, cum ex corde recitanda discitur, a dicta- toribus ordinatis discentibus interpretatur.* (Corpus Consuetudinum Monasticarum I, 1963, 441).

It throws light on Haito's character that in his fifty-sixth year he resolutely renounced all his offices in Basle and Reichenau, in order to apply himself unreservedly to life after and subject to the Rule. At one moment we see the aging abbot busied in sending letters in every direction, in order to incorporate, name by name, every magnate, bishop and monastery in the Empire of which he knew into long lists for a brotherhood of prayer, as if he was trying to convoke a diet of the prominent people of his century in the hereafter. At the next, he was sufficiently impressed to note down the visions of Limbo and Hell that had visited his pupil Wetti on his deathbed in 824. Walafried Strabo, his greatest pupil, turned his prose into verse, and thus into a model for Dante's *Divina Commedia*. Haito seems to have been a Carolingian churchman of the type we often find in the eighth and ninth centuries, with a yearning for extremes.

On the plan the monastery was clearly demarcated into four main areas. This may be seen as the novelty of Haito's arrangements. He was inspired by the Synod of Aachen, and surely also by the building ventures of the imperial court, to re-think the whole institution of the monastery in terms of its functions.

The first of these areas was that of the claustrum, or monastic enclosure round the cloister – the cut-off world composed of dorter to the east, refectory to the south, and cellar to the west. There was only one means of access to this zone, the undisturbed setting of days passed strictly according to the Rule, and that was through the monks' parlour, where, following the Rule, even guests' feet were washed. Subsequently in Cluny, but perhaps already here, the whole place was to be called the *mandatum*, after the words of Christ that the monks sang during the foot-washing: '*Mandatum novum do vobis: ut diligatis invicem*' – 'a new law I give you, that you shall love one another'. It is already indicated on the plan as '*exitus et introitus ante claustrum ad conloquendum cum hostibus et ad man- datum faciendum*' – the entry and exit to the cloister for talking to guests in and performing the *mandatum* ('maundy'), or footwashing. The buildings round the cloister form the monastery within a monastery, the enclosure. The plan shows the dorter with its seventy-seven beds on the upper floor, the refectory with its tables – including that of the abbot – on the ground floor, whilst the chapter was not yet thought to need a special room. The monks gathered to read the Rule on the benches in the arm of the cloister alongside the church. Inscrip- tions disclose that under the dorter was the day-room of the monks, the warm- ing room, and above the refectory, the wardrobe; further, that in the cellar wing, a larder for bacon and other 'necessities' was to correspond above to the cellar below. The cloister is exactly a hundred feet square. The placing of col- umns, arcades and buttresses betrays concern for the greatest regularity and exact symmetry. Internal regimentation was to be reflected aesthetically.

This shut-off area of peace to the south of the church is balanced by a second area to the north of the church that was open to the world. There were to be found buildings for distinguished guests, the school for laity and strangers, the abbot's house, and the house for his kitchens and bath. A large kitchen building with a brewery and bakery for the guests alone was also anticipated. The Emperor and his court might be among them. It reminds us that the Rule had laid down that the abbot was to eat with them and not with the monks. When Monte Cassino was rebuilt in the eleventh century the abbatial palace and guest- buildings were also arrayed to the left of the church (*vide* Pl. 26). Centuries later the state court of Baroque monasteries was to develop, out of this open area,

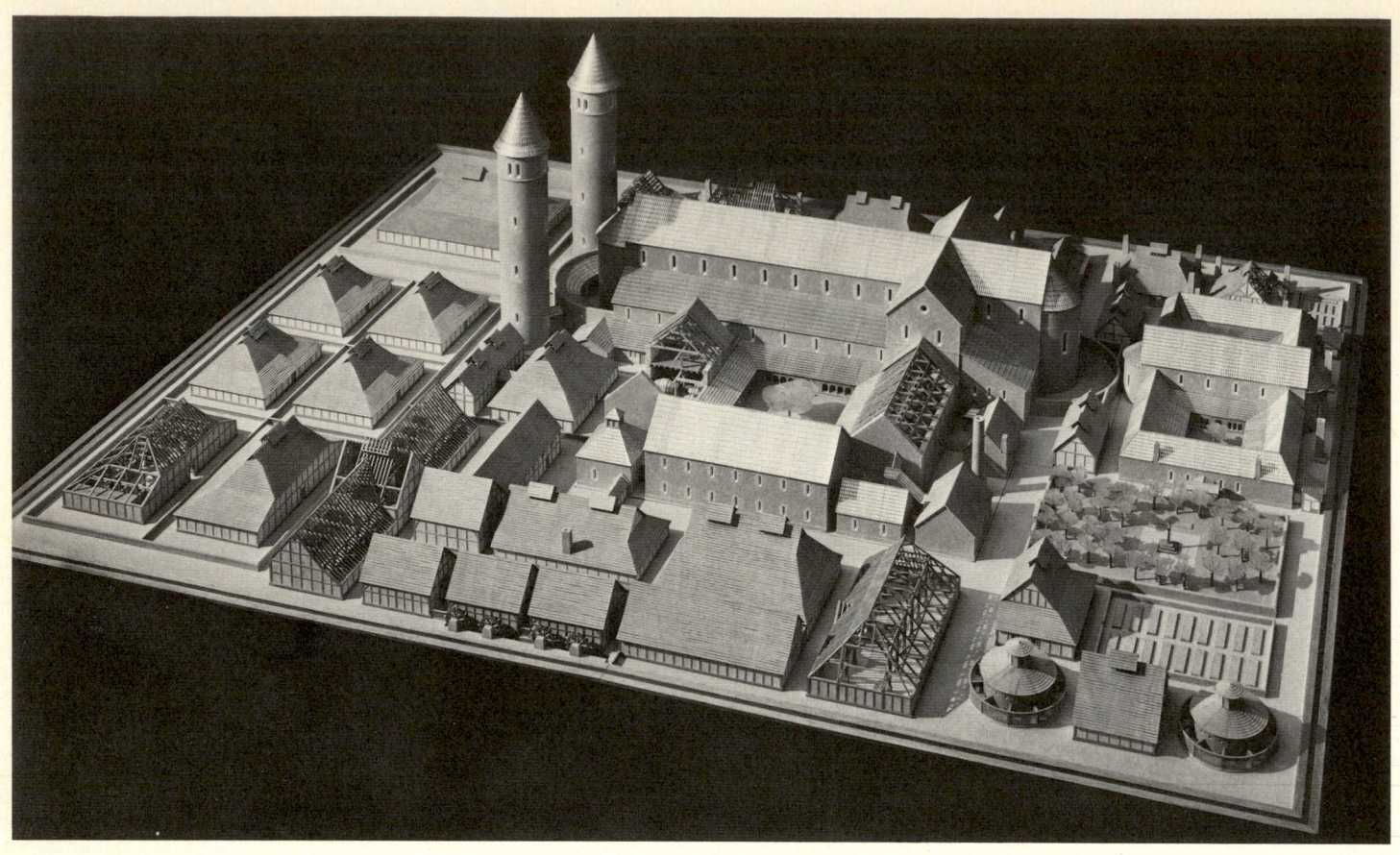

29 Model made from the St Gall plan by Walter Horn and Ernest Born. This view is orientated in the same direction as the plan itself reproduced on p. 38

mostly to the left of the church, balancing the conventual court, as in Weingarten (*vide infra* p. 207). In St Gall the ground-plan already tells us that the abbot's house was to be a stone palace, with fireplaces in the two large ground-floor rooms, and arcaded and columned passages opening outwards along the sides – a consciously representational effect, making it the most important piece of secular Carolingian architecture that we can recreate, besides the Royal Hall at Lorsch and the Palace of Aachen.

The remaining two areas are those of the domestic buildings, in which the craftsmen and menials lived, in their workshops and alongside the animals, and for the sick and the novices behind the church, i.e. those no longer or not yet bound to observe the strict life of the Rule.

Later centuries were to develop, just as for the state court, a rigid schema for this domestic court, in front of the church and to the south near the conventual buildings (*vide* pp. 212ff.). Here the draughtsman was more intent on comprehensiveness in including all the activities necessary to the running of the monastic city than on their subordination to an architecturally conceived whole that also took account of the functional coordination of barns, stalls and workshops. We may be sure that Haito and his draughtsman were also aware that these domestic buildings lacked the necessary space, i.e. the actual courtyard. Their preoccupations are manifest in the thoroughness that went into thinking out this Noah's Ark of a monastery – with geese- and hen-houses to the right and left of the house of the caretaker of fowl; a drying-kiln, a thresher and a mill; stables for the horses and oxen where the menials also lived; a sheep-cote with shelter for the shepherds, a similar arrangement for the goats and goatherds; a cow-byre with shelter for the dairymen; a piggery also sheltering the swineherds; and finally, a stable for pregnant mares and their foals, again with a place with a hearth for their grooms. The very striving for completeness and the insistence on the rigorous allocation of all the stalls, stores, and workshops to distinct buildings lends this plan its Utopian character and numbers it amongst princely amusements, like the equally Utopian town-plans and ideal fortifications of future centuries.

The commissioner of the plan gave especial attention to the fourth zone, that of the novices and the sick. For both the embryonic monks and the old and sick a miniature monastery was envisaged behind the conventual church, each with its own cloister and chapel and its own bath-house and kitchens. Next to the sick-zone lay the house of the doctors and the blood-letting theatre in which operations were also performed. The doctors – of whom there must have been at least two, for there were two separate lavatories at their disposal – were also responsible for tending a small garden of simples. The inscriptions speak of a *domus medicorum*. They specify that the chronic sick were to sleep there too (*cubiculum valde infirmorum*), and even where the senior doctor was to live (*mansio medici ipsius*), and where his medicine-chest was to stand (*armarium pigmentor*). To keep journeys short, the graveyard was as close as possible to the infirmary. This monastery *in parvo* even had like the main one a dorter, a refectory, a storeroom and an arcaded cloister. By 800 this last went without saying in a Benedictine monastery.

There were buildings and groups of buildings belonging to none of these four zones, and here especially one can admire the cunning with which they are so sited as most rationally to implement their function. Among them are the large hostel for the retinue of the distinguished guests, and the houses (almonry) for pilgrims and the poor, to whom the monastery traditionally owed hospitality. They are deliberately put near the church and near the porter's lodgings (e), whose job it also was to look after the pilgrims. The monks' brewery and bakery were so arranged that they could reach them without crossing the courtyard (9). Their baths and lavatories were also only to be accessible from the dormitories. It is typical of the then current outlook that no lavatories were envisaged for the menials and retinue, whereas these *necessaria* were plenteously provided for the distinguished guests, the abbot's house, the monasteries of the novices and the sick, and even for the operating-theatre. Directly attached to the church on the side of the abbot's house were, on the ground floor the scriptorium, and above it the library, whilst the sacristy and vestry were planned on the

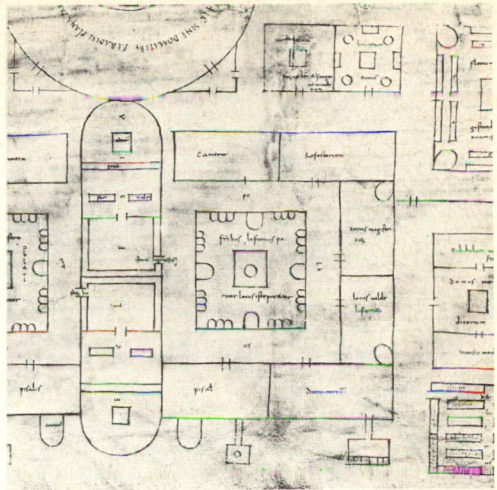

30, 31 St Gall. The infirmary and novices' cloister, seen from the east in the original (above) and model. This whole complex, a separate monastery in miniature, lay behind the east end of the church. The two chapels form one continuous range in the centre, with cloisters on either side. Note the chimneys and latrines in the foreground

opposite side. The library would not retain its place here. It was transposed in later monasteries to the cloister beneath the dorter: its place opposite the abbot's house in St Gall may have been determined firstly by his desire to have these treasures constantly under his eye, and secondly for his being able to show them to distinguished strangers as the real treasure of the monastery. It is indicative of the care devoted by Haito to every detail, that he provided to the right of the sacristy for a special building for the preparation of the host and the reservation of the sacred oil.

Counting the beds in the dorter depicted on the plan suggests that seventy-seven monks were envisaged. The refectory tables would have seated a yet greater number. Even the abbot's house would have had beds for at least eight people. The house for distinguished guests had four separate rooms in which a prince might have lodged with his retinue. There were besides two antechambers for bodyservants. It is noteworthy that the horses here would have to have been led through the common-room to reach their stables. For none of the guests wanted to sleep apart from his horses.

Two questions have repeatedly provoked research: the size and shape of the church, and the reconstruction of the timber and half-timbered buildings that would have surrounded it. In his model Walter Horn arrived at ancillary buildings for which he drew on the study of all the sources for medieval wooden architecture. As far as we can judge the model reproduces all the significant aspects of the design. A supposed contradiction between the given measurements and the drawing of the church has inspired numerous theories, which mostly only succeed in convincing their inventors. The latest suggestions by Adolf Reinle are no exception (Bibl. 55). He thought it possible to deny the whole problem by an alternative translation of the crucial inscription, AB ORIENTE IN OCCIDENTE LONGIT PED CC – PED, taking PED not as *pedum*, but as an abbreviation of *pedare*, thus – 'from east to west measure the length two-hundredfold'. But this translation is undoubtedly wrong. The earlier view should be trusted, that these measurements refer to a later proposal attempting to reduce the size of the church, which would have led to subsequent alterations to the whole plan. For the whole plan employs a module, based on the breadth of the nave, of forty Carolingian feet, corresponding to $2\frac{1}{2}$ inches on the ruler used by the draughtsman ($\frac{1}{16}$ of an inch on the plan is equivalent to 1 foot as built). This gives the classic dimensions for the cloister of a hundred feet square, denoted as appropriate not long after by Hildemar of Corbie.[9]

But in another respect A. Reinle has taught us to look at the plan more closely. I owe to his article the information that the two miniature monasteries of the novices and the sick are drawn using not the Carolingian foot of 32·16cms, but instead the smaller Capitoline foot of 29·6cms, which has always been usual in Italy. We apparently encounter in them an arrangement borrowed from an earlier sketchplan with a different destination. It is probable that this depicted a double monastery for monks and nuns, such as was frequently built in the early days of monachism. The difference in absolute size, compared with that of the Carolingian project, is evidence of the boom based on the victories of Charlemagne. The existence of such a model forces the conclusion that regular monastic layouts were also prevalent in the south by the eighth century. Thus the strict separation of zones, down even to the chapels, which had no means of communication, would have derived from considerations less of hygiene than of morals. The existence of such a model makes it clear that the St Gall plan was not unique. In the Frankish Empire, where monasteries were everywhere being founded, enlarged and rebuilt, the most diverse plans must have been swapped amongst the abbots.

One final consideration: the plan is not only a monument of the striving toward *perfectio*, but thereby also of Carolingian spirituality and piety such as served as an example to the later Middle Ages. These are apparent in both the inscriptions and the proportions, and are also suggested by the choice of the titular saints of the altars and the disposition of the latter in the church.

For a fifth area demands attention alongside the four that we have described. The church was made so long, because it had to serve not only as that of the monks, but also as parish or pilgrimage church. The cloister only abuts on the eastern half of the nave, and the monks penetrated the church, unobserved, by the transept, either from it or from their dormitory. Only the abbot and the visiting monks had similarly discreet access to the church. The sole solemn entry to the church was at the same time the main entrance to the monastery, a broad way, described thus by an inscription:

OMNIBUS AD SCM TURBIS PATET HAEC VIA TEMPLUM
QUA SUA VOTA FERANT UNDE HILARES REDEANT
THIS IS THE WAY TO THE HOLY TEMPLE FOR THE MULTITUDES, WHITHER
THEY OFFER UP THEIR PRAYERS, WHENCE THEY MAY JOYOUSLY RETURN.

They were greeted at the entry by two high towers dedicated to the Archangels Michael and Gabriel, and having altars to these in their upper storeys so as to convey their blessing far and wide. The people assembled in the open atrium, called on the plan the Field of Paradise, with the distinguished guests coming from the left and the pilgrims from the right. Their portion of the church stretched from the altar of St Peter in the west apse to the altar of the Holy Cross in the centre of the church. They possessed, besides the font, altogether nine altars, for the multiplicity of intercessors and beneficent saints were to come together in an imaginary choir.

32 St Gall. Another view of the model looking north-east. In the foreground are farm buildings, at the back the church, with the claustral ranges in between. The kitchen occupies the corner

The actual monks' church began two bays before the crossing. In this part stood the ambo and the two lecterns for the Gospel and the Epistle. The crossing is given prominence as the choir in which the psalms were chanted at the Hours. To the left and right seven steps ascended to the High Altar. On the middle of them stood the altars of SS. Benedict and Columban, the founders of the Benedictine Order and of the earliest cell at St Gall respectively. The High Altar is consecrated to the Virgin and St Gallus himself, whose sarcophagus stands behind it. The sequence of the Redemptive Way through the church reaches its climax in this stirring tableau formed by the altars of those saints especially claiming the monks' allegiance. Furthermore both the pilgrims, via the entry on the right hand side, and the distinguished guests, through that on the left, could go past all the side altars directly to St Gallus's grave, and thus realize the object of their journey – direct contact with the conferrer of blessings in the darkness of the crypt.

Patrons and draughtsmen have always conceived of the whole monastery as a unity, with its four zones clustered round the church with its constellation of altars. The patron saints of the altars were for them visibly present like those of a 'Sacra Conversazione' in later panel-paintings. But this unity would have appeared incomplete, were it not anchored in hallowed proportions. The length and breadth in feet of the various parts on the plan was the subject of profound consideration. This meant that they must have striven to express architectural status through the very purity of the proportions used. The more elevated a building, the more lucid and beautiful had the figures governing its proportions to be. The *point du départ* for all observers is the module supplied by the church crossing, 40 : 40 feet. It governs not only the dimensions of the church, but also those of the buildings round the cloister, and this itself. What proportions were crucial for the patron, i.e. had a special significance for him, is hard to say. Reinle has composed series suggesting ordinance deriving from the triple ratio of the simple, so-called Golden Rule (Bibl. 55). They are as follows:

40 : 80 : 120 = Breadth of the nave : Breadth of the nave and aisles : Length of the transept.
80 : 100 : 180 = Breadth of the nave and aisles : Length of the cloister : Length of the nave.
120 : 180 : 300 = Length of the transept : Length of the nave : Length of whole church.

This table can be read horizontally or vertically. Such proportions not only reveal the will to absolute harmony, but also a spiritual approach that sought a religious symbol in every number. Three times three pointed to the Trinity, and in the horizontal and vertical equivalence of the central columns of figures the Cross appeared, to eyes used to the *carmina figurata*, the emblematic verse, of the age. This monastery plan was a network of complex interrelationships. Only once it embodied the Rule functionally, whilst the sacred received expression in numerical laws, could Haito rest content. In the light of all this we can give a literal interpretation to his letter to Abbot Gozbert. Haito begged him in studying the plan to exercise his intellect. I should like to give the reader his letter in its entirety, and as well as translating it, reveal its significance:

Haec tibi dulcissime fili cozberte de posicione officinarum paucis exemplata direxi quibus sollertiam exerceas tuam, meamque devotionem utcumque cognoscas. Ne suspiceris autem me haec ideo elaborasse, quod vos putemus nostris indigere magisteriis, sed potius ob amorem dei tibi soli scrutinanda pinxisse amicabili fraternitatis intuiti crede. Vale in christo amen.

I have sent you, Gozbert, my dearest son, this modest example of the disposition of a monastery, that you may dwell upon it in spirit . . . and know my love toward you; think not that I laboured at this design because we believed that you had need of instruction, but rather believe that we drew it through the love of God out of fraternal affection, for you to study only. Farewell in Christ, Amen.

Haito presents his brother abbot with an 'idea' on which he can exercise his intellect. He does not want to teach him, but to do him a loving favour, that will be seen as pleasing to God. Just like the Rule, but in this case for the abbot alone, the plan is to promote meditation upon the meaning and worth of the monastic life. Its very perfection elevates it above the practically useful into a work designed to further the monastic idea and glorify life in a monastery. In the same way that reflection on the purposes of a monastery is associated with meditation on the Rule, the elaboration of ideal designs in the Middle Ages must have challenged the imaginative powers of abbots just as much as in the Baroque. The St Gall plan belongs to an old tradition, and there were undoubtedly constantly letters from abbot to abbot with designs for monasteries appended.

4

Cluny

HISTORY

One monastery of the tenth and eleventh centuries towered above all the others, and resolutely raised itself to become the capital of a monastic empire – Cluny in Burgundy. This, the largest monastery ever built in the West, controlled in the twelfth century around 1,500 abbeys and priories in every part of Europe. Under Cluny's lead a centralized monastic state grew up in place of numerous and powerful individual abbeys. Its abbots, among them four great monastic leaders of sagacity and even genius, achieved a princely status. Its enemies compared them ironically with kings; super-abbots we might call them. The brethren of innumerable monasteries professed before them, not before their own abbot. They were counsellors and judges not only in the monasteries adopting their reforms, but also in the secular sphere. Emperors, Popes and Kings sought their verdict.

Cluny owed its rise and special status to three factors: firstly, to its situation in a 'power vacuum' (Walasch), an area neither belonging to the Empire nor subject to the French monarchy; secondly, to the dynasty of its four great abbots, each ruling almost a half-century; thirdly, to a new spirit of monasticism. This last also gave rise to distinctive features of the Burgundian Romanesque, that proto-Renaissance, whose finest achievements are the capitals of the columns in the choir of the third church, with representations of the nine tones, which in form and subject are the best description of what Cluny was striving to achieve.

The spiritual revival was one aspect of a general movement that changed the course of European history in the last third of the eleventh century. The various estates grew apart; Pope and Emperor became conscious of their opposing interests, the aristocracy became worldlier and bishops less so, burghers more bourgeois and monks more spiritual. Great overriding aims held sway, and it soon emerged that not only did Cluny have to adopt policies toward them all, but that it had to go beyond this and take the lead for the sake of their realization. The former counsellors and supporters of the Ottonian and Salic Emperors became defenders of the new might of the Papacy. Monasteries, dedicated to the renunciation of worldly affairs, took the van in urging Crusades in the East and the *Reconquista* in Spain. One furthering the other, both their worldly and their spiritual power grew. They became immeasurably rich and influential.

The story of Cluny reads like that of the rise of a small town to being a great power (Bibl. 59, 68, 76). From the beginning of the tenth century to the middle of the twelfth the setbacks were marginal. In 909 William of Aquitaine donated a farm with a chapel in the valley of the Grosne, a tributary of the Saône, to start a monastery. The new foundation was not to be subject to the bishop or the duke, but to the Pope alone. But the papacy in the tenth and early eleventh centuries was in no position to guide or to protect. Instead the monks rapidly became the helmsmen of the papacy. The Cluniacs also attested their attachment to Rome by dedicating virtually all their new churches to St Peter, whereas the Cistercians were to show the colour of their piety by consecrating all theirs to the Virgin.

33, 34 Cluny. Two eighteenth-century views before the destruction of the monastery after the Revolution. Above: view from the north-east. The farthest tower, over the south transept, is the one that still survives. Below: interior of the nave, looking east

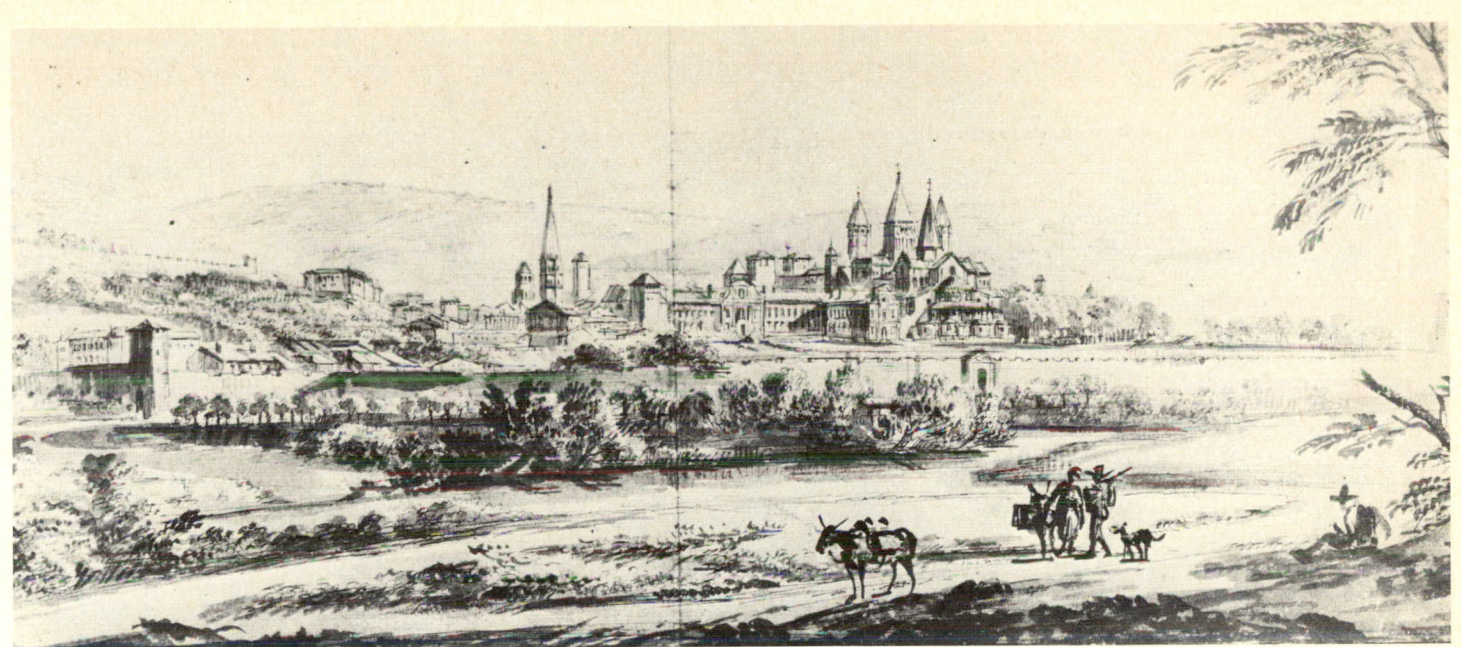

35, 36 Cluny. Two more pre-Revolution watercolours. Above: a distant view from the east, showing the church with its chevet of chapels on the right, and the monastic buildings extending to the left. Below: the west front, which led not into the church proper but into the narthex

The founding abbot was Berno of Baume (910-26), who built the first church for his twelve monks, and found his final resting-place behind its altar of St Benedict. His successor, Abbot Odo (926-44), received from the Emperor Henry I the privilege of subordinating other monasteries to his. Abbot Majolus (954-94), a friend of Otto the Great, replaced the first modest church with another, known to art historians as Cluny II. His predecessor had already begun the revolutionary work toward 950; in 981 it could be consecrated. The apogee of the Cluniac movement fell during the abbacy of his two successors, Odilo (994-1049) and Hugh of Semur (1049-1109). It was almost a symbolic act that Henry II bequeathed the abbey his imperial orb. In the parent monastery alone the number of monks rose from 73 in 1063 to over 300 in 1122. Expressive of its new power and spiritual vigour is the building of the third successive church (1088-*c*. 1120), Cluny III. It was at one and the same time the largest Romanesque church, the largest French church, and the largest abbey ever built.

In the course of the fifty-five years of his abbacy Odilo had complemented the church of Cluny II with new monastery buildings, the marble cloister of which amazed contemporaries. Yet Hugh of Semur was forced to see that it still could not contain the rising number of monks. For a whole century the enlargement of the colossus was constantly being projected. Plans for rebuilding and lesser interventions accumulated. The incumbency of the vain Pons de Megeuil (1109-22) was a setback, as he was expelled from Cluny and died excommunicate in Rome. Not till his second successor, Peter the Venerable (1122-56) – Hugh II only ruled a few months – could the gigantic task reach a certain stage of completion. This is not the place to go into the lives of the four great and saintly abbots. Majolus ruled forty years; Odilo for fifty-five; Hugh of Semur achieved exactly sixty, and Peter the Venerable thirty-six. History knows of no elective monarchy with such an unbroken record of success. One must also remember that the building and rebuilding of the church and conventual buildings was never the focus of attention. Building was done with the left hand, whilst the right ruled an empire. And building was to one end only: the life of a monk was to be almost exclusively devoted to the celebration of the liturgy, to such long drawn-out services, that by comparison meditation and study were virtually, and bodily labour wholly, neglected. Chants and litanies filled the whole working day. This 'art for God's sake' now seemed the sole purpose of the monk. The few fragments of building or works of art that we know of or survive evince the exemplary character that was intended for them. Cluny gave the lead both as an order and in its artistic achievements. The monastery must have showed itself at the peak of its powers at the encounter of Pope Innocent IV and Saint Louis in 1245. Glowing with pride, the monks relate that they were in a position to lodge the Pope's retinue of twelve cardinals and twenty bishops, as well as the King and his court, his mother and his brother, not to mention the Byzantine Emperor and his train, without having themselves to give up their dorter, refectory, chapter-house, or indeed any key building.[10] As early as the twelfth century we learn that up to 1,200 fathers and brothers could be accommodated in the dormitories and dining-halls. The church held thousands.

'Cluny is the greatest creation of the Middle Ages', wrote Emile Mâle. 'To persevere is harder than to start afresh', Peter the Venerable had prophetically riposted to his friend and opponent, Bernard of Clairvaux. Decline set in immediately after his death. It led in 1252 to the renunciation of independence and the submission of the monastery to the King's protection. Thereafter the abbots were no longer freely elected. Most of them resided, like Richelieu and Mazarin who were both to be *Abbés commendataires* of Cluny, in Paris. Even as a congregation Cluny was absorbed into the congregation of St Maur (1634-44), and subsequently into that of St Vanne. The last *Abbé commendataire* was Cardinal Dominique de la Rochefoucauld (1757 onwards), who, on his sporadic visits to Cluny, lived in a special château and no longer in the monastery.

Cluny suffered severely from the onslaughts of the two eighteenth-century movements hostile to anything medieval – the Enlightenment, with its classical

38 *Cluny. Interior of the south transept as it exists today. Squinches in the central bay form the octagon supporting the tower*

37 *Cluny. The south transept, the only substantial part of the great church now standing*

mania for regularity and uniformity, and the French Revolution. In 1727 the old monastery buildings were torn down. The Paris-produced plans for rebuilding, which would have given a château-like appearance to the whole, were only partially executed around and after 1750. The townsfolk of Cluny began to break up the huge church immediately after the secularization in 1790. Their gall was roused by these witnesses to an archaic power. The new belief in progress wanted to liberate itself from all traces of the past. The campaign of restoration begun in the twenties of the nineteenth century had no more than rubble to rescue. And though French archaeology has ever since laid stress on the grandeur of the original achievement that was so destroyed, the French public has up till now always sided with the Revolution. This is linked to the fact that large-scale excavations have never been conducted, and that the new owners impede inspection of the remains. Following several attempts to redeem what still survived in the nineteenth century, it has remained to the American architect, Kenneth J. Conant, to endeavour the task of reconstruction, at least in plans and models, in decades of idealistic effort. His output contains no less than twelve articles on Cluny between 1929 and 1965, and the final summing-up is still outstanding (Bibl. 77-86). Conant has bit by bit tried to piece together a picture of the whole complex, using trial trenches, interpretation of the written sources, and speculations on possible mathematical and geometrical regularities. He has constantly been forced to revise his opinions in the course of his studies. The evidence for determining many details is inadequate. Odilo would undoubtedly no more have accepted the compromises shown in Conant's plans of Cluny II, than Peter the Venerable would have in Cluny III. Though it is certain that every individual building was conceived of as it related to the whole plan, we still do not know whether there really were for the monastery buildings, as for the church, only two overall designs. It is tempting to suggest that, in the case of a gigantic complex stimulating projects throughout two centuries, successive plans were superimposed, so that Conant's reconstructions propounding one monastery by Odilo, and another by Peter, can only be abstractions.

Nonetheless, in the present state of our knowledge these two reconstructions contain everything of importance built or completed in the early eleventh and the late eleventh and twelfth centuries respectively. Here our most fruitful sources are the general plan of the monastery done from measurements made before the destruction of 1623, and another of about 1710 (terminus post quem 1698, & ante quem 1727). The church and the greater part of the monastic buildings were little changed in the intervening 500 years. Nonetheless, these plans can only give an incomplete answer as to which buildings were put up or renewed between the twelfth and the seventeenth centuries. Comparison with Conant's plan of the monastery of Peter the Venerable shows up a series of new buildings and rebuildings. The detailed history of the architecture of Cluny has yet to be written.

In investigating the St Gall plan we spoke of four zones that were brought together in the ideal design. Three of them recur in Odilo's monastery. Only the domestic buildings were, save for a few workshops, omitted. The monks no longer worked in the fields. Cluny farmed through tenants. The spheres of the distinguished guests and of the pilgrims are clearly distinguishable to the left of, and in front of the church. The tendency toward the subsequent 'State Courts' of the Baroque has made a great advance. The conventual buildings round the cloister agree in their disposition with those of the St Gall plan. The only additions are the chapter-house, with the Lady Chapel attached, and the parlour for conversations, since the Cluniacs required unconditional silence in the cloister, dorter, and refectory. As in St Gall the infirmary and cemetery lie to the east of the church, the latter hard against the chevet of the abbey. The monks sought their last resting-place in the very shadow of the Almighty. More significantly, the infirmary was separated from the noviciate, which was situated in the south to the right of the cloister. The separation is innately logical, and will doubtless have been employed in practice in the Carolingian period.

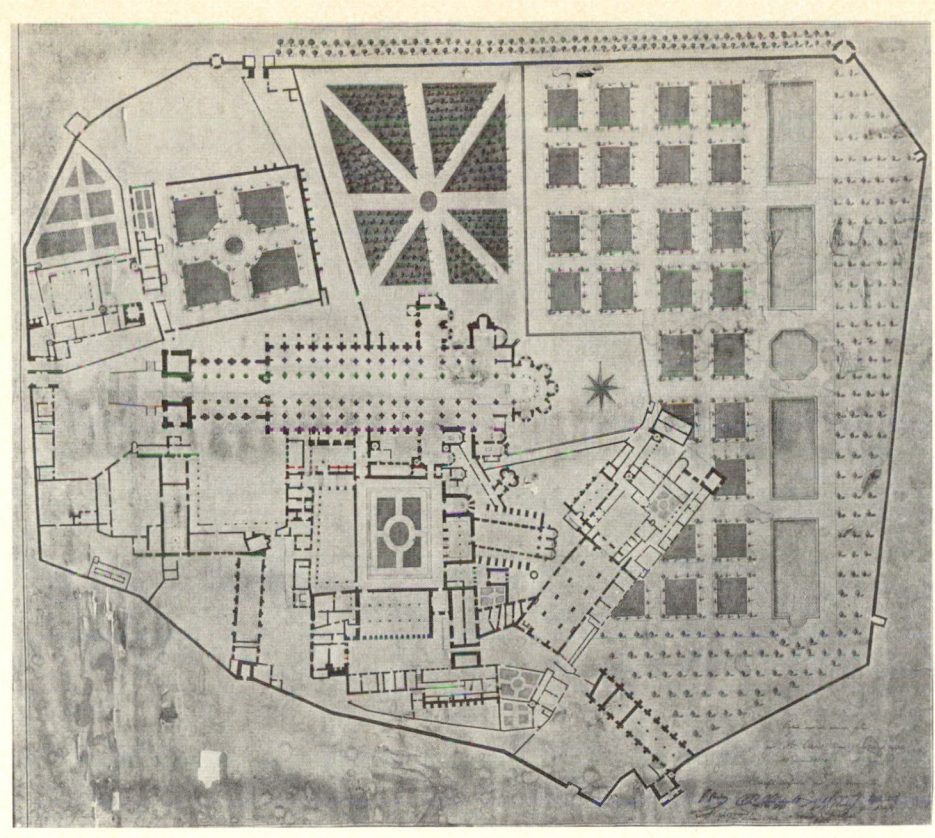

39 Cluny. Plan of the monastery (Cluny III) engraved in 1710. It had changed little in the previous five hundred years

But the most important innovation is to be found in another element first palpable on Conant's sketched reconstruction – the buildings for the serving brethren, the long, narrow range demarcating the monastic precinct to the west. The ground floor was for the horses of both the monastery and strangers, the upper floor contained the dorter and refectory of the lay-brothers and *conversi*. With the Cistercians this section was to become an important element in monastic architecture. It should not be confused with the domestic buildings of the older monasteries, which in the case of the Cistercians was to spread outside the realm of the lay-brothers. Instead it betokens a general development in western monasticism, which was variously allowed for by the Cluniacs and the Cistercians, as well as by other Orders.

As in Benedict's time, in a Carolingian monastery there were still relatively few ordained priests amongst the brothers. Even great scholars and monastic leaders like Alcuin and Paul the Deacon were content with minor orders. The monks, both priests and brothers, performed all the chores together, leaving only such work as would have detained them from the Offices – for instance, tending the cattle – to menials, who were often serfs. Subsequently a 'clericalization' of the monks occurred, in that ever more became priests. But even amongst those declining to take orders, a less robust attitude prevailed. They no longer worked in the fields. At the same time humbler folk, who were neither capable nor desirous of training for even modest capacities, sought the monastic life. The monastery servants themselves aspired to be accepted into the community of the religious. Hence in the course of the eleventh and early twelfth centuries a new class of monk, the *conversi*, grew up on the periphery of the monastic community, bound by eternal vows and having their own rules. It was also known for members of the higher orders, knights and counts, even priests and bishops, to be moved by penitence and the desire for humility to prefer the simpler habit of the *conversi* to that of a full monk. *Conversi* as a deliberate institution go back to the foundation of Camaldoli by St Romuald in 1012. The Cistercians were to refine on the idea yet further. *Patres* – if the distinction may be allowed – were joined by *fratres*, to whom all menial functions were soon left. Special buildings were set apart for them in the monastery, and special pews in the church. Cluny II and Cluny III as built, show that their integration was not then completed, nor their incorporation into the monastery thoroughly thought out.

Do Conant's reconstructions of the monasteries of Abbot Odilo of 1043 and that of Peter the Venerable of 1154 stand up to critical analysis? Undoubtedly they do in their general layout, but they are open to doubt in many details. Nor are the stages of rebuilding known with any exactness. The monks were forever faced with the task of amplifying and improving on their huge complex without for a single day disturbing the course of the Rule. The author has gone over the possibilities with students of architecture, without coming to any firm conclusions. It may be accepted that between 950 and 1150 building was always going on somewhere in Cluny, alternating between the church and the conventual buildings. The earliest church of Cluny I must have been succeeded by improvements to the monastery buildings before the major project of Cluny II was undertaken. The monastery appropriate to this church was erected by Odilo in the early eleventh century. But plans for a third church did not follow immediately on the completion of the second monastery. Around and after 1080 a situation arose of sporadic building on both church and monastery. By the death of Hugh of Semur the institution was on such a scale as to make constant maintenance work necessary. The Middle Ages never ceased to convert, renew and add to sections of this gigantic complex. After the middle of the twelfth century the burden of building overstretched the declining resources of the monastery. The maxim applies equally to Cluny, that great buildings are first completed when the zenith of the institutions that sustain them is past.

ODILO'S MONASTERY (CLUNY II)

All attempts to reconstruct Odilo's monastery suffer from the fact that, save the church, all that can be verified are a few walls by means of trial trenches; but they are furthered by the written sources which, in the light of subsequent rebuilding, leave no doubt as to the general layout.

The *Life of the Abbot* reveals that, with the exception of the walls of the church, he thoroughly rebuilt the monastery within and without (Document VII). A contemporary observer stood in these buildings filled with admiration, and recorded a few features (Document VIII). The rules of the monastery provided for visiting ecclesiastics to see the conventual buildings. Laymen were not allowed access. It is the first account to suggest that the age thought not only the church, but also the monastery buildings worthy of a visit. There was a set tour, led by the prior. It was stipulated that the hours after Mass should be chosen for this, whilst the fathers were still praying in the church and would not be disturbed in their rooms. The path of the visit permits no doubt as to the rightness of the main lines of Conant's plan.

The tour began from the almonry (No. 16 on the plan), the *domus elemosynaria*, where the St Gall plan had already specified that the guests' feet were to be washed. The guests were first shown the storehouse (15) and kitchens (13, 14), then the refectory (10), from which the noviciate was visited (21). Then back to the cloister to see the dorter (5, 6). The text does not mention the chapter-house (4), whose situation close to the church is known to us from other sources, but it will not have been left out, not least because it gave access to the Lady Chapel (19). The tour ended with a visit to the infirmary (20). The church and guest-houses were not included, as they would be anyway familiar to visitors. Nor were the workshops mentioned (22), since they were not rated worthy of a visit. It is noteworthy then that the refectory was not directly visited from the cloister, but that cellar and kitchens were taken in on the way. They must have been interesting structurally. That the noviciate and the infirmary to the south and to the west were inspected, demonstrates that the object was to reveal the internal

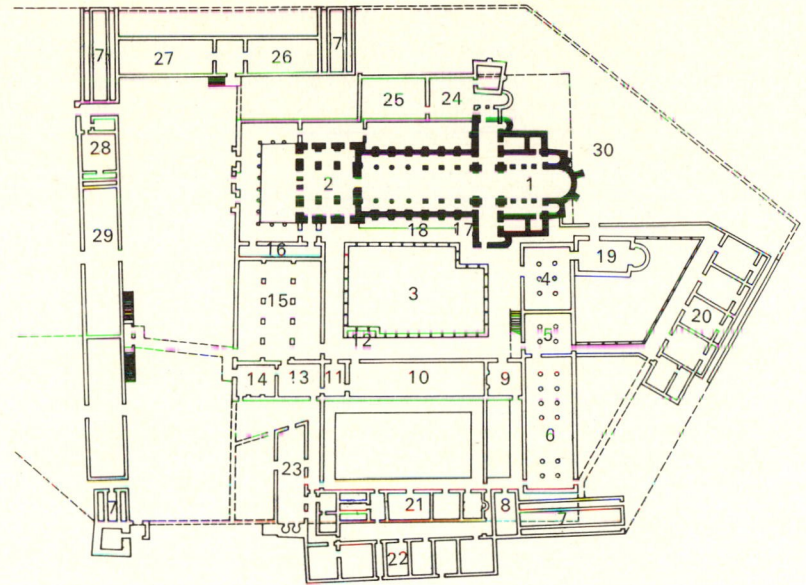

logic of the monastic complex. It was to show that Cluny fulfilled every particular of the Rule, and to present the pattern of a perfect monastery.

We are in the happy position of possessing an eleventh-century travel diary of a monk who went on this tour. He was a Roman cleric, who describes the journey that he made to Cluny in the retinue of Cardinal Peter Damian in 1063 (Document VIII). He was impressed by the size and beauty of the monastery, most notably by the extent of the dorter and the refectory. He particularly noticed that there was running water everywhere in the monastery, carried in concealed conduits. Such installations demanded new feats of planning, and it is probable that solutions were facilitated by the knowledge of Moorish models in Spain, that would have become known to the Cluniacs through their introduction of the Roman liturgy in Navarre, Aragon and Castile after the *Reconquista*. Peter the Venerable's commissioning of the first translation of the Koran from the Englishman, Robert of Ketton, in 1143 testifies to a like preoccupation with Arab culture.

These reports on Odilo's monastery shed light upon the most important written source, a description of a model Cluniac monastery, dating from about 1042, inserted into the second book of the *Disciplina Farvensis*, the constitutions of the monastery of Farfa, north of Rome (Document VI). It was labelled the *Ordo Farvensis* by Julius von Schlosser in 1889. Since the middle of the nineteenth century it has repeatedly been seen as a description of Odilo's monastery. Mortet, in his famous *Recueil de textes relatifs à l'histoire de l'architecture en France au Moyen Age* of 1911 simply refers to it as the *Ordo Cluniacensis*. Mabillon had already seen the connection. Conant's reconstruction of the guest-houses and the lay-brothers' tract stands or falls with this assumption. The prologue to the first book of the *Disciplina* confesses that a description of a monastery, written by an Apulian monk called John after a visit to Cluny, lay before the author, a monk by the name of Guido. Analysis of the text itself and of certain associated texts, such as the inventory of sixty-four books that were to be distributed to sixty-four monks to read in Lent, and whose titles are all those of books found in Cluny library in the twelfth century, makes it improbable that with this model monastery any other than Cluny can have been meant.[11] The conjecture is supported by general historical arguments. The supposition that Farfa itself is presented as the model monastery is excluded by details of the description. The two towers over the narthex of the church are a feature of Cluny that would have been impossible in eleventh-century Italy. The large, long building of the lay-brothers before the west front could never have existed in Farfa, but may very well have done so in Cluny, in the form shown by Conant's reconstruction.

Farfa, the highly favoured *Reichskloster* of Charlemagne, had only begun to revive from its destruction by the Saracens at the end of the first millennium, following the introduction of the Cluniac reform. Odilo himself had been in Farfa, and the constitutions of 1049 stood wholly under the influence of Cluniac devotion. The description of the monastery must be seen in the light of the St Gall plan in order to be rightly understood. Just as the one came as a model from Reichenau to its neighbouring monastery, so the other may have come as a descriptive pattern from Cluny to Farfa. In the description, a series of buildings that are indicated as already standing are followed by others where the form of words suggests that they were still to be built. It has therefore been concluded that at the point when John of Apulia was in Cluny, not all Odilo's buildings were completed (Document VI). That question must be left aside.

Conant's reconstruction is rooted at almost every point in this description. Twenty-five buildings are named, whose size is always, and whose situation is mostly, given. The author begins with the church, the length of whose foundations is almost exactly that of Cluny II – 140 feet (1). He gives an exact description of the chapter-house (4), as having three windows to the north and four to the east, as well as twelve arcades supported on slender double columns toward the cloister. In his earlier reconstructions Conant had only foreseen a single row of supports, and only in his most recent ones of 1959 and 1963 the more probable double row of columns. Adjoining the chapter-house are the monks' parlour (5) and their common- or study-room (6), whilst the dorter, longer at 160 feet than the church, took up the upper floor. It was 23 feet high. The ninety-seven narrow, six-foot high windows are specially mentioned. It was Benedictine usage for every bed or group of beds to be well lit by its own window, so that the monks could read during the siesta, as the Rule allowed (Cap. 48). This thick array of windows is always a pointer when there is doubt as to the purpose of a building, as in Mont-Saint-Michel (p. 187 and note 42). With a width of 34 feet, a double row of supports is likely here, even if the room was not vaulted. Visualizing the proportions, one can understand that the Roman monk of 1063 was so impressed (Document VIII). It is suggestive that visitors of 1042 could not measure the height of the windows high over the beds, but only estimate it. Just like the chapter-house, one can more easily imagine the long chamber, with its quantities of serried, high, slender apertures, in the context of eleventh-century Burgundian architecture, than in Italy. The same phenomenon greets us in Cistercian buildings surviving from the twelfth century.

The description dwells lovingly on the depiction of the large latrines (7), mentioning their forty-five seats, each ventilated by a *finistrella* above. It then turns to the warming room (9), the refectory, the two kitchens for the monks and lay-brothers (13, 14), joining up with the tour at the storehouse (15) and the almonry (16) – more a corridor than a room, of which it expressly says that its length was that of the width of the storehouse. The author's reliability in always giving the size of the buildings is convincing. He does not mention the cloister that he traversed, but he does give the distance between the entrance to the church and the warming room (9), 75 feet. Odilo's new cloister of 1042 was anyway not yet finished. We know from other sources that the monks did not enter their church directly from the dorter, but through a majestic door onto the cloister. It is a notable aberration from the St Gall plan that the ranges round the cloister were of uneven breadth. This is a sign that the builders had to accommodate their plans to an existing complex. They were restricted in many particulars by the preceding buildings, not least because they could not construct everything at once, but only section by section. It also stands out that this monastery was rather too large for the church than vice versa. One has the impression that it virtually demanded the rebuilding of the church. The impression given is of medieval variety, in contrast to the classical uniformity of St Gall.

The description forsakes the cloister for the Lady Chapel (19) and the cells of the sick-bay (20). No building for the doctor is as yet mentioned. Four wards are envisaged, each with eight beds. The remarks of Hildemar in his commentary to the Rule (Document v) suggest that provision for four wards was in conformity with earlier usage. A further room was used for blood-letting, and another as laundry for the linen of the sick. Arab influence may also be detected in this unexpectedly hygienic arrangement, as early as on the second monastery.

The author describes the large guest-tract (26, 27) and the long range for the lay brethren (29) at great length. He calls the latter *famuli*, showing that he had not recognized their special status. Even the furnishing of the buildings receives mention, in particular the comfort of the house for forty noblemen (27) and thirty noblewomen (26). Conant's reconstruction of the latrines (7), near the monastery gates and the cemetery for the laity, is improbable. They must have lain to the north behind this building, and what was done when they were broken up in consequence of the rebuilding of Cluny II is not clear from the reconstructions. The long stable range (29), with the dining-hall and dormitory of the lay-brothers in the upper storey, formed, with the church and the guest-tract, the sides of a forecourt, which was numbered amongst the gems of secular Romanesque architecture. The representational character of the palatial buildings for the guests is brought out by the observation of the document, that on feast-days it was to be hung with curtains (*cortinis*) and rich stuffs (*pallis*). The long stretches of the façades were relieved by the two towers of the ante-church (2) and the gateways. In Cluny III this forecourt was to be yet more elaborate. The plan itself hints at the diversity of the buildings. Their air of worldly magnificence and variety was in deliberate antithesis to the calm of the conventual court, and the harmony of its arcades.

The document concludes with the buildings to the south of the cloister. It details the twelve bathrooms – *cripta* – and their twelve tubs (8), the noviciate (21), the workshops and quarters of the goldsmiths, enamellists and stainers (22). It refers to a number of buildings stretching as far as the mill and bakery (23). This passage is clear in naming and describing each individual building, but not in accounting for their position in relation to one another and to the novices' cloister, which goes unmentioned. These obscurities are the reason for Conant's repeated changes of opinion about the disposition of the various parts of the noviciate and the baths, excavations being of no greater help to him. The description encourages the view, not supported by the relative lack of space, that in Cluny the classroom, refectory and dorter of the noviciate (21) were disposed round a small court. The monks' bath-house will certainly have lain to the east near the dorter, and no less surely will the bake-house have been built by the kitchens. The conduit, so admired by the visitor in 1063, must have been channelled past the latrines and the baths to the fountain sited by Conant in a corner of the main court (12). Interlopers within this well thought-out complex are the more delicate crafts' workshops (22) – those of the goldsmiths and enamellists and the *magistri vitrei*. The latter perhaps point to Cluny's role in the development of stained-glass windows, banished by the Cistercians later, but which reflect the Cluniac love of symbols. These workshops are absent from the plan of Cluny III, as is the similarly inappropriate insertion of the tailors' and cobblers' room (25) to the north of the church by the sacristy (24) – itself rather out of place opposite, rather than alongside, the entry of the monks.

Are the description and the plan sufficient to do justice to the architectural achievement as a whole? Odilo's marble cloister impressed contemporaries as much as the concealed water-supply responsible for the scattered fountains. The rationality of the design is self-evident. We have mentioned the picturesqueness of the forecourt. The long chamber of the dorter with its rows of windows must have been a forward-looking achievement. One thing is curious: that the place for the scribes was in the exposed north arm of the cloister (18), with the book-cupboard in a nearby corner (17). Did these copyists really work in the open, looking out onto the columned court and the toing and froing of the monks?

The monk John's description of Odilo's chapter-house raises the question of the origin of this type of building. The identifying characteristics of this type of building are its position adjoining the transept of the church, its medium size (at Cluny 45 feet by 30), and its arcade opening on to the cloister. The document mentions *XII balcones*, calibrated by double columns. The intent was to allow novices, and other members of the community not admitted to the chapter, to witness the proceedings. This requirement, to enable an audience to stand, protected against the weather, in the cloister and participate in a particular item of the day's routine, was to be for centuries a spur to architectural inventiveness. The first time that we hear of a special *domus* for sessions of the chapter is in Ansegis' description of the monastery of St Wandrille. But it is likely that here only the arm of the cloister alongside the church was meant (Document IV). The oldest chapter-house, whose foundations at any rate survive, is in the monastery on the Heiligenberg near Heidelberg. It is dated to about 1030, that is, scarcely any earlier than that of Cluny, for which Conant proposes a date of 1035, ten years before Odilo's new cloister of 1045. One must assume that the situation, dimensions and basic shape of chapter-houses were common to most Benedictine monasteries from the beginning of the eleventh century. It is also probable that cathedrals borrowed the motif from monasteries, and not vice versa. Its elaboration in Cluny will undoubtedly have made a great contribution to its crystallization as a type.

From the very first chapter-houses served as the burial-place of the abbots, more rarely of the founders. This may have been one of the reasons for joining the back of it to a Lady Chapel serving as mortuary chapel. The motif first crops up at Cluny, and was copied by various monasteries, such as Hirsau, that were under Cluny's influence. It may have been inspired in Cluny by the position of the somewhat older Lady Chapel of 1032, to which the chapter-house formed a kind of vestibule. The Cistercians would occasionally, as in Maulbronn, build onto the chapter-house its own small choir and altar in this place, and this was to prove especially fruitful in Italy right up to the threshold of the Renaissance (cf. the Pazzi chapel). It is more surprising that the great abbots of Odilo's Cluny had not merely no palace, but also no bedroom or study of their own. The layout has the severity and clarity of the early Romanesque, but from the very first the growth of the Order had rendered parts obsolete. Complaints of constriction were not stilled throughout the century.

THE MONASTERY OF PETER THE VENERABLE (CLUNY III)
As if they wanted to make a votive offering of unsurpassed grandeur to God with outstretched arms, the Cluniacs marshalled all their efforts from 1088 to around 1130 into erecting the massive abbey, to the north of the old church and outside the monastery, which was to be both the mirror of the might of their resources, and the visible expression of their devotion, their idealism and their artistic urge. It was a bold, even foolhardy plan. They did not want to build as was customary on the hallowed site of the old church, but right the other side of it on virgin ground. The foundation-stone was laid by a papal legate on 30 September 1088; it was ready for the final consecration by Innocent II in 1130. By 1121 the nave of Cluny II had been demolished. The church must therefore have been structurally complete within thirty years. The receipt of 10,000 gold pieces from the Spanish king, out of the booty won from the Arabs with Toledo in 1085, was the probable incentive. An interval of three years for the planning of something utterly new may seem rather too short than too long. The boldness of the conception did not reside only in its structure and dimensions, though the built-over area was rather more than ten times that of the old church. The greatness of the undertaking is affirmed by the fact that the new project was put so far to the south that during the whole construction-time not a single one of the old buildings had to be torn

down. Shielded by the earlier church, life in the monastery could go on undisturbed the whole time. Even the noise of the building-site will hardly have penetrated the cloister. The monks were not content with just rebuilding, enlarging or renewing, or bit by bit replacing each section with a greater – as in the rebuilt cathedrals of Cologne, Amiens, Beauvais or Florence – but instead aspired to build unhampered something on a totally different scale and plan. The old monastery became in spirit a workshop ancillary to the huge site, concentrating on this project with its hands and its resources, and yet continuing to pursue its avocations. Late eleventh-century France appears in a new light with the realization that it was capable of this church.

The plan of the new church is supposed to stem from Gunzo, the Abbot of Baume, who spent his last years in Cluny. The *Life of Hugh of Semur*, composed around 1120, relates that the command to build a new church came to the sick abbot from SS. Peter, Paul and Stephen in a vision, in which the saints themselves marked out the plan of the church with ropes (Document IX). A miniature of about 1180 from Saint Martin des Champs depicts the event. For contemporaries it was incontestable. We are more impressed that the fantasy life of a sick abbot was dominated by plans of rebuilding. Not just in the monks' dorter, but also in the sick-chamber, there were dreams of a huge church that would surpass any ever built in Christendom.

The same Life of St Hugh speaks of the constraining want of room in the monastery, and of the decision 'to lay more spacious foundations'. In 1146 Peter the Venerable's monastic constitutions refer to a *novum monasterium*. Conant was posed with the problem: which parts go back to Hugh of Semur and antedate the church, and which to Peter the Venerable and postdate it? The sources supply few clues. The plan of 1710 puts the question even more acutely: which buildings belong to the eleventh and twelfth centuries at all? Which have been renewed later, almost without touching their configuration, and what has been displaced by new buildings? Did the thought of venturing on fresh buildings, unconnected to the old and outside the existing precinct, first emerge with the plan of the new church? Was there a predecessor in the abbey lands?

The new Lady Chapel (33) was consecrated in 1085. This enlargement may be seen in conjunction with that of the cemetery (30), for which it acted as the mortuary chapel. The old infirmary would have to have been torn down to fit it in. But the thirty-two sick-beds listed in the *Ordo Farvensis* would have ceased to be adequate long before, especially when many alien monks, like Abbot Gunzo of Baume, found not only their spiritual home but also a quiet end to their days in Cluny. The idea of building a new infirmary zone to the east beyond the existing one had so much to commend it, that one should accept Conant's hypothesis that it was finished by 1082 (35). These extensions to the east were complemented by others to the west. The memory of the new stables built by Abbot Hugh always remained alive in the monastery (39). It was a remarkably ambitious conception. Conant supposes that these stables and the rooms over them, as well as the associated guest-houses, were completed in 1078. The basic idea was to thrust back one half of the large lay-brothers' building, and bound the thus enlarged court with a third range. The impression cannot be dismissed out of hand that this enlargement was already to accommodate the new atrium of the church, though this was still not finished a century later. A palatial ensemble was created amongst which, of all the earlier buildings of the monastery, the guest-range (26 and 27, it is true known only from the *Ordo Farvensis*) alone was able to assert its place. There is an excellent sketched reconstruction by Kenneth Conant. The details may have appeared otherwise, but it must capture the picturesque grandeur of the whole. A few decades later this grouping was given its dominant note by the abbot's palace, which was erected in and over the galilee (2) of the old church (38). One text mentions the *Domus Superiores*, later referred to as the palace of the Pope. In the purlieus of this abbot's palace a series of buildings were superimposed on the old storehouse and the almoner's corridor (15, 16). This opened up great new opportunities for sheltering guests and pilgrims. The

41, 42 According to legend, Cluny III was commissioned by SS. Peter and Paul themselves who appeared to Gunzo, Abbot of Baume, and marked out the plan with ropes (above). Gunzo related his dream to Abbot Hugh of Cluny (below). Illustrations from a manuscript of c. 1180

43, 44 Cluny III. Above: bird's-eye view of the new accommodation for guests, looking south-west. In the foreground is the abbey church. The ranges of buildings beyond are those numbered *39* and *29* on the plan opposite. Below: bird's-eye view of the whole monastery from the east. Both drawings by Professor Conant

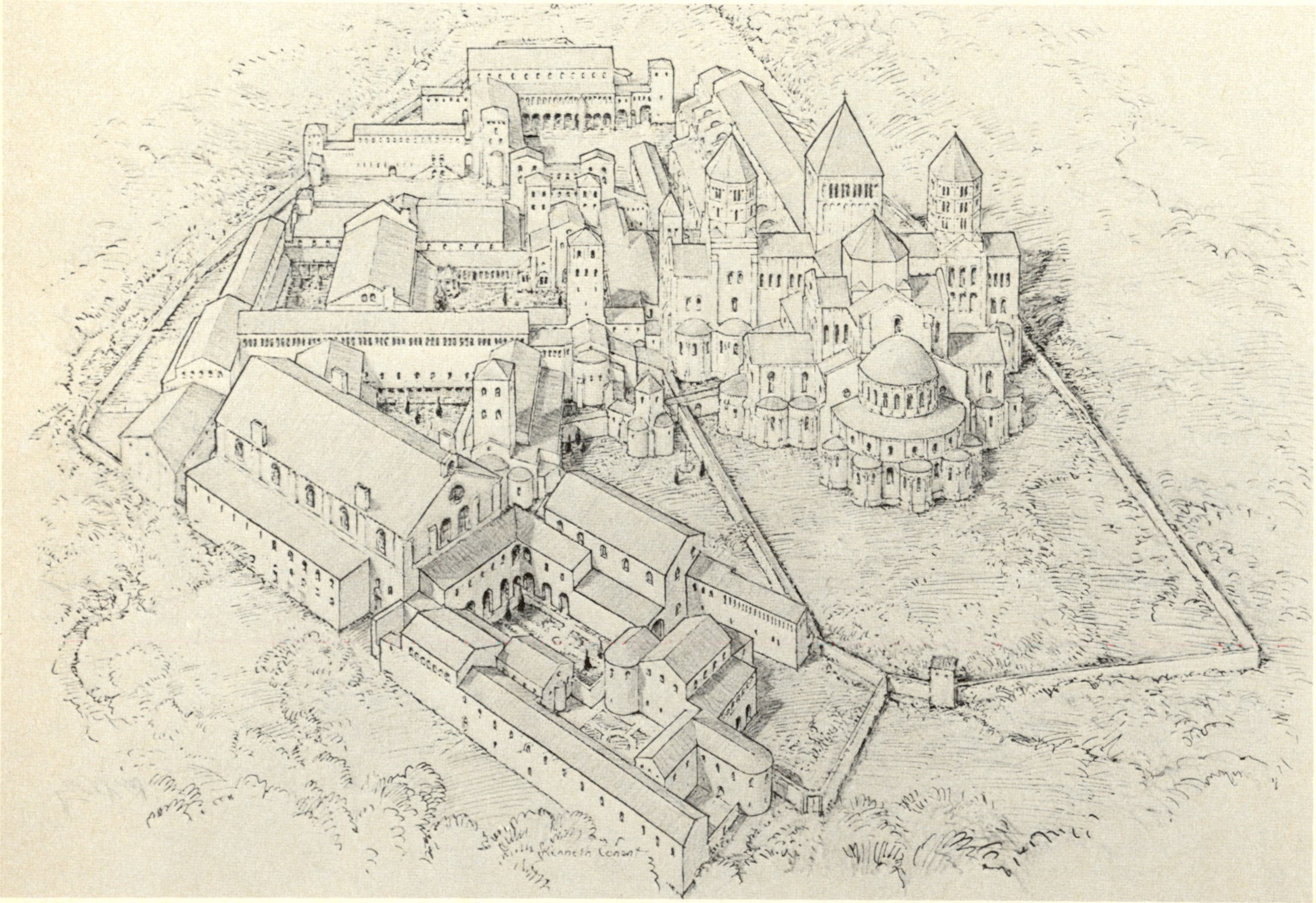

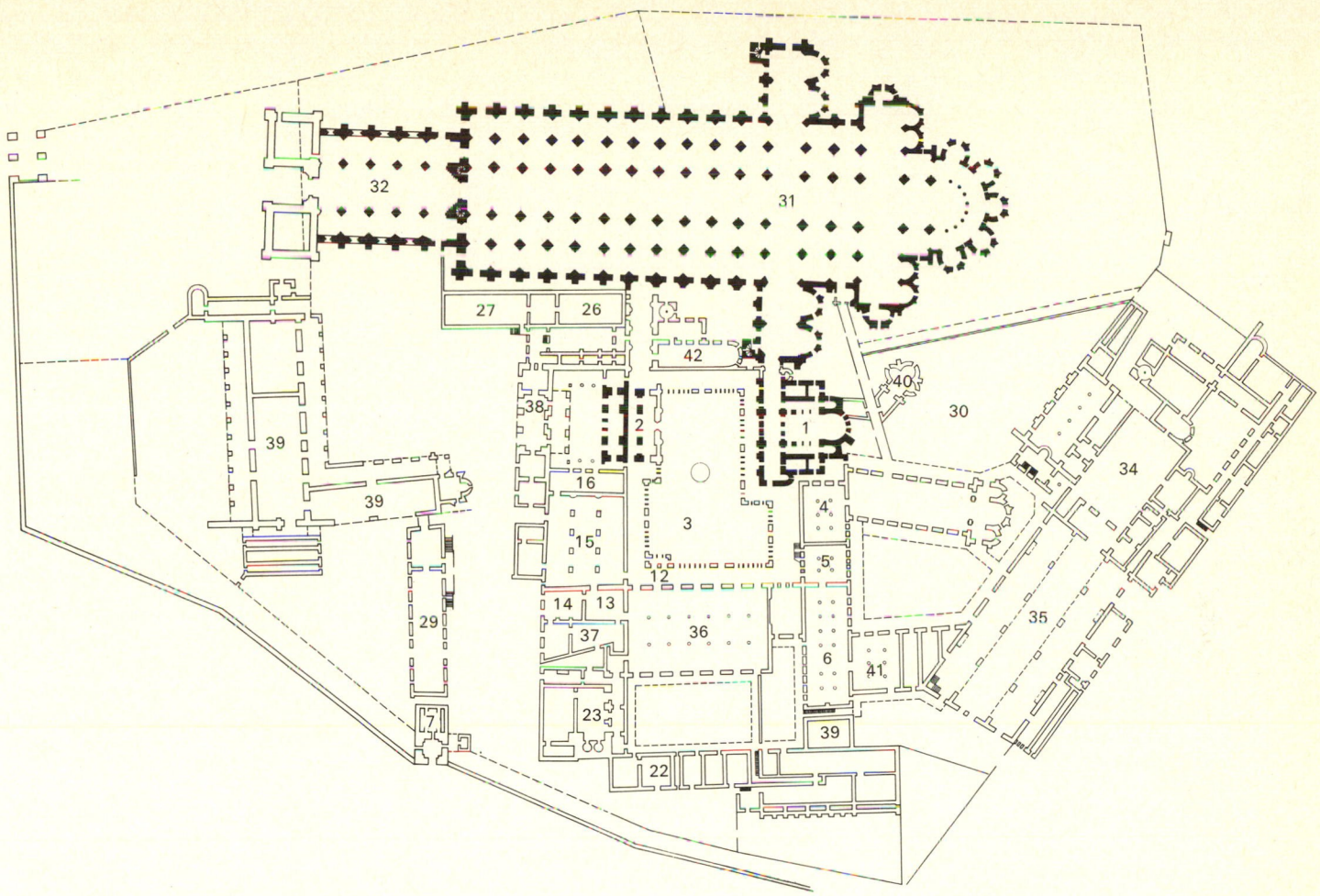

45 *Cluny. Plan of Cluny III, the monastery as it was about 1150, reconstructed after Professor Conant*

Parts remaining from Cluny II (using the same numbers as pl. 40):

1 *Choir of the old church (Cluny II)*
2 *Narthex of old church*
3 *Cloister (enlarged by taking in the old nave)*
4 *Chapter-house*
5 *Monks' parlour* ⎫
6 *Monks' common room* ⎬ *dorter above*
7 *Latrines*
9 *Warming room*
12 *Fountain*
13 *Kitchen*
14 *Lay-brothers' kitchen*

15 *Storehouse*
16 *Almonry*
22 *Workshops*
23 *Bakery*
26 *Women guests*
27 *Men guests*
29 *Stables, lay-brothers' quarters*
30 *Cemetery*

New buildings:

31 *New church (Cluny III)*
32 *New narthex*
33 *Lady Chapel*
34 *Infirmary court*
35 *Infirmary*
36 *Refectory*
37 *Kitchen*
38 *Abbot's palace*
39 *Hospices and stables*
40 *Cemetery chapel*
41 *Dorter extension (?)*
42 *Abbot's chapel*

stables and great hospice (39) also possessed a portico. It is probable that this great guest-house of Cluny, which according to Conant's reckoning created places for up to 2,000 people, was the model for the *Aula Nova* shown on the plan of Canterbury. These buildings in Cluny made up the first recorded 'state court' – an inner courtyard of imposing size and variegation.

It is recorded that Hugh built a new refectory (36), put around 1080 by Conant. It was undoubtedly not only in the same place as Odilo's, but also as that shown by the description of 1632 and the plan of 1710. Was it the same in appearance? Odilo's refectory, if we can trust the dimensions given in the *Ordo Farvensis*, was 100 feet × 28 feet, or 2,800 square feet. It was only possible to lengthen it on

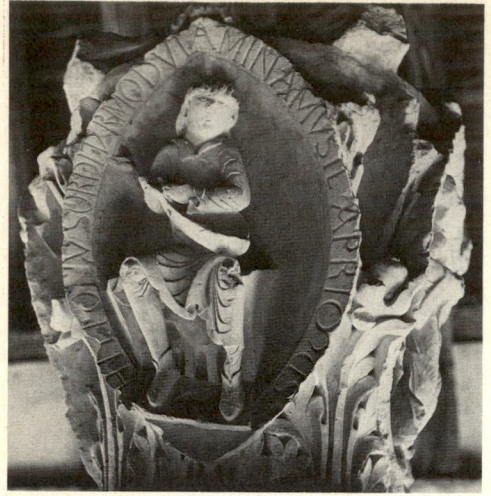

the same cloister by displacing the pantry from between the refectory and the kitchens (37), a gain of only about 16 feet. The width of the cloister stayed constant up to the eighteenth century. So Hugo must have aimed at getting the extra room by widening outwards. Now the *Chronicon Cluniacense*, which was written around 1500, reports that the refectory then measured 38 paces by 24. Taking the pace as about a yard, that corresponds to the measurements of the seventeenth-century buildings. This was a real hall, whose end was adorned by a wall-painting of the Last Judgment.

Summing up, we see that in the eight years between 1078 and 1086 the monastery put up a new infirmary – subsequently amplified by the new priory – the new hospice buildings, the new Lady Chapel and the new refectory. We have less certain information as to the date of the extension of the dormitory to the south and, by an accretion, to the east. The old area of roughly 172 feet by 36 feet could not possibly have sheltered the growing numbers of over 300 monks. Conant's assumption of accretions, based on later descriptions and plans, does not imply any disruption of the old sleeping arrangements.

In 1121, once the choir and nave of the third church were complete, the nave of the second could be torn down and the cloister enlarged. At the time it was thought preferable to preserve the choir and transept of the old church (1) and accept the consequent irregularity of the cloister. Room was also found between the old and new churches for a special abbot's chapel (42), consecrated in 1118. Only later were new buildings put up to the north and west of the church for the abbot, guests, and their retinue, thus repeating on a large scale an ensemble already set out in Odilo's monastery of 1050. There arose the palaces of the abbots Jean III de Bourbon (1456-85) and Jacques d'Amboise (1485-1510), with their terraces and gardens. Only the fifteenth century was callous enough to pull down the transept of the second church. The chapter-house and, finally, the dorter were renewed, and the cloister itself straightened out. But these measures only form part of Cluny's history, not of that of the Cluniac movement.

Studying the reproduction of Conant's plan and that of the eighteenth century, one is forced to realize that only the extrapolated buildings put up on the far side of the old walls of the monastery could succeed architecturally; that is, in the first instance the new church to the north, and then the infirmary zone with the adjoining administrative buildings to the east, and the great hospice and stables to the west. The refectory as such was doubtless very fine – broad and well-lit. But the harmony of the cloister and of the buildings bounding it on the other three sides was broken up by the rebuilding. A typically medieval, ragged patchwork of bits of buildings from different epochs resulted. The treasured early eleventh-century marble columns in the cloister were not replaced by some that were stronger and with more richly sculpted capitals. Even the new cloister will not have been vaulted. I am not able to say how it would have looked. Would it have appeared light and delicate, or already have had the squatness and exuberance of the Romanesque? Any radical solution was ruled out by respect for the old choir and its abbots' graves. There was also a reluctance to disturb the core of the conventional buildings; the chapter-house, parlour, common-room and large dorter above. The great operation of rebuilding the body of the monastery with the life of the community going on all around it failed in the interior. The same builders, who in the church created the greatest work of the Romanesque, were forced here to sacrifice unity to variety. The rebuilding of Cluny II was a precedent. Buildings grew outward from the cloister to which they had originally clung. As in the seats of medieval government, the pristine order was obscured by a mass of miscellaneous buildings, tracts, towers and gateways. It is easy to detect a palimpsest of plans and projects. It is a huge 'machine for living', in which the diversity of uses obscures its inner logic. Only Clairvaux was to restore the situation.

Cluny remains a *fata morgana*. All the efforts of Conant do not suffice to reduce it to the sphere of artistic reality. If we ask what this monastery did for the development of Western architecture, the reply must be: a tremendous amount with its churches, and its huge buildings for guests, the sick and the abbot. The Cistercians levelled their criticism against this world-oriented monumentality. Amongst the actual conventual buildings only details counted – possibly the huge size of the dorter, and beyond this the novelty of the conjunction of chapter-house and Lady Chapel, the provision of a parlour and a monks' common-room. One thing is certain: that Cluny was the first place where the buildings round the cloister really achieved the status of conscious architecture. However richly Carolingian monasteries were built – a Centula, a Fulda, a Saint Wandrille or Jumièges – they never attained the scale or lavishness of Cluny. Here for the first time floors, walls, doors and windows were of stone. Here for the first time a care was lavished on each detail that was previously only thought appropriate for churches. I am referring to Odilo's monastery as it appeared in the *Ordo Farvensis* and to the visitor of 1063. It set the scale for many monasteries of the second half of the eleventh century. And yet even it was outmatched by Hugh's rebuilding.

This prodigality in the service of a new devotion occasioned Emile Mâle's above-cited judgment that Cluny was the grandest thing produced by the Middle Ages. Through a happy chance, out of all its features the very works survive which most faithfully embody this devotion – the choir capitals from the third church, with representations of the nine tones. This is a remarkable and novel theme for capital sculptures. Nothing comparable is known. The Cluniacs, who sacrificed all the other callings of the monastic estate, both the *lectio divina* and the *opus manum*, to the *opus Dei* – the celebration of the liturgy – chose to depict a musical system in the sanctuary of their new church. Even ascetically strenuous monastic leaders like Peter Damian criticized the practice of celebrating the chief festivals in the church throughout the night and often through the following day as well. Like the church, the list of canticles steadily expanded. These masterpieces of early Burgundian classicism from the beginning of the twelfth century have as their subject neither the attributes of the Evangelists, nor the symbolic or fabulous imagery of the Romanesque so vehemently criticized by Bernard of Clairvaux in 1124 (Document x). They show the unshowable, the tones, something both sensuous and supersensuous, in which the temporal encounters the eternal without disjunction.

Where there is a preoccupation with musical harmony, there is mostly also preoccupation with architectural proportions and their higher significance. In his last study of Cluny in 1963 Conant tried to resolve its measurements and arrange them into a numerical system. That there was such a system is almost as evident as the fact that it was one of the governing preoccupations of its builders. Beauty emerged through just proportion. The history of monastic architecture should also embrace the history of these numbers and their significance, but the basic work on them largely remains to be done.

THE CLOISTERS OF MOISSAC AND LA DAURADE

The 'nine tones' of the choir capitals of the new abbey of Cluny are the most sublime piece of monastic sculpture of the Middle Ages. The new Cluniac Romanesque, which was later attacked by St Bernard (Document x) emerges more clearly with the aid of the sculptural programme of the portal and cloister of Abbot Durand de Bretons (Abbot of Moissac 1048–72) and his successors. They are masterpieces of Romanesque expressionism, produced by the marriage of motifs from prehistoric art with the late classical sculptural tradition. Durand was appointed abbot during a visit of Odilo in 1047. He subsequently also became Bishop of Toulouse, and as such contrived the affiliation of La Daurade to Cluny. Soon after 1100 appeared the related group of sculptures in Saint Sernin and La Daurade in Toulouse, and in Moissac. They herald the sculpted commentaries on the world and salvation found in the cloisters of the southern French and Catalonian monasteries jostling one another to the right and left of the Pyrenees. A map of these monasteries would show how close to one another they are. The monumental entrance portal survives in Moissac, the first to adopt an innovatory apse-composition of Cluny's and to turn it into a relief spread out

49 Abbot Durand of Moissac, one of the first monasteries to reflect the new Cluniac Romanesque that culminated in Cluny III

46–48 Cluny. Three sides of a capital from the choir of Cluny III, c. 1088–95, representing the tones of Gregorian chant

50 *Moissac, the cloister*

51 *Saint-Trophîme, at Arles, the cloister*

52 *Santa Maria, Ripoll, the cloister*

53 *Moissac. Tympanum over the main entrance, showing Christ with the symbols of the Evangelists, and around them the twenty-four Elders of the Apocalypse, c. 1130*

like a great fan above the lintel of a door, showing Christ in Majesty between the four Beasts, and above the twenty-four Elders of the Apocalypse. This transfer of the *majestas Domini*, from the final stage of the pilgrim's progress through the body of the church, to its beginning, presupposes the changed meaning, inspired by Cluny, given to the actual church. More important for our investigation is the appearance of the cloisters of Moissac, La Daurade, and Saint Sernin. In the latter the chapter-houses, which are entered from the cloister, are given a figured portal such as we otherwise only encounter on churches. The twelve Apostles are represented there in Saint Sernin, in token of the twelfth century's derivation of the cloister from the hall of Solomon's Temple in which, according to the fourth chapter of the Acts of the Apostles, the latter first committed themselves to a *vita communis*. In Moissac a whole-length relief figure of the departed Abbot Durand is placed before the chapter-house. The abbot was thus not only buried in the chapter-house, as already in the ninth century in Fontenelle, but also depicted before the entrance to it. It may be assumed that in Moissac as well the adornment of the portal played upon the theme of the room within. The twelve Apostles were depicted in similar reliefs on the pillars of the cloister, but only nine survive. The capitals of the columns bore a whole encyclopaedia of scenes and figures from the Old and New Testaments, and from the deeds and sufferings of the saints. Through these the cloister became a place of edification and contemplation; the coloured reliefs breathed an air of pomp and festivity characteristic of the self-confidence and self-regard of Cluniac Benedictinism. It is hardly

54, 55 *Two capitals from Toulouse churches – Saint Sernin (above) and La Daurade (below)*

erroneous to assume that here the age put forth the highest flights of its 'art of living'. The monks moved in an area totally permeated with works of art. It is true that even in the early Middle Ages the cloister was the object of special attention, but with Odilo's cloister in Cluny of shortly before 1050 a new pitch seems to have been reached. The cloister was liberated to become the chief architectural feature of the monastery. In the coming centuries its almost unlimited potentialities, both architecturally and as a vehicle for painting and sculpture, were exploited by all enterprising monasteries. The cloister became increasingly the spiritual home of the monks.

Cluny, and subsequently even more emphatically Cîteaux, schooled itself against the individualism of powerful monastic personalities. Diversity was to yield to uniformity – and this applied just as much to the Rule as to buildings. But the third monastery of Cluny was itself richly individual both as a building and as a social system; so much so that it could not be emulated by any later monastery. The architectural influence of the new church is a favourite theme of art-history; but the influence of the monastic complex is untraceable – unless by antithesis, in the buildings of the movement which fought the alleged extravagances of Cluny, that is, in the plans of Cistercian Clairvaux and its dependent monasteries. St Bernard and the Cistercians were also responsible for the new aesthetic which gave rise to the Gothic monasteries.

56, 67 Santo Domingo de Silos. Above: capital with fantastic animals. Below: the two-storeyed cloister

5

The Cistercian Monasteries

THE NEW ORDER

Cluny's antithesis in the twelfth century world was Cîteaux. It embodied the attempt to extract Benedictine monasticism from the worldly role which had fallen to it in the course of the years. How can a monk flee a world that is to a large extent dominated and led by monks? Can the individual realize the aspiration of poverty, if his community as a whole has become inordinately rich? Benedict of Nursia and his monasteries were not faced with these conundrums in the context of the collapse of the Roman Empire. Benedict of Aniane had to propound them to his fellow-abbots in the reforming Synods of Aachen in 816 and 817. They were given fresh actuality by the emergence in the eleventh century of the *Reichsklöster* and of the Cluniac Reform. Reality contradicted the purity of the theory. Even the Cistercians were to experience this in the course of their own history. They had withdrawn to remote and barren parts, but their credo of work had made the lonely valleys and marshes flourish. Once it was clear by the beginning of the thirteenth century that even they could not sustain the grace of poverty, because it was irreconcilable with the injunction to work, St Francis was rather for renouncing work than poverty. But then his successors recognized that in that case they ought to have renounced monasteries themselves (*vide infra* p. 130).

The new reformed Order was precipitated in 1075 by the flight of one Robert and seven monks from his monastery of Saint Michèle de Tonnère to the forest of Molesme. Twenty-two years later, in 1098, it was apparent that even this retreat had become a centre of attraction, and they fled yet further to the marshes of Cîteaux. In the Burgundy of this quite other-worldly century, sanctity was hard to hide under a bushel. This time twenty-three monks had banded together, among them the Englishman Stephen Harding, who drew up the aims of the new foundation in a small masterpiece of Latin prose, of scarcely six pages, roughly 1,680 words. This *Carta Caritatis* was confirmed by Pope Calixtus II in 1119. It was supplemented by the *Consuetudines*, or new monastic constitutions ascribed to Alberic, the second Abbot of Cîteaux (1099-1109). Its three sections contain provisions for the order of Offices, the life of the monks, and the life of the *conversi*. There is a third document of the early community, giving an account of their withdrawal from Molesme and life in Cîteaux up to 1115, the *Exordium Cisterciensis Cenobii*, later called the *Exordium Parvum* to distinguish it from the *Exordium Magnum*, which depicts the subsequent history of the Order up to about 1180, mingled with many tales of miracles (Bibl. 99). The three early texts are rounded off by the *Instituta*, or the decisions of the annual General Chapter, which were written down in 1134, and supplemented by a few paragraphs in 1152. The aim of the *Instituta* and *Consuetudines* was to restore the pristine sway of all St Benedict's Rule. Everything not expressly allowed by it in the way of indulgence in clothing, housing or food was to be forbidden. It had become apparent that in most abbeys, of the three duties of the monks – worship, reading the

58 *Page from the Bible of Stephen Harding, one of the early abbots of Cîteaux. The centaur on the left forms the letter H of HIC. On the right a white Cistercian, gripped in the talons of St John's eagle, makes up the letter I of IN PRINCIPIO*

59 *St Bernard preaching in the chapter-house of Clairvaux and (bottom) being tempted by a devil; a page from the fifteenth-century Hours of Etienne Chevalier, by Jean Fouquet*

Scriptures, and bodily work – only the first two were still cultivated. In Cluny liturgical celebration alone was left, whose proliferation and length claimed virtually every minute. Stephen Harding had entitled his work the *Carta Caritatis*, because its prime concern was the loving fellowship of all monks far beyond the bounds of the single monastery. It was aimed against the individualism and autonomy of the great abbeys. All the abbots were to appear once a year at the General Chapter, and submit themselves to twice-yearly visitations by the abbot of their mother house or his deputy. An abbot was now no more than overseer in his own monastery. Even the Abbot of Cîteaux could be brought to order and even dismissed by the abbots of its four oldest daughter houses. The all-powerful Order now displaced the single abbey in eminence.

This centralism must have been more conspicuous in what was built than with the Cluniacs. Since life in Cistercian monasteries was supposed to obey the same laws day by day, all their monasteries should theoretically have looked the same. Most of them were indeed alike in their basic units. For this reason it is possible to set out for the Cistercians alone a binding schema on which all executed monasteries were variations. In it the evolution of the medieval Benedictine monastery reaches its climax and its culmination. The rationalism of this architecture sets a new touch to our picture of Romanesque construction.

The decisive event in the Order's history was the entry into Cîteaux of Bernard of Fontaines (1091-1153) with thirty noblemen, including four of his brothers, in 1112. One has the impression that everyone in the way of Burgundian nobility who had withstood the inducements of the Cluniacs was now entering the monasteries. Even his own father was to follow him with his youngest son in 1120. Three years later Bernard was able to found Clairvaux with twelve brethren. Seventy-two personal foundations are reputed to have followed in barely forty years. This most medieval of all medieval religious figures must have exercised a compelling power of conviction. His character embraced theological acuity and boundless energy, with an equally limitless asceticism. Every word he uttered or wrote is shot through with a lyrical power, which fired the youth of a whole age with the monastic idea. Bernard's boundless spiritual forcefulness made his century that of the white habit. His monks sought out all the remotenesses of Europe as the seed-ground of new monasteries, from Ireland to the borders of the Russian Empire. Sixty-nine monasteries sent their abbots to the General Chapter of 1133; there were 343 at Bernard's death, and 742 at the end of the Middle Ages, not to mention the 761 nunneries whose location we know. Of the monasteries, 525 sprang up in the twelfth century and 169 in the thirteenth. Thereafter the movement ebbed. In the fourteenth century there were only 18 more, and in the fifteenth century 20, most of them in the present-day Netherlands. Altogether, France possessed 246 monastic settlements, England 76, Scotland 13, Ireland 41. In Italy there were 95 Cistercian monasteries, in Spain 59, in Portugal 13, in the present-day Belgium 18 and Holland 14. The crusaders founded 15 in Greece and the Holy Land. Over a hundred lay in Germany and the neighbouring territories of the Slavs. The best presentation of the location and number of these monasteries is to be found in the superb maps and statistics of Frederic van der Meer's *Atlas of the Cistercian Order* (Bibl. 101). The offshoots of Cîteaux and its four original daughter-houses, La Ferté (1113), Pontigny (1114), Morimond and Clairvaux (both 1115) spread like a tree. Clairvaux had 355 daughter-foundations, Morimond 193, Cîteaux itself 109, Pontigny 43 and La Ferté 17. Europe was parcelled out between them. It was amazing what trust was reposed in many of their precocious brethren by the abbots of the great monasteries, who sent them out year after year into the unpeopled and unknown with a team of twelve equally young companions to found new settlements. By the end remote places were scarce in Europe. The General Chapter of 1152 required every new foundation from then on to be licensed. None might be set up closer than 15,000 paces to the next one.

The spirit of the new foundations was that of unrelenting self-sacrifice. The asceticism of the monks reduced their mean expectation of life to twenty-eight

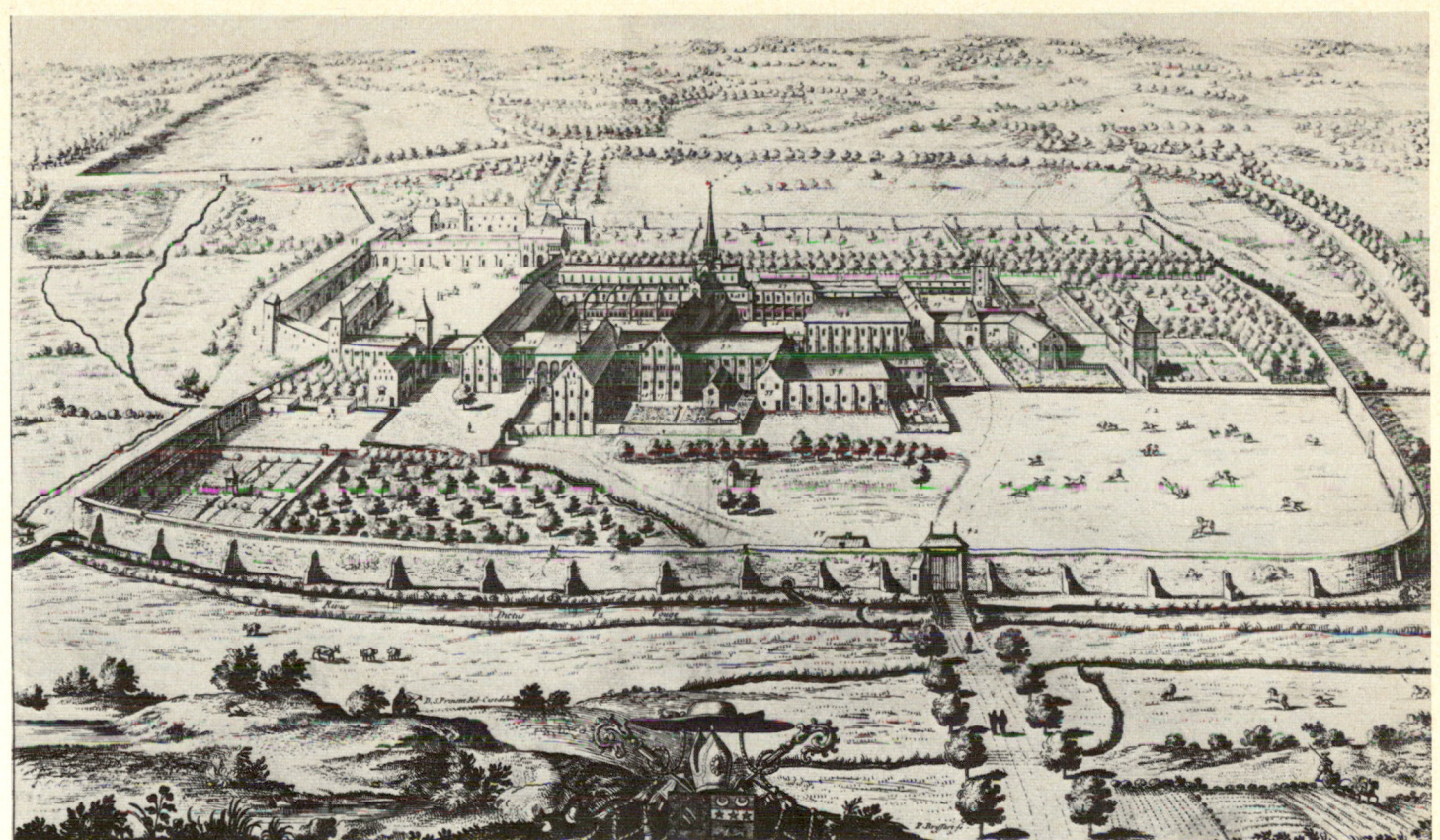

60 Cîteaux, the parent house of the Cistercians, was destroyed in the French Revolution. This eighteenth-century drawing shows it as it existed then. The church is on the far side, with the cloister and projecting refectory easily recognizable

years. If one reflects that these youths never entered a monastery before their fifteenth year, and often like St Bernard only at twenty-one, this means that Cistercian asceticism was on average only supportable for about a dozen years. When receiving the novices into Clairvaux St Bernard said, 'If you are impatient to realize your selves, then leave your bodies outside. Here only souls enter. The flesh is good for nothing'. Despite this, in 1148 around 700 monks and *conversi* lived in Clairvaux, the capital of the Cistercian state – more than had ever lived in Cluny. It is disputable which involved the more misplaced idealism, the Knights' Crusades or the monks' foundations. Both belong together, and both are the fruit of the same exciting and excitable decades. Bernard described himself as the 'chimaera of the century', half monk and half knight. This Christian saint and poet compared himself to a classical monster, yet he would have rejected its depiction in art (Document x).

The Order's struggle against all display, against anything tending to distract from the contemplation of God, was fanatical. Its very fanaticism united the youth of the twelfth century, and kindled the belief that the world could be saved through the extreme renunciation of all worldly goods. Individuals competed in communities in the stages of asceticism. The struggle was directed equally against knowledge, literature and representational art. It lasted more than a hundred years, but failure was a foregone conclusion. Asceticism was constantly threatened by the desire for artistic expression. The General Chapter repeatedly attempted to stem the tide through specific regulations. These, when collected, present a vivid picture of the laws governing the inevitable growth of art from the desire for perfection and order. 'No abbot, no monk, and no novice is allowed to write new books without the permission of the General Chapter', it went, as early as 1134 (Bibl. 91). A special decree of 1199 arranged for all versifiers to be removed from their monastery to a stricter one (do.). No-one might dare to expound 'rhythmos'. Nor did the novices receive any instruction. The lay-brothers were to read no book, and to learn nothing but the Lord's Prayer, the Creed, the Miserere and a few other prayers, which they were to sing by heart. They were never even to look at a text. The list of prohibited pictures and sculptures created in the various monasteries is immense. It remains to be shown why the simplicity of the early buildings did not endure.

Two episodes typify the spirit of the movement. The first was a victory won in Germany, the second in England.

TWO EPISODES

In 1123 Camp, the first Cistercian monastery on German soil, was founded. From the first it was puny and threatened by malformation. The new Burgundian monastic idea had not been grasped. Then in 1132 the twenty-year-old Otto of Austria visited Morimond on his way back from his student years in Paris with fifteen companions from the highest German aristocracy. The youthful monastic settlement must so have impressed this grandson of Henry IV, the half-brother of Conrad III and uncle of Barbarossa, that his whole party resolved to stay in Morimond and take the white robe of the Cistercians. If one reflects what ideas must have filled the head of this prince on returning from Paris, where he had probably attended the lectures of Abelard (1079-1142), and certainly those of Hugh of St Victor (1096-1141), and if one conjures up the shock this step must have given to the Babenberg Margrave Leopold III in Austria, then the real gravity of the decision becomes apparent. Leopold had founded the college of Klosterneuburg for his son, and had already had the boy elected Provost in 1114. The revenues of this foundation supported his studies abroad. It is ascribable to Otto's influence that Leopold inspired the foundation of the Cistercian monastery of Heiligenkreuz in 1135, undoubtedly to prevail on his son to come home. But in 1136 the latter had already become Abbot of Morimond at twenty-four. During the six years that he remained there most of his companions themselves fanned out and founded new Cistercian monasteries in Germany. It is the great youth of these bands of monks that most impresses the imagination. It was with reluctance that as a twenty-six-year-old the prince gave up the claustral peace of Morimond and the work of training in this youthful community, to ascend the episcopal throne of Freising in 1138. But the success of the Cistercian movement in the Empire was already assured. In 1147, before he had yet followed Conrad III on his fateful crusade to Jerusalem, Otto described the indispensable tasks of monasticism for the survival of the world, in the seventh book of his *Chronica sive Historia de duabus Civitatibus*.[13]

'On account of the multitude of our sins and the foul sinfulness of these most troublous times, we believe that the world cannot much longer endure, unless it be saved through the merits of the monks, the true citizens of God's kingdom, whose manifold, well-ordered brotherhoods blossom in great number throughout the world.' He goes on: 'They live concealed in this world, coveting no increase of their fame, and lead already on this earth a life of heavenly and angelic purity . . . they live in common, laying themselves down to sleep with one accord, rising to pray in unison, taking their meals together in one room, and busying themselves day and night with prayer, reading and work.' Otto closes this piece with the memorable characterization: 'Thus equipped within and without, they have spread over the whole earth in rich and fruitful profusion, and in the shortest time their merit is as hugely swollen as their number; now they gleam with the refulgence of their signs, and illuminate with their miracles; they are often singled out by divine manifestations, and they are yet more frequently comforted in departing this life by the appearance of an angel or of the Lord. They heal the sick, expel demons, and sometimes, so far as is possible on this earth, they attain through contemplation a foretaste of the delight of the heavenly fatherland, and thus watch the whole night through with the singing of psalms, hymns and holy songs, though faint with work, exhausted by lack of sleep, and wasted by fasting; in this like the crickets, which shrill the more when they are hungry.'

Is it for the historian or for the psychiatrist to intrude here with explanations? For those seeking heavenly approval, Cistercian architecture provided the necessary seclusion. Under its firm array of vaults, an ascetic emulation took place which gave these bands of young men the exultant feeling of participating in a communal movement, in which love of one's friend was given vent as love of God. One must allow the sources to speak, for it is hard for modern language to convey the incidents with delicacy. The Cistercian movement is penetrated by both tenderness and severity. The second episode brings this out particularly well.

In 1132 a crisis broke in the abbey of St Mary at York, arising out of criticism of the lives of the monks and the lead given by Geoffrey the abbot, by Richard the Prior and twelve followers. One can be certain that it was knowledge of the precepts of Cîteaux which brought it home to this group of radicals that they were no longer living according to St Benedict's Rule. We know of these goings-on from a stirring account dictated by a Cistercian monk called Serlo, when he was almost a hundred years old, to a fellow-monk in 1206 (Bibl. 17, p. 232). Serlo came to St Mary's in 1132 as a young cleric in the retinue of Archbishop Thurston of York, and a letter from the Archbishop himself to his colleague of Canterbury confirms that the aged monk remembered down to the last detail the events of his youth which had determined his life. The climax was when the Archbishop himself was barricaded in the church of St Mary's with the thirteen rebels, whilst in the cloister the monks and their abbot called for exemplary punishment. The tumult lasted several days. Finally, on 17 October 1133, Thurston was enabled to return home, taking the thirteen monks with him. They remained in his palace at York for about three months.

In the meantime Bernard's advice had been sought in Clairvaux. At Christmas Thurston went to Ripon, where he had great estates, and handed over a piece of unreclaimed wilderness to the thirteen who had forfeited their monastery. Such were the origins of Fountains, which after initial hardship rapidly achieved unusual success (Bibl. 119). In the early period it enjoyed a close relationship with Clairvaux. Both its first abbot, Richard, the strikingly energetic Prior of St Mary's, and its second, also a Richard and once sacristan of St Mary's, went there several times, the latter even dying there in 1144, whilst the first Richard died in Rome in 1139. Richard II was one of the great contemplatives amongst the monastic leaders of the twelfth century, and it is attributable to the simple power of his love, that the influx of monks was so swift that a great number of new foundations sprang from Fountains in the space of a few years. His successor Henry Murdac swept away the last remaining customs of the St Mary's tradition in favour of the new discipline of Clairvaux. Fountains is also one of the first abbeys to have adhered without deviation to the Burgundian model in the placing and character of its monastic buildings. The plans were brought by a famous builder/monk from Clairvaux, Geoffroy d'Alaine.

Contemporary with Fountains was the development of Rievaulx, the second great Cistercian centre in the North of England. Bernard had sent his own secretary, St William, as founder-abbot in 1132. It began with 25 monks and *conversi*, by 1142 there were 300, and in 1165 actually 740, 100 of them monks and 600 *conversi*. By Bernard's death thirty-two new foundations had sprung from the earliest three monasteries (Waverley was the third, in Surrey), twelve of them from Rievaulx alone. The monastery owed its success to the achievements of St Ailred, the Bernard of England, who governed it from 1147–67. Ailred had a genius for friendship. His two most important writings, the *Speculum Caritatis* and *De Spirituale Amicitia* are both paeans to friendship. His whole being was filled with the endeavour to reconcile loving friendship for his fellow-monks with the love of God. Thus the *Speculum Caritatis* was written in response to the blow of the death of a younger monk called Simon: 'I remember how often, when my eyes strayed hither and yon, the mere sight of him filled me with shame. . . . Our Rule forbade us to speak with one another, but his bearing, his gait, his very silence, spake to me.' It would be wrong to read into this homosexual inclinations. Each monk saw in the other his exemplar in the path toward meditation, and the built seclusion of these islands of stone in the wilderness was symbolic of the emulation in the young communities. Raised with King David's son, Henry I, at the Scottish court, Ailred filled the office of seneschal when, on his way back to the see of York in 1134, riding one day over the hill of Rievaulx, he was overcome by the desire to make his profession there, just like Otto of Austria at Morimond two years before. He could not resist the enticement represented for him by the mere sight of a monastery. In the years he spent there as monk and abbot, the monastery was transformed from a wooden one to the stone one whose ruins we see today. Contemporary with Clairvaux, and similar to it in many respects, of all those surviving, it best reflects the ideal.

VOW OF POVERTY AND BAN ON LUXURY

In the final analysis there were four preconditions for the novel physical appearance of Cistercian monasteries: the ideal of poverty; the desire to escape the world; the insistence on affiliation; and a new spirit of regulation, inspiring a new functionalism, which went so far as to appoint a precisely determined set of buildings appropriate to the *conversi*. Just as the *Regula sancti Benedicti* was the origin of all these, so the Benedictine monastery was the basis of everything built.

The ideal of poverty, requiring not only each monk, but also the monastery and its church to be poor and make a show of their poverty, inspired severe condemnations of any form of architectural or artistic luxury. In every monastery the same simple rooms were to hold the monks, and the same simple utensils to be at their disposal for their services – crosses only of painted wood, chalices and patens of plain silver, unembroidered vestments of light linen, iron candlesticks, and copper thuribles. The churches were to possess no towers, the windows to display only colourless patterns, and the sole piece of sculpture allowed was a Madonna (Document XI). All the walls were to be left unplastered, all the architectural members to be devoid of figural, and in a rigorous interpretation even ornamental, decoration. In this primitive age, when sculpture was being called upon everywhere to give graphic expression first to the fantastic visions of the Romanesque, and before long to the Gothic desire for expressiveness, when the preference everywhere was for paintings and stained-glass in glowing, often violent, colours, the Cistercians demanded bare, unadorned stone. The dark habit of the Cluniacs had been set off by cinnabar-red, ultramarine-blue and siena-green walls and wall-paintings; the Cistercians should be pictured in grey-white, woollen and linen cowls, neither bleached nor coloured, in the midst of light-grey walls. Their habit was to be as simple as their buildings. St Bernard's lyrical fanaticism made no concession to Peter the Venerable's view that both tradition and decency spoke for the black habit. To chasten the eyes he forbade even colour to this colour-sated generation, maintaining that it was vain luxury, and distracted the senses. In his famous *Apologia ad Guillelmum* of 1124, directed against the Cluniacs, and probably also against Abbot Suger of Saint-Denis, he damned everything that we call Romanesque (Document X). With the same stroke he cleared the way for Gothic art.[14] Bernard found fault with the dimensions of the new churches, the splendour of their wall-paintings, the costliness of their sacred vessels, but reserved his real spleen for the sculptural carving of the cloister capitals: '*Caeterum in claustris coram legentibus fratribus quid facit ridicula monstruositas, mira quaedam deformis formositas ac formosa deformitas?*' ('What are those laughable monstrosities doing in the presence of brethren reading in the cloister, such extraordinary perverted beauty and such accomplished ugliness?') The saint names the unclean apes, the wild lions, the horrible centaurs, half-men, fighting soldiers, figures with one head and many bodies, and others with many heads and one body. He conjures up the whole wealth of Romanesque sculpture. We learn that these things were famous even then, and on account of their fame became the object of worldly interest. Bernard condemns the worldly element in all art, which vitiated it for the soul intent on God.

The history of the Cistercian Order reveals that poverty is far less heritable than wealth. These monks wanted to live from the work of their hands in the solitude of wooded valleys, and for the first, and often for the second, generation they did so. They forbade furs and woollen cloaks, bed-linen and body-linen; they spurned tenantry and menials, superfluous mills and superfluous woods, any churches outside the monastery walls, and any houses. But however much they sought out the loneliest, most barren combes for their new foundations, however many decades they lived off roots and oatcakes, the hard work enjoined on them, in conjunction with the poverty, inevitably brought prosperity. A level of education and an educative drive superior to that of any peasant, and indeed any knight, led them to gather and transmit experience in farming and forestry that only accelerated the process. They were the best agronomists, the best stockbreeders, and the best foresters of the later Middle Ages. They were experts in fisheries and the use of water, and the valued pioneers of mining and smelting. St Bernard's theological prescience was blind to the connection between work, self-sacrifice, and wealth. The whole age lacked the insight into economics which would have disclosed that the pious bequests praised everywhere as good deeds were bound to entice the monastic communities into the world again. The Second Crusade of 1147, fomented, even in person, by Bernard and his pupil, later Pope Eugene III (1145-53), spurred on both the crusaders and those left behind to a spate of donations to Cistercian monasteries in particular. Many knights bequeathed their fortunes to the monasteries. Maulbronn in Württemberg shows how much a young community could owe to the Crusade. Soon after the turn of the century it owned properties in over a hundred different places. Worldly obligations grew with prosperity in the guise of rights to be protected, as everywhere in the Middle Ages. In the thirteenth century we encounter Cistercian monasteries that were richer than most of those of the Cluniacs. They disposed of extensive estates, leased farms, possessed whole villages, saw-mills in the woods, mines and mills. The self-same Morimond before whose poverty Arnold of Carinthia, a brother of Archbishop Frederic of Cologne, had fled in 1124, and whose ruthless asceticism had captivated the young Otto of Freising in 1133, possessed a century later 4,000 acres of land, sustaining 700 oxen and cattle and 2,000 pigs on farms and smallholdings.

The insistence on retreat was supposed to further the fulfilment of the vow of poverty. Both had to be seen in conjunction with our third precondition, the system of affiliation. The Cistercians aspired to build their monasteries in total isolation from any town, any village, or any castle. They wanted to avoid the possibility of a village community growing up round the monastery. For this reason they preferred narrow combes for their foundations, so long as there was running water, which was held indispensable by their Rule. Everywhere they were to be on virgin, preferably uncleared ground. They greeted unusual impediments put in their way by the first clearings as furthering their self-chastisement. Marshes, grudging soil, rocks, gullies and impenetrable undergrowth they joyously christened as the 'Valley of God', 'the Virgin', or 'Grace'. The choice of locations also implied a jealous independence of any bishop or lay lordship. Hence their reluctance to reform existing houses. They were the first to designate the institution of new monasteries as a task of the monks themselves. Monastic communities testified to their divine zeal by the foundation of daughter-houses, that were to remain attached to them for ever, like children to their parents. This is the meaning of affiliation. The diffusion of the Order over the whole inhabited globe was one of St Bernard's goals. An abbot was constantly to see himself put in the position of starting again in a new wilderness with twelve monks. It was a system which inevitably exhausted the area available. The map of expansion via affiliation conveys the process by which this great upheaval eventually petered out (Bibl. 101). Nonetheless, right to those in the furthest east the new monasteries maintained their connection with the Burgundian homeland.

It is only with our fourth precondition, the new spirit of regulation and functionalism within the monastery, that we return to our theme. The chief spirits behind the reform thought more closely about St Benedict's Rule in the light of changed times and circumstances. The annual cycle of the monks' day was re-examined hour by hour. In order to re-establish the balance between *opus Dei*, *lectio divina* and *opus manuum*, which had been neglected by the Cluniacs, the regime and the tasks of the *conversi* were also set out. In the *Dialogus inter Cluniacensem monachum et Cisterciensem de diversis utriusque ordini observatis* the Cistercian points out that his abbot is master of two houses, that of the monks and that of the *conversi* (Bibl. 89, Part v, Col. 1584). For both, the shape, size and place of the buildings were so precisely laid down, that it has proved possible to draw a standard plan for them. The new regulatory drive aimed at greater simplicity, clarity and precision. Just as the commandment to work inevitably produced wealth from poverty, art flowered from the desire for order. Everything superfluous was forbidden, and what was built was to be plain, chaste and lasting. Attention was consequently paid to the stone, to its careful dressing and fitting, and to the proportions of the rooms that it defined. Everything was built from the same pale, smooth-hewn stones. There were stone floors, stone door- and window-frames, stone walls and stone vaults, replacing wooden ceilings even in unimportant rooms. In the wider halls the urge to vault brought about a central row of columns, expressive of solidity. Even the roofs were often tiled with stone. Stone is always more suggestive of permanence than wood or plaster, more rigid and solid. One receives the impression that the monks have fixed themselves for ever in these expanses of vaulting. Here nothing gets out of place. It is both dungeon and paradise.

The Cistercian aesthetic unfolded in this world of stone, leading on to the Gothic. Once figural sculpture and colour were banished, the handling of stone reached new heights. Simplicity and geometric clarity were elevated into an ideal. Dammed-up artistic impulses flooded into new channels. It was no more possible to sustain utter simplicity, than poverty. In an artistic century, the insistence on work and perfection meant that a gain in art inevitably followed from a gain in effort. The geometric simplicity of ashlar survived until around the 1147 Crusade and the death of St Bernard in 1153. Thereafter, exemplified as early as the cloister of Fontenay, forms become more substantial from decade to decade, as if in obedience to an inevitable law of history. Severity is relaxed, plasticity takes hold. Leaf-capitals burgeon and ornament gains in body. It could by all means be said that the monastery goes along with the century, but the converse is also true. Every sphere is gripped by growth.

Pictures and monumental sculpture were for long still avoided. In obedience to the *instituta* neither façades nor towers were built. But instead, columned rooms were adopted for quite ordinary purposes. In the thirteenth century Cistercian monks erected the finest conventual buildings of the whole Middle Ages. In Poblet in Spain, Casamari in southern Italy, Maulbronn in Württemberg, or Eberbach in the Rheingau, the chapter-houses, dorters and refectories of both the monks and the *conversi* surpassed even the church-buildings of earlier times in their size and splendour.

THE STANDARD CISTERCIAN PLAN

Every Cistercian monastery lay by a stream in a valley, never on a mountain, nor by the sea, nor on an island, nor beside a lake or big river. The typical Cistercian situation such as we find it at Clairvaux (Document XIII), Fontenay, Maulbronn or Himmerrod is at the head of a vale opening toward the west, and closed by hills or mountains to the north, south and east. There, at the very point where a stream or river enters the plain, the abbot and the twelve monks built their new monastery. Repeatedly, as at first in Clairvaux, they went too high up, too much into a defile. They were then often compelled to shift an enlarged monastery toward the west and into the open. As a rule the layout exploited the site in a masterly way. By reducing the site to an ordered array of architecture a monastic landscape was produced, and the valley – it is hard to find another word for it – was *sanctified*. Some towns also lie where a river debouches from the mountains

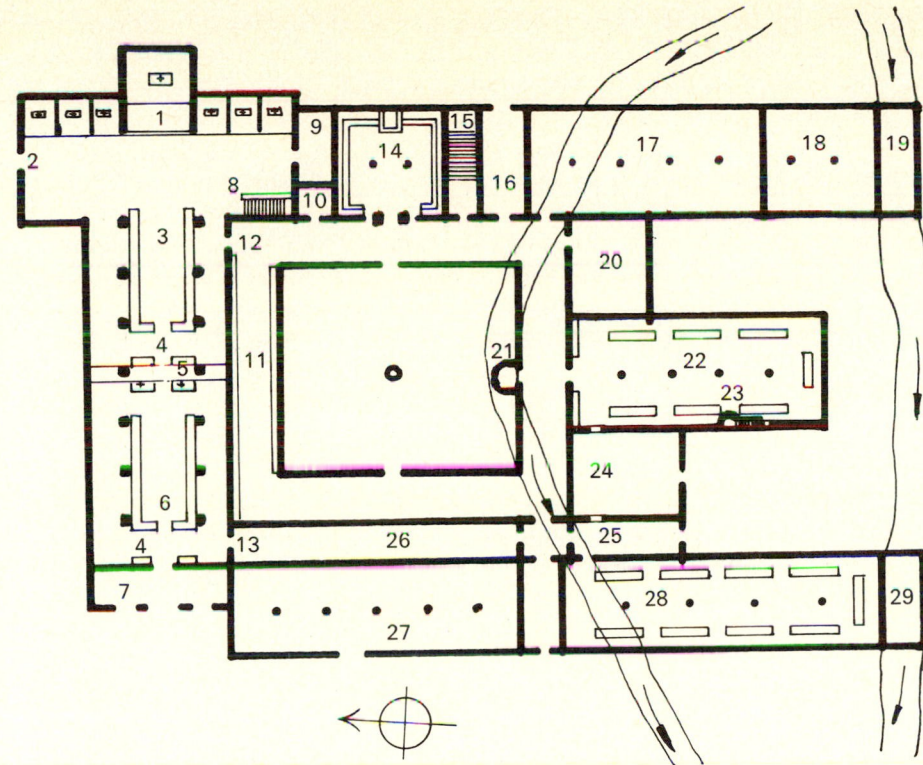

61 *The ideal Cistercian monastery, as presented by Aubert and Dimier.*
One of the prime requirements was a stream which could be diverted to provide
water for the fountain (21) and the two latrines (19, 29)

into the first piece of plain, between three ridges. Florence is an example. The Cistercians' rigid adherence to a predetermined plan, the monumentality of their buildings, and the fact that theirs was mostly the only architecture within sight, create an even more powerful impression. One sees nature tamed by civilization. A garden, terraces of vines, ploughed land and fishponds grow up round about. And as the land bears fruit, the architecture lends it a spiritual dimension.

Marcel Aubert in 1943, and Father Dimier in 1962, presented a plan of the ideal Cistercian monastery to which we have only found it necessary to make trivial additions. We can see in our mind's eye a fully evolved complex in which everything was provided for, nothing was superfluous, and which was composed of a series of uniform elements, amongst which the church only stood out thanks to its greater size. Right-angles predominated; the articulation of the monastery was firm and clear. Following Benedictine custom, the church was wherever possible erected to the north and the cloister to the south. The unconditional necessity of siting the watercourse adjacent to the refectory arm of the cloister occasioned so many exceptions to this that the rule almost ceases to apply. The church was intended for the monastery alone. There was no room for the populace or pilgrims, and for a long time they were not given access. On this account the standard Bernardine church as reproduced here provided for no façade nor wide west portal. A vestibule was allowed, as far as which guests might go. The schema stuck to the simple pillared basilica with a transept in the east and, following earlier Burgundian usage and in conformity with a stipulation of St Bernard, with a small rectangular choir. The monks could read their private masses in the four, or more often six, simple chapels of the transept.

A rood-screen (5) divided the church into the monks' choir (3) and that of the *conversi* (6). Two benches for the sick were allocated to each part (4). Whilst the monks followed the service at the High Altar, two side-altars against the rood-

1 Sanctuary
2 Lych-gate, the door through which bodies were carried from the funeral service to the graveyard
3 Monks' choir
4 Benches for the sick
5 Rood-screen, separating the monks' choir from that of the conversi
6 Choir of the conversi, or lay-brothers
7 Narthex
8 Night-stairs from the church to the dorter
9 Sacristy
10 'Armarium' (aumbry), where books were kept
11 Benches for reading, and for the 'maundy' ceremony of foot-washing
12 Monks' entry
13 Lay-brothers' entry
14 Chapter-house
15 Stairs from the cloister to the dorter, which extended over the whole range 14–19
16 Parlour
17 Monks' common-room
18 Room for novices
19 Latrine (used from the upper storey)
20 Calefactorium, or warming-room
21 Fountain, for washing
22 Refectory
23 Pulpit, for reading during the meal
24 Kitchen
25 Cellarer's parlour
26 'Lane' or 'alley' of the lay-brothers
27 Cellar, or store-room
28 Lay-brothers' refectory. The dorter of the conversi, or lay-brothers, extended over the whole range 27–28
29 Latrines of the lay-brothers' dorter

screen were provided for the lay-brothers, the altar of the Virgin and the altar for masses for the dead. Monks and *conversi* entered their choirs by different entrances, the monks from the cloister (12), and the *conversi* via the narrow passage (13), or 'lane', whose chief purpose was to ensure an area of quiet between their sphere and the cloister. The monks were neither to hear nor to see the lay-brothers. At night the former had a further means of access to the church, the steep stair (8) to the dorter down which they went to Matins at one or two in the morning. They had been sleeping for six or seven hours fully dressed on their plank-beds, and now had to last out another six or seven hours of choral service in the unheated church. The only thing common to monks and lay-brethren was the exit (2) through which the dead, immediately after their death and a short service, were borne into the open and the graveyard, hard behind the church. This door had no other purpose.

The Cistercians were content with a small sacristy (9), for even the unornamented vestments were kept in the altar-chapels and put on before the altar. Room 10, the *armarium*, held the library, and access was from the cloister, not the church. As in earlier Benedictine monasteries stone benches lined the north arm of the former against the church (11), on which, in proximity to the book-cell, the monks were to read in the open air. There also their feet were washed by the two monks who in the past and the coming week were responsible for the catering. Unlike St Gall or Cluny, no bath-house was provided. The *Mandatum* was also sung here during foot-washing. The chapter-house (14) adjoined the sacristy as usual. Then came the stairs to the large dormitory in the upper storey (15), and the prior's parlour (16), which the monks entered one at a time. There they were allocated their work and utensils. It gave directly onto the garden to the east of the monastery. The provision of a monks' common-room (17) was taken over from Cluny. It took the place that might easily have been set aside for the noviciate. It was created in most Benedictine monasteries merely through a fact of construction: the dorter, elongated so as to receive the growing number of monks, brought with it a lower storey which could not be filled by the chapter-house, parlour and dorter stairs alone. Bernard had specified no especial use for it. It is unlikely that under his supervision the monks were as yet allowed to work there too. A further small chamber for the novices (18) and the latrines (19) might be attached to it.

The calefactorium (20), as the only heated room in the monastery, had special uses. In some monasteries there were even two rooms, the smaller summer-room and a larger winter-room. There the monks might warm themselves, prepare parchment and inks, grease their shoes, and dry out after rain. There their hair and beards were cut, seven times a year in the early days, subsequently twelve times. Four times a year they underwent a bloodletting there. The calefactorium was also only accessible from the cloister. It is to be observed that the Cistercians put back amongst the conventual buildings those which for reasons of hygiene were specially housed outside them on the plans of St Gall and Cluny. Everything specified in the Rule was to take place round the cloister.

The Cistercians made an innovation in the placing of their refectory (22). It was built at right angles to the cloister, probably less for the commonly asserted reason of giving it more light, than to leave room for a kitchen (24) between the refectory and the house of the *conversi*. Its shape was borrowed straightaway by certain Benedictine monasteries that had accepted the Cluniac reforms. A famous example is the great refectory of Saint-Bénigne in Dijon, for which we possess plans and descriptions from the seventeenth century. We know that St Bernard had close connections with this monastery in the capital of his homeland, in which his mother, the blessed Alette, was buried. The new idea had caught on immediately (Bibl. 13). The sub-division of the upper storey in this whole wing was never settled. Sometimes a wardrobe was installed above the calefactorium. No second storey was possible above the kitchen. The detached situation of the refectory cried out for the monumental treatment, that was achieved for example in the *Herrenrefektorium* (that of the full monks) of Maulbronn. The hall

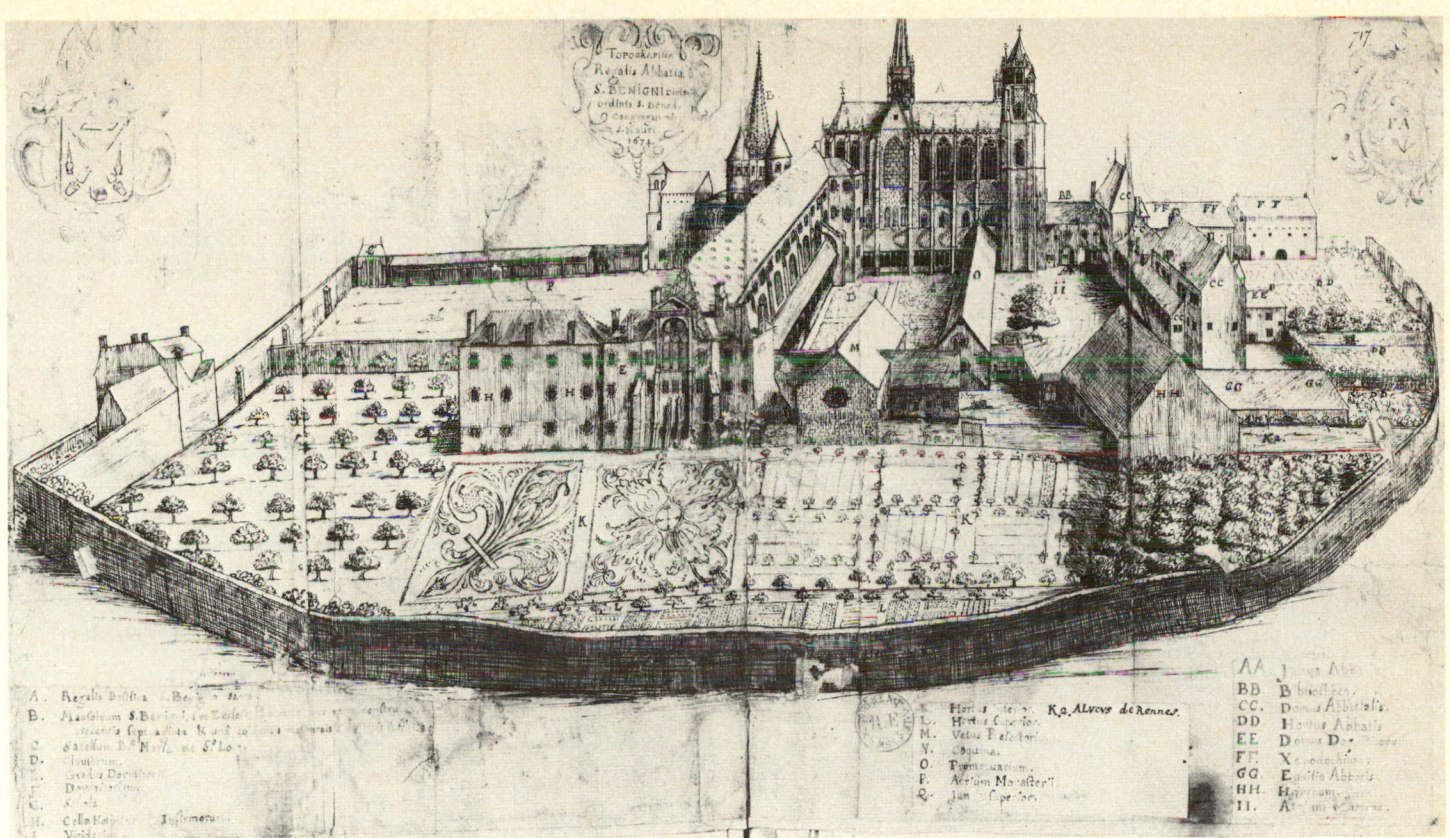

62 *The Benedictine abbey of St Bénigne at Dijon, as it appeared in the seventeenth century. St Bernard knew this monastery well, and it was probably from here that the Cistercian position of the refectory (M) was borrowed*

was taken up through two storeys, almost to church height. It was part of a general development not restricted to the Cistercians, that in the course of the twelfth century a fountain was built out from the cloister opposite the entry to the refectory (21). The same thing is found on the plan of Canterbury of about 1160. With the Cistercians the lavabo had to do duty for a bath. They washed their head each day, and their hands at every meal before entering the dining-hall. They were moved less by the thought of hygiene – in St Gall a survival from Roman bathing *mores* – than by cleanliness. To the right of the refectory was the kitchen (24), with a hatch both to the monks' refectory and to that of the *conversi*. It could naturally be entered and supplied from outside. From Easter to 14 September there were meals twice a day, at midday and in the evening. In summer lunch was pushed back to two o'clock so as not to interrupt work in the fields. From mid-September the monks were satisfied with only one meal a day, at two o'clock, pushed back to six o'clock after Vespers in Lent. Breakfast was unknown.

A contributory factor to the siting of the kitchen was the endeavour to associate a monastery for the brothers with that of the fathers, with a clearly defined relationship to the church and the cloister. The monks wanted it near at hand, yet set apart from theirs. The *conversi* themselves wanted to turn their back on the world like the monks, but their work required more frequent contact with it. For this reason they were allocated the west of the church and the cloister. The layout of the monastery of the *conversi* testifies to the instinct for order behind the planning. In Cluny all of this was still at random. The *conversi*, like the menials, lived over the stables. They had long been delegated the supervision of the great cellar to the east (27). They now achieved their own refectory through the extension of this cellar (28). Only once their eating-habits were precisely regulated

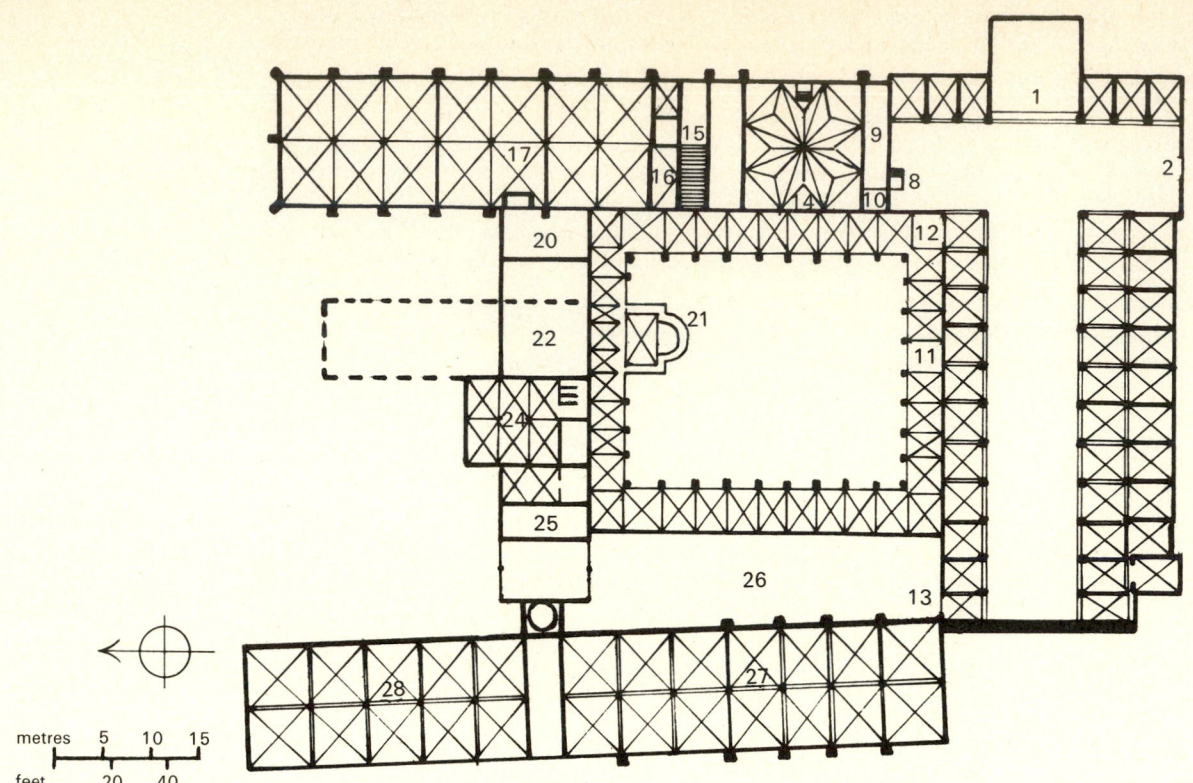

63 Eberbach. The same numbers are used as those given for the ideal plan on p. 75

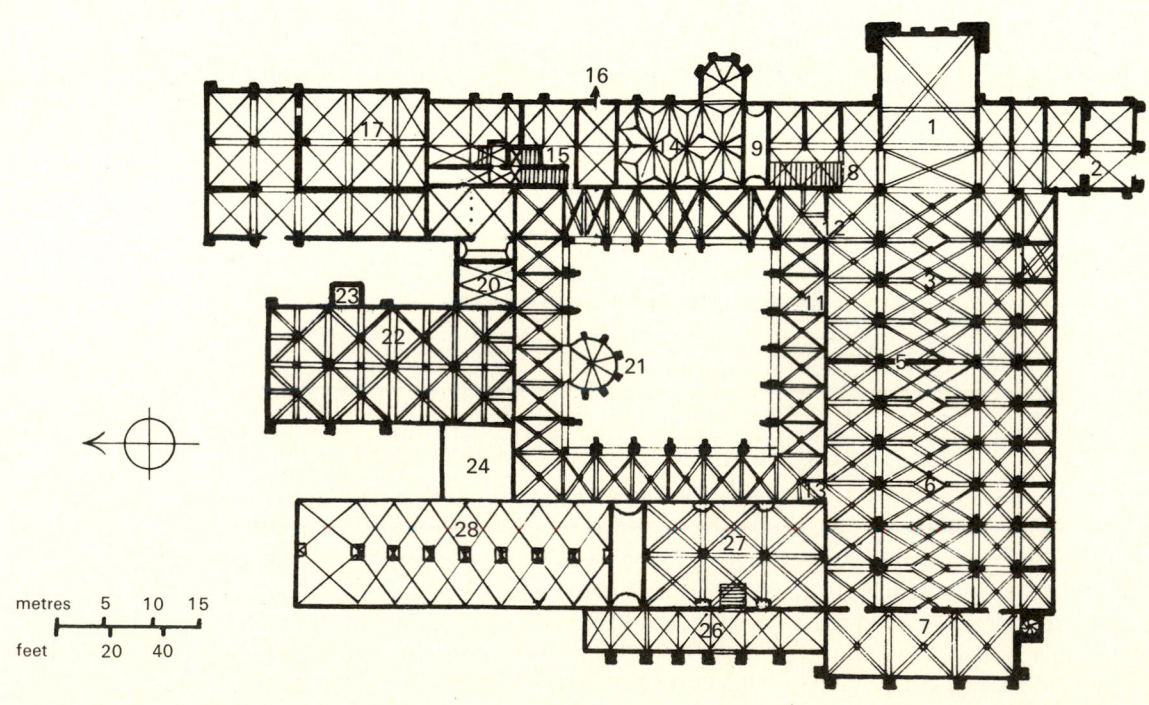

64 Maulbronn. For the key see p. 75. At both Eberbach and Maulbronn the monastic buildings are on the north side of the church instead of the more normal south, shown on the ideal plan

– the times, quantity and type of food, as well as the grace said before and after meals – did the servants of the monastery become true members of the community. Regulation of meals entailed appropriate architecture. Whether the dorter of the *conversi* extended the whole length of the wing, or only over the refectory, depended on the number of brothers. No-one ever ventured to take their dining-hall too through two storeys.

I must return once more to the alley of the *conversi* (26). It stands here, as it were, for the great court of Cluny, separating the menials from the monks. It exemplifies the whole problem of a class-division in the monastery. The *conversi* had to be admitted to the church, but not to the cloister. The 'lane' was indeed not built in all monasteries. It was provided for from the beginning on the plan for the enlarged second monastery of Clairvaux.

Outside the dictates of any schema were the buildings to the east, with the infirmary situated in their midst, and those to the west, comprising the hostels and domestic buildings. None of them belonged to the standard Cistercian plan. Though the Rule enjoined care of guests and the sick, these tasks were not easily reconcilable with Bernard's picture of the life of a monastic community. Here, as in earlier abbeys, spontaneous growth could occur. But the conventional buildings now cut themselves off more drastically from these 'lower' zones. Rarely was the infirmary, and never were the guests' and domestic buildings, 'major' architecture.

CLAIRVAUX AS MODEL

The description of the standard plan has left the question of its historical origins open. This is bound up with two problems, that the information given in our sources is not sufficient to elucidate. The first concerns the question of the relative shares of the monks and of outsiders in planning and executing what was built. A twelfth-century author, Odericus Vitalis, states that 'all Cistercian monasteries were built in remote places in the midst of woods and were constructed by the monks with their own hands' (*Hist. Eccl.*, Migne, *PL* 188, col. 641). But wherever we have more detailed information, it reveals that many of the builders in charge and the mass of the workmen were outsiders. This is demonstrable both from the style of the ornament and from records of payments to secular stonemasons. Links with the local schools of architecture were everywhere close, and absolute in the case of the first group of Burgundian foundations. Yet we must still assume that, just as the abbots bore the responsibility for the overall plan, monks and *conversi* bore the brunt of its execution. The first wooden buildings of the new settlements were their work. In the nature of things the transformation of this wooden architecture into stone must have been their doing in the early period. An increase in experience and manual ability will have gone hand in hand with the increase in scale. It is also natural that the sources record transactions with outside craftsmen, but only rarely the contributions of the monks and *conversi*. Scholarly opinion, which originally made the assumption that monasteries as a whole were the work of monks, now tends to underrate their part, in the light of these sources and analysis of the influence of local schools of building.

The issue is related to our second problem, which we have already encountered in considering Cluny. How is a small monastery rebuilt on a greater scale, and how are simple wooden tracts converted into stone halls, without upsetting the daily routine? If we picture to ourselves for example the architectural history of Maulbronn between 1147, the date of the re-siting of the monastery in its present position, and the end of the thirteenth or even well into the fourteenth century, there were decades of repeated and often total rebuilding of either church or conventual buildings. In this particular instance we know that most of the architects and craftsmen were outsiders. But we must still assume that the monks and the *conversi* had to accept improvised arrangements from time to time, in the cause of the finer, larger and more lasting construction of the cloister and the buildings round it. The monastery saw to its own expansion. It evolved from

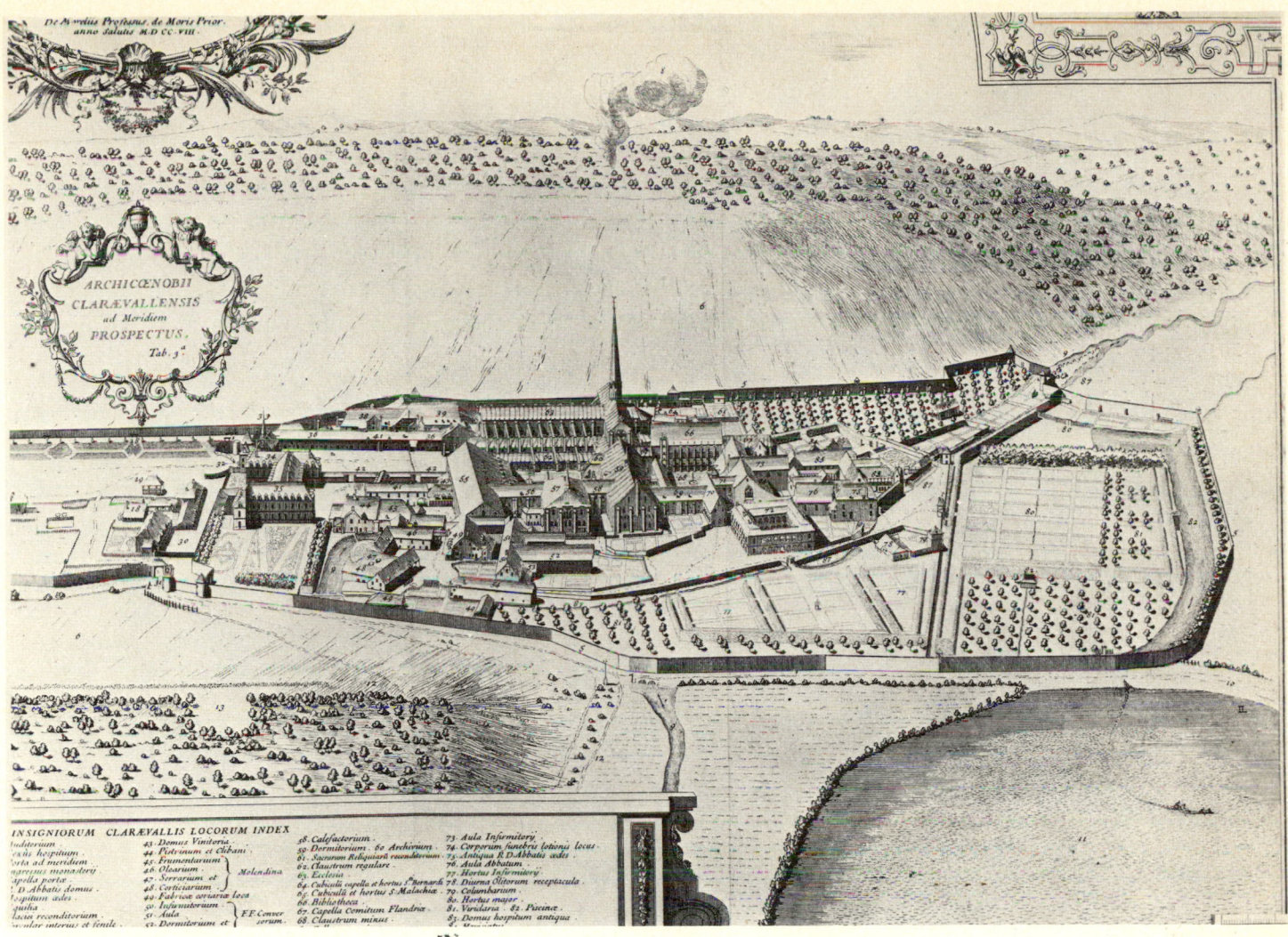

65, 66 Clairvaux: plan (left) and bird's-eye view (above) from Lucas's engravings of 1708. By this date it had expanded enormously from St Bernard's monastery, which consisted only of the buildings round the cloister

within, and not through interference from without like later monastic complexes.

Of the four parent foundations, Clairvaux – Bernard's own abbey – best answers the question of the historical origins of the new monastic plan. The monastery was unfortunately to a large extent destroyed by the fanatical devotees of Reason in the French Revolution, but we can piece together successive details of its appearance from the description in the *Exordium Magnum* of about 1180, from the first *Life of St Bernard* (Document XII), from the precise description by Joseph Meglinger, the Swiss Cistercian from Wettingen, of 1667,[15] and above all from the plan by the English Benedictine, Milley, of 1708, engraved by C. Lucas. We also know that, even whilst it was being built, the plan of the new monastery served as a model for others, which, above all like the two English abbeys of Fountains and Rievaulx, at any rate survive as ruins. Abbots of other foreign monasteries came to send their architects to Clairvaux to take the precise measurements of their paradigm. Aubert informs us of Abbot Wigbold from the Dutch monastery of Aduard, who sent a *conversus* and his son to Burgundy for this purpose in 1224 (Bibl. 105, p. 97). This lay-brother subsequently made such a perfect job of building the monastery and its church, that he was accorded the rare honour of a burial-place before the High Altar.

For eighteen years, from 1115 to 1133, Bernard and his monks lived in exceedingly simple and humble surroundings. These are still to be seen on the plan of 1708 to the east of the later monastery, revealing that the buildings were then employed as workshops – *artificum mansiones*. They consisted of a rectangular church, to which only one building was attached, containing the refectory and kitchen below, and the dorter above. There were two dark little cells under the stairs, with no room to stand upright, used as St Bernard's room and a guest-chamber. There will undoubtedly have been outhouses. Bernard himself mentions the cunning water-conduits (Document XII). He also states that the buildings were erected with great effort in stone. It was as yet not a Benedictine monastery in the strict sense. When Bernard was staying in Rome in 1133, his cousin Godefroid de la Rochetaille as Prior of the monastery, and the novice-master Achard who was himself an architect, clearly supported by the famous specialist in monasteries, Geoffroy d'Alaine (whom Bernard used to send to advise new foundations), proposed a plan for rebuilding it about 300 yards westward, on the banks of the Aube. I have reproduced the conversation, in the course of which Bernard was only very reluctantly persuaded to sanction the project (Document XII). He could not evade the point that the old site was simply too constricted for the steadily mushrooming number of monks and *conversi*. Funds and offers of help came from every side. The *Vita Sancti Bernardi* depicts the rapid progress of the undertaking. The monastery was caught up in the new task. The church was ready to be consecrated in 1145. The conventual buildings will have been ready for occupation at the same time. The *conversi* were at first allocated the old monastery to the east. But the shape and length of the nave make it certain that from the very first their building was planned for where it was finally built, some time before the saint's death in 1153. In the nave six bays were allotted to the 400 *conversi*, as against five to the 300 monks. In 1667 Meglinger counted 316 seats for the *conversi* against only 138 for the monks.[15]

The two most important innovations of the Cistercian Order, the realignment of the refectory, and the building for the *conversi* with its lane, were both

67 Fontenay from the air. The church is on the right, with the dorter wing extending in the foreground to the left. Facing this across a yard is the impressive forge

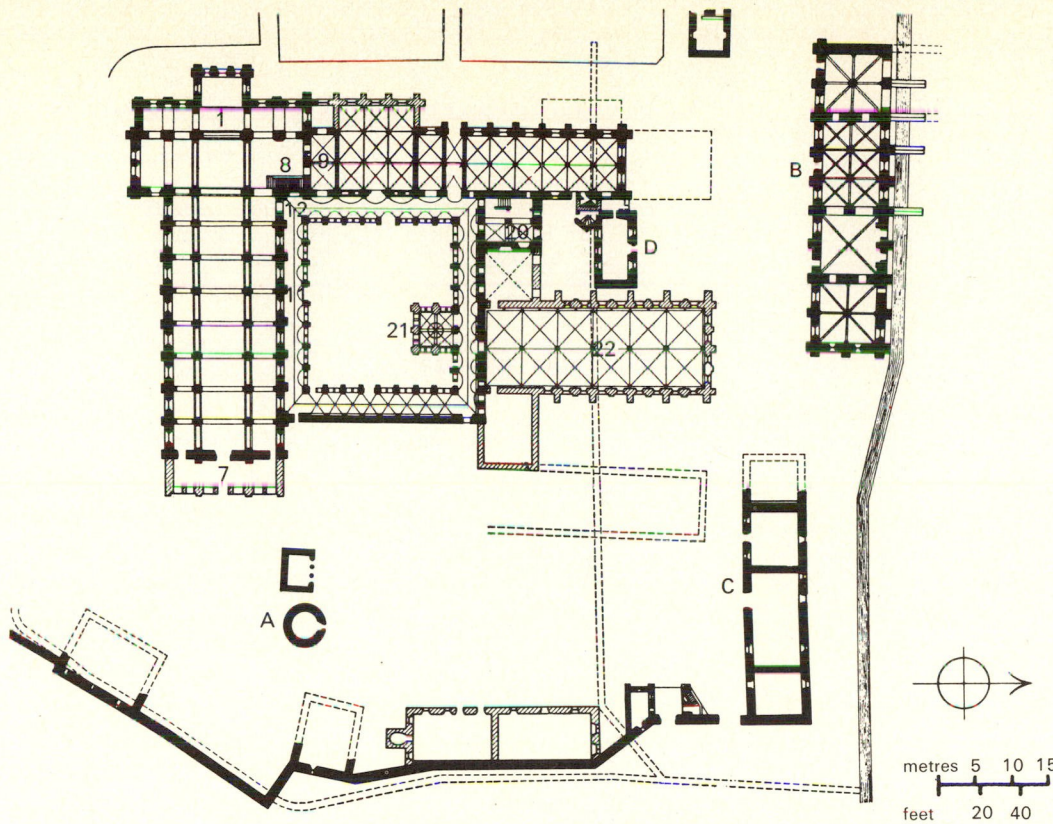

68 Fontenay. For the key to the numbers, see p. 75. Additional features are as follows: A, Dovecote; B, Forge; C, Guests' lodgings; D, Prison

contained in the plan for rebuilding of 1133. At that time the sub-dorter was still supposed to be used as the noviciate, and only as a new noviciate was built to the east at the end of the century under John II (1186–91), was it re-allocated to the monks as a common-room. Experience had taught that the cloister would thus be relieved of activities that disturbed its discipline and quiet. The length of the wall, 2,870 yards, which enclosed the whole monastery and was the first thing to be built, indicates that the grandiose plan incorporated sufficient space for the ancillary buildings – the sick-zone and a place for the scribes in the east, and areas for craftsmen and guests in the west. Furthermore, in Clairvaux itself the monks had almost twenty years to reflect upon possible improvements. In the very years around and after 1130, when the Order began the process of penetrating beyond the boundaries of France, into England, Germany, Italy and Spain, and when the annual decisions of the General Chapter were first published in the form of edicts, the perfect monastery was evolved in Clairvaux, and rapidly became the norm.

A prototype, and certainly an equally distinguished creation, survives in the shape of Fontenay. The same Godefroid whom we have encountered as Prior of Clairvaux founded this monastery in 1118 on the instructions of Bernard. It was the second daughter of Clairvaux. As with the latter a little later, it was found necessary in 1130 to shift it about half a mile down-river, from a too narrow valley. The site had been presented by an uncle of Bernard's, Rainard, the Lord of Montbard. The total cohesion of the complex suggests that it was complete in plan before Godefroid's return to Clairvaux in 1130. However the building of the church was only prosecuted energetically after 1139, thanks to the donations of an English prelate, Everard of Arundel, Bishop of Norwich, who had retired not far from the monastery. This, the oldest surviving Cistercian church in France, was consecrated by Eugene III in Bernard's presence. Only a detailed investigation of the structural ornament of the cloister and chapter-house could yield any certainty as to the point in the mid-twelfth century that

69 Fontenay, the abbey church, looking across the nave into the south aisle

70, 71 Fountains, plan and air view from the west. Most of the features shown in the plan are still visible. The key to the numbers is given on p. 75. The letters stand for the following:

A   *Abbot Huby's tower, built in defiance of Cistercian rules in the sixteenth century*

B   *Chapel of the Nine Altars; this parallels the rebuilt east end of Clairvaux and Pontigny, to provide extra altars*

C   *Infirmary*

D   *Infirmary chapel*

E   *Infirmary kitchen*

F   *Lay-brothers' infirmary*

G   *Guests' lodgings*

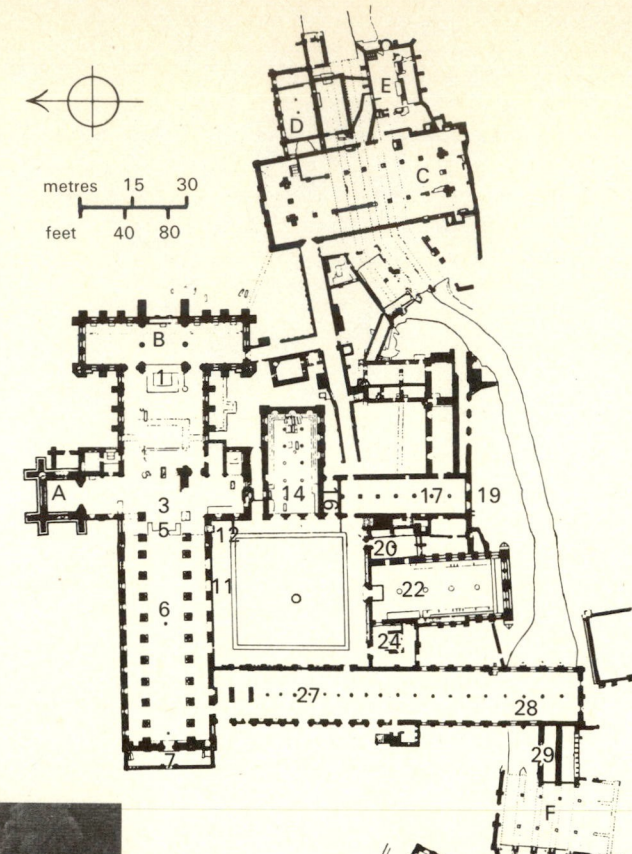

these were built. The most able men of the Order were concerned with planning it at the same time as, if not earlier than, Clairvaux. What was executed shows how Clairvaux must have looked. We know of the chapter-house that in plan at least it agreed with that of Fontenay.

In 1135 Bernard sent his architectural expert, Geoffroy d'Alaine, from Clairvaux to Fountains. We owe it to the fact that Henry VIII's England pursued the work of demolition less systematically than the France of the Enlightenment, that these ruins give a better picture of the original complex. They have also been more thoroughly researched (Bibl. 119). Apart from the enlarged chapter-house, Fountains reproduces the Clairvaux schema in every detail. The monastery which Bernard's former secretary William began to build in Rievaulx around 1132 also makes it clear every detail was fixed by the early thirties. Calefactorium, chapter-house, fountain, house of the *conversi* – they had all found their ultimate position. Even before the edicts of the General Chapter of 1134 had specified what was prohibited (Document XI), what was allowed was there for all to see. Clairvaux, Fontenay, Fountains, and Rievaulx are all manifestations of the same design. Cîteaux followed suit somewhat later. At the beginning of the fourth decade of the twelfth century, a group of young monks from St Bernard's circle was gripped by the same enthusiasm for the built realization of the perfect monastery that we saw on Reichenau in 816/20, or at Cluny or Hirsau in the eleventh century. They were the truly creative years. The essentials were developed and perfected between 1130 and 1140. The pattern was now completed. The next three centuries merely fiddled with the trimmings.

The course of the wall round Clairvaux, as it is shown on the 1708 plan, reveals that from the very first it was intended to allow for expansion alongside the river, that is, from east to west and not from south to north. Running water also kept company with the monastery in Fountains, from the monks' infirmary and its kitchen in the east, to the infirmary of the *conversi* in the west. Amongst the reasons cited by Bernard against the rebuilding of his monastery was the existence of perfectly good channels taking the Aube through the old monastery. Nowhere else does the same author, in describing the new monastery, lay as much emphasis as on the canalization of the river, which served to drive mills and pounders in several places, before the canals were reunited with the bed of the river at their exit from the monastery (Document XIII).

73, 74 Fountains. Above: the undercroft of the lay-brothers' range (27 and 28 on the plan). Below: looking from the chapter-house (14) across the cloister to the entrance of the refectory

72 Rievaulx from the air. The nave of the church is completely ruined, but the transepts and choir still stand, as does the refectory on the opposite side of the cloister

75 *Fountains, the nave and north aisle*

76 Rievaulx, the rebuilt thirteenth-century choir

77 The 'corona' of chapels round the choir had been given new currency by Abbot Suger at Saint-Denis. Both this, and the pointed arch and rib-vault, were quickly adopted by Cistercian architects

We saw how the art of the water-engineer was admired in Cluny, whilst the plan of Canterbury (Pls. 194–6 and *vide infra* p. 164) was specifically designed to show it off. The arrangement of the water-supply in the rebuilt Clairvaux presupposes that at the time of the reconstruction of the conventual buildings a general plan of the future monastery was already in existence, comprising the sick-zone and scribe's place to the east, and the workshops, domestic buildings and hostels (with a special chapel for the guests, who were not allowed into the abbey church) to the west. Bernard's brethren had become fully aware of what was involved in building large monasteries. Monastic life was only possible in all its rigour when the business of supply and services was handed over to others. A large piece of ground was marked out on the far side of the conventual buildings for extensions to the monastery. We know that John II (1186-91) built a special infirmary court, to which another for the scribes was added a little later. On his visit in 1667 Father Meglinger was astonished at the number of buildings provided for every branch of craftsmanship. Besides smiths and weavers, cobblers and carpenters, he mentions painters and sculptors. The growth of the

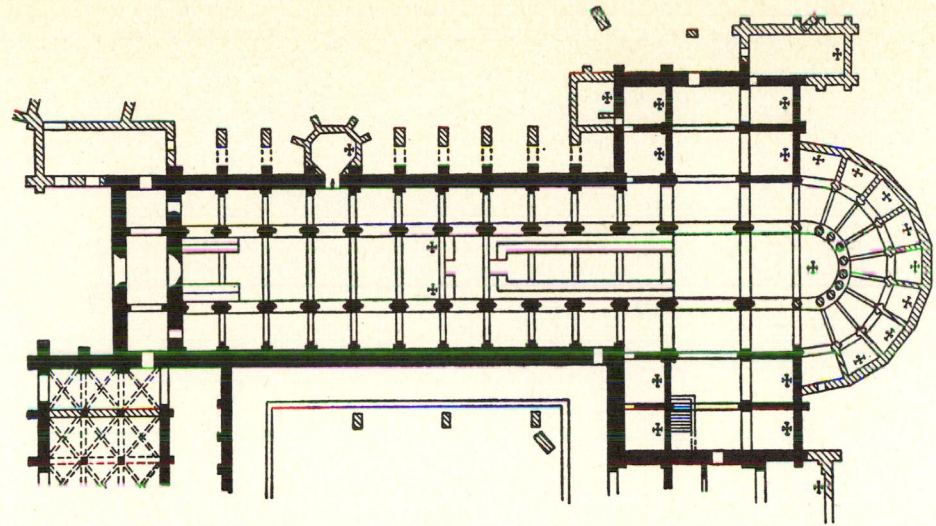

*78 The church of Clairvaux, showing the rebuilt choir. It originally had a square
east end like Fontenay*

institution could not be restrained. The plans for rebuilding Clairvaux in 1133
reveal that there was a group of monks round Bernard who, like many of the
disciples of St Francis of Assisi on a later occasion, thought more realistically
about the earthly necessities of monastic life than the saints who launched their
movement.

SUBSEQUENT DIFFERENTIATION

Even the sturdiest renunciation of the world cannot rescue a single artefact from
the stamp of its time or from the marks of the culture that it was created in. All
Bernard's stipulated uniformity of monastic architecture could not prevent its
being Burgundian in Burgundy, Swabian in Swabia and English in England.
Features evolved everywhere in response to the same laws of style. Cistercian
architecture was no exception to the progression from Romanesque to Late
Gothic. The precepts of the Order only provided the trellis-work on which,
from the twelfth to the sixteenth century, new fruits constantly ripened. Whatever attempts were made to prune them back to the norm, fresh offshoots repeatedly sprang from the old stock. Seven hundred and forty-two times, to
count only monasteries, was the Cistercian house built on the same plan, and in
the course of the centuries altered, renewed, enlarged or wholly rebuilt. Neither
in the Middle Ages nor in the Renaissance was there any attempt to alter the
number or placing of the rooms round the cloister: neither the cloister itself, nor
the chief buildings, such as the church, the chapter-house, the monks' common-
room, the refectory and the house of the *conversi*, nor yet the lesser places – the
parlour, the calefactorium, the kitchens and the fountain. There has been no
other formula in the history of European architecture, at any rate none so complex, which has been the object of such constant and consistent treatment.
Whatever time and the nations brought forth by way of stylistic discoveries
throughout the various phases of Romanesque and Gothic, the monks took up,
converted to their use, and embroidered upon, so as to refurbish their stone mansion in ever fresh variations on the same basic theme. The weight of particular
tracts and rooms in the total composition remained constant. They might be
large, like the refectory; middling, like the chapter-house; or small, like the
calefactorium. Nor were any fundamental changes made in the proportions;
change was purely stylistic. A community might live for centuries in the same
habitation, generations being satisfied with the familiar. Then an abbot might
be faced with the necessity of renewal – *renovatio* – , and so there were the stonemasons, from the monastery itself or from outside, 'reforming' the fountain, the

Three early Cistercian monasteries:
Pontigny, Heiligenkreuz and Le Thoronet.
For the key to all numbers, see p. 75

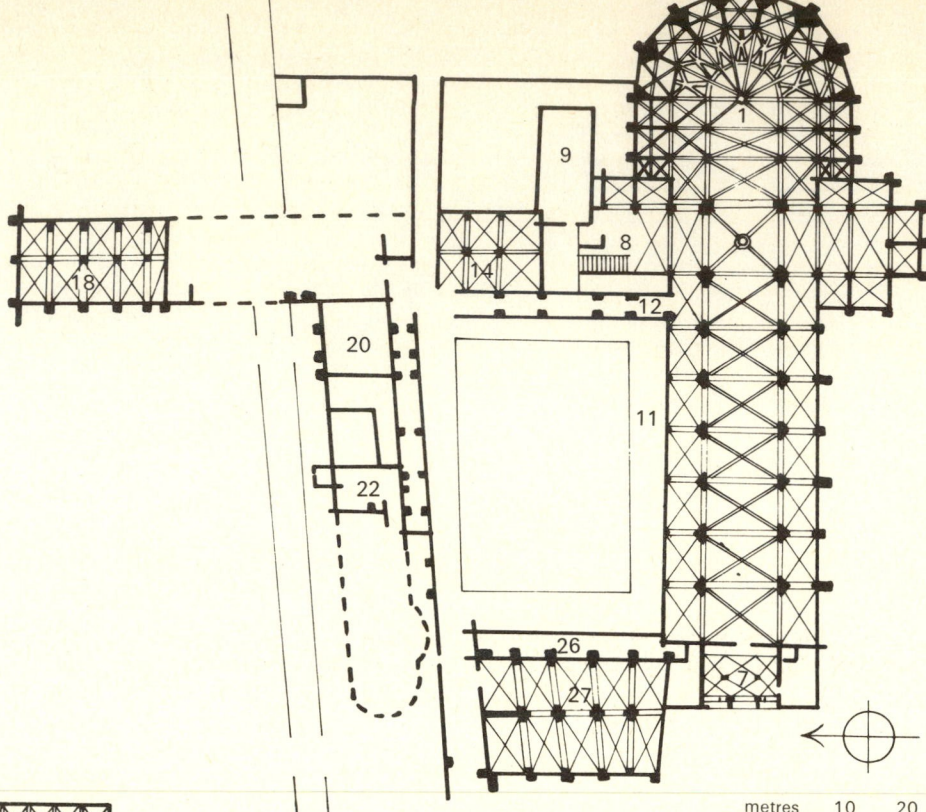

79 *Pontigny. The east end, originally*
square, was rebuilt on the same lines as
Clairvaux

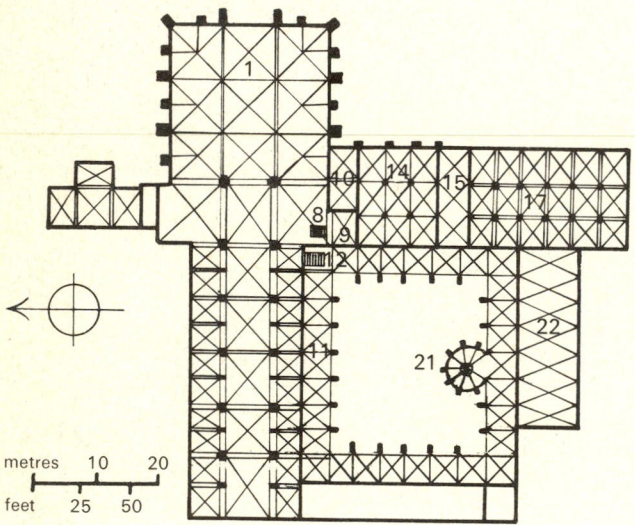

80 *Heiligenkreuz. The choir here is a*
'hall-church', see pl. 84, opposite

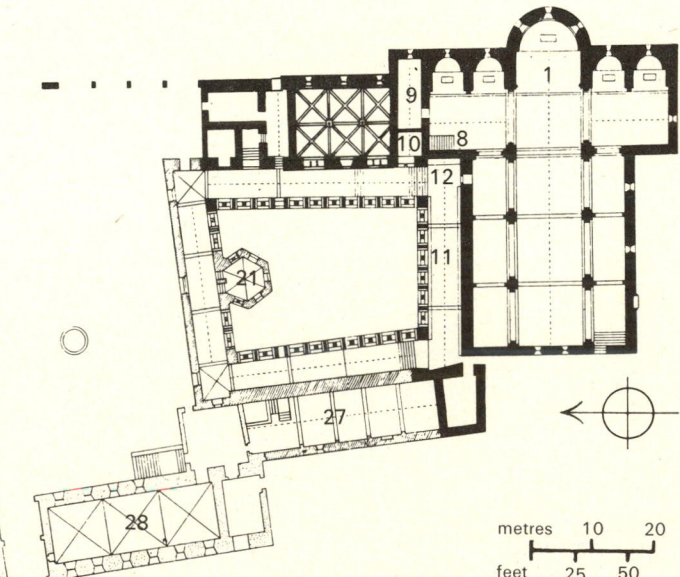

81 *Le Thoronet, where expansion*
practically ceased after 1200

cloister vaults, or some other place, according to the latest fashion. The old theme was given fresh instrumentation, but such variations still echoed the original spirit. Only like this was each monastic ensemble able to evolve its own architectural personality. Each forms a synthesis of components that one can trace. The Cistercian component is always only one, though the most important of these; others might be French, English, German, Spanish, Italian, or even Polish. For since each motif – from the church and all its features to the chapter-house, cloister, fountain or refectory – displayed unlimited adaptability, every style or artistic school had its contribution to make. We shall be able to show how conformity to Cistercian precepts had less a constraining than a stimulating effect on creative endeavour.

Our first example may be taken from church architecture. The rectangular choir of the Bernardine Abbey of Clairvaux was rebuilt, both enlarged and altered, immediately after the death of the saintly abbot. The Bernardine schema only allowed for a simple rectangle with an altar-table in the middle. K.H. Esser has stressed that Bernard himself insisted on this straightforward solution for Cistercian choirs.[16] For him the church was not in fact the House of God, but an *oratorium*, the place of the soul's communion with God, as specified in St Benedict's Rule. In 1135 Achard put up the church of Himmerrod in the Eifel precisely according to Bernard's principles, and on the very spot ordained by him in person on an expedition from Trier. The monks said their private masses at the altars of the transept chapels, of which there were only eight at Clairvaux, and six at Himmerrod. In keeping to the principle that only one mass might be said at each altar per day, each individual from amongst the great number of priest-monks only rarely had the chance to do so, which many complained at. An answer was found in Cîteaux, on the one hand by lengthening the transept so that there was room for three chapels on each arm, and on the other by mantling the rectangular choir with an ambulatory with room for ten further chapels. Clairvaux in 1154 adopted the old idea of an ambulatory with a corona of chapels, which had been given new life by Abbot Suger of Saint-Denis with the help of the Gothic method of vaulting a few years beforehand. And so a high, light-filled sanctuary appeared at Clairvaux, which contained the germ of the soaring Gothic choirs of both the Cistercians themselves and of future cathedrals. This step would lead to the generous choir-arrangements of Pontigny (c. 1185-1208), Royaumont (1228-35), Altenberg (1255ff.), or Doberan (1294-1368). The tall, light-filled sanctuary prevailed against every Cistercian tradition, to become in the end distinctive of their own architecture. The ruins of the choir of Heisterbach (c. 1210) and the 'hall-choir' of Heiligenkreuz (1288-95) are two more examples among many. These choirs satisfied both the needs of the Cistercians, and the architectural aspirations of the century. The *oratorium* had once again become an *ecclesia*, a place less for the praying monks, than for the presence of the worshipped God.

The history of the standard monastic layout illuminates another aspect of the innate conservatism of the Order's architecture, though this is obscured by the multiplicity of examples, each displaying some variation on the basic idea. There are small monasteries which expanded no further after their initial success, such as Thoronet. There are others which were constantly enlarged and altered, like Maulbronn; and there are several which rapidly became dilapidated, and could not thereafter be completed in stone. There is a final group of those that were the work of rich patrons, and were built at one go in their mature form. Such a case is Royaumont, which St Louis of France had built from 1228 onwards in fulfilment of the last wishes of his father. The church was ready to be consecrated after

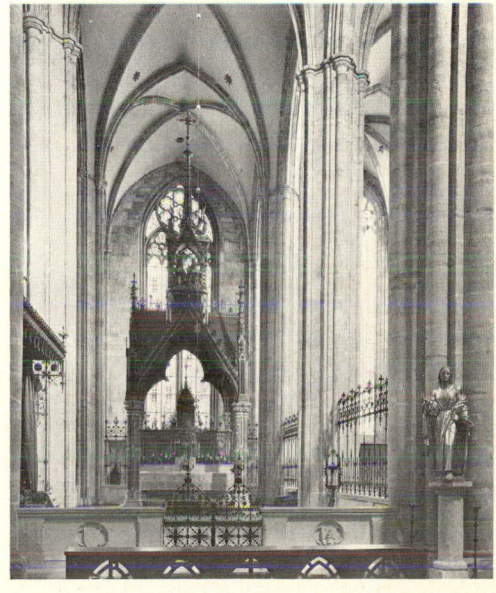

82, 83, 84 Right: three variations in the arrangement of the east end of Cistercian churches. Top: Altenberg, with the corona of chapels. Centre: Heisterbach, with apsidal niches opening off the ambulatory. Bottom: the 'hall-choir' of Heiligenkreuz

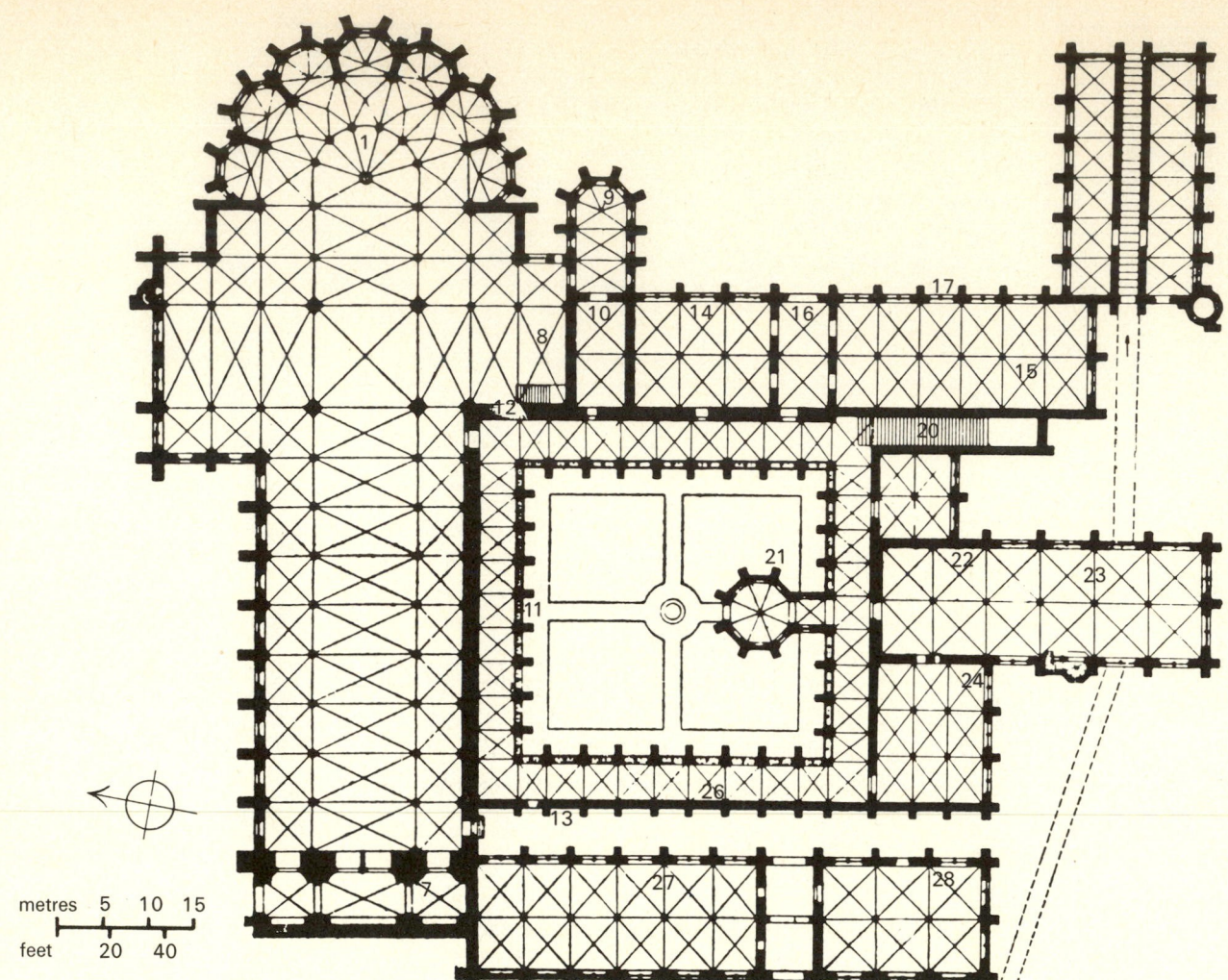

85 *Royaumont. For key to the numbers, see p.75. Here the elaboration of chapels round the choir reaches a climax*

seven years, in 1235, and the conventual buildings must have been completed not long after. The abbey was the preferred burial-place of several members of the royal house. Apart from the church, it largely survives. The plan reveals that a Cistercian monastery could now be produced on the drawing-board. Everything is formed out of the same components, in the same style. Sober rationalism and crystalline clarity prevails. In its charm, in the hair-fine and slender proportions of each part, in the constant recurrence of the same elements, as if they were prefabricated, the abbey is a classic example of the first phase of the *Style Saint-Louis*. The Sainte-Chapelle of 1247 makes a courtly counterpart to it. Here even the latrines with the stream funnelled through them to the south-east (19), the kitchens (24), and the lay-brothers' lane (26), were given an imposing appearance. It is the epitome of a High Gothic monastery, to which, as in a cathedral of the same period, nothing can be added, and nothing taken away. Almost exactly a century had passed since the plan of Clairvaux. Cistercian art never improved on this plan. What came later brought only local variants on it.

The Cistercians remained true to their schema for four centuries, which becomes apparent by juxtaposing the plan of Royaumont with the picture of the Flemish monastery of Duinen, or Ter Duinen, painted in 1580. This place, which was taken over by the Cistercians in 1138, and visited by St Bernard himself in 1139, seems to have been wholly reconstructed or rebuilt in the first half of the sixteenth century. It was burnt down in 1566 by *Les Gueux*, plundered in 1577, 1590 and 1593, and lay deserted after 1628. The inmates had withdrawn to Bruges and made a new monastery there. The old buildings were then torn

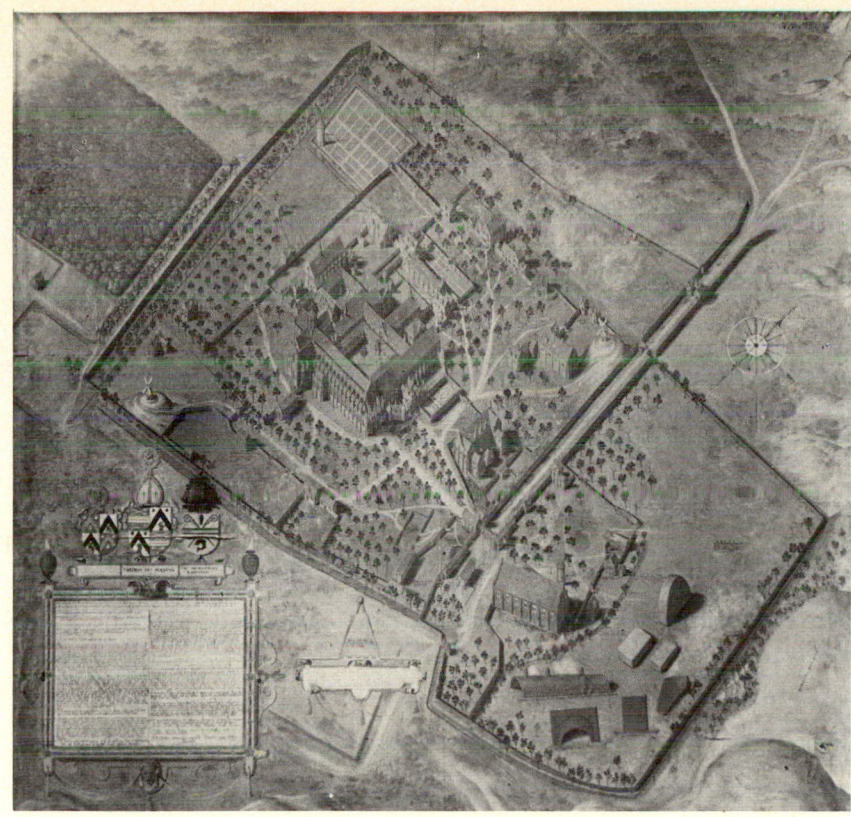

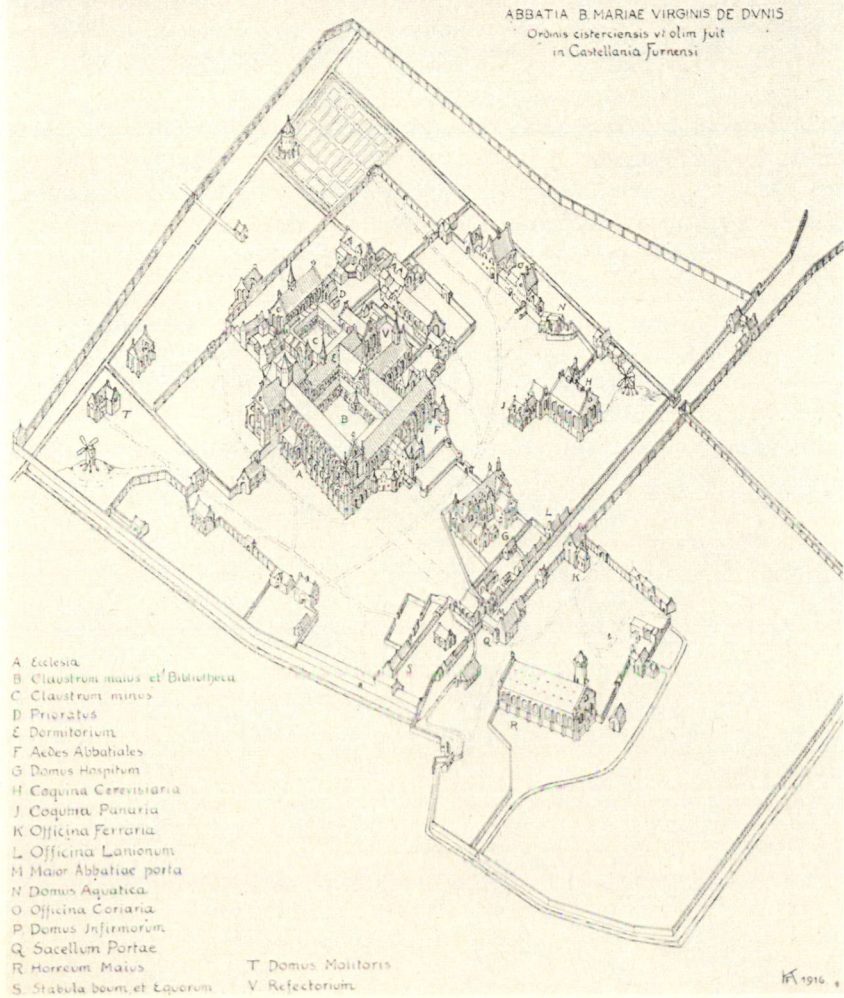

86, 87 *The Flemish monastery of Ter Duinen, as portrayed by Pourbus in 1580 (top) and after Sanderius in 1640 (bottom). The Latin key to the latter may be translated as follows:*

A *Church*
B *Large cloister and library*
C *Small cloister*
D *Prior's lodging*
E *Dorter*
F *Abbot's lodging*
G *Guests' lodging*
H *Brewery*
J *Bakery*
K *Smithy*
L *Butchery*
M *Great gate*
N *Pumping station*
O *Leather curing house*
P *Infirmary*
Q *Rear gate*
R *Great granary*
S *Stables for oxen and horses*
T *Miller's house (by the windmill)*
V *Refectory*

down. In 1580 Pourbus painted the monks an imaginary picture of their monastery, which at this period, after having been burnt and plundered, can hardly have been as complete as it is shown here. When Antonius Sanderius incorporated the etching by Creites in his *Flandria illustrata*, it was no more than a commemorative picture, and this fact would explain the false designation of the gallery (17) as an infirmary.[17] Not one of the chief buildings had changed its position from that on the standard schema – neither the dorter in the east (11), nor the refectory in the south (12), nor the house of the *conversi* in the west (15). The kitchen building stands free between the refectory and the house of the *conversi* (13), and as at Royaumont the large latrine (10) stands against the dorter. To the west was the prelate's precinct, with its own garden, and a miniature Gothic palace – a Bruges burgher's house. In front of it is the large *gasterie* (19). Corresponding to these western buildings, in the east – as in Clairvaux, and for that matter in Cluny and St Gall – are the infirmary (16), with its own cloister (8), shared by the noviciate, which was housed in the little buildings on its north side. It was already traditional for the administrative head of the monastery, the prior, to have his house near the infirmary – this was the case with the palace of the second man after the abbot in Cluny. Further to the south and west there was ample room for a multitude of domestic buildings.

If one looks more closely at the picture of the monastery and its inscriptions, one sees that the desire for completeness had given rise to several novel buildings. The monastery had a special wing housing a gallery (17), 206 feet long according to the inscription, where the genealogy of the counts and countesses of Flanders was set forth, in other words a hall of honour for the founders. The monastery was plentifully provided with domestic buildings and stables. On the far side of the great walled way leading through several gateways up to the western entrance to the church, a large new workyard was created, with notably geometrical workshops and a brick-kiln behind them. There was a large vegetable garden with a tower in the south-east corner of the site, and at its northerly edge small buildings were strung out, going from the abbot's stables, through two huts for the almoner, to a mill and a house for the miller. The buildings serving the water-supply were of major significance here too. One would expect them in the east, and that is where they are to be found. There is a water-tower (*'t waterslot*) connected up to two pipes and, under the number 20, a waterworks (*'t waterhuis*) with a horse-turned waterwheel of great size from which, the inscription relates, conduits went to all the main buildings – to the church, the refectory, the prelate's precinct, the kitchens, the brewery, the bakery, the slaughterhouse, and to the covered threshing-floor.

One can see that the selfsame basic ideas as in the twelfth century are here taken up and embroidered on in the sixteenth. The river is made serviceable and cleanses, offering itself and then returning to nature; it becomes a friend and an example to the monks and even a symbol of their regimen.

In all Cistercian monasteries the greatest attention was paid to the water-supply, whose history however seems to me beyond the reach of research. It is hard to distinguish what was borrowed from the Arabs, and what from earlier discoveries, and what refinements were then made from the twelfth and thirteenth centuries right up to the seventeenth. Cleanliness was inherent in Cistercian aesthetics. It is to be found both in the use of patiently smoothed stones and in the provision of washrooms; the covered fountains opposite the entrance to refectories became increasingly elaborate in response to this use. They are symbolic of the importance of the role played by water in the monastery.

88 Detail of the Pourbus painting showing the buildings round the cloister. The numbers are explained in the text above

SALVE · REGINA · MISERICORDIE ·

89 Diptych commissioned by Christian de Hondt, Abbot of Ter Duinen, in 1499, showing himself kneeling before the Madonna in his own room

90 The refectory of Saint-Martin-des-Champs – a princely hall in striking contrast to the meagre fare which formed a Cistercian meal

Everything had been thought of, it all looks new, it is all ready. Just as in the appearance of Bruges today, the proximity of the large to the small shows each to advantage. The monks had installed themselves so well in this institution that they might hope that their day would run like clockwork.

Through the storeys all being on the same level, the continuous roof, the glazing of the cloister, and through compactness of building, conventual life could be carried on wholly indoors in this sixteenth-century rebuilding. One also knows that in the case of the Cistercians each monk and each *conversus* by now disposed of his own cell. It was not only through the eyes of the painter but in their whole approach, that the monks were becoming bourgeois; and this was reflected architecturally. In the interiors one would have encountered wainscotted, richly furnished suites of rooms. In such comfortable and *soigné* surroundings the late medieval art of living attained one of its high points. Thomas à Kempis's (1379/80-1471) *The Imitation of Christ* was read by the fireside. Paintings were hung in the panelled rooms. Christian de Hondt, the thirtieth Abbot of Ter Duinen, had himself painted as donor before the Madonna in front of the fireplace of his own chamber in 1499 (Antwerp, Musée des Beaux-Arts). Yet the insistence on the unalterable arrangement and co-ordination of every building still obtained, and lent meaning and stature to the whole ensemble.

The path which led from great Cistercian complexes like Clairvaux, via Royaumont, to Ter Duinen possesses many further stops on the way, and equally many divagations from it. To tread these and describe them would distort the picture that I have tried to delineate. We have not even mentioned the Cistercians in Italy, Spain or Eastern Europe; such splendid monasteries as Zwettl, Lilienthal and Heiligenkreuz in Austria have not been touched on. Let these few examples then at least serve to underline the fact that medieval monasteries surpassed any other kind of building in the rigorousness of their planning, and the diversity of structures that were thus welded into a superior whole. To illustrate the evolution of their interiors we may draw on a fresh set of examples. The urge to use stone in any second campaign of building following Bernard's insistence that it should replace wood, and the consequent partiality for columns and vaulting, revealed itself as remarkably fruitful. It acquired yet further importance through the truth to materials induced by the ban on pictures and colouring. In the course of time stone replaced wood even in the domestic buildings. Barns, threshing-floors, mills, blacksmithies, bakeries and breweries claimed the status of architecture. Kitchens and water-towers were built on a heroic scale. Vaulted halls and columns, albeit of the simplest type, seemed suited to every purpose, because they embodied greater permanence. The physical character and stone-carving of any building with claims to artistic significance regularly put a gloss on its place and significance in conventual life: they were 'message-bearers'. Thus fountains became receptacles of living water, dorters became chambers of sleep, chapter-houses enshrined the gravity and solemnity of chapter-sittings, and refectories the importance ascribed to the common meal in the regimen of ascetics. The meagre fare was eaten in princely dining-halls, which sometimes rivalled churches in their size and magnificence. It is true that the Cistercians invented no new type for any of these buildings – the proportions of all of them were basically similar in Cluny – but the use of stone and the renunciation of pictures assisted their purist bent toward preciser formulations.

Enough specimens from the twelfth to sixteenth centuries survive in the countries that traditionally make up Europe to compose respective histories of the five main sorts of building – cloister, chapter-house, fountain-house, refectory and dorter. The over-riding importance of the churches has unjustly distracted attention from the conventual buildings. The history of the various sorts of building is particularly stimulating because, whilst the type remains constant, each particular example of it reliably reflects the differing period and local context that it was produced in. There creators operated within narrow limits. The higher the quality of each particular feature, the more informative it is about the exact time and place in which it was produced. Just the few examples that I have managed to select for this book disclose what slight variations are necessary, in order to express differing architectural impulses of the very highest order.

The monastic cloister is a particularly happy invention, because it makes it possible to align delicate arcading in front of the bases of massive buildings of different dimensions – as the church and conventual buildings are – to produce

91 Le Thoronet, the east walk of the cloister

92 Fontenay, the cloister looking south, 1139–47

93 Royaumont, the north walk of the cloister looking east, 1231–35

the effect of a mighty load over something fragile, and a variety of masses over a uniform band of columnar or pillared arcades. The Cistercians moreover everywhere arranged things so that the succession of columns, pillars or windows all rested on a continuous base and, wherever the monastery flourished for any length of time, that they bore a solid vault. The stonemasons were wholly in their element, as from decade to decade they gave the arcading an ever lighter appearance. Thus the chaste Romanesque of Le Thoronet was succeeded by the more florid Romanesque of Fontenay, and this in turn by the noble Gothic of Royaumont, only to culminate in the filigree of Late Gothic tracery – the climax of a development in which mass was progressively reduced, whilst detailing increased. Less stone was called for, but more labour.

The construction of the chapter-house was also a promising field for especially beautiful feats of architecture, because at the entrance end it could use the same architectural vocabulary as the cloister, in that it usually opened onto this via a three- or five-bay arcade, composed of two or four windows plus the portal. It was almost always square or rectangular, with a vault supported on two, four, or more rarely six, columns or pillars. Only a few, though important, examples made do with a single column in the centre (e.g. Eberbach). The monks always sat along the four walls on one to three steps, that were originally always stone-hewn. In many monasteries the floor enclosed by these steps was actually lower than that of the cloister, so that one stepped down in stepping into the chapter-house. But in the chapter-house of Fontaine-Guérard near Evreux we are confronted by a thirteenth-century building whose architect ventured to pierce it with three portals toward the cloister, with no change of level, thus imbuing it with a new solemnity.

94 Maulbronn, the chapter-house, looking out into the east walk of the cloister. The vault is fifteenth century

95 *Eberbach, the chapter-house, c. 1345*

96 *Fontaine-Guérard, the chapter-house, thirteenth century*

97 Zwettl, 1138

98 Noirlac, c. 1170

Cistercian chapter-houses of the twelfth century

99 Bebenhausen, c. 1200

100 Fossanova, c. 1200

Emphasis was always placed architecturally on the capitals and vaulting with, as was customary with the Cistercians, great weight being given to the matching of ribs and capitals. The capitals themselves were of every kind: those with strong projections, as in Zwettl or Bebenhausen, alternating with others pared to the minimum, as at Noirlac. Or Gothic might be infused with classicism, as at Fossanova, and ornament be enlivened by flowers. In each instance one is amazed at the expressively distinctive character that could be given to each separate capital.

It is remarkably exhilarating to note how the selfsame windows and arcades that are immediately crowned by vaulting in the cloister, stand in a quite different relationship to the broad, high vaults of the chapter-house, though these usually employ the same artistic vocabulary. The place was mostly illuminated by windows on the rear wall as well as by the arcades at the entrance end, but with the Cistercians the former was almost never extended to receive an altar. It is nonetheless remarkable what variations the stonemasons drew out of this theme in the course of the centuries, giving vent to differing local traditions of stone-masonry as much as to stylistic changes. Fossanova is as Italian in its treatment of columns as Fontenay and Senanque are French. Poblet is quite Spanish, whilst Zwettl and Eberbach are rooted in Austria and the Rheingau. Nowhere, save in some English monasteries (p. 170–1), could the builders go very high – and this is the chief difference from the requirements of the refectory – for the long wing containing the dorter extended over every chapter-house. Nonetheless a particu-larly broad and well-lit chamber was created in Eberbach, for example, through the use of only one column, whilst Fossanova achieves classic proportions.

The Cistercians created the fountain-pavilion in front of the refectory using identical constituents to those of the cloister in the middle of that arm of it. Its architectural effect is more potent when it is seen in conjunction with the chapter-house. For whilst the latter opens inward from the cloister, the former projects

101 St Remi, Rheims, the chapter-house

102 Ossegg, in Bohemia, the chapter-house

103 Fontenay, the east walk of the cloister, looking into the chapter-house

104 Senanque, the chapter-house, end of twelfth century

105 Poblet, the chapter-house, c. 1200

outwards from it. The Cistercians mostly made the little pavilion hexagonal, though sometimes square, with in the middle the circular basin of the fountain, from which water was never to cease to flow. The columns, arcades, balconies and tracery of the cloister undergo yet a third transposition owing to the new relationships set up within this small structure. These fountain-pavilions are the smallest sort of centrally-planned buildings in stone conceived by the Middle Ages. Romanesque arcades gradually develop into traceried windows. The fountain becomes a glass-house, whose door to the cloister echoes the five windows. Every variety of arcade, column and pillar found in the church recurs there too. National characteristics can be especially marked here; compare for instance the Italian Fossanova with the Portuguese Alcobaça, and this in turn with the Swabian Maulbronn. Even the form of the basins varies; these were mostly shaped with the greatest care, and many are masterpieces of the mason's art.

As long as Benedictines and Cistercians adhered to the principle that the whole monastic community was to sleep in one room, they had to create huge halls as dorters. As a rule the dorter would be the largest secular building in the monastery; sometimes it even surpassed the nave of the church in length. There were mostly two means of access, one giving immediately onto the transept of the church, and the other onto the cloister court or latrines. Right from the very earliest known examples of the seventh century, it was thought appropriate to put it in the storey above the chapter-house and the later monks' common-room. For this reason it could never be of great height. As we saw in Cluny, what was required was a moderately wide, exceedingly long, and relatively low hall, lighted by a great number of windows, for it had to be possible to read lying on one's bed during the day. The Cistercians aspired everywhere to vault it, smaller monasteries making do with a barrel vault, whilst the larger ones opted for ribbed vaulting supported on short, stocky columns. For an eye used to the soaring vaults of churches these modestly high chambers have an especial charm; one should visualize them filled with their flat, narrow beds to capture the full effect of these wide, long, low dormitories. The total quiet enjoined in them is reflected in the avoidance of any dramatic effect in their features.

Whereas the dorters were of necessity kept low, the refectories could, and were encouraged to, be high. They are at ground level. No upper storey was envisaged for any purpose by the Rule. Thus, with a roof-ridge almost level with that of the dormitories, they could be almost double their height. I have already emphasized that it was less a question of lighting than the need to situate next to them the kitchens and calefactorium which led to their being put end-on to the cloister

106–09 Four Cistercian fountain-pavilions, placed near the entrance to the refectory, where the monks washed before meals. Above: Le Thoronet (c. 1175) and Heiligenkreuz (end of thirteenth century). Left: Fossanova and Alcobaça (both thirteenth century)

110 *Poblet, the dorter (dormitory) of the novices, end of the thirteenth century*

111 *Le Val, the dorter, thirteenth century*

112 *Eberbach, the dorter, 1270–1345*

instead of, as in earlier Benedictine monasteries, side-on. They were always vaulted, and mostly two-, or more rarely three-, aisled. By contrast with the dorters they had tall, slender columns, but in many monasteries the bases and capitals of these were deliberately kept chaster than those of the chapter-house. The windows are shaped like church windows, and are as tall. The lectern was almost always up a small flight of stairs built into the wall.

For roughly half the year the monks only entered these resplendently vaulted stone halls once a day, and the rest of the year twice a day, in total silence; they prayed long and vigorously before they sat down and, still in silence, were read to whilst, without haste, they consumed their meagre ration. They were to show no trace of appetite or pleasure on their faces. They sat at two or three long, low tables, headed by a crosswise table with the abbot and a few of the brethren or guests.

The monks' refectory of Maulbronn is the most ambitious thirteenth-century dining-hall to survive. Its features date it to about 1220. It is a masterpiece of the transitional period of Hohenstaufen art; that is to say, of Gothic proportions and Gothic construction, using forms of Romanesque grandeur. Seven columns, three stout and four more slender, and all with shaft-rings, support the strongly stilted and vigorously profiled rib-vault. This gives four sexpartite bays in the centre and two heptapartite bays on either side of them. The place is lighted by four windows on the outer end wall, and by five along each side; a sixth was supplanted by the stairs by which the reader climbed to his high pulpit. Such solemn and elevated splendour can only have been meant as an encouragement to give the food, following veritable orgies of fasting, the higher meaning

113 Le Thoronet, the dorter, 1160–65

114 Royaumont, the refectory, c. 1250. Note the pulpit for reading

115 Santa Maria de la Huerta, the refectory, fourteenth century

116 Oliva, near Danzig, the refectory, late sixteenth century

117 Poblet, the refectory, c. 1200, now used as the library

ascribed to it in St Augustine's Rule (*vide* p. 12). Eating became a ceremony, and its *locus* enshrined a diet imbued with exalted significance. The Franciscans and Dominicans were to achieve the same effect through wall-paintings of the Last Supper. The columns and vaults in Maulbronn are vehicles of a message similar to that depicted in Leonardo's picture in Santa Maria delle Grazie in Milan (*vide* p. 146). It is this intermediate position, between profane and sacred art, which gives all monastic architecture its special flavour.

The infirmaries of the Cistercians demand special treatment. We saw how in Clairvaux and Cluny, just as on the St Gall plan, a special area detached from the actual conventual buildings, but still inside the monastery walls, was reserved for the sick. In St Gall it was a small monastery within a monastery. The importance attributed by the Rule to the care of the old and sick (Document 1, Cap. 31) inevitably stimulated specialized architecture for them. The farmery hall often surpassed the refectory in size, and the chapter-house in elaboration. Care of the sick justified the highest standards. The infirmary was mostly supplied with its own kitchens, chapel, and latrines, besides the great hall. The finest surviving examples of infirmary halls are those of Ourscamp, of about 1210, and Eberbach, of roughly a decade later. The *Salle des Morts* of Ourscamp, as it was once called, is the sole building from this famous abbey to survive, and is now used as a church. It is a high, three-aisled, rib-vaulted building of no less than nine bays. The portal and windows are on a grand scale. The upper storey windows consist of two narrow rectangles surmounted by a circular opening. They were glazed and could not be opened. They were complemented at ground level, serried over the beds, by a row of small windows which only had wooden shutters, and were hence exclusively for ventilation. This separation of lighting and ventilation is typical.[18] Similar, though on a more modest scale, was the Hospital of Eberbach. It lay, together with its chapel and with subsidiary rooms for the kitchens, lavatories and a ward for the dying, round its own cloister. These Benedictines appreciated that the sick also felt the need of surroundings in which they felt at home; for sick brethren they therefore created a monastery *in parvo*.

118 Maulbronn, refectory, c. 1220

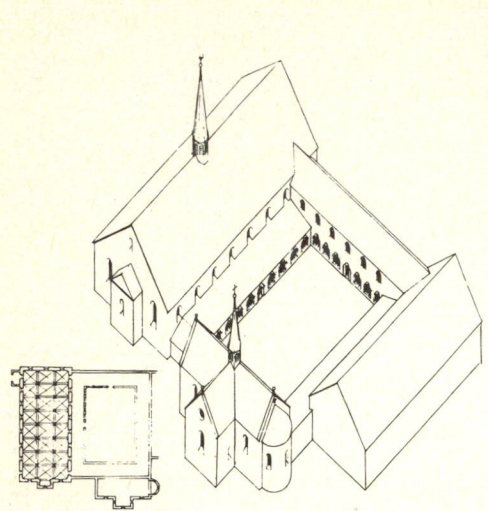

119   *The hospital of Eberbach. The hospital proper is the large block on the left. It has its own cloister and chapel, the small building at the bottom*

120 *Eberbach, interior of the hospital*

121 *Ourscamp, the infirmary, c. 1210, pessimistically known as the 'Salle des Morts'*

122 *Gloucester, the 'lavatorium', another form of washing area, c. 1370*

123 *Fontevrault, twelfth century, the kitchen, much restored*

The White Monks, and not only they, also evolved lesser types of building with special characteristics. Art-history has neglected to pursue the evolution of the kitchens, monastic gateways, rere-dorters and lavatoria. The farm buildings also cry out for attention – stables, hay-lofts and granaries of incredible dimensions, often masterpieces of wooden construction. Walter Horn has made these buildings the object of special study (Bibl. 122). Apart from some non-monastic tithe-barns in England, farm buildings of comparable monumentality survive in no other context. We shall find them given even greater importance in the domestic courts of the princely abbeys of the Baroque (*vide* pp. 203–4). Even here the monks built for eternity. Here as elsewhere, the Rule looked for perfection and not cost-effectiveness.

Have we done justice to the Cistercian monastery in this survey? A French writer who was showing Le Thoronet to a group of foreigners drew attention to the management of light, to the acoustics, and to the proportions, which, he said, owed their beauty to old and forgotten laws. He spoke of the three secrets of the Cistercians; that of light, that of number, and that of sound. This is a romantic way of describing the special emphasis laid by the monks, to whom pictures and sculpture were denied, upon the fundamentals of architecture. They saw to it that light was manipulated in accordance with function; they constructed their buildings using the traditional ratios transmitted since Vitruvius, but now endowed with new symbolic meanings; and they strove for acoustics that would accentuate the clarity of the antiphonal singing of their choirs. It is impossible to fit the principles behind the management of light into a scientifically rigorous schema, but an eye schooled to sensitivity to the degrees of brightness in their colour-free interiors notices the care taken in choosing the number, size and location of the windows. By moderating the intensity of light, its values could be played with; and hence gloomy tracts alternate with others in which the light appears soothingly mild. Nowhere does light stream in to produce glaring brightness. We have as yet few exact analyses of the ratios used in building by the Cistercians. An introduction to the problem is supplied by Hanno Hahn's book on the church of Eberbach (Bibl. 109). There can be no doubt that each proportion was carefully calculated and subordinate to the laws of the idealist mathematics that steadily increased its influence in Gothic theology.

124 *Bury St Edmunds, the gate-tower, c. 1130*

It is beyond my powers to elucidate this. Cistercian sources themselves are more forthcoming about the attention paid by the monks to anything that might further the singing of the liturgy. St Benedict's Rule is nowhere so thorough as in underlining the importance of this singing. It was the fulfilment of the *opus Dei*. 'Let us then consider how we should comport ourselves in the Presence of God and his angels, and so stand in choral prayers that our soul may be in harmony with our voices.' After all, these men did sing for altogether at least four hours a day. We learn that Bernard himself undertook the task of composing an antiphonal purged of every error. Any slip in choral singing was severely punished (Document 1, Cap. 45). In the performance of the daily liturgy Cistercian aesthetic aspirations achieved their apotheosis. There are no available measurements of the acoustics of Cistercian churches, but every one of their choirs acts as a resonating chamber through which sound is both held and muted. Echoes were avoided, each word was to ring out firm and clear. Since silence was the chief injunction during most of the day, an acute sensibility was developed for the melodic intervals of the chant.

125 Chorin, the brewery, gatehouse and kitchen wing, built of brick, thirteenth century

126 Fontenay, the so-called forge, used as a smithy and metalwork shop, early thirteenth century

6

The Charterhouse

The European Middle Ages only succeeded in formulating one wholly novel type of monastery to put beside that of the Benedictines in its achieved form, as developed through the efforts of the Cluniacs and Cistercians in the eleventh and twelfth centuries – the Charterhouse. The founder of the new Order's inspiration was to combine the hermit's existence and the common life in one monastery. St Bruno (c. 1032-1101) realized that the greatest temptation of monasticism, the desire for meditation in total seclusion, could only be combated by making the eremitical life possible within an actual monastery. There were precedents; Camaldoli and Vallombrosa are instances. But in those days they were only colonies or villages of hermits, not monasteries. Repeatedly we hear of fresh attempts to concentrate these colonies into fewer, more centralized settlements. We shall later investigate such an attempt by the Hieronymites in Spain. The monastery of Montserrat also originated in the endeavour to bring together into one unit all the hermits living on the bleak rocks of the mountain ridges. The Carthusians were however the first to succeed in a synthesis of the anchoritic *laura* of the East with the coenobitic organization of the West (Bibl. 130). Whereas the Benedictines were never alone, the Carthusians wanted almost always to be so. Their founder regarded it as a necessary antidote that they should meet at precisely fixed times in the church, the chapter-house, and in the refectory. What form of building could accommodate this dual aspiration?

After several initial failures, St Bruno, a native of Cologne, withdrew in 1084 with six companions to a rocky wilderness about 3,250 feet up and 15 miles from Grenoble – the *Chartreuse*. The new settlement was favoured by local potentates. It gained the name of *La Grande Chartreuse*. It was first described by a visitor, Abbot Guibert of Nogent, in 1104. He mentions the cells which lay round the cloister: *cellulae per gyrum claustri*. Peter the Venerable, who visited the Chartreuse in 1126, reports that the monastery was built on the model of those of the early Egyptians: *more antiquo Aegyptiorum monachorum*. This could have meant merely a courtyard round which *laura* lay. The reality was more impressive.

St Bruno left no Rule. But there can be no doubt that the eighty chapters of the Carthusian *Consuetudines* written down by his fourth successor Guigo I in 1127, and often added to later but never altered, encapsulate the cardinal ideas of the founder (Bibl. 131). Their starting-point was the Benedictine Rule. The Charterhouses were to house only twelve monks, thirteen with the prior. Later there were double Charterhouses. The Grande Chartreuse was itself enlarged into such a double house in 1324, and in 1595 it even received a third *ambitus*. Each monk lived by himself in his own cell. He only joined the others in daily Mass, Matins and Vespers. At all other times he prayed alone. On Sundays and certain feast-days meals were taken together in the refectory and a lesson read. On Sunday mornings meetings in chapter were allowed. Only very belatedly was permission given for the exchange of experiences of the spiritual exercises in the cloister one hour a week. It was a purely contemplative Order. Any outward-

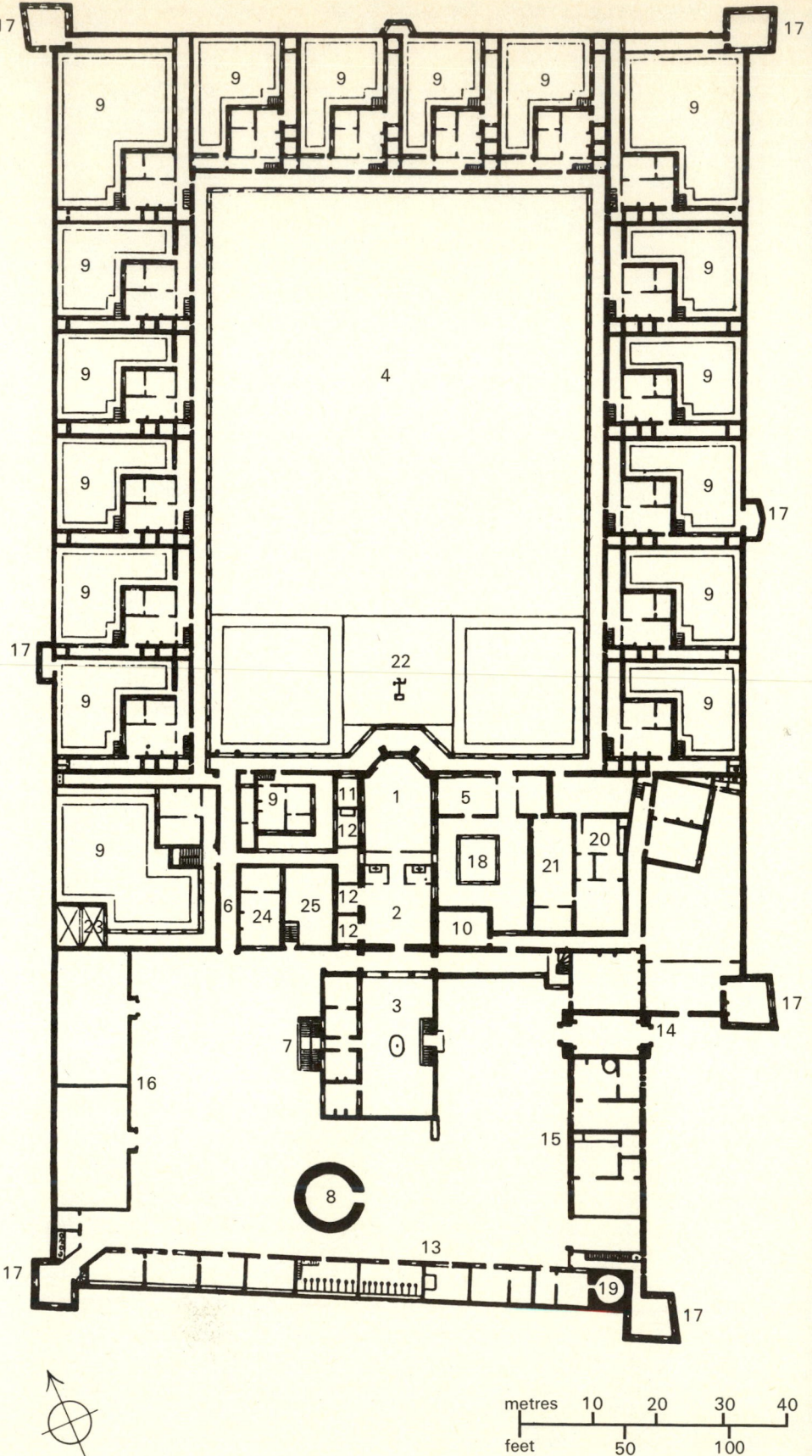

127 *Clermont. Plan of the Charterhouse, after Viollet-le-Duc*
 1 Monks' choir
 2 Lay-brothers' choir
 3 Prior's forecourt
 4 Great cloister (claustrum maius)
 5 Chapter-house
 6 Passage to the great cloister
 7 Prior's house
 8 Dovecote
 9 Individual cells, each with garden
10 Chapel of Pontgibaut
11 Sacristy
12 Chapels
13 Stables and rooms of donati
14 Gate
15 Guest-house
16 Barns
17 Watch-towers
18 Small cloister (claustrum minus)
19 Bakehouse
20 Kitchen
21 Refectory
22 Cemetery
23 Prison
24 Sub-prior's house
25 Sub-prior's garden

going work like proselytizing or preaching was wholly inhibited by the circumstances of eremitical life. Solitude entrained silence, which might only be breached a few hours a week. Like Cistercian monasteries, Carthusian priories were subject to annual visitations. Once a year also, the priors assembled in the Grande Chartreuse for a General Chapter, in which they submitted everything to the decision of the Grand Prior of the mother house. The monks inherited the Benedictine obligation to work. But the location of this was only to be their own cell and a tiny garden in front of it. It was therefore necessary to institute a separate organization composed of *conversi* and *donati*, that is to say lay-brothers, to supply the needs of the monastery. The *conversi* were bound by eternal vows, whilst the *donati* were not, but both were committed to life in single cells.

It would appear to have been the same Guigo I that wrote down the *Consuetudines*, who worked out the final version of the Carthusian priory. He saw himself compelled to shift Bruno's earlier monastery owing to the danger of avalanches. When the 'Customs' were committed to paper in 1127 the cloister of the new monastery was still under construction. The church was consecrated in 1132. These were the very years in which the developed Cistercian monastery emerged at Clairvaux. St Bernard himself was at the Chartreuse not long after. This, the chief monastery of the Order, was so often renovated, and furthermore never thoroughly investigated, that archaeological proof of its primacy is not forthcoming. But the numerous Carthusian priories agree in character in such a way as to presuppose their common prototype by this point in time.

The Romanesque rationalism and the desire for systematization, which characterize pictorial and intellectual endeavour in the twelfth century, were also the preconditions for both the Cistercian and the Carthusian monastery. The challenge was to weld the three distinct areas of life in the monastery into one whole. By these three areas I mean the monks' cloister and its dozen cells; the group of community buildings comprising not only the refectory, chapterhouse and library, but also the church and the prior's cell; and finally the precinct in which the *conversi* and *donati* not only saw to the needs of the monastery and received its guests, but also shielded the monks from the world. For into this area were shunted all the worldly dealings, without which even the humblest monastery could not get by. Begging, which was adopted by new Orders in the thirteenth century, stood in the way of strict seclusion. The security afforded against the intrusion of the world by such a third sphere is responsible for the Carthusians' want of any special stipulations as to the localities best suited to their new foundations. There are Charterhouses in valleys and in the mountains, in villages, outside large towns and not infrequently even within town walls.

The plan of the Clermont Charterhouse, appended by Viollet-le-Duc to a project for its restoration in 1858, shows a classicizing reduction of the ideal Carthusian priory. Here we have a very large complex, the fruit of a long development, and one which in many particulars no longer adheres to Guigo's strict statutes. Nonetheless, it teaches us to see the functional character of Charterhouses.

The monastery was strongly fortified and enclosed by a wall strengthened by seven towers. The complex was entered by a gate in the south-west (14), strategically covered from two of the defensive towers. This gave onto the large domestic court of the monastery with the prior's house in the middle (7), backing onto the prior's forecourt (3), which looked out onto the church (1, 2). This first court was bounded by the guest-house (15), the stables, and the cells of the *donati* (13). To the left of the church lay the house of the sub-prior, and to the right of it the small monastery court, round which were grouped the conventual buildings – the chapter-house (5), the refectory (21), the kitchen (20), and a chapel (10) endowed by the Pontgibaut family, who were great patrons of the monastery. This cloister (18) – it was called the *claustrum minus* – corresponded in many of its details to the Benedictine schema. It could only be entered from the large cloister. At the same time it communicated with the church at the height of the rood-screen, which we shall come to shortly. This church was subdivided into a fore-

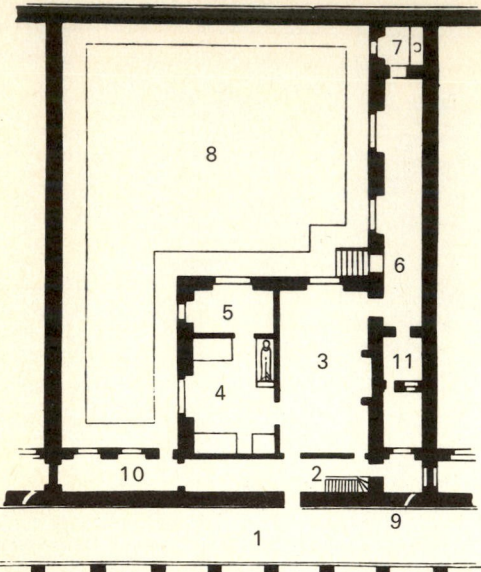

128 A typical Carthusian cell – a small self-contained house and garden

1 *Cloister walk*
2 *Corridor, isolating the monk from the noise of the cloister*
3 *Ante-room*
4 *Main room*
5 *Second room*
6 *Corridor to latrine*
7 *Latrine*
8 *Garden*
9 *Aperture in wall, through which food was passed*
10 *Door to garden*
11 *Larder*

church (2) for the *conversi* and *donati*, and a monks' choir (1), by this very rood-screen. Following a later reform two altars were available in the forechurch and only one, which was originally the only one allowed, in the monks' choir. The Carthusians were the first to make do with a single-naved oratory in place of a basilical church. The laity, who were originally excluded, were subsequently allowed access to a modest gallery over the entrance.

On the far side of this middle portion containing the *claustrum minus* and the church lay the *claustrum majus* (4). This consisted of a quadrangle, with a passage off which lay eighteen cells (9). Here dwelt the monks, doubly protected against the world. They had their cemetery (22) behind the church, so that they always had it before their eyes. The silence of the living echoed the peace of the dead. Pictures were originally banned from the cloister, but a few late examples show that citations from the Bible were occasionally written up over the cell doors. S. D. Mühlberg cites the instances of the Charterhouses of Hain and Margarethenthal in Basle (Bibl. 130). Large-scale architecture was quite alien to the Charterhouses. Yet even this one plan reflects the fact that an ensemble of great beauty was created by the repetition of the same small elements. Such a symmetrical layout, centred on the axis of the church, would be produced by Orders only in the Baroque. The Carthusians realized a form of ideal town-planning in their priories that would have remained a Utopia in any other context. There is also no other Order that would have given such vivid expression to the special role of its abbots or priors, who were expected to sacrifice their solitude for the good of the community, by placing the prior's house in front of the church and in the court of the *conversi*. Here in embryo lay great scope for further treatment, inviting fresh variations and additions. Circumstances were most favourable when Nature herself, as with the Certosa di Galluzzo near Florence, raised the whole complex aloft like a citadel on a plateau of rock. Precisely because the organization of the monastery was reflected with especial clarity in the disposition of the buildings, each new establishment wanted to think the schema out afresh, and thus developed a separate character of its own.

The Carthusians' functionalism extended even to the construction of the cells in which the monks severally lived. They each comprised a small house and a garden. They are carefully thought-out miniature dwellings which are unique in the context of medieval architecture. I base my remarks once again on a drawing of Viollet-le-Duc's.

They formed a kind of housing estate strung out round the passage or cloister (1). House and garden were even shielded against the slightest noise in the cloister by a corridor (2). A *conversus* used to put the bare minimum of nourishment – bread, very occasionally a jug of wine, and other food not available from the garden – through a slit (9). Even this slit communicated only with a closet. The prior alone was allowed to pass through this corridor to the door of the garden (10). The layout took account of the monk's need for solitude in every particular. He did not only want to be alone, but also to feel alone. The house itself consisted of three rooms – the heated ante-room (3); the cell (4), in which stood four pieces of furniture, the only ones allowed (a wooden bed, a bench, a table and a bookcase); and a small chamber (5). (11) was used as a larder, and (6) was a corridor leading to the latrine (7). The garden (8) was three or four times as large as the whole house, and girt by a high wall. What each monk might possess was narrowly laid down – a straw mattress and pillow and two blankets for the bed, little and simple table ware, tools for repairs, sewing-kit, a comb and a razor, writing utensils, and no more than two books to read. A crucifix was the only artistic object available.

The consequence of the renunciation of large-scale architecture was that Carthusian priories were, to a far greater extent than Cistercian monasteries, purely variations on one and the same theme. Apart from a few princely foundations, none merit the attention of the architectural historian. The Order might justly pride itself that it was 'never reformed, because never deformed'. For the same reason there were no attempts at architectural innovation. The best survey of the Order's layouts, S. D. Mühlberg's unpublished thesis (Bibl. 130), which it is true only deals with the Germanic territories, and indeed chiefly with the province of Franconia, therefore only succeeded in demonstrating variants on one schema, which were in any case in greater part due to the site and to local fashions in building. The monks never encouraged, and were even slow in accepting, stylistic changes, insofar as this lay with them. The focus of attention was always the nexus between the *claustrum majus* and the *claustrum minus* and also that between the realm of the monks and the forecourt turned toward the outside world, of which the modest church was the pivot. Here the monks, who entered the church singly and not, like the Benedictines, in procession, were chiefly exercised by the problem of access. Their deliberations resulted in taking the cloister passage through the church as a rood-screen, instead of alongside it as with the Benedictines.

Let us use the plan of the Charterhouse of Buxheim in Swabia to illuminate the issue. Baroque rebuildings have here made multiple alterations to the schema as a whole, not least because after 1548 Buxheim was the only *reichsunmittelbare* Charterhouse, the only offshoot of the Order whose prior was also sovereign in his own territory. Furthermore, the sad fate that the establishment underwent after the secularizations, and before Don Bosco acquired it for the Salesians, led to the demolition of numerous buildings. But the great rectangle of the inner court, around which the cells of the monks were, and in part still are, disposed, remained intact.

The Carthusians pursued their lives in an area defined, not to say enclosed, by architecture. In contrast to the Benedictines they never left the monastery. They did not go out to work in the fields, visited no brother-foundations, did not meet in synods, and never preached to the populace. Missionary activity was as foreign to them as it was to the Cistercians. They maintained no schools. Save

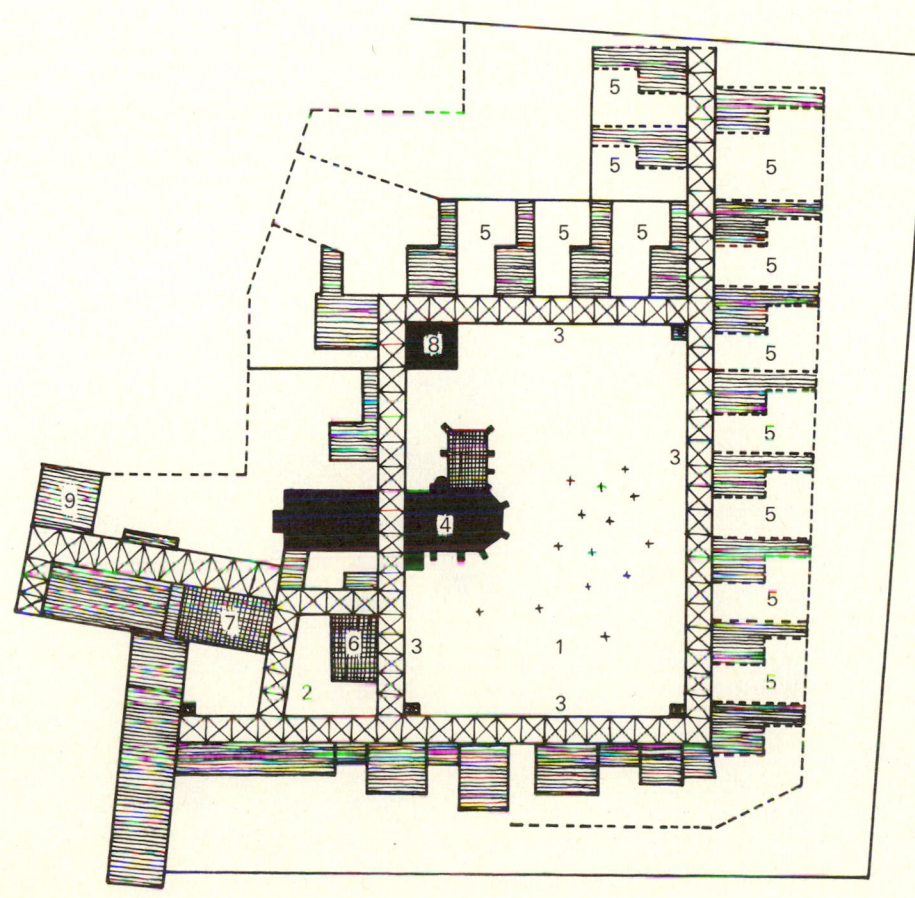

129 *Buxheim. Plan of the Charterhouse as it was before the Reformation*
1 *Claustrum maius (also the cemetery)*
2 *Claustrum minus*
3 *Cloister walks*
4 *Church, bisected by the west cloister walk*
5 *Cells, with gardens*
6 *Library*
7 *Refectory*
8 *Chapel of St Anne*
9 *Prior's quarters*

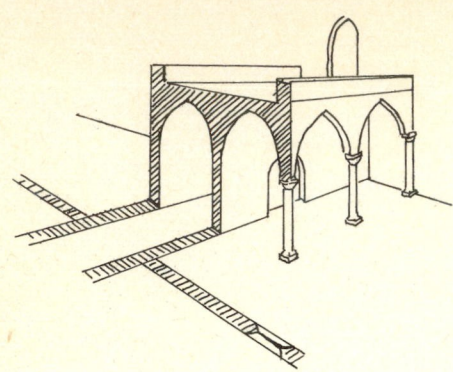

130 Passage through a Carthusian church, forming a rood-screen

131 Hinton, Somerset. Chapter-house and library of Charterhouse

in their wall-girt gardens, they never went out into the open. Even in the cloister they were still bounded by architecture. One can no more envisage them standing in the middle of the courtyard than in the square before the church. They trod a beaten track from their cell to the church and to the little court surrounded by the chapter-house, refectory, and library. Keeping to it, they never left the tiled floor of the cloister. It is not easy to pin-point the moment and the place at which the idea took shape of henceforward taking this passage into and through the church itself at the dividing line between the priests' and the lay-brothers' choirs. In consequence, the passage also formed a rood-screen. From Mühlberg's compilation it would appear that the oldest surviving passage-cum-screen is that of St Catherine's, Valeria, in Sion (Switzerland), dating from the middle of the thirteenth century. This was not a Carthusian church but it was in a region not so remote from the Grande Chartreuse. The idea recurs at Mauerbach in Carinthia, in the first quarter of the fourteenth century. It is subsequently found in the Charterhouses of Cologne, Nuremberg, Danzig, Basle, Ittingen and Jülich. Buxheim is the only good surviving example, admittedly Baroquized in the eighteenth century. It is probable that the motif arose in connection with the sanctioning of a second altar for the lay-brethren near the middle of the thirteenth century, and the balancing of this by a third altar for the private masses of the ordained monks through a supplement to this statute in 1276. In fact, it was almost bound to occur once it was decided that the priests' choir should, as in Buxheim, project into the monks' court, and that of the lay-brethren into their realm. Only once they had the passage-cum-screen were the Carthusians able, like the Benedictines, to enter the church for the nocturnal Matins without going out into the open. It was typical of the rationality governing their architecture that they could enter it, each by the shortest way, from both sides.

The Order did not proliferate with the whirlwind pace that so impressed us with the Cistercians, and will do so again with Franciscan and Dominican friars.

132 Hinton, Somerset. Refectory of the Charterhouse

The founder originally only contemplated a single settlement. At his death no more than two others had adopted the rigorous Rule. By about 1200 there were altogether thirty-seven Charterhouses in the West, and of these only two were in the Holy Roman Empire, and only one, at Witham in Somerset (founded in 1181), was in England. In the following century and a half, only one further house was established here, also in Somerset, at Hinton in 1227. If one reflects that each monastery only housed twelve monks, with the prior as a thirteenth, in terms of numbers they were insignificant in the context of the monastic movement of the High Middle Ages. It was the age of mysticism, the fourteenth and fifteenth centuries, which stands out as the halcyon time of the Order. The number of priories now grew to 195, 58 of them in Germany, Austria and Switzerland, and a further 7 in England. The Carthusian priories were centres of spiritual resistance in the Reformation. These recluses were not to be left in peace. They produced an astonishingly large number of martyrs, including three priors and three monks from English houses. It is attributable to this constancy that by the end of the eighteenth century there were 295 houses. Then they were struck at once again, by the fury of the Enlightenment. Joseph II of Austria ordered the dissolution of all their priories. However, in Europe today there are once more 19 houses – 7 in Spain, 6 in Italy, 4 in France, and one each in Germany and England.

133 Galluzzo, Italy. View of the Certosa from below showing the backs of the cells

From the fourteenth century onwards a number of Charterhouses came about as princely foundations. Actually the earliest German priory, and the fifteenth belonging to the Order, Johannestal at Seitz, was founded by the Styrian Margrave Ottocar V. This was followed in 1314 by the Charterhouse of Allerheiligental in Mauerbach, founded by Duke Frederick the Fair of Austria on the occasion of his election to the throne of Germany. The Certosa of Galluzzo near Florence of 1342 was also a princely foundation, built on a plateau of rock by Nicola Acciaiuoli, one of the richest men of his time. It is typical of the

134 Galluzzo, the Great Cloister

135 *The Certosa of Pavia was founded by Giangaleazzo Visconti as a burial place for the Dukes of Milan. In this detail of a fresco by Bergognone he is shown presenting the monastery to the Virgin*

religious approach of the later Middle Ages that it was not left to the initiative of monks to seek out places of retreat for themselves, but that they were garnered from the establishments of other Orders and impressed into the new foundations. Many of these foundations were, as the burial-places of, and monuments to, their founding families, sumptuously embellished with works of art. The most striking examples are the Charterhouse of Champmol in Burgundy, founded by Philip the Bold in 1385, and the Charterhouse of Pavia, set up by the Visconti in 1390, and then even more highly favoured by their successors, the Sforzas. Several of these donors, particularly the Visconti, were amongst the cruellest and most ruthless princes of their time. It is hard to read Jacob Burckhardt's depiction of the nature of their misdeeds without shuddering. It leads to the impression that on the one hand they were setting up great powerhouses of prayer to outweigh their guilt, and on the other hand wanted to make an extravagant artistic display of their desire for atonement – easily paid for by fresh exactions from their subjects.

The charters of Champmol, together with details of its appearance and furnishings, shed further light on these associations. The plan goes back to 1373. The means for its execution were only gained by Philip the Bold in 1385 with the death of the father of his wife, Margaret of Burgundy. 'There is nothing more efficacious for the soul's salvation than the prayers of pious monks who, out of the love of God, have voluntarily embraced poverty and renounced the vanities and pleasures of the world', so run the words of the charter of foundation. The Duke is conscious that none but the best, in both art and prayers, will do for one of his rank. The document goes on: 'Since the Carthusians pray tirelessly night and day for the salvation of the souls and the prosperity of the commonwealth and princes', so he was willing '. . . from his own means to found a Charterhouse

136 *Pavia. The Great Cloister of the Certosa, showing the individual cells, each with its chimney*

137 The Charterhouse of Champmol, near Dijon, was founded for similar reasons by Philip the Bold of Burgundy. The church (above) contained his tomb and that of his son

1 Altar
2 Tomb of Philip the Bold
3 Tomb of John the Fearless
4 'Angel' chapel
5 Chapel of St Peter
6 Chapel of St Agnes
7 Door to small cloister, with tympanum

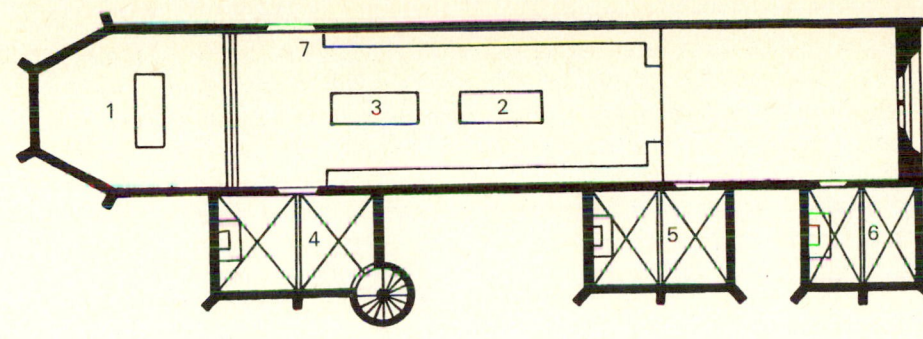

in honour of the Holy Trinity for twenty-four monks, five lay-brothers, and their prior'.[19] This was then a double house, in order to multiply the praying-power of the monks. The king's architect, who was occupied on the Louvre, Drouet de Dammartin, received the command to prepare plans for the monastery with the greatest despatch. The church, which was ready for consecration by 1388, was intended as the burial-place of the dynasty. Sluter and Broederlam, the foremost names of the age, were called on to decorate it. The idea was – in an almost frivolous exaggeration of the desire for redemption – so to situate the princely graves between the monks' stalls in the choir of the church, that the antiphony of prayer went through them back and forth, and away up over them. The graves are those of Philip the Bold and of his son, John the Fearless and his consort, which were mutilated in the aftermath of the secularization in 1789 of

138 The tomb of Philip the Bold, now in the Museum of Dijon

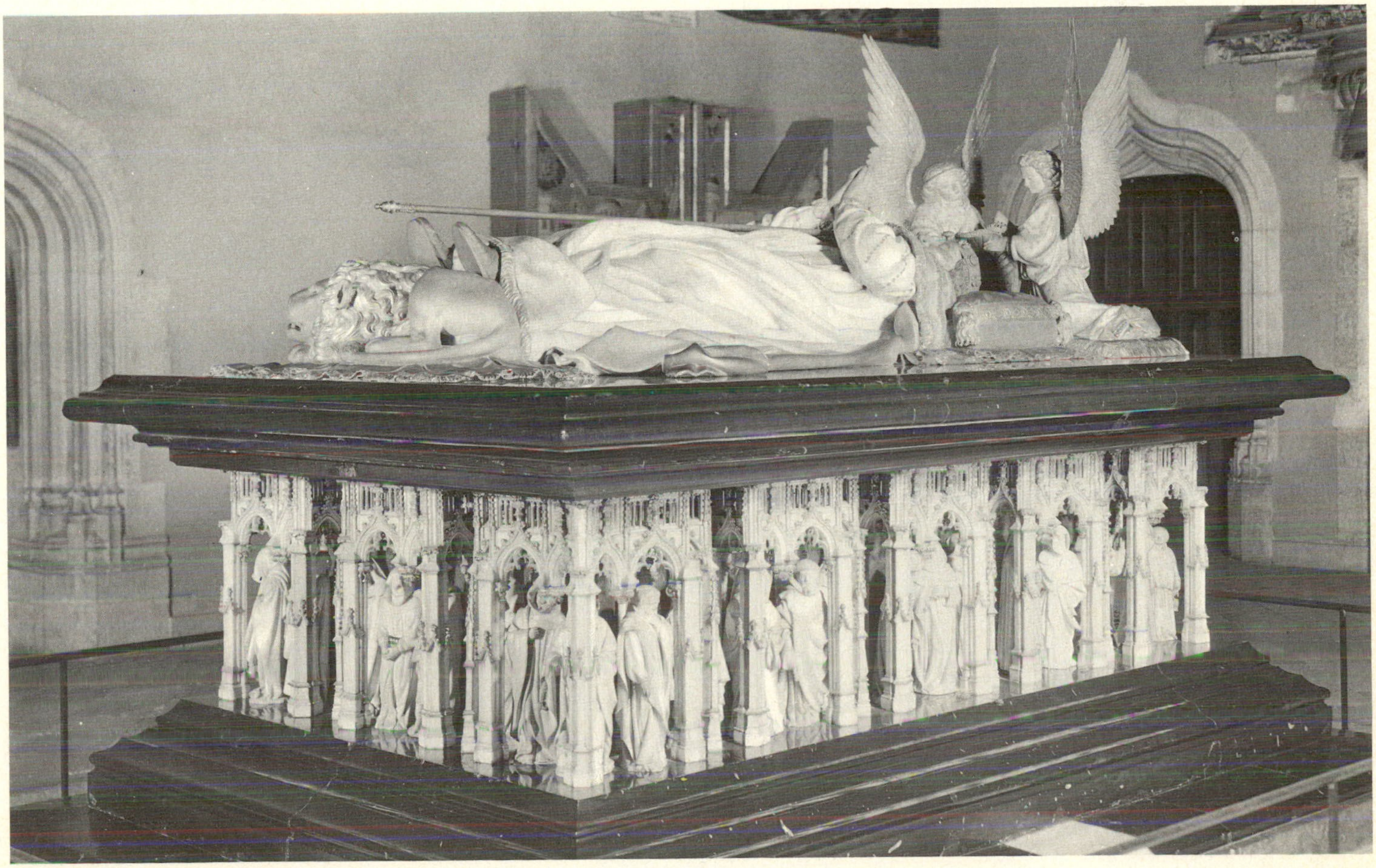

139 Weepers on the tomb of Philip the Bold, by Claus Sluter

140 Head of Christ, from the Puits de Moïse, by Sluter

141 Moses and David, from the Puits de Moïse, by Sluter

this and sixty-seven other French Carthusian priories, and are now in Dijon museum. As *pleurants* – mourners about the bier of the Duchess – the monks with their cowls drawn right up over their heads have earned their place in art-history. The idea had spread that for as long as masses were said for the departed, the flames of purgatory were quenched. This conviction was to prompt Margaret of Austria more than a century later to endow her aunt's, Margaret of Bourbon's, foundation of Brou so richly, that enough monks were available for a perpetual mass to be said for the soul of her prematurely departed husband, Philip the Fair. A moving correspondence survives from the confused period of secularization, in which the expelled monks beg their brethren in surviving Charterhouses to join in taking over their often centuries-old obligations of prayer and masses, till finally the handful of monasteries was overwhelmed by the accumulated onus of prayer.

It is likely that the iconographic programme of the *Puits de Moïse* from the middle of the cloister was controlled by a similar idea. The elaborateness of this form of mystic Calvary is unique in the history of monastic art. Claus Sluter created a well in the middle of the cloister, and raised a Crucifixion Group above it, thereby signifying the Cross and the Blood of Christ as the fount of all Grace. He fused the motif of the well in the middle of the cloister with that of the graveyard Cross, doubtless aware that the Carthusians sought their last resting-place in the area between this fountain and the choir of the church, in the midst of the living. The coats of arms of Flanders and Burgundy adorn the structure's pediment, betokening the ruling houses that hoped to be bathed in this flow of Grace. Six grave figures from the Old Testament solemnly surround this base, from amongst whom Moses may be remembered as the man during whose prayer on the mountain-top Joshua prevailed in the plain beneath. For as long as Moses held his arms aloft the enemy fell back, until at dusk they were defeated. Sluter depicts Moses otherwise. The comparison must not be taken literally. Nonetheless the biblical account tallies exactly with the role intended for the monks by Philip the Bold in his administration. The most rigorous of the Orders could alone serve him in this way. The artistic effect of this piece, revealing both courtly refinement and sheer joy in the imitative discovery of Nature, was heightened by its contrast with the asceticism of the life around it. The splendour of this princely intrusion was enhanced by the gulf separating it from monastic poverty. Seen like this, both the High Altar of the church, with its carved retable by Jacques de Baerze and painted wings by Melchior Broederlam, and the side-altars of Jean Malouel and Henri Bellechose, have an altered significance. Astonishingly, even the chapter-house, which may be regarded as a treasury of Burgundian court art of pre- and circa 1400, contained an intricately carved altarpiece. Philip further arranged for each cell to have a devotional picture. Amongst them may have been the small panels of Christ's Passion by Simone Martini in the Louvre, the Berlin Museum and in Antwerp, all of which came from Champmol, and also the Berlin triptych of the Trinity from the end of the fourteenth century, Jean Malouel's *Grande Pitié* in the Louvre, or Jan van Eyck's *Annunciation* in Washington. Each of these small panels is an encouragement to mystic rapture and theological reflection. The monastery owned a picture-gallery of the highest order.

Episcopal sees and free cities also maintained their Carthusians. There were a great number of Carthusian monasteries inside town walls. Paris had a renowned Charterhouse, and so did London. There were priories in Cologne, Nuremberg, Würzburg, Mainz, Basle and Prague. They lie in areas of comparative tranquillity at the edge of the cities, but mostly still within the old walls.

The Nuremberg Charterhouse was relatively well-preserved once its remains had been put at the disposal of the Germanisches Nationalmuseum in 1857. Much was inevitably destroyed in the Second World War. It was originally endowed by a Nuremberg merchant. The council licensed the building in 1380; in 1383 it was already complete. Citizens of Nuremberg undertook to pay for particular tracts of it, and individual families to underwrite a cell. Thus inter-

142-43 The outer panels of the Champmol altar-piece (above left) were painted by Melchoir Broederlam with scenes of the Annunciation, Visitation, Presentation in the Temple, and Flight into Egypt. When opened, the altar revealed carvings by Jacques de Baerze (above right)

144 One of the side altars of the church of Champmol: the martyrdom of St Denis, with Crucifixion, by Henri Bellechose

145–47 Three paintings commissioned by Philip the Bold to go in the cells of the Champmol Charterhouse. Above: Jan van Eyck's Annunciation. Above right: 'Grande Pitié' by Jean Malouel. Right: Christ carrying the Cross, by Simone Martini

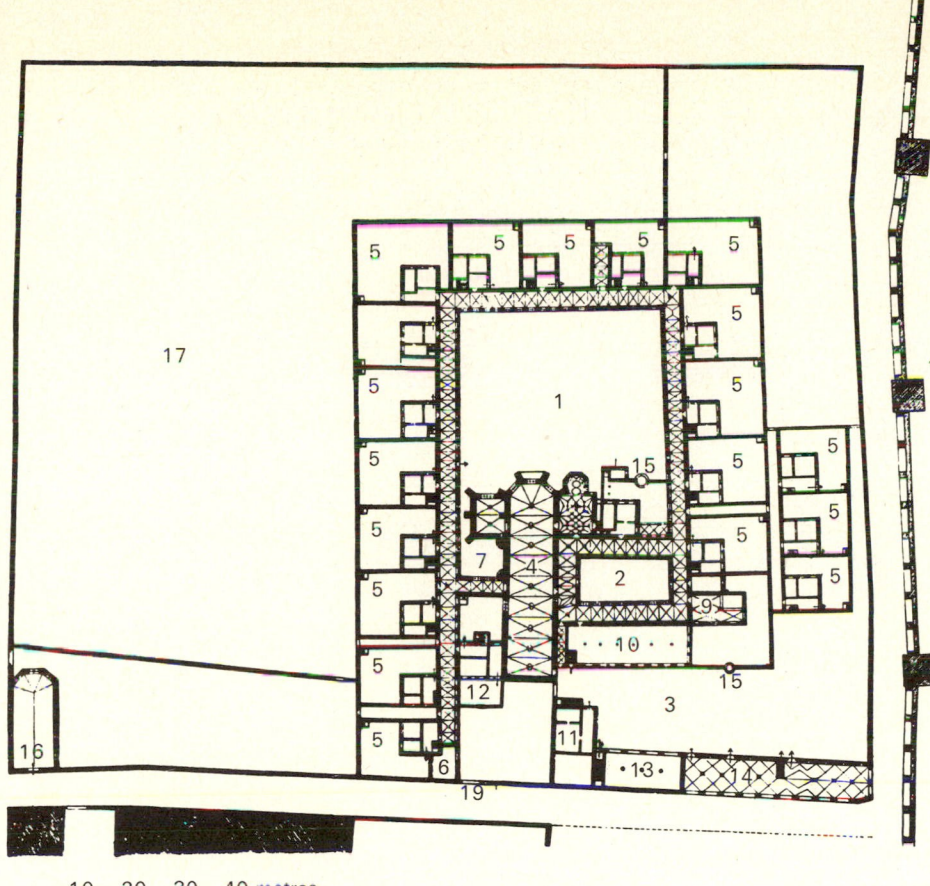

10 20 30 40 metres
25 50 75 100 125 feet

cession for each of them became the responsibility of a monk. There is an interesting instrument by which the council subordinated the monastery to itself. It did not want to forego the presence of pious monks in the town, yet it wanted to avoid the emergence of another exempt institution. The prior had to accept six conditions. He might only accept twelve monks, each one of them subject to the city's permission. All his undertakings were to be submitted to the council for approval. He was forbidden to petition the Emperor or kings for special liberties. Peasants or subjects were to pay their dues to the city and not to the monastery. Finally, the prior was to declare his readiness to allow the monastery, which lay between the inner and the outer fortifications, to be broken up should the strategic situation demand it. It was on a site where building was ordinarily not allowed. That these conditions were not so narrowly interpreted emerges from the fact that twenty-three cells were in fact subsequently allowed. There were too many families that wanted to endow them. The Charterhouse lasted no more than 150 years. Its prior went over to the Reformation as early as 1525. The cells fell to the city, which used them as widows' almshouses until, with the loss of its imperial freedom, they were degraded into a magazine and crumbled.

The plan, which follows the reconstruction proposed by Essenwein, the Director of the Museum, in 1892, is not wholly accurate. One should also remember than this urban monastery had to incorporate numerous rebuildings and additions, testifying to the continuing participation of the founders' kin. The fitting of the life of the community into the interior of the monastery was complemented by its minutely considered insertion into its setting. Its site outside the actual town walls facilitated the enclosure of large grounds, including extensive gardens, the beautiful chapel of the Twelve Apostles in the north-west corner, and a garden for simples in the south-east corner. Looking closely at the hermitages round the great cloister one sees that the builder omitted the protective corridor in front of them. The small cloister is surrounded by the conventual

149 *Nuremberg Charterhouse, the interior of the church; now part of the Museum*

buildings, amongst which the chapter-house stands out on account of its complex lierne vault. Originally this church too had a passage-cum-screen, one of whose entries is still visible to the left of the church. Stables and sheds were situated on the street side to the west, and one can safely assume that there was accommodation for guests in their upper floor. The disposition of the three courts is very fine, each sited according to its role; the large court to the east, the conventual court in the centre, and the domestic court, split in two by the prior's cell, to the west. It is apparent, and this view would be greatly strengthened by the comparison of a large number of Carthusian plans, that these institutions offered wide scope for differences in arrangement. The bourgeois Charterhouse of Nuremberg would, like the princely Champmol, have been enlivened by innumerable buildings and works of art, commissioned from the foremost craftsmen by the merchant aristocracy. There was a work by Dürer himself in the chapel of the Twelve Apostles.

The schematic layout of the Order was laid down in such close detail that even the nineteenth and twentieth centuries have seen no occasion to propose alterations. England's only Carthusian priory, St Hugh's Charterhouse at Parkminster in Sussex, owes its origins to the need of French Carthusians to assure themselves of a refuge abroad when they were threatened with expulsion. It was built in the Neo-Gothic style from 1876 onwards. There was no shortage of money. A double house was built, on the exact lines of an old one. The aerial photo brings out the three courts between which the church is held. The only innovation to be seen is that the cells are set back from the cloister, behind their gardens. Not that the houses have any windows looking outward. Even the cemetery kept its old place by the church. Only one concession to Neo-Gothic taste was felt necessary; the church was given a tower, at whose base the arms of the cloister merged. It was thought to be more important that the monks saw the church towering before them as soon as they set foot in the cloister, than that they should feel themselves close to the Host in the choir of the church.

150 Parkminster, Sussex. Air view of the Charterhouse of St Hugh, a nineteenth-century foundation following the traditional plan

7

The Mendicant Orders

How can art be produced when one renounces possessions? How can a monastery – a church and communal buildings – be built, when for St Francis (1181-1226) the most miserable hut on its own plot of land already seemed a betrayal of Lady Poverty? Francis had no intention of founding a new Order, for in his eyes life in imitation of the Son of Man, who had nowhere where he might lay his head, had nothing in common with life in monasteries and suchlike foundations. There everything was planned in advance, here one trusted in God to provide; there one strove behind high walls, here out in the open. For the wandering friars every place that they entered with the greeting taught them by Francis, 'Peace be on this house', was their home. Were not his last instructions that his body was to be perfunctorily buried on a rubbish-dump in the circumvallations of the town?[20] It was these instructions that led to the massive substructures supporting the church and the monastery over his funeral vault.

151 Assisi, air view of San Francesco. In front of the church is the long piazza for pilgrims, behind it the monastery, built up on buttresses above the valley

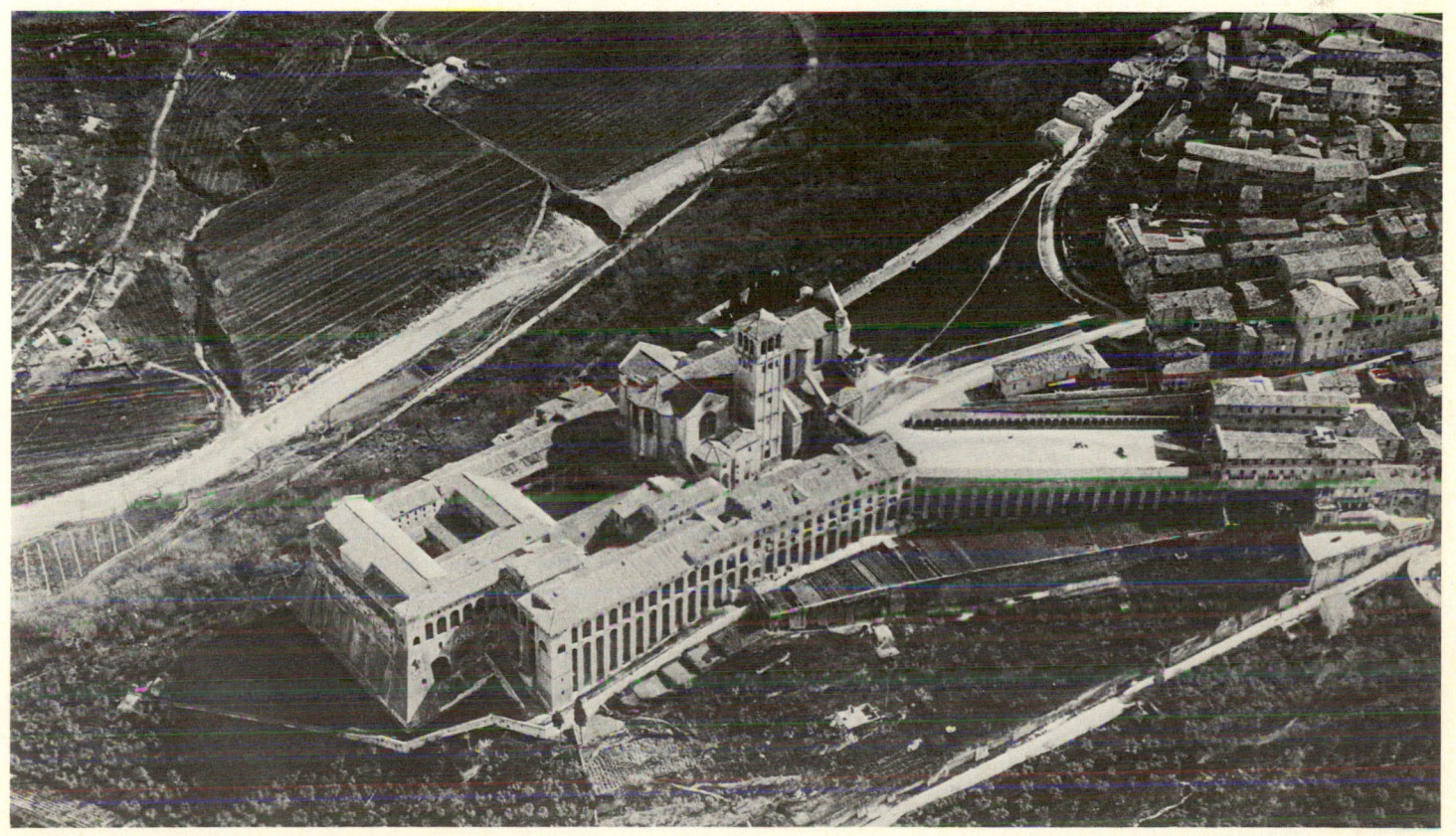

152 Assisi. The Great Cloister

St Francis wanted to be forgotten. Despite this, his followers commissioned the monumental fresco-cycle depicting his life on the walls of the Upper Church of San Francesco, giving visible expression to the *Fioretti* through the brush of Giotto and his pupils, in a position where up till then one would only have expected to find the *Gesta Christi* according to the Gospels. The monastic idea and the desire to perpetuate his legend pictorially proved mightier than the precepts and admonitions of their founder. San Francesco is the physical embodiment of a process which occurred in many parts of Europe in the course of the thirteenth and fourteenth centuries. It should be seen in conjunction with the religious movements of the High and Late Middle Ages (Bibl. 142). These movements were also the vehicles for artistic changes that led, through the art of mysticism, to the art of the Renaissance.

St Dominic, of Spanish birth (*c.* 1170-1221), created a militant organization of poor but free priests who, standing outside the constricting hierarchies of bishoprics and foundations, though before long in the service, and under the protection, of the papacy, entered the lists against the break-up of a Christianity subject to ever more radical interpretations. In the midst of burgeoning wealth and luxury they aspired to share the poverty of the poor; money was not to be accepted. Land-based revenues were repudiated, but St Dominic allowed his Order to accept revenues in cash, because whilst the possession of land burdened the organization with work, money freed them for their scholarly and pedagogic avocations. The priestly fraternities set themselves up outside the forms of social organization that had dominated the High Middle Ages. They did not seek their home in monastic citadels or estates, but rather in hall-like churches on the edge of towns. St Dominic supplied them with the old book of the Austin canons as

153 *Assisi, view of San Francesco from the piazza, showing the entrances to the upper and lower churches*

154 *Assisi, the lower church, looking north from the entrance*

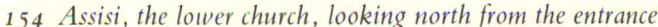

155 *St Francis receiving approval of his Rule from Pope Innocent III, one of the frescoes in the upper church attributed to Giotto*

their Rule, save that for them the outward-going activities of the pulpit and the confessional, and not choral worship, were to be the focus of their lives. A fresh activity, that of study, was enjoined by their founder. Deeper learning was to equip them to confound heresy. Albertus Magnus and Thomas Aquinas were to be the greatest teachers belonging to the new Order. At the same time the Inquisition arose; St Dominic's successors were prepared to employ any means to attain the goal that he had set himself.

St Francis started out from different preoccupations. It is no more possible to overlook the fact that the new community grew great in Italy, or in Umbria to be more precise, than to overlook the French origins of the Cistercians or the Spanish origins of the Dominicans – though here the ingredient of French logicality was later to be added, making them the true heirs to the Cistercians. Their devotional approach is different: the clear-sightedness of French spirituality dominates St Bernard's Order, Spanish intensity and religious zealotry governs St Dominic's communities of priests, whilst Franciscan lyricism derives from the Italian desire for submission. These tendencies were converted into architecture and images in innumerable ways. St Francis was himself imbued with the same spirit of radical Christianity which led the Cathars, the Albigensians and the Waldensians at the end of the twelfth century into courses that brought about their inevitable exclusion from the Church. When St Francis came before the Pope with his eleven companions in 1209 or 1210 in order to win the confirmation of the first of his three Rules, the Curia was bound to be suspicious of him as yet another such radical rebel, whose Gospel-inspired opposition to any form of possessions was also a threat to any form of institutionalized priesthood. What had been refused to Waldes by Pope Alexander III in 1179 was achieved by St Francis through the mediation of the subtle Benedictine cardinal, Giovanni Colonna. The Curia grasped the fact that it was better to encourage the young community in the hope of using it to win back the mass of the people. St Francis was also able to point out that his Rule made no innovations, since it was almost exclusively composed of sentences from the Gospels. The ban on new Orders persisted, but he had always insisted that his community of brethren was not an Order. The Franciscans did not want to be monks, they never tried to withdraw from the world into monasteries. They regarded even an eremitical existence as no more than a preparation. They called themselves 'lesser brothers' – *fratres minores* – to distinguish themselves from all the higher ranks of the clergy. Nonetheless St Francis was willing to be tonsured, denoting that he was, if not a monk, then still a cleric. It is attributable to the influence of Honorius III that these successors to the Apostles finally did become an Order. The transformation was heralded by a bull of 1220, taken further by the Rules of 1221 and 1223, and completed in this form by a bull of Gregory IX of 1230. Like the Dominicans before them and the Jesuits after them, the Franciscans swore utter obedience to the papacy. Their organization furthered the march of centralism in the Church. The new Orders of the Franciscans and Dominicans should be seen as becoming a two-pronged political instrument, with St Dominic taking the field against the heresies of his century from without and St Francis trying to enlist the people from within, before they had even succumbed to the more radical tendencies. At the outset the two Orders complemented one another, but they soon came to confront one another as rivals, so that almost everywhere where one established a house, the other quickly ensconced itself too. We encounter them as pairs in the context of urban Europe.

Both drew their strength from the sudden increase in population, that is to say in the number of artisans, in the thirteenth century. In contrast to the Cistercians the preaching Orders chose heavily-populated towns as their testing-grounds. From the late twelfth century up to the time of the Black Death of 1348–52 the number of towns, as of their inhabitants, steadily increased. Whilst, for example, there were scarcely fifty walled cities in Germany around 1100, there were more than a hundred in 1200 and almost five hundred in 1300. Soon there was both a Franciscan and a Dominican friary in nearly every town. As a rule they lay on the outskirts of the populated areas near the town wall, where land was cheap and there was good scope for expansion. In statistical terms the achievement of the Franciscans and the Dominicans is no less impressive than that of the Cistercians (*v.s.* p. 68). In 1277 there were 414 Dominican houses, in 1358 there were 635, and in 1720 there were actually 1076. This was their apogee. In 1316 the Italian provinces of the Franciscan Order comprised 567 friaries and 198 nunneries, the French provinces in the same year 247 friaries and 47 nunneries, and the German provinces 203 friaries and 47 nunneries. In the late thirteenth century the number of entrants into the nunneries was particularly disturbing. The number of sisters bore no relation to the economic strength of the houses. The Order had long fought shy of nunneries. St Francis had tolerated no more than a loose association with one alone, St Damian's, where St Clare was. It was even harder to maintain the vow of poverty for the nunneries than for the friaries. St Clare had managed to defend the *privilegium paupertatis* up to her death in 1253, but then the dam burst, as it already had for the Dominicans in 1245, owing to the personal intercession of Amicié de Monfort with Pope Innocent IV in Lyon. In the very same year the convent of St Agnes and no less than five other Dominican nunneries in Strasbourg were incorporated into the Order. The ideal of devoting oneself to meditation in total poverty began to depopulate the burghers' houses. It was a means of escape from the burdens of the century. The towns fought against the transfer of ever larger properties to the friaries, and the withdrawal of the supply of labour in favour of meditation. Satiety was reached, of

156 *Franciscan and Dominican, the former with a devil on his back: a satirical illustration, in the margin of a fourteenth-century treatise on poverty*

whose dangers contemporaries were quite aware.[21] The nunneries of both Orders were forced to close their doors to impoverished would-be postulants. Hence came the associations of the pious who belonged to no Order – Beguines, female Penitents and the like. St Francis's noble idea had soon been taken *ad absurdum*. It must be remembered that the difference in the style of life between the mendicant friaries and nunneries was far greater than that between the older monasteries and nunneries. The activities of the priests and brothers were all directed into the outside world, at the people. The nuns were however in the main themselves the object of pastoral care. They lived in strict seclusion save where, as in the case of the Poor Clares, they also took on the care of the sick. Besides these, there were the confraternities of prayer in both communities, whose members, known as tertiaries, often recruited great sections of the urban population – burghers and their wives, committed to a life of asceticism, prayer, and good works. As a result of the missionary activity of the Mendicant Orders the dividing line between the laity and clergy became blurred. Even tertiaries could, like St Catherine of Siena, wear a religious habit.

The devotional tone of the second half of the thirteenth century and of the first half of the fourteenth was set by Dominicans' and Franciscans' piety, just like that of the twelfth century by the Cistercians. In an immensely impressive way, one took over from the other. The old Orders continued their existence; the Dominicans turned the experiences of the Cistercians and Premonstratensians to account in constructing their own organizations. A. Hauck calls this the most perfect achieved by the Middle Ages.[22] Not infrequently, the Benedictines still produced notable works of art and of the intellect, but it was the buildings of the Dominicans and Franciscans, and the painting and sculpture created for their churches, that set their mark upon the age. Even episcopal sees had forfeited their creative urge after 1250. Where new cathedrals arose, they were due more to the urban bourgeoisie than to the higher clergy. Such was the case with the west façade of Strasbourg Cathedral and the cathedrals of Milan and Florence. The term 'minimal Gothic' has been used to describe what was created under the aegis of the mendicant Orders, but the expression is misleading, because it was not just the case that the structural complexity characteristic of the cathedrals was reduced, but that their elements were imbued with fresh meaning and conveyed a new form of spirituality. Richard Krautheimer has pointed out that in the churches of the mendicant and preaching friars the 'magic element' receded (Bibl. 143). This involved a process of increasing secularization, which did however set architecture a new role and open up new possibilities for it.

The clash between the principles of St Francis's life and teaching and the harsh realities of administering an Order broke out into the open immediately after his death. It led to the schism in the young community between 'spirituals' and 'Conventuals'. San Francesco in Assisi was one of the first objects of dispute. The Spirituals wanted to go on as St Francis had done, renouncing all possessions as itinerant preachers of the Word. They refused to acknowledge that the Order should evolve in response to the pressures due to the sudden influx of numbers. They condemned the extravagant buildings of the monasteries, the size of the churches, painting and sculpture, and also secular learning. The Franciscan statute of 1260 accepted some of their demands – for instance in only permitting pictures of the Crucifixion, the Madonna, and SS. John, Francis and Anthony (Document XIV). But it would appear that these decrees were never carried out. They were impracticable in the face of the dependence of the friaries on a munificent merchant aristocracy, without whose support the large urban communities were not viable. The Spirituals made enormous sacrifices in constant fresh attempts to stem the tide of a development that was ineluctable and irresistible. This resulted in banishment to distant missions in Syria and Armenia, in the disappearance of hundreds in monastic confinement, and even in the odd auto da fé. The papacy made several attempts to mediate. The Conventuals prevailed everywhere in the fourteenth century, so that churches such as Santa Croce in Florence or Santa Maria Gloriosa dei Frari in Venice could be reared aloft

157 Santa Croce, the great Franciscan church of Florence

158 Santa Maria dei Frari, Venice, another example of the grandeur of later Franciscan building

unimpeded, if not uncriticized.[23] Even if they still did no farming, the Franciscans now ran estates and rented out houses. Later movements opposing these tendencies were more successful than the Spirituals in that they did not stand in opposition to growth itself, but tried to steer it. The most important of these were the Observants in the fifteenth century. Their name was an affirmation of their desire to observe the Rule in every point (*observantia regularis*). Great popular preachers such as Bernardino of Siena assured them of success, and by 1500 the Observants had more establishments than the Conventuals, sheltering 30,000 brethren in all. But even they had finally to bow to the world and its dealings. The pawnshops that they opened in many towns with the purely charitable purpose of affording loans – called *montes pietatis* – developed into banking-houses. Movements became institutionalized; what was once inward and spiritual, took to architectural and pictorial manifestations.

It was inherent in organizations that gave up the *stabilitas loci* insisted on by St Benedict for a life of peregrination from establishment to establishment, that they split the spheres of activity of their Orders up into provinces. In 1218, three years before St Dominic's death, the Dominicans had twelve such provinces, whose boundaries reveal that from the very first the whole of the West and its outposts were regarded as their field of activity. These became eighteen in 1303, rising to twenty-three in 1484, since the increase in the number of establishments forced the banding of ever smaller areas into administrable units. Whilst the Cistercians had won adherents bit by bit, expanding outward to the south, north and east from their Burgundian base, the aim of the Franciscans and Dominicans was right from the start that of holding the whole of Christendom in their grasp. It was only seldom possible to realize the ideal of going out as missionaries, so they did not attempt to penetrate fresh ground, but concentrated on changing the infrastructure of existing Christian communities. The conception of provinces also reveals that each particular house was left incomparably less freedom of

*159 The Pazzi Chapel, added by
Brunelleschi to the cloister of Santa Croce,
occupies the traditional position of a chapter-
house*

action than, for example, the old Benedictine abbeys. The organization of both
Orders was centralized, with a General at their head, who did not for long
persist in calling himself, as had St Francis, the servant or menial of the brethren.
Subordinate to him were the provincial priors, nominated in the case of the
Franciscans, elected with the Dominicans. The principle of the visitation of all
friaries was adopted from the Cistercians, but it was conducted not by the priors,
but by specially appointed brothers, sometimes Inquisitors. This is not the place
to go into the problem of the contradictions arising out of superimposing provinces on congregations which had begun as voluntary associations of divers
establishments gripped by a spirit of reform. The Franciscans not only looked on
their town and friary as their spiritual home, but also on the province, the wider
sphere of their activity – that was their larger unit. Similarly, the lesser unit was
not so much the friary as the single cell from which they went out into the world
and to which they returned. The organization of the individual friary was of
less importance to them than their spiritual mission in and for the world. Their
communal buildings, in particular their churches, ceased to proclaim themselves as bastions of faith, and became halls for the preaching of the Word. The
precisely thought-out monastic institution was replaced by the dynamic contrast
between the single cell, in which the friar composed and prepared himself, and
these public halls, where he exercised his gifts.

Neither St Francis nor St Dominic reflected upon the layout of their houses,
nor did the question possess any greater importance in the eyes of their successors.
The fruit of this casualness towards what they considered superficial was the
adoption of the traditional Benedictine schema for all their establishments. The
extant was accepted without question. At first the friars installed themselves
using the ready-made set-up of the monks. The cloister was retained, as were the
positions round it of the church, the chapter-house, the dorter and the refectory.
The absence of an abbot, and the fact that it was merely a prior who ran the
community, led as a rule to the disappearance of any stately abbatial tract. With
no farming, a domestic court was superfluous, and the storehouse or *cellarium*

160 The Pazzi Chapel, view from the Great Cloister, with church on the left

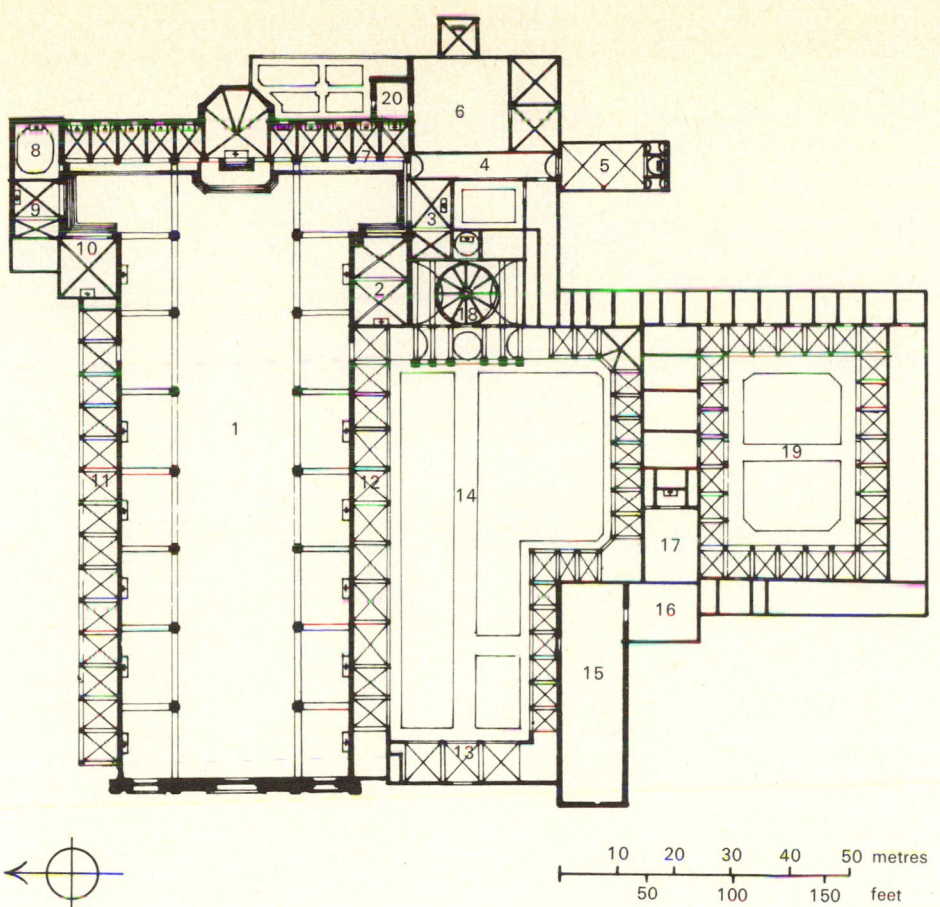

```
        10   20   30   40    50 metres
   |----|----|----|----|----|
          50      100     150    feet
```

was done away with, or thrust into the background. The friars lived off the alms of rich burghers, or from purchases at shops in the town. Even the distinction between lay-brethren and priests had little influence on the physical appearance of the convents. At the outset no Franciscan and every Dominican was in orders, and though this soon changed in both cases – the Dominicans had lay-brothers for menial work, and several Franciscans were priests – it never led to separate establishments as with the Cistercians. Lastly, the infirmaries quickly developed into huge institutions also serving the local inhabitants. The friars mostly elected to operate in already-existing infirmaries, the Hospitals of the Holy Spirit.

Whereas the Benedictines and Cistercians had no liberty to depart from the monastic schema once it was established, owing to the exigences of the joint processions incumbent on their communities on specified occasions, the mendicants, each of whom lived in his own cell and went about his own business, had greater scope. The schema itself remained mandatory, but the various buildings could be squeezed together in novel combinations to suit the site and the space available. In San Francesco in Assisi the sharp fall of the ground required the monastery to be built on two levels, one above the other, behind the choir of the church. The differing levels of the Upper and Lower Churches were a creative challenge to which this fertile century rose with one of the most remarkable solutions, transforming nature into architecture and the monastic schema into a multi-faceted whole. Monasteries on mountain peaks, in narrow valleys, on broad plains, on islands and in the bends of rivers we have met with already, but a large monastery on a sheer hillside was something new. Here too the architectural history of the friary, as distinct from that of the churches, remains to be written and is anyway not a very promising subject, since one plan overlays another, and the effect of the labyrinth of courts and passages is more of a picturesque medley than an organized whole. Its chief feature is the massive underpinning elevating the church and the conventual buildings on interlocking levels.

Taken on their own, neither the chapter-houses, refectories, nor cloisters of the mendicants differ from their Benedictine form, but the new ranges of cells make a dorter superfluous. The Capellone degli Spagnuoli, as the chapter-house of the Dominican friary of Santa Maria Novella, Florence, sticks as rigidly to the traditional location for one as to the received proportions. Even Brunelleschi's Pazzi Chapel fits into the Franciscan friary of Santa Croce as a typical chapter-house by virtue of its form, function and decoration. Its rectangular shape parallel to the cloister, its association with a chapel, the stone benches running round the body of it, and even the construction of its porch like a fragment of cloister, reveal that Brunelleschi was mindful of tradition. It reflected the new ethos of the Order, that the distinction between ecclesiastical and more strictly conventual buildings had become so minimal. I shall return to this point in another connection. The finest Dominican church in France, that of Toulouse (planned 1245, began 1260, consecrated 1292), has been compared to a giant chapter-house. The builder decided on a twin-naved hall, which till then, barring its abnormal height (the cylindrical columns are seventy-two feet high), was a form used only for the secular refectory. At the same time chapter-houses became chapels, most decisively – and here not in the case of the new Orders alone – in England.

Innovations in the way of building were due to sheer numbers, necessitating several cloisters in some establishments, and to the desire for each monk or friar

162, 163 The church of the Dominicans – the Jacobins – in Toulouse: interior and cloister

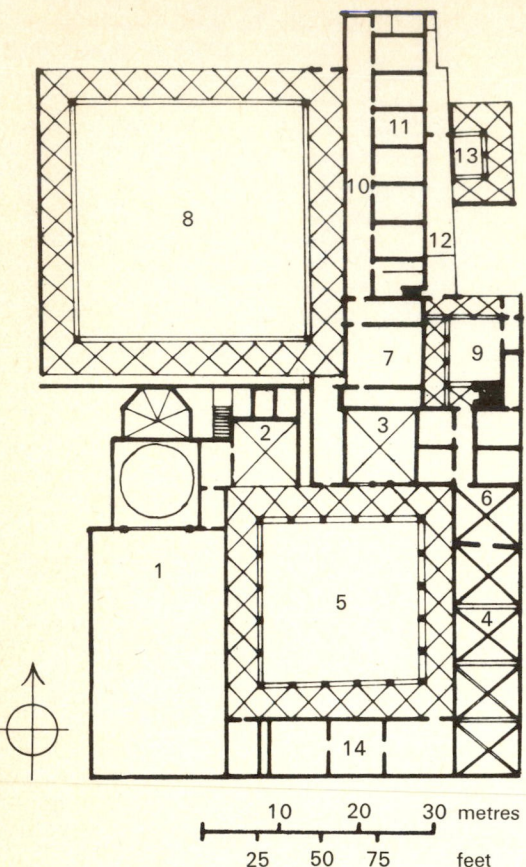

164 *San Marco, one of Florence's two Dominican friaries*

1 *Church*
2 *Sacristy*
3 *Chapter-house*
4 *Great refectory*
5 *Chiostro di San Antonio*
6 *Lavabo*
7 *Small refectory*
8 *Chiostro di San Domenico*
9 *Chiostro della Spesa*
10 *Corridor of the former hospice*
11 *Former hospice*
12 *Corte del Granajo*
13 *Chiostro de' Salvestrini*
14 *Former hospice, now Museo Fra Angelico*

to have his own cell. A common dormitory was relinquished almost everywhere in the late fourteenth and fifteenth centuries. In cases of rebuilding this call for single cells inexorably led to radical upheavals in the traditional schema. The amount of room required for cells, classrooms, and before long yet larger libraries, inspired the wish for a uniform structure including cells in the upper storey of each of its three sides round the cloister. The process has not been subjected to detailed analysis, but it is clear that the creation of single monk's cells, connected by an open loggia-like passage which would have been quite superfluous in the case of the common dorters of the Cistercians, was responsible for two-decker cloisters. The year 1419, that in which Martin V conceded single cells to the Benedictines, may be taken as the nodal point of a long drawn-out process. One of the earliest examples of the new type of monastery was Cosimo Vecchio's foundation of San Marco in Florence for the reformed community of San Domenico in Fiesole, which rose to fame through its great inmates, St Antonino, Blessed Fra Angelico, Savonarola, and Fra Bartolommeo. Michelozzo created in San Marco in 1433/34 an integrated complex in which the chapterhouse, the refectory and the administrative buildings were deprived of their architectural autonomy at a stroke by the single cells crowning them on the floor above. Nor did this re-arrangement remain peculiar to the mendicants; Benedictines and Cistercians began to install themselves in single cells around the same time, and thus to extend their living- and sleeping-quarters round all three sides of the cloister within a uniform overall structure.

Even if neither the Dominicans nor the Franciscans formulated decrees covering the architectural modifications needed to accommodate their altered role and particular way of life, their friaries were logically bound to adapt themselves from within to the new routine. Mendicant friaries of the thirteenth to sixteenth centuries look quite different from Benedictine monasteries built in the same period. It is interesting that in the following account we can draw almost exclusively on Italian examples, just as we drew chiefly on French examples to illustrate Cluniac and Cistercian art, and shall draw on German ones for the

165 *The main cloister of San Marco, Florence. The side of the church is on the left; cells of the friars occupy the other three sides of the upper storey*

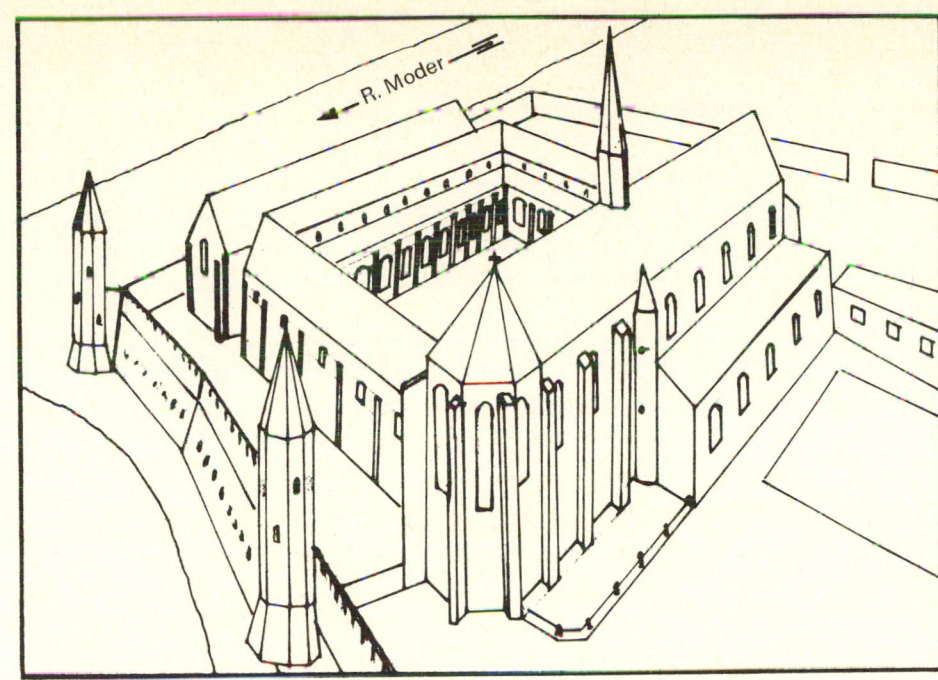

166 *Dominican friary of Hagenau, a new town, where the friars were given a strategic site on the town wall*

Baroque. In each case there was a shift in the centre of the monastic stimulus to artistic activity. The largest of the friaries, such as the Dominicans' Santa Maria Novella and the Franciscans' Santa Croce in Florence are imposing in their spaciousness. 'Cities within the city' they were already termed by Giuseppe Richa in 1754.[24] We cannot pursue here their importance in the urban scene. In many cases they formed new concentrations on the outskirts, that existed in symbiotic rivalry with the old centre formed by the cathedral and the town-square or market-place. They often dovetailed their massive substructures with the fortifications of a town. San Francesco and San Domenico in Siena are instances of this, as is the parent house of the Franciscans in Assisi itself. This phenomenon is particularly noticeable in the case of new towns, where the Black Friars and the Friars Minor were given strategic positions on the town wall from the outset, as exemplified by Wiener Neustadt and Hagenau. At the other extreme, in the case of small foundations like the Franciscan friary in Fiesole, there is something touching in the idyllic picture of each brother in his tiny, flower-girt cell. The administrative urge to give monumental expression to a community yielded to the need to create an appropriate ambiance for the individual. We have seen that the heart of the monastery was no longer the cloister, but the cells in which the friars not only slept but worked. An element of privacy insinuates itself; individuality gains in importance in the very place for which the qualifications were humility and self-sacrifice. The friar arms himself for his mission privily, and not in the midst of the community. The cell in San Marco, from which Savonarola directed the whole of Florence, is the incarnation of this attitude. Many friars were able to acquire, if not equal, then at least comparable influence to Savonarola's, for Franciscan and Dominican mysticism was the governing force in the cultural climate of the municipal republics and free cities of the fourteenth and fifteenth centuries, and outstanding preachers played a decisive part in the spiritual and imaginative life of the urban population. Thus it repeatedly happened in the 1230s and after that a preacher would win such power over one of these municipal republics that he would attempt to revise its constitution according to mendicant ideals: such was the case in Parma with the Hohenstaufen Emperor Frederick II's supporter, the Franciscan Fra Gerardo; or with the Emperor's opponent, Brother John of Vicenza, who stayed first in

167 *Cloister of the small Franciscan house at Fiesole*

168 Savonarola's cell at San Marco, Florence

Bologna and then in Verona, where he was acclaimed duke and rector until his utopian form of communism collapsed after a few months. Individual Dominicans like Peter Martyr indulged in a reign of terror as they presided over the nascent Inquisition. He succeeded in persecuting and executing not only heretics, but respected townsfolk as Cathars. But he in turn was soon overtaken by his own dread fate. Today he is venerated as a martyr, because he is supposed to have been hewn down by some Cathars.

We must forego mentioning here the movable works of art that were created in response to the desire for rapt immersion in the mysteries of faith especially for the cells of the friars, particularly in Germany. By contrast with the cells, the conventual buildings such as the chapter-house, refectory and church become public or half-public in character. They are accessible to the public, or at least on certain occasions. It is there that individuals sway a congregation. There can be no greater contrast than that between a Cistercian church, destined exclusively for the monks and *conversi*, to which laymen, and especially women, were denied access, and the preaching-halls of the Dominicans and Franciscans, which were the especial resort of the laity and above all of a female congregation, whilst the brethren themselves withdrew for their Offices into a small choir behind the altar. Santa Croce and Santa Maria Novella are examples of this too. Those who bore the costs of these churches were also chiefly laymen, from the urban aristocracy, who consequently not only acquired a burial-place in the chapel financed by their kin, but frequently also the right to particular places in the church itself. Chapter-houses too were often the gift of rich families, who had the right to be buried there. It was by no means exceptional for the Dominicans of Santa Maria Novella to have put theirs at the disposal of the Spanish retinue of the Grand Duchess Eleonora of Toledo as a private chapel, whence its name. The new friaries did indeed take their cue from the Benedictines in their regulations concerning the Offices, the order of meals and the division of their day – the Dominicans more so than the Franciscans – but the decrees of both concentrate more on exemptions from the Rule than on tightening it up. It was thus possible for the refectory to become the scene of sermons, discussion and study, as well as the place where the leading men of the town ate together with the brethren. Laymen

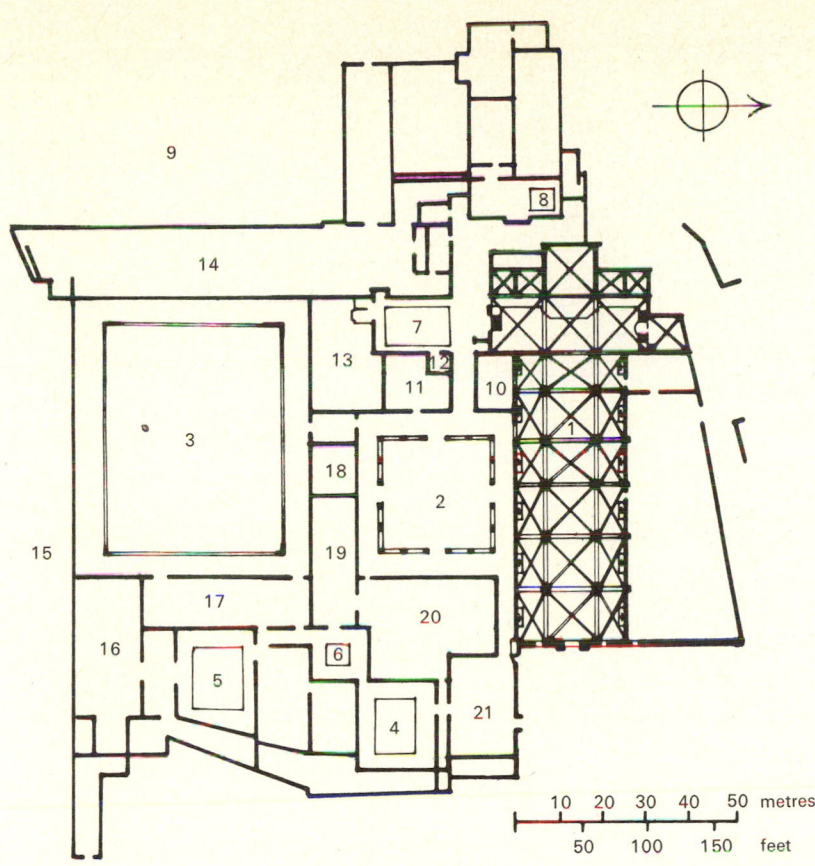

169 *Santa Maria Novella, the larger Dominican house in Florence*

  1 *Church*
  2 *Chiostro Verde*
  3 *Chiostro Grande*
  4 *Chiostro della Porta*
  5 *Chiostro dell' Infermeria*
  6 *Chiostro Dati*
  7 *Chiostro dei Morti*
  8 *Minor cloister*
  9 *Monastery garden*
10 *Sacristy*
11 *Capellone degli Spagnuoli (Spanish Chapel)*
12 *Chapel of Our Lady of the Annunciation*
13 *Dorter*
14 *Dorter 'della Capella'*
15 *Guest house with papal hall*
16 *Chapel of St Nicholas*
17 *Infirmary*
18 *Capitolo del Nocentino*
19 *Refectory*
20 *Domestic rooms*
21 *Forecourt*

170 *Santa Maria Novella, the Chiostro Verde ('Green Cloister')*

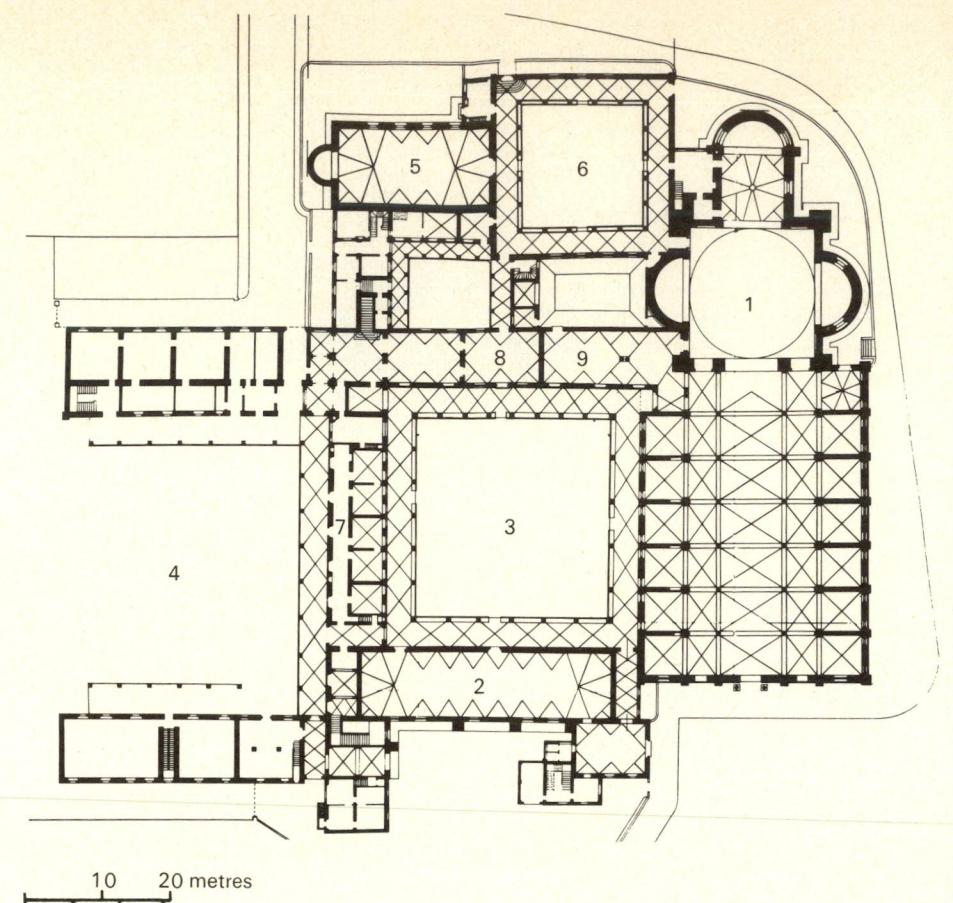

171 Santa Maria delle Grazie, Milan. Here Bramante built the east end and crossing, with its dome, and the small columned third court
1 *Church*
2 *Refectory (containing Leonardo's Last Supper)*
3 *Chiostro dei Morti*
4 *Great Cloister*
5 *Sacristy*
6 *Sacristy cloister, by Bramante*
7 *Cells (library over)*
8 *Chapter-house*
9 *Lady Chapel*

10   20 metres
20 40 60 feet

172 Opposite: Cloister attributed to Brunelleschi at Santa Croce, Florence (no. 19 in the plan on p. 133)

could, like Cosimo dei Medici in San Marco, retreat to the friary for a period of days or weeks in order to live in common with the friars. The obverse of this was that the religious had their friends, or partisans even, when it came to the external affairs of their house. Whilst I noted earlier that the churches of the new Orders were the result of a process of increasing secularization, the chapter-houses and refectories experienced *per contra* a reconsecration.

Wherever documents are available – and Florentine and Venetian friaries once again supply good examples – we learn that every single portion of the friaries, every cloister, refectory, dorter, noviciate, guest-house and chapter-house, every detail of decoration even, was endowed by some citizen. A friary was the work of a town; the size and splendour of an establishment were determined not merely by its needs but also by the general readiness to contribute towards it. Moreover the extent of a friary depended less upon the number of its own inmates than upon how the town ranked as a rendezvous for brethren from several provinces, as a home of the *studium generale*, and as a field for the greatest preachers. Hence there was no reluctance, whenever the number of visitors, the insistence of benefactors or some other reason required it, to attach a second or even a third cloister to the first, though these were then no more than open spaces held in by the new ranges of cells and guest-houses. Plate 169 shows that Santa Maria Novella ended up with seven cloisters. The houses of the Franciscans and Dominicans simply expanded outwards, without involving the destruction of earlier parts, as was the case at Cluny or Clairvaux. Court was added to court, and cloister to cloister, just like cells. All construction was conceived of in terms of individuals and their aggregates, and not in terms of the routine of a fixed, definable group. Occasionally in the Renaissance the cloister was employed as a pure work of architecture for its own sake. Bramante created a third small columned court of unparalleled harmony for Santa Maria delle Grazie in Milan, which was originally only intended to act as an atrium to the equally marvellous sacristy chapel.

Even the second cloister of Santa Croce, which has been attributed to Brunelleschi, was built more on its own account than because of the buildings round it. It is designed to be a model piece of architecture, an utterly fresh version of an old and venerable motif – a cloister for a cloister's sake. The place of the friary in the urban commune means that the evolution of particular architectural features can only be understood in conjunction with those of cathedrals and private buildings. Whereas with the Cistercians the onus of building was borne mostly by their own monks and *conversi*, the Franciscans had a regulation stipulating that these tasks should be left to the guilds. The object was for the friars to devote themselves entirely to their spiritual duties. It made no difference whether the architect was a monk who also built regularly for the city, like Fra Jacopo Talenti, the builder of the Spanish Chapel, or a civil architect who worked for a friary, like Brunelleschi for Santa Croce, or Michelozzo for San Marco. It was of greater moment that in all these friaries the private sphere of the friars, the semi-private sphere of the conventual buildings, and the public arena of the church and the open square before it, stood in a new relationship to one another, which is less detectable in the buildings themselves than in their decoration.

We embark on a subject here that has never been systematically dealt with before, not least because too few examples have come down to us in good condition. In most friaries architecture played a subordinate role to pictorial decoration. Rooms were to be above all spacious and empty. Wall-paintings depicted the ideals of conventual life and the message of the sermons. What artistic decoration was thought appropriate to a cell? It is hardly possible to exaggerate the gulf between the cubby-holes in poor monasteries and the rooms in San Marco, painted by Fra Angelico. What iconography was appropriate to the cloister, and what to a chapter-house or refectory? Little information and few examples from the older Benedictine houses survive. They are not enough for us to arrive at conclusions about the formulation of a binding programme.

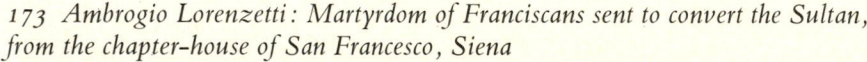

173 Ambrogio Lorenzetti: Martyrdom of Franciscans sent to convert the Sultan, from the chapter-house of San Francesco, Siena

174 Luca Signorelli: Scene from the life of St Benedict, in the cloister of Monte Oliveto, near Siena

Neither the surviving paintings of the chapter-house of Brauweiler near Cologne, with episodes from the Old Testament associated with martyro- and christological scenes (pre-1149),[25] nor the reported depiction of the Last Judgment in the new refectory of Cluny (*v.s.* p. 62) appear to have had any particular bearing on the function of the building. According to a description of the latter in 1485, it had pictures from the Old and New Testaments as well as the monumental figure of Christ in Judgment, and so must have been quite tapestried with pictures.[26] Ambrogio Lorenzetti painted famous scenes of Franciscan martyrdoms for the cloister and chapter-house of the Franciscan friary in Siena, those of the chapter-house being later transferred to the church. Ghiberti described the far more extensive cycle of about 1326 in the cloister, which was destroyed, as a masterpiece of the new realism. It seems as sensible to have been reminded of the merits of their brethren in the cloisters and chapter-houses, as to have wanted to put a monument to them there. The earliest example of such a series of pictures that we know of is a report of twenty-four scenes from the life of St Gallus painted for the cloister of the monastery of St Gall between 980 and 990. Ekkehard IV composed the tituli for this series at the behest of the abbot, Purchart II (1001-22). Thereafter we frequently encounter pictures from the life of St Benedict in Benedictine houses, the frescoes of Signorelli and Sodoma in the abbey of Monte Oliveto near Siena (founded 1313) being the best known. The Late Renaissance and Baroque produced hundreds more.

The earliest distinctive programme for a chapter-house to survive was painted by Andrea da Firenze from 1365 onwards for the Dominicans in the Spanish Chapel. The basic idea goes back to a work of a prior of Santa Maria Novella, J.

175 Interior of the Spanish Chapel, Santa Maria Novella, Florence, with its frescoes by Andrea da Firenze. On the altar wall: the Crucifixion. On the wall to the right: the Triumph of the Dominican Order, showing the friars (symbolized by dogs – 'domini canes') guarding and helping the estates of the world to Heaven

Passavanti (*ob.* 1359). It must surely have reflected an established tradition that the Crucifixion was depicted opposite the entrance. Fra Angelico was to paint his famous *Crucifixion* in San Marco in the same spot. In the Spanish Chapel it is supplemented by the *Bearing of the Cross* and the *Descent into Hell* below and the *Resurrection* in the vault. It is clear that the four frescoes in the severies of the vault must be seen in conjunction with those of the walls beneath. Nor is it surprising to find at the back on the entry wall scenes from the lives of the greatest Dominican saints, Dominic and Peter Martyr, the latter having once delivered his searing sermons in the piazza in front of Santa Maria Novella. What are novel are the frescoes on the sides, that on the left showing personifications of the sciences forming the Dominican *studium generale* and the *Triumph of St Thomas Aquinas*, and that on the right picturing the *Church Militant* or the *Triumph of Repentance*, with Peter shown walking on the waters in the vault above. Passavanti stated that without God's Grace men would be engulfed like Peter by the ocean of their sins. Florence Cathedral appears as it would have looked if it had been completed according to one of the projects of those years, and beneath it the ranks of Christian society upholding the Church; abbot, cardinal, pope, emperor, king and count. At their feet the people are depicted as lambs guarded by piebald dogs

176 *On the opposite wall of the Spanish Chapel, Andrea da Firenze painted the Triumph of St Thomas Aquinas, the most famous Dominican theologian. Above him are flying Virtues; beside him Evangelists and Prophets; beneath him, in Gothic pews, the Arts and Sciences with a leading practitioner of each*

– the *domini canes* – who are harried underneath to the right by wolves, that is to say heretics, whilst Dominic, Thomas Aquinas and Peter Martyr refute their teaching and compel them to burn their own books. The Dominican Order has here created a memorial to itself. Only post-Giottan Florence was capable of giving visible expression to its religious convictions in this way. The great expanses of the walls and vaults were intended for frescoes from the outset, the architecture was no more than a shell. The unbroken severies of the vaults between the massive ribs and the omission of a central column were meant to offer as much surface as possible. The relationship of the four walls to one another and to their vaults embodies the conception of a *Summa* of belief and doctrine. The point of the representation lies in its immediacy as a whole, which could never be attained by the sequential logic of a treatise. It synthesizes the Dominican certainty of salvation.

The decoration of refectories was apparently accorded greater importance than that of chapter-houses. In the case of Florence alone, we discover the 'Last Supper' no less than fifteen times in the refectories of the various religious houses (sometimes in a wider iconographic context),[27] from the earliest representation of about 1340 in Santa Croce, up to the middle of the sixteenth century. Surviving monuments scarcely allow us to pursue the theme of the Last Supper back beyond the Florentine wall-paintings of the fourteenth century. A single example encouraged Emile Mâle to suppose that the theme was first adopted in Cluniac houses: there is a tympanum depicting the Last Supper over the arched entrance to the refectory of Saint-Bénigne in Dijon, deriving from the middle of the twelfth century. By means of this tympanum the refectory as a whole is likened to the chamber of the Last Supper, but, as we know from letters of the Benedictine fathers to Mabillon, its interior was decorated with portraits of the popes, cardinals, saints and great abbots of the Benedictine Order, betokening less a Hall of Fame than a collection of exemplary men. The building dates from shortly after the fire of 1137, and the names of those represented makes it probable that this programme was envisaged from the very first.

The earliest known Last Supper in a refectory, that of Santa Croce, is also the most impressive. Its figures are life-size. It lies at the west end of the large hall, which is lit by six high Gothic, church-like windows along the sides, over and behind the prior's table, and underneath Taddeo Gaddi's illustration of the *Allegory of the Cross* from Bonaventure's *Tractatus qui lignum vitae dicitur.* This is based on the legendary identity of the Tree of Life and the wood from which the Cross was carved. Agnolo Gaddi was later to tell the story of this wood as related in the 'Golden Legend' in the choir of Santa Croce, just as Piero was to do in that of San Francesco in Arezzo. It was a Franciscan theme; the very name 'Santa Croce' conjured up an important image of Franciscan mysticism. Art historians can best study these connections through Werner Cohn's exhaustive analysis of the panel of the *Lignum Vitae* by Pacino di Bonaguida in the Florentine Academy.[28] From the trunk of the Tree, amalgamated with the plain wooden Cross of the Crucified Christ, supposedly hewn from the Tree itself, spread boughs, from which hang the twelve fruits of Faith enumerated by Bonaventure – episodes from the Life of Christ, from Daniel's vision of his birth up to his eternal reign in heaven. Pacino actually depicted these fruits, but Taddeo only cited them on scrolls, whilst showing the twelve Apostles on the twelve boughs, and the four Evangelists displaying their scrolls amongst the branches above and below. The saints of the Order are dispersed at the foot of the Tree: Bonaventure writing, Francis embracing the trunk, in addition to Anthony of Padua, Louis of Toulouse and, in commemoration of their fraternal feeling toward their rivals, Dominic. The pelican is put at the top of the Tree as a symbol of self-sacrifice. Love of God and of one's neighbour are represented to the left of the centre picture by the stigmatization of St Francis above and by the feeding of the poor by St Louis in Santa Croce below. To the right of it God's provision for mankind is exemplified by the legend of the Priest who was reminded by a vision in the course of his Easter meal of the privations of St Benedict, and brought him food. Underneath, the Love of God is celebrated in a depiction of the Magdalen at the feet of Christ at the feast in the house of Simon the Leper in Bethany.

The Last Supper, representing Christ's institution of the Eucharist and the riddle of his betrayer, points to the paradox of the human condition, poised between grace and guilt, that was and is ultimately the message of every sermon. At the same time it confers on the friars' meals that higher meaning, which for the Cistercians the architecture alone could suggest (*v.s.* p. 97). Taddeo Gaddi undoubtedly takes up the theme of an older tradition beyond our ken. In his turn however he begins a tradition which was to be enriched by Andrea del Castagno, Perugino, and Ghirlandaio, before reaching its apogee in Leonardo's *Last Supper* in the refectory of the Dominican Santa Maria delle Grazie in Milan in 1497/98, and fading out with Andrea del Sarto's version of 1527 in San Salvi. Fresh light is even thrown on Leonardo's *Last Supper* when it is seen in the wider context of the Dominican friary. The semi-public character of this refectory is expressed by the fact that it does not lie in its wonted place facing the church, but near its entrance. Ludovico il Moro, as founder, commemorated himself and his dynasty in it; he had himself depicted with his family under the Crucifixion covering the wall opposite the *Last Supper.* Leonardo synthesized the artistic endeavours of

177 The end wall of the former refectory of Santa Croce, Florence, is occupied by a large fresco by Taddeo Gaddi showing the Last Supper and above it the Vision of St Bonaventure (a follower of St Francis) of Christ Crucified on the Tree of Life. The four smaller pictures show scenes from the lives of St Francis, St Louis, St Benedict and St Mary Magdalene

centuries, in that he fused place and image into one, at the same time as asserting different orders of reality between the harmonious hall of the community and the timeless perfection of the picture. The friars sat down to table in a room of dignified solemnity, in truly elevating silence. The high windows, the harmonious curves of the vault, the alternation of frescoes with light, unornamented walls, and the combination of softness with precision in all the details, reveal the unerringness with which his genius availed itself of what was already there to create a work entirely his own, yet faithful to its old purpose. We may recall at this point that the Dominicans had adopted St Augustine's Rule, and that they were especially well-versed in his prescriptions for conduct at table: 'For ye shall not take your nourishment with your mouths only, but your ears shall hunger after the Word of God.'

178 *The theme of the Last Supper continued to be the accepted decoration for monastic refectories until the mid-sixteenth century. Above: the Last Supper by Castagno, for the refectory of S. Apollonia, Florence*

179 *Last Supper by Ghirlandaio, in the refectory of the Ognissanti, Florence*

180 *Last Supper by Leonardo da Vinci, in the refectory of S. Maria delle Grazie, Milan*

181, 182 *Two feasts painted for refectories by Paolo Veronese. One (above) for the Dominican
friary of SS. Giovanni e Paolo, Venice, was formerly called the Last Supper; the name was changed
to the Feast in the House of Levi in order to escape an Inquisition charge of sacrilege. The other, the
Feast in the House of Simon the Pharisee, was painted for the Servite Franciscans, Venice*

183 Fra Angelico: the Transfiguration, in a cell of San Marco, Florence

184 *Fra Angelico: the Crucifixion, in the chapter-house of San Marco, Florence. On the right are Dominican saints and St Francis; beneath, in medallions, more beatified and canonized members of the Order*

Venetian convents of the late Cinquecento went yet a step further. Tintoretto, as is known, no longer painted his famous representations of the Last Supper for refectories, but mostly for the chancel of churches. It is indicative of the changed spirit of monasticism abroad in the early Baroque that Paolo Veronese and others substituted for the Last Suppers of the refectories those great pictures of feasts, in which we see Christ sitting down to receptions whose lavishness leaves nothing to be desired. In 1573 Veronese replaced Titian's *Last Supper* in the refectory of the Dominican friary of SS. Giovanni e Paolo, burnt in the fire of 1571, with the *Feast in the house of Levi* now occupying the whole end wall of the large room in the Venice Accademia. It had been preceded by the *Feast in the house of Simon the Pharisee* for the refectory of the Servite Franciscans, which of all her pictures the Serenissima chose to present to Louis XIV. Somewhat earlier still he had painted his first representation of this subject for the Benedictines of SS. Nazaro e Celso, Verona (Galleria Sabauda, Turin). In 1572 the Franciscans serving the pilgrimage church of Monte Berico outside Vicenza received a *Feast of Gregory the Great*, in which Christ appears as a pilgrim whilst Pope Gregory feeds twelve of the poor with a sumptuous feast. These scenes display everything that the age could offer in the way of princely banquets, in order to emphasize the hospitality meet for a visit from Christ. Nothing but the best seemed proper to these convents; but one should not draw any conclusions about their way of living. The allegories and emblemata of early Baroque show-pieces are more remote from modern sensibility than, for instance, the grave architecture of Maulbronn refectory. Their intent can only be appreciated by using the idiom of an era transformed out of all recognition.

The fortunate coincidence of several circumstances in the 1440s produced the only convent painted throughout to survive from this period, the Dominican

185 *Corridor in San Marco, Florence, with Fra Angelico's Annunciation on the left*

house of San Marco in Florence. Michelozzo produced a building whose plain, unfussy construction cried out for pictures. In Fra Angelico the Order itself possessed the leading painter of the city in this decade, and one moreover with an efficient workshop. Cosimo dei Medici patronized him by paying for the whole cycle of paintings. It is clear here, as in other instances, that monks and friars could only employ their own talent when someone else met the expenses. In this case not only were the cloister, chapter-house and refectory frescoed, but in addition every single cell. The Life of Christ was portioned out amongst the various cells, whilst the smaller ones were adorned with a fresco of St Dominic at the foot of the Crucifix, instead of with the usual Cross. The friars painted the saint with his finger upon his lips above the doors of the cloister as a reminder of the vow of silence. A large Crucifixion was painted in the chapter-house, with the greatest saints of the Church at its foot, and round it the honourable company of the canonized and beatified members of the Order in medallions. Whilst only one panel-painting survives from the decoration of the first refectory that now serves as a museum, Ghirlandaio depicted the Last Supper in a subsequent dining-hall. The only room lacking pictorial decoration is the architecturally proudest – Michelozzo's library. The monastery as picture-Bible – this is the ultimate step, and also an interpretation of the monastic idea characteristic of the early Renaissance.

186 The library of San Marco, Florence, designed by Michelozzo

8

The English Cathedral Monasteries

Two features distinguish English monastic culture from that which we find on the Continent. Firstly, ten of the largest monasteries were simultaneously bishops' seats – that is to say, in ten of the seventeen dioceses of the country the bishop's residence was in a monastery, and the cathedral church was a monastery church.[29] Nine of these were Benedictine: Bath, Canterbury, Coventry, Durham, Ely, Norwich, Rochester, Winchester and Worcester; and one, Carlisle, was a house of Austin canons. Not only were there no comparable institutions in Europe, there were none in Scotland, Wales or Ireland (save Downpatrick, to which monks came from Chester in order to found a monastery around 1185: Bibl. 18, pp. 619ff.). It sometimes happened in the early Middle Ages in the mission areas of Germany that the abbot of a missionary monastery was conjointly bishop of the burgeoning town. Regensburg, where this personal union endured until the end of the tenth century, was the last case of this. Rulers might also procure the appointment as bishop of the abbots of their chief monastery. Thus, after 1176 the Abbot of Monreale was also Bishop of the neighbouring Palermo, and as late as 1744 the Abbot of Fulda was consecrated bishop. But in neither case was the extent of the diocese greater than the original area of the monastery or of its jurisdiction.

Our picture of British monastic life is coloured by this distinctively English institution, the cathedral monastery, because it alone, though in a reconstituted form, withstood Henry VIII's dissolution of the monasteries. That is the second feature. The bishop remained; dean succeeded prior, and the monks were replaced by canons. Bath was the only exception; the abbey became a parish church, partly because the bishop resided in Wells. Part of the monastic buildings could always go on serving comparable purposes, and so be spared from decay or destruction. There were also cases of monastery churches, such as Chester and Gloucester, only then receiving cathedral status, thereby getting the same protection. Medieval England was remarkable for the profusion and importance of its monasteries (*q.v.* Statistical survey in Bibl. 16, pp. 359ff.). Benedictine monasticism spread in three waves. The first age extended from the beginnings in Canterbury under St Augustine in 597 until the Danish raids, that began with the plundering of Lindisfarne in 793 and were constantly repeated till the middle of the tenth century. Lindisfarne too had been a bishopric, till the see was transferred to Chester-le-Street and finally to Durham. There exists a series of investigations into the simple churches of these early monasteries. Canterbury may be pictured as similar to Old St Peter's.[30] But we have virtually no reliable account of the monastic buildings; nothing survives, and practically nothing has been excavated. It is unlikely that the Benedictine monastic layout such as we have seen it in the plan of St Gall had time to establish itself. Not one monastery, with the possible exception of Canterbury, came through these troubles. Despite this, the second wave of monastic foundations in numerous instances chose the same locations: ground once hallowed remained holy. This second wave began with the new foundations by St Dunstan (959-88), Abbot and Archbishop of Canterbury, and minister and counsellor of Edgar the Peaceable (958-75). He was supported by two important bishop-abbots, Ethelwold, Bishop of Winchester (963-84) and Oswald, Bishop of Worcester (961-92) and from 972 also Archbishop of York. Oswald had made his profession at Fleury, the later Saint-Benoit-sur-Loire, and it may be assumed that he there became familiar with the Benedictine monastic layout. The monastic rule of Fleury formed the basis of Oswald's *Regularis concordia anglicae nationis* (Migne *PL* 137, 475/502), used as the formula for all new foundations. By the end of the tenth century thirty Benedictine monasteries and nine nunneries had been founded, including Ely and Ramsey in the Fens, Peterborough and Westminster. In the course of the eleventh century several of them accepted Cluniac customs. So it is highly plausible that, in keeping with continental monasteries at the end of the tenth and the beginning of the eleventh century, they adopted their most significant novelty – the shift of the meeting-place of the chapter from the arm of the cloister adjacent to the church to its own room, the chapter-house, on the west arm. Four of these new foundations were already cathedral monasteries before 1066: Canterbury, Winchester, Worcester and Sherborne (which later lost its bishop).

The new young bishops that came to England in the train of William the Conqueror could scarcely have much sympathy at first for this English form of monasticism, least of all when it was just these Anglo-Saxon monasteries that remained the most tenacious centres of resistance to Norman hegemony. National singularity was deliberately cultivated. The turning-point came with another remarkable monk, Lanfranc of Canterbury (1070-89), who perceived the potential usefulness of episcopal monasteries for the assertion of Norman rule. The third wave of monastic foundations began under him, reaching its apogee under Henry I (1100-35). Fifty Benedictine monasteries were counted at his death, and no more were ever founded. Three later bishops were inspired to make their sees monasteries – Gundulf at Rochester (*c.* 1080), William at Durham (1083) and Herbert at Norwich (*c.* 1096). The endeavours of the Norman rulers to translate episcopal sees from country areas to defensible towns brought the abbey in Bath into the possession of the bishops of Wells (1088), and Coventry into the possession of the bishops of Lichfield/Chester (*c.* 1090). A small diocese round Cambridge was carved out of Lincoln and richly endowed by giving the new bishop the prosperous Abbey of Ely for his residence (1108/9). The point had been grasped that by closely interlocking episcopal sees and Benedictine monasteries, so presenting every abbot and prior with the chance of ending his career as a bishop, numerous prelates would be bound more tightly to the throne.

We have already seen how at this time all those seeking out monasteries as places of retreat and asceticism were drawn to the new foundations of the Cistercians. The history of monastic architecture was strongly affected by the fact that in the later towns also it was monastery and abbot that were first on the scene, and not the bishop. Only in two cases (Norwich and Rochester) did a monastery grow out of an episcopal see; it is the sees which grew out of monasteries. Durham is the sole instance of the foundation of both together.

The fact that a bishop had quite other political and military duties to fulfil in his diocese than those of an abbot in his monastery inevitably gave rise to manifold difficulties. Unavoidably, bishops were frequently absent from their monasteries, and even when they were there they could only participate to a limited extent in the conventual life of the brethren. For its part, the community both asserted its right to the free election of the abbot-bishop – but with no power to back this up – and even more emphatically, its right to elect the prior as representative of the abbot and director of the community, though the Rule of St Benedict stipulated his nomination by the abbot. The latter right was won everywhere after hard struggles in the course of the thirteenth and early fourteenth centuries. The separation of the incomes of the bishop from those of the community was also achieved. There was episcopal land, just as there was land allocated to the monks (Bibl. 18, pp. 255ff.). Time and again distinguished monastic leaders appeared among the bishops, and stood out against any tendency towards the divergence of episcopal residence and monastery, but in the end such tendencies prevailed. Almost everywhere the bishops had their palace and court built outside the monastery walls, and almost everywhere priors became the true heads of their communities. In the course of the thirteenth century each of them became entitled to the *pontificalia* (i.e. the same status and liturgical garments as an abbot), together with total jurisdiction over the monastery. In certain places like Worcester the prior even became archdeacon of the town churches. But one thing none of them could attain: unlike the abbots, they were not separately invested with land and rights, that is, with a baronial fief (Bibl. 18, pp. 250–58). Nonetheless their position was sufficiently imposing for historians to use the expression 'cathedral priories' in preference to 'cathedral monasteries', whilst I have nowhere found mention of a 'cathedral abbey'. In the course of the centuries they lost the character of abbeys, and each split up into an episcopal see and a priory.

To what extent was the building programme of these institutions affected by these struggles over power and organization between the prior and community on one side, and the abbot-bishop on the other? The innovations upon the traditional Benedictine monastic layout must be sought in three main areas. An abbot as bishop needed buildings with a far greater degree of independence in relation to the monastic complex, and which could be of a sumptuousness quite inappropriate to an abbot acting merely as father to the community. One recalls that the question of the independence of the abbot's palace and kitchen had already been raised in the synods of Benedict of Aniane in Aachen in 816/17, and that this problem recurrently preoccupied many communities up to the end of the Middle Ages (*v.s.* p. 40). For his part, the prior of a cathedral monastery, as often the sole presiding head of the community, had to enlarge his own accommodation, incorporating buildings for the reception of distinguished guests, who might include the king himself. He built a hall and a chapel alongside his own lodgings; but in no case did a prior go so far as to build himself a palace comparable to those of the abbots of the great monasteries. One will look in vain in cathedral monasteries for a prior's house on the scale of the seat of the Abbots of Westminster by the West Door of the abbey, or the comparable abbatial palace at Cluny. Their dwellings were differently located and differently built. The third area of innovation becomes apparent in considering how a cathedral monastery fitted into a town. They all had to lie within the walls, whereas in almost all other cases the chief Benedictine abbeys were in the countryside, like Monte Cassino, Cluny and numerous English examples now showing up merely as ruins in the midst of farmland in aerial surveys,[31] or they were constructed outside the walls on a town's perimeter, like St Augustine's, Canterbury, or the monasteries ringing old Paris – Saint-Germain-des-Prés, Saint-Martin-des-Champs and Saint-Denis. A Benedictine monastery within a town posed its builder with problems of urban planning not found with a monastery beyond the walls. Often it was older as a foundation than the town itself, which then grew up in its purlieus. How was the monastic precinct set off from the townspeople without actual severance? A cathedral monastery could not totally cordon itself off like the monks in Tournus, or as those in St Gall had largely done. As a rule – the town plan of Canterbury gives the best example – the monastic complex took up a whole quarter of the town, abutting on the town walls and set off from the townspeople by its own wall, which was however pierced by a number of gates. The notably fine gatehouses characteristic of English Benedictine monasteries proclaim this accessibility. For the cathedral churches could not stand apart; they served the brethren, but they served the local population in equal measure, as the regular place of pontifical ceremonies on great occasions, although never as parish churches. It is my guess that the distinctive shape of English cathedrals, with their elongated monks' choir, and nave of roughly the same length, evolved in response to this double task.

187 *Durham Cathedral and Castle,*
formerly the residence of the Bishop
  1 *Cathedral church*
  2 *Galilee*
  3 *Chapel of the Nine Altars*
  4 *Chapter-house*
  5 *Prison (old dorter above)*
  6 *Prior's quarters*
  7 *Undercroft of refectory*
  8 *Kitchen*
  9 *New dorter (above), later library*
10 *Fountain*
11 *Bishop's castle*
12 *Kitchen*
13 *Great Hall*
14 *Tunstall's gallery*
15 *Tunstall's chapel*
16 *Keep*

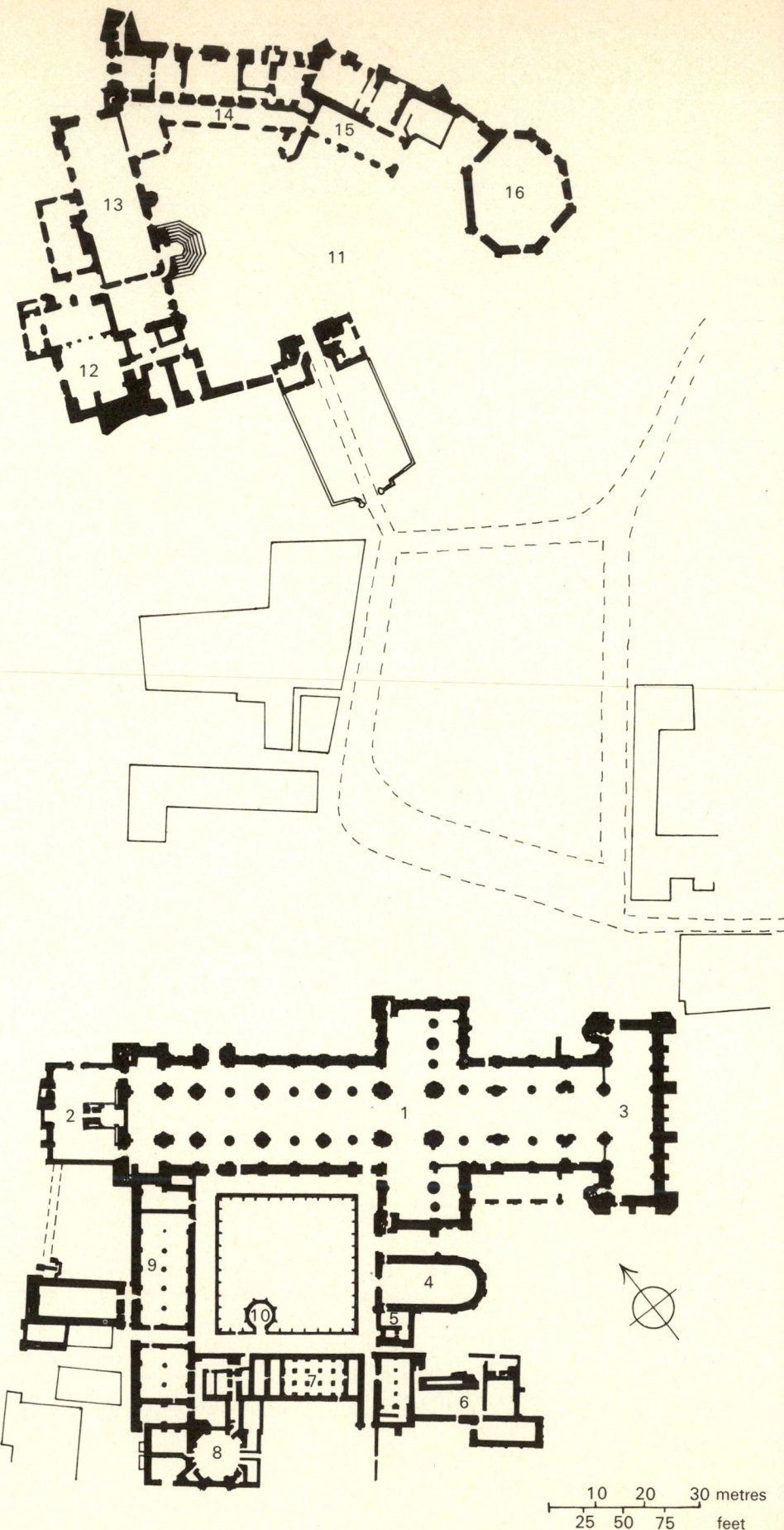

188 *Air view of Durham Cathedral and Castle*

189 Durham, the former dorter, now the library

But even this simple observation raises two difficulties. The ten cathedral monasteries of England form entities whose comparability is strictly limited. The diversity in political standing among the sees was almost as great as that in their situations, which set the builders their chief creative challenges. Durham on its escarpment, where the bishop was a territorial ruler comparable to a German *Reichsbischof*,[32] was a very different case to Canterbury in the plain, whose archbishop played an important role in the politics of both church and state. The Bishop of Bath, as we noted, resided after 1206 mostly in Wells, and the Bishop of Worcester resided as a rule in York. This is the first difficulty. The second derives from the fact that we are wholly in the dark as to whether certain innovations that we come across in cathedral monasteries also had their origin there. Inspiration came also from the leading monasteries; but equally, bishoprics that were never monasteries adopted elements from the repertoire of monastic buildings. In the fourteenth century the Bishop of Bath and Wells had a cloister erected at Wells for its own sake, never enclosed by monastery buildings. On the other hand Westminster Abbey, thanks to its royal function, attained a shape similar to that of the cathedral monasteries. And when from the thirteenth to the sixteenth century Westminster placed its renowned polygonal chapter-house at the disposition of the Commons for their sessions, this recalls the fact that

190 Durham, the chapter-house

similarly richly decorated chapter-houses in the English cathedral monasteries were the very places where an abbot as bishop could preside over assemblies, whose resolutions were directed far beyond the sphere of the monastery. The chapter-house at Canterbury suggests a royal throne-room much more strongly than a place for monks to assemble to meditate upon the Rule of Saint Benedict. But with this reference I am jumping ahead of the course of our investigations.

In Durham, the political circumstances surrounding the origins of the see are clearly legible from the town plan and aerial photos. The naturally fortified river-girt escarpment had been the refuge of monks fleeing the Danes. In 995 the shrine of St Cuthbert had been transported there for safety. The Normans similarly valued the strategic worth of the place in their feuds with Scotland. Within the diocese the new bishop was vested with unique rights, equivalent to those of the king outside it: '*Quicquid rex habet extra, episcopus habet intra*'. His actual residence was the citadel, which was made into an impregnable fortress and a magnificent castle; but we need not concern ourselves with that here.

The building progress of the great cathedral likewise lies outside our theme. From west to east it dominates the heights of the tongue of land in the bend of the river. Nave, transept, and monks' choir form the most important work of early Norman architecture in England (1070–1140). The western galilee (*c.*

191 Durham, the fourteenth-century kitchen, with on the right the former refectory

192 Durham, the east walk of the cloister, looking towards the Prior's door into the church, and with the triple entrance to the chapter-house midway on the right

1170–75) stretches right to the sheer bank of the river. The Chapel of the Nine Altars (1242–*c.* 1290) turns its choir face to the main street of the town, the North Bailey. It fulfils the role of a Lady Chapel; its architecture is of courtly delicacy and princely splendour. It bespeaks the bishop in his capacity as premier noble of his diocese. To the south of the church unfold the extensive monastery buildings; to the north lies the bishop's castle, also entrusted with the defence of the bridges over the river. The total disposition is perfect, a classic case for topological study. A topographical description betrays the stamp of the historical forces that created this seat of government.

The monastery falls into an inner zone around the cloister and an outer zone round the abbey garth. The former was the sphere of the prior, whilst the bishop, as we saw, had erected his residence, with fortifications, palace and administrative buildings, directly on the opposite side. They met in the middle, in the cathedral itself, or occasionally in the nearby chapter-house – but here the prior customarily presided.

The monastery buildings kept closely to the Benedictine norm, each one in its appointed place on one of the four sides of the cloister: the parlour, the chapter-house with the lock-up for lesser offenders beside it, the adjoining warming-room (which was later altered). The large refectory had its wonted place along the south side of the cloister. The oldest pieces of Norman architecture in Durham are preserved in its lower storey. Kitchen and cellars were also where one would expect, save that the later kitchen shown on our plan, John Lewyn's remarkable building of 1366–77, was detached from the frontage, to rear up as a free-standing structure in the gardens, whence it could also supply the guest-house. The fountain took up its inevitable place in front of the entrance to the refectory. The buildings on the west arm of the cloister served originally in part as the monks' workshop, and in part as a storeroom. Under Bishop Skirlaw (1398–1404) the dorter was transferred from the east to the upper floor of the west side, resulting in the huge chamber with the mighty wooden roof, 194 feet long and 39 feet wide, that now serves as museum. Behind the dorter the sizeable rere-dorter was built on bold underpinning, flushing its waste directly into the river beneath. It is likely that, as in Worcester (*v.i.* p. 168), hygienic considerations contributed to the decision to alter the traditional siting of the dorter. It doubtless went against the grain with the monks, who were thus compelled to traverse the whole nave in order to reach the choir for their nocturnal orisons. The late-comers, in whose favour even the Cistercian *consuetudines* connived at the slower singing of the first psalms, could no longer creep into their seats. But the expansion of the priory, with its new hall, new palace and new chapel also made the move necessary.

Within the monastic complex, the prior's group of buildings are strategically situated for the fulfilment of his functions. They still adhere to the inner zone near the cloister, whilst facing outwards toward the garth, which was encompassed by farm buildings, store-houses and guest-blocks. Regarded from the church, the prior lived at the back, not like the abbots of Cluny or Westminster, out at the front. His house was not the representative focus of the monastery, but its hidden, private centre. Seeing it in conjunction with the chapter-house, refectory, guest hall and the abbey gates, we become aware that from here all the

193 Canterbury, air view. The circuit of the monastic wall can still clearly be recognized. In the distance are the ruins of the abbey of St Augustine

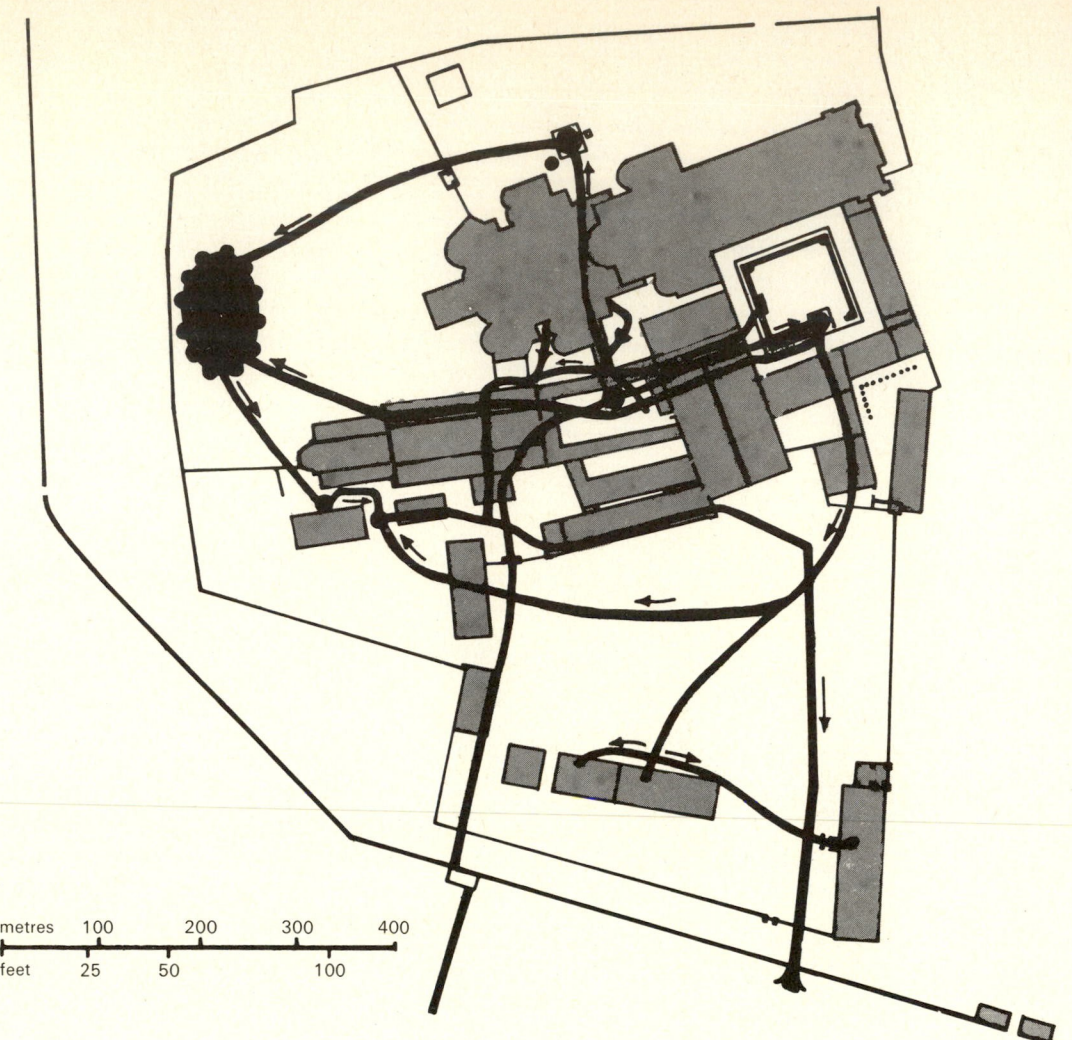

metres   100   200   300   400

feet   25   50   100

194-96 Canterbury. Above: the monastic buildings with the water-pipes superimposed from the twelfth-century plan. Right: a redrawn version, by Professor R. Willis, of the twelfth-century plan, of which the original is reproduced as the endpapers of this book. The plan is described in detail on p. 164

reins were in the prior's hands. Here he was the master, and hither the bishop could not follow. It was not only the key position but, as his subsequent successors the deans would realize, it was also the most beautiful in the monastery. Yet basically the priors never forsook their old cell at the edge of the dorter, the little room from which, elsewhere, a sub-prior would come to supervise the sleeping arrangements of the monks. In a centuries-long process priors just steadily bettered their quarters. Where the abbot was a bishop, the prior was in a special position, which found architectural expression just like any other slight alteration in living conditions in the monastery.

Now let us turn our gaze from the furthest north of England to the furthest south, to Canterbury. The cathedral monastery of Canterbury is not only the best preserved, but thanks to the plan of about 1160, also the best explained monastery in England. This is the sole surviving complete plan of a monastery, between that of St Gall and the bird's eye views of the sixteenth century.[33] It is a unique document both for the history of perception[34] and of monastic architecture. It was drawn up owing to Prior Wibert's (1151-67) insistence on a new water-supply (Bibl. 19, p. 58) more in accordance with St Benedict's Rule than before (*v.s.* p. 88). And it owes its preservation to having been bound up with one of the most notable manuscripts of the Canterbury school, the Eadwin Psalter now in Trinity College, Cambridge (Cod. R. 17). This plan shows that

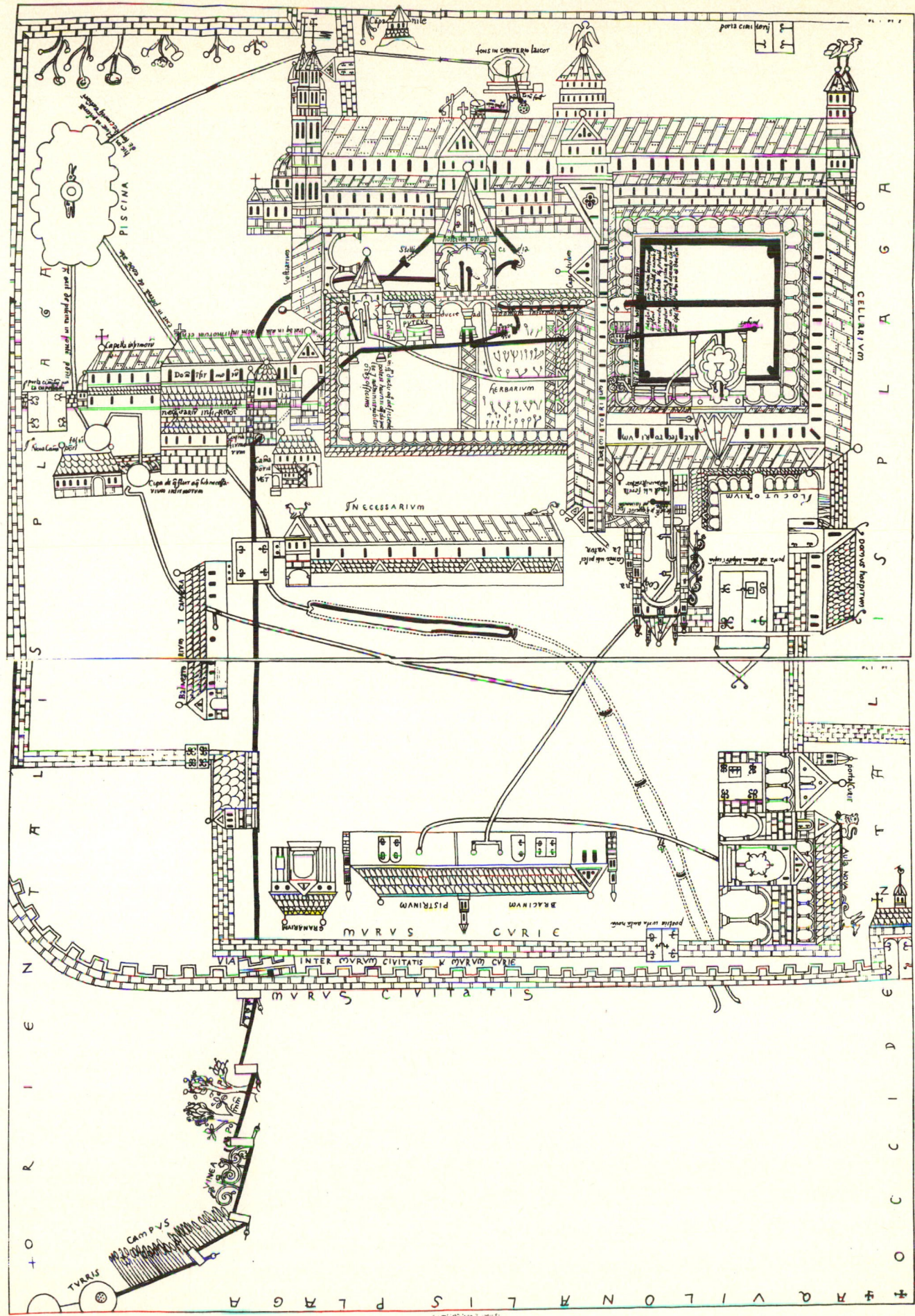

even the twelfth century, in making a working drawing and not an illustration of an abstract idea, could be accurate down to the last detail. It should be read with the aid of modern plans, though these all show the monastery from south to north, whereas the old plan depicts the buildings from north to south.[35]

Beginning at the bottom edge, we see first the battlements of the town wall, and then the monastery wall running close alongside it, before turning off to enclose the whole monastery, but leaving the south side of the cathedral free. Two drains flow under the pair of walls to discharge into the river which runs from west to east. We gather from a document of the time of Edward II 'that Prior Wibert caused to be made the conduits of water in all the offices within the court of the priory, and that water taketh its source about a mile out of the City, which wholly under the ground by pipes of lead he caused to come into the Church' (Bibl. 19, p. 67). This inlet is not marked. It issues into a pumping station – of which there are altogether five on the plan – at the left edge behind the farmery chapel. This supplied the large basin to its left, whence in turn pipes led round the choir of the church to the fountain on the far side of the monastery wall in the city cemetery, and others to the farmery hall and to the water-tower in the centre of the farmery cloister, the main distribution-point. But from the pump at the entry of the water-supply a further branch appears to have gone off to the right to serve the prior's 'New Lodging' and, through a second pumping-station, the immense rere-dorter, or lavatories, with fifty-five seats. If one examines the plan thoroughly it will be apparent that many other buildings besides the main fountain in the main court and the kitchen had water laid on, including the poor pilgrims' hostel, which is the prominent *Aula Nova* on the lower righthand edge, and the bakehouse and the brewhouse in the centre underneath. This plan makes it clear that the layout of the monastery was laid down by 1160. Whatever may have been destroyed in the great fire of 1174 was in every case rebuilt on the same spot. With the exception of the archbishop's palace, outside the monastery wall to the right, and a guest-house for the greater nobility to the left, made possible by an enlargement of the monastic precinct in the fifteenth century, we find all the buildings traceable in a modern reconstruction already present.

The sketched reconstruction displays the utterly rational arrangement of this monastery. From about 1075 to its dissolution in 1538 no attempt was made to tamper with its coherence. As in Cluny, there was probably always building going on somewhere in the church or monastery, with each archbishop and most priors seeking to set their mark upon them. But the great monks' quarters shown on this plan were only renovated, never altered. The conventual zone, disposed in classic fashion round the cloister – the chapter-house and dorter to the east, the frater with the kitchen complex behind to the north, the *cellarium* to the west – stayed unchanged as regards both the placing and the proportions of its buildings. From the very first the cloister had the hallowed dimensions of the heavenly Jerusalem – 144 feet square (Revelations Ch. 21, vv. 16-17, cubits having been read to mean feet). The dorter is the largest in England, 148 by 78 feet: 'A massive wall pierced by twelve arches divided it longitudinally into two apartments and supported a double roof; the sub-vault of each half was divided into three aisles which were vaulted throughout. As the chapter-house intervened between the dorter and the transept there were no nightstairs, and for the night Offices in the choir the monks had to pass from the dorter along a gallery of the farmery cloister to a doorway in the choir transept' (Bibl. 19, p. 67). This was still not so far as in Durham.

The next largest complex to that of the monks was that for the sick. They were the special responsibility of the sub-prior, who had his chamber there. It is a singularity of English cathedral monasteries that the large farmery halls all had their own chapel. They also had their own kitchen (not shown on this plan) and their own frater, or refectory, called the flesh-frater, because only here might meat be eaten. Here, provision for the sick went far beyond the needs of the monastery. Laymen could clearly not be admitted, but it does seem as if the archbishop could use them to treat part of his clergy.

Surprisingly, neither on the 1160 plan nor on the reconstruction are there traces of buildings for the novices, such as we regularly encounter from the plan of St Gall to Cluny III. By contrast, guests could find lodging in three different places, according to their rank. The 'poor pilgrims' were lodged in the *aula nova* or north hall. The porter saw to their needs. The almonry and almonry chapel lay in front of their hostel. Guests of middling station were looked after by the cellarer. From 1394 a three-storied house next to the cellarer's hall, called Chillenden's Chambers, whose predecessor is visible on the 1160 plan, stood at their disposal. The prior lodged the finest guests, the king and his court, in the new building behind the infirmary, which for more than five hundred years has borne the name of Meister Omers. A forerunner is shown on the 1160 plan, again near the infirmary. Lists of many of the guests who stayed there still exist. Almost every English court did so on its pilgrimage to the tomb of Thomas Becket, and many also summoned political gatherings there.

The archbishop dwelt in his extensive palace outside the monastery. The site of this group of buildings makes it improbable that he could ever have entered the monastery any other way than through the church. He came only on some official occasion. Were the cloister and its chapter-house adapted for his visits? Did he rather than the prior have the right to preside over the community in chapter? The form and ornament of the cloister, like the size of the chapter-house,

197 Canterbury, ruins of the infirmary. We are looking east along the south aisle; the further row of piers is that of the infirmary chapel

198, 199 Canterbury. Above: detail of the cloister vault, showing some of the 820 heraldic bosses bearing the coats-of-arms of Kentish gentry. Right: the new fourteenth-century chapter-house

whose famous wooden roof is next in size only to that of Royal Westminster Hall, make it probable. The 820 heraldic bosses of the Kent gentry in the cloister vaults (*c.* 1400) made this into an aristocratic hall of honour. It was completed by Archbishop Arundel in 1414. The first chapter-house, which was erected in about 1075, was almost the same size as the one today, and Archbishop Lanfranc will certainly have presided there. The present building stems from the fourteenth century, but here two priors, and not an archbishop, are recorded as builders. The triple arcades over the throne are like a baldachin. Arcades over the seats of the monks and the higher clergy from the archbishop's curia lend prominence to each one of them. The huge high window diffuses the refulgence of a royal throne-room. Yet must not the prior also have headed the house's assemblies there? Must he not have been bent on making this chapter-house throne his counterpart to the throne of St Augustine in the choir of the cathedral, which was reserved to the archbishop alone? It is not possible to answer this unequivocally, because the dispute between the archbishop and the prior varied in outcome according to the century and the personalities involved. Demonstrably, both archbishop and prior did preside there. It was the contest between them that gave rise to dimensions that have no peer upon the continent. In England both monasteries and secular cathedrals created great chapter-houses that betoken both the

200 Worcester, the abbey gatehouse, or Edgar Tower

high self-esteem of the heads of these institutions, and their wealth and taste. In a study of monastic architecture these English chapter-houses demand especial attention. We must begin by considering the oldest surviving of the polygonal chapter-houses, that at Worcester. It is also probable that it was the earliest that was ever built.

In Worcester the articulation of the monastery is again intimately linked with aspects of its site and hierarchy. After the Danish raids St Oswald had refounded the monastery on the original spot high above the west bank of the Severn. St Wulfstan (1062-95) was the sole bishop-abbot to retain his see throughout the Conqueror's reign. An aerial view shows up the church, the cloister with the polygonal chapter-house, and the large frater. As in Durham, the dorter was shifted to the west side by the river, but here, contrary to all normal usage, it was erected at right angles to the cloister over the infirmary, whose ruins are still visible. The proximity of running water, essential to the *necessarium*, was the reason for this realignment. A row of arcades belonging to the old guest-houses are perceptible behind the chapter-house, and further back the big gatehouse, now known as the Edgar Tower. Neither the abbatial palace nor the priory have survived. The round chapter-house was completed around 1120, certainly before 1150.[36] It was re-vaulted in the fifteenth century and given a decagonal exterior. To allow a high, brightly-lit construction here, the dorter had to be transposed to the west side of the cloister or, as in Canterbury, set back from it. What circumstances were responsible for this new form? It is permissible to

201 Worcester, ruins of the guest house

interpret it merely as a happy inspiration of the architect's, or did it have a special purpose?

The history of these centrally-planned buildings, which take this form only in England, is well researched.[37] But there is only one investigation that I have found which broaches the problem of the relation of form to function.[38] Their form derives from the special responsibilities of both monachal and canonical chapters. They were not only gatherings to reflect upon the *capitula* (chapters) of the *Regula Sancti Benedicti*, but councils taking decisions affecting far wider circles than just their communities. It was not inappropriate that the Westminster chapter-house was used as the Commons' Chamber from the fourteenth to the sixteenth century. In neither monastic nor secular cathedrals was an abbot-bishop or bishop's claim to primacy in the cathedral ever disputed (Bibl. 17). Yet we hear of arguments over his relationship with the dean or prior almost everywhere down the centuries. There buildings pose still more insistently the question which arose over Canterbury: could an abbot-bishop, or in secular cathedrals the bishop, also preside in chapter? In the case of monastic cathedrals the question cannot be answered with any certainty, but in many of the secular cathedrals the dean prevailed. In both cases the huge, light-filled chapter-houses express an assertion of power; neither the bishop on one hand, nor the prior or dean on the other, were content to preside in some low and dingy claustral chamber, but instead demanded an ample, high hall like a throne-room; whether rectangular as in Canterbury or Durham, or polygonal as in Worcester.

202 Worcester, the chapter-house, first of a long line of comparable English chapter-houses

203 Worcester, air view. The cloister lies to the right of the cathedral, with the chapter-house on the far side, and behind that the ruins of the guest house

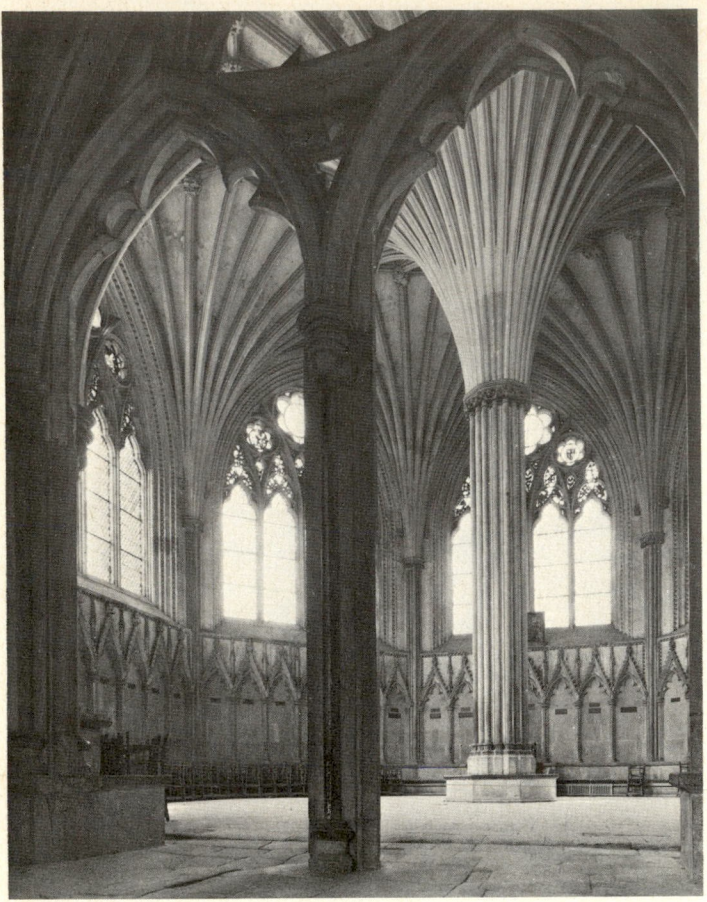

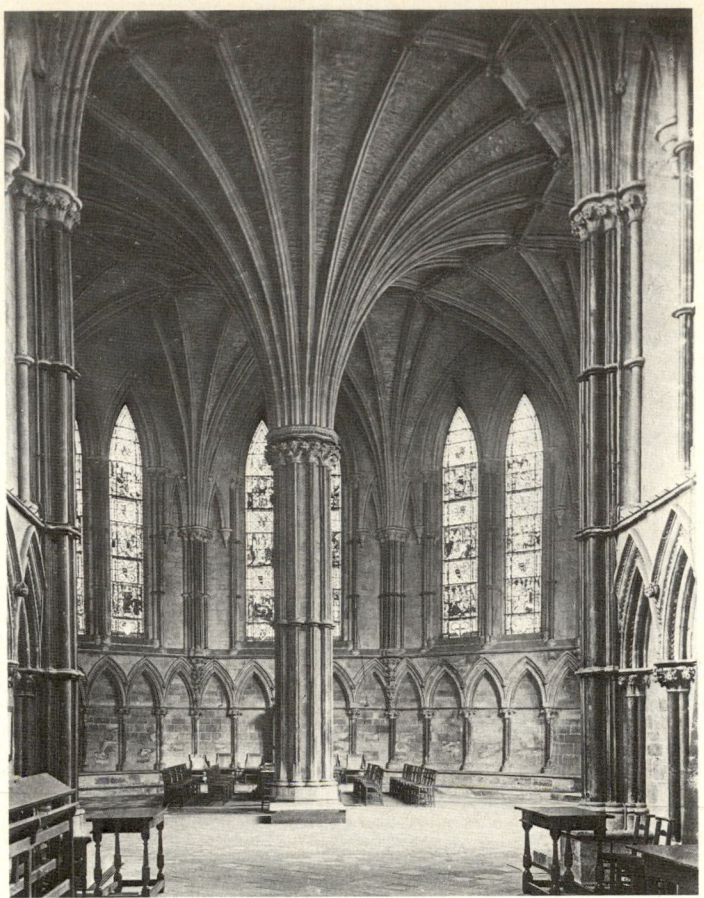

204   *The octagonal chapter-house, an English speciality. Wells, early fourteenth century*

205   *Lincoln, begun c. 1235*

206   *Westminster, 1245-53*

Twelve polygonal chapter-houses survive in England, and thirteen more are known from ruins or engravings. They occur in monasteries, and in both monastic and secular cathedrals. They chiefly originate from the thirteenth century. The first, and for a long time the only one, was, as we saw, at Worcester. The shape was adopted at the end of the twelfth century in two Cistercian monasteries, Margam and Abbey Dore, but they remained isolated cases of its use by this Order. The first secular cathedral with a polygonal chapter-house was Wells. It was begun in 1220, though admittedly only completed, as the last major example of the type, in 1320. But as we saw, the abbot-bishop of Bath presided there. The large Lincoln chapter-house (begun *c.* 1235) was demonstrably built under the influence of Worcester. The builder, Bishop Grosseteste of Lincoln, was a friend of Bishop Walter de Cantelupe, and Alexander the architect had previously been occupied in Worcester.[39] Of somewhat later are the most famous chapter-houses, of Westminster (1245-53), Salisbury (1263-84), Lichfield (1239-59) and York (1280-before 1295). Uniform in size – Westminster and York are 58 feet in diameter, Salisbury and Lincoln 56 feet – and closely related in appearance, they affirm that each of the ruling English prelates, whether abbot or bishop, commissioned a comparable room of state.

There is another point. By no means all of these chapter-houses lie traditionally to the left of the cloister by the transept as at Worcester and Winchester. Some of the most important of them, like Wells, Lichfield, Lincoln and York, stand in isolation on the north side of the cathedral. Belonging to secular cathedrals, they were not bound by the constraints of monastic layout, but could face deliberately outward to the world. But even here there was reluctance to forego the associated cloister.

207 Salisbury, 1263-84

208 Lichfield, 1239-59

One development had taken place in all Benedictine monasteries since the late eleventh century, until its apparent completion by the end of the twelfth: 'The abbot was no longer the paterfamilias of the Rule, but is rather the prelate, almost the bishop of his monks, and the representative of his abbey to the outside world. . . . The growth of the communities and their offices, the responsibility for widely scattered properties, the many calls made upon the abbot by the public life of the country and by the duties of hospitality – all these, added to the separation of establishments due largely to feudal claims, tended to withdraw the father of the family from the life of the house, and to deprive him of any adequate knowledge of the characters and spiritual needs of his sons.' (Bibl. 18, pp. 300ff.). The thought suggests itself that this new attitude of his towards the community was responsible for the common council chamber acquiring a throneroom-like appearance quite different in size as at Canterbury, or quite different in shape, as at Worcester, to that of the chapter-houses of the older Benedictine or Cistercian monasteries, and even of Cluny. Here is another English peculiarity for which there are few parallels on the continent: cloisters are emancipated from their functional role. They were adopted by secular canons, who probably realized the amenity of such a place to pace up and down in before meeting in chapter. The earliest of these 'abstract' cloisters was built in Salisbury at the same time as the chapter-house, as a kind of forecourt and atrium to it. It would have been far simpler to have had just a covered way from the chapter-house to the church, as was done with much slighter means at York or Lichfield. Lincoln is an example of a chapter-house on the north side of a cathedral being associated with a cloister; whilst old St Paul's was unique in putting the chapter-house in the middle of a small cloister. Both thus confer new dignity on the chapter-house. It

209 York, 1280-95

*210   Wells Cathedral, from the east. The
chapter-house is not in its usual monastic
position, opening off the east walk of the
cloister, but, as with several English
secular cathedrals, is attached to the north
transept*

*211   Lincoln Cathedral, from the west. The
cloister is on the north side, but the chapter-
house is in the normal relation to it*

too is emancipated from its traditional role and becomes a room of state for the bishop and/or abbot, and his rival, the dean or prior. Wells is a special case, inasmuch as here the chapter-house is to the north, and the cloister to the south of the church, so that they forego even their connection with one another. It illustrates a tendency observable in many branches of high art – what has long been done of necessity, is ultimately done only for aesthetic effect. A thirteenth-century cathedral feels incomplete without the ancillaries of cloister and chapter-house.

I must deal once more with the abbatial/episcopal palace. In almost every case the prior kept his lodgings at the south-east of the cloister. The position reflected his sphere of duty; thence he could devote equal attention to monastic routine and administration, and to the sick. There was even space to lay out his own garden. Equally consistently, bishops laid out their palaces outside the monastery walls – where possible, as in Canterbury, to the west of the cathedral, for there by tradition lay the abbot's palace. It was still envisaged to the north in the St Gallen plan, and this variant was often adopted. In Cluny it lay in the west, associated with the guest-house, and this was retained in Westminster. Every abbey guide gives a sketch reconstructing the appearance of Westminster in the years immediately before its secularization by Henry VIII, that graphically shows dependence of buildings upon their historic use. The millrace, diverted from the Thames and flowing back into it, encloses a rectangle. Four gateways lead to bridges spanning it landwards and townwards. Within, five zones gird the abbey. Firstly, the monks' zone round the cloister (8), to which the chapter-house (7), frater (10), outward-facing kitchens (11), and the priory (12) belong. The sick-zone is closely attached to this in its usual place (16, 17). It has its own garden (18) in which, as on the plan of St Gall, medicinal herbs were particularly grown. The site of the infirmary is, as in most monasteries, part-determined

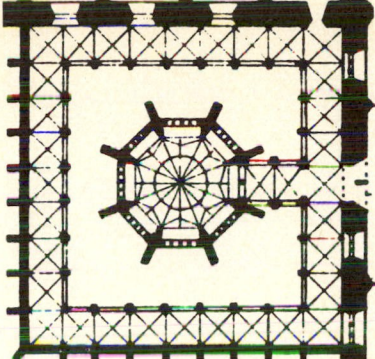

212, 213 At Old St Paul's, London, the chapter-house was placed uniquely inside the cloister itself. All trace of it was destroyed in the Fire, but seventeenth-century engravings (below) preserve its appearance

214 Salisbury Cathedral: cloister and chapter-house in their normal position, though there was no monastery

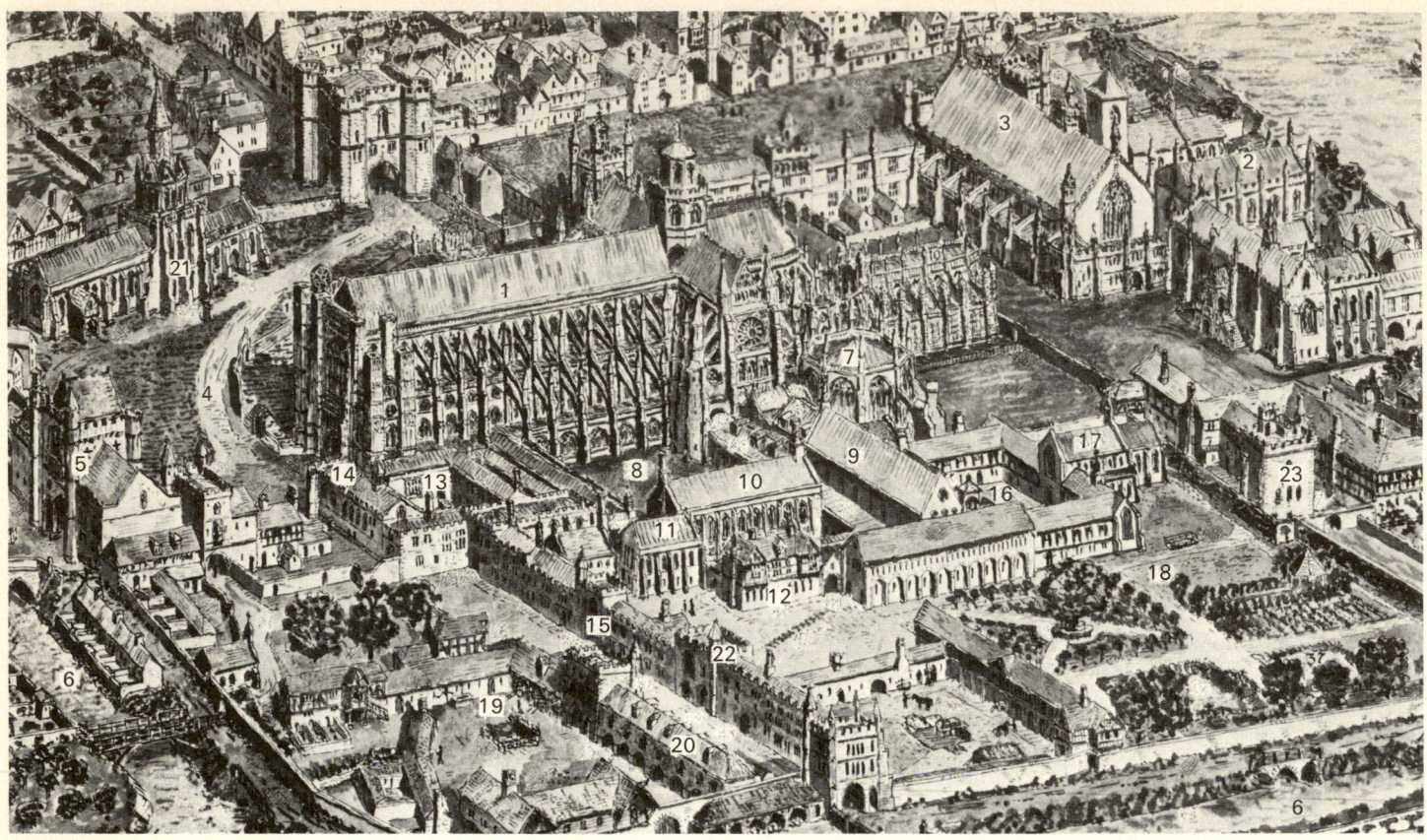

1 *Westminster Abbey*
2 *Palace of Westminster*
3 *Westminster Hall*
4 *Sanctuary*
5 *Gatehouse*
6 *Mill Stream*
7 *Chapter-house*
8 *Cloister*
9 *Dorter*
10 *Frater or Refectory*
11 *Kitchen*
12 *Prior's lodging*
13 *Abbot's lodging*
14 *Jerusalem chamber*
15 *Guest house*
16 *Infirmary cloister*
17 *St Katherine's Chapel*
18 *Infirmary garden*
19 *Home farm*
20 *Granary*
21 *Belfry*
22 *Grammar school*
23 *Jewel Tower*

215 *Westminster Abbey and Palace, a reconstruction as they probably appeared just before the Reformation*

by the proximity of the graveyard, which lay near the choir of the church. The third zone is that of the abbot (13, 14), associated with the guest- and school-buildings (15, 22), in front of the cloister to the west. It recalls the association of the abbatial palace, the school, and the range for distinguished visitors in St Gall. On the far side of the abbatial zone toward open country, one sees at the picture's lower edge the garth, with the home farm (19) and granary (20). This was the lowly end. At precisely the other end of the monastery, between the Thames and the church choir, one penetrated the royal zone, containing the Palace of Westminster (2) and Westminster Hall (3). This arrangement was the work of centuries. Prior (12), abbot (13) and king (2) built their house or palace on the exact spot where rank and function decreed it. One could go further, and complete this hierarchy of the monastery by including Christ, its Lord, in the church, and even more convincingly Mary, in the Lady Chapel. It is a religious body expressed in stone. In Westminster, as elsewhere, political, religious and practical considerations governed the putting of each building in its rightful place.

9

Monastic Republics, Cities, and Citadels

ABBEYS AS UNITS OF GOVERNMENT

The Cluniac, Cistercian and sundry other reform movements chiefly arose as a reaction against the kind of powerful and aristocratic establishment that had evolved its own version of communal life, which may indeed have been based on St Benedict's Rule, but that had so modified it as to allow for the special functions that these monastic cities, citadels and residences had assumed in and for the world. They governed territories, administered estates, served as royal and princely residences, acted as the strongpoints of a defensive system that harnessed both the defensive potential of their stone architecture and the spiritual might of Christianity and the watchfulness of the monks. Whereas a monastery's own role inclined its architecture towards unity, its worldly role impelled it toward diversity.

This applies even to reformed houses. It is still more the case with the free abbeys of Germany (*Reichsabteien*), the royal Spanish monasteries, the monastic cities of Italy and the monastic citadels of France. Fulda, St Gall, Lorsch, and St Emmeram come to mind when one speaks of this kind of state institution in the Middle Ages. Since the seventh and eighth centuries the Frankish abbots and the monastic leaders of England and Ireland had been great men who had taken over the direction of a monastery for the sake of secular power. Some of them were members of ruling houses. This also applies to the abbesses of aristocratic nunneries – Essen, Quedlinburg, Gandersheim, and in the southern Germanic lands, Zurich, Lindau and Buchau. Abbots and abbesses ruled great territories, and the external affairs of their abbeys tended to prevail over their internal affairs. Many monasteries usefully housed kings or emperors on their travels. They were often used by them as their residences – particularly in Spain, where the Escorial is the crowning instance of a monastery turned royal palace, and a royal palace turned monastery. Many monasteries are thus Janus-faced. The abbot's outward pomp and duties stand in contrast to the demeanour of the monks within. Monastic government was often beneficial to the country and its peasants, but also frequently pernicious, and we constantly hear of popular uprisings against it. Whilst the previous chapters have concentrated on describing the essentially conventual buildings of a monastery, we now turn to the accretions necessitated by their worldly obligations. The best results are achieved where the architecture is a successful synthesis of the two. The epitome of this is the fusion of monastic and defensive architecture on Mont-Saint-Michel.

The fate of a monastery as a political institution depended upon such factors as its geographical location, the favour of princes, and the ability of its abbots. The founding of monasteries is a rarely considered branch of surveying. All politically successful monasteries are in locations already favoured by nature. They dominate a mountain, a valley, the course of a river or an island. It has often been observed how well the monks installed themselves in the landscape that they colonized. More than towns and villages, comparable alone to, but often more systematically than forts and castles, the monasteries knew how to exploit the features of their situation in order to provide a suitable setting for what they built. 'In Bavaria', remarks Goethe at the break of the first day of his Italian Journey, 'one is straightaway confronted with the Abbey of Waldsassen – delicious possession of the religious, who were wise before other men. It lies in a saucer-, not to say bowl-like depression, amidst fine meadows and surrounded by gentle, fertile slopes. The monastery has possessions for miles around.' The architecture of the monastery is a monument to the discipline that won it its realm. The efficient is combined with the sacred, and the economically vital with the defensively useful.

Most monasteries lie well. Exceptional situations tempted their founders from the earliest Middle Ages. Whenever and wherever missionaries and monastic leaders renouncing the world explored virgin and uncharted land for a suitable location for a monastery, they always plumped for some unusual, and sometimes quite extraordinary site. Think of Weltenburg, of Reichenau, of Melk, or of the nunnery of Gandersheim. 'For the place was welcoming with its meadows and groves and, protected by thick woods and marshes, afforded great security to the dwelling of God's fair champion', we read of the foundation of Gandersheim in Thangmar of Hildesheim. Often it was the lonely beauties of Nature themselves that were read by princes, bishops and abbots as an encouragement to found a monastery out in the wilds. For what else could have prompted the numerous and repeated tales of apparitions of the Virgin in the course of a hunt, of eagles circling constantly over the same spot, and of the Crucified Christ revealing himself in a clearing? They were often places that had long been hallowed by an earlier cult of the Germans, Celts or Romans. Blaubeuren, by the Blautopf near Ulm, may be cited here as an example of a formerly sacred spring being converted into a monastery. The extraordinary natural phenomenon of the deep blue water was first interpreted as a sign of the presence of gods, and then as a pious challenge. In this case the external situation did not allow of further expansion. Nonetheless throughout the centuries patrons were found to favour the house. The sheer multiplicity of examples makes it impossible to formulate a law to cover the causes determining the political rise of a monastery. Wherever it occurred, it took shape as architecture. The result is the quite incomparable succession of monumental works of architecture that tower up in the open countryside. They testify no less to the numerous modes of highly civilized rural existence of a kind that could only have come about in the monasteries.

MONASTERY AND CITY

Not merely the restrictions of this survey, but also the desire to present a manageable picture, make it essential to illustrate the dependence of the physical appearance of a monastery upon its political role and status with but a few examples. We begin with the question of the relationship of town and monastery. What are the signs of the political and legal relationship of one with the other, and of which of the two had the upper hand? In the provinces of the Holy Roman Empire particularly, monasteries and towns strove for independent status, and were for this reason constantly intent on outflanking each other's rights.

We were able to point to numerous monasteries in the fifth to eighth centuries that were founded on the main roads into former Roman towns, or at any rate within their jurisdiction (*vide* p. 21). Such foundations were more frequent outside than inside the walls of a town. Paris, Lyon, and Le Mans are cases in point, as are Cologne, Trier and Regensburg. We can only assess the size and importance of a town in these centuries by the number of its monastic institutions. It was subsequently to fall to an ascendant bourgeoisie to incorporate these complexes within their ever more extensive town walls. For Merian at the beginning of the seventeenth century the importance of a town was still indicated

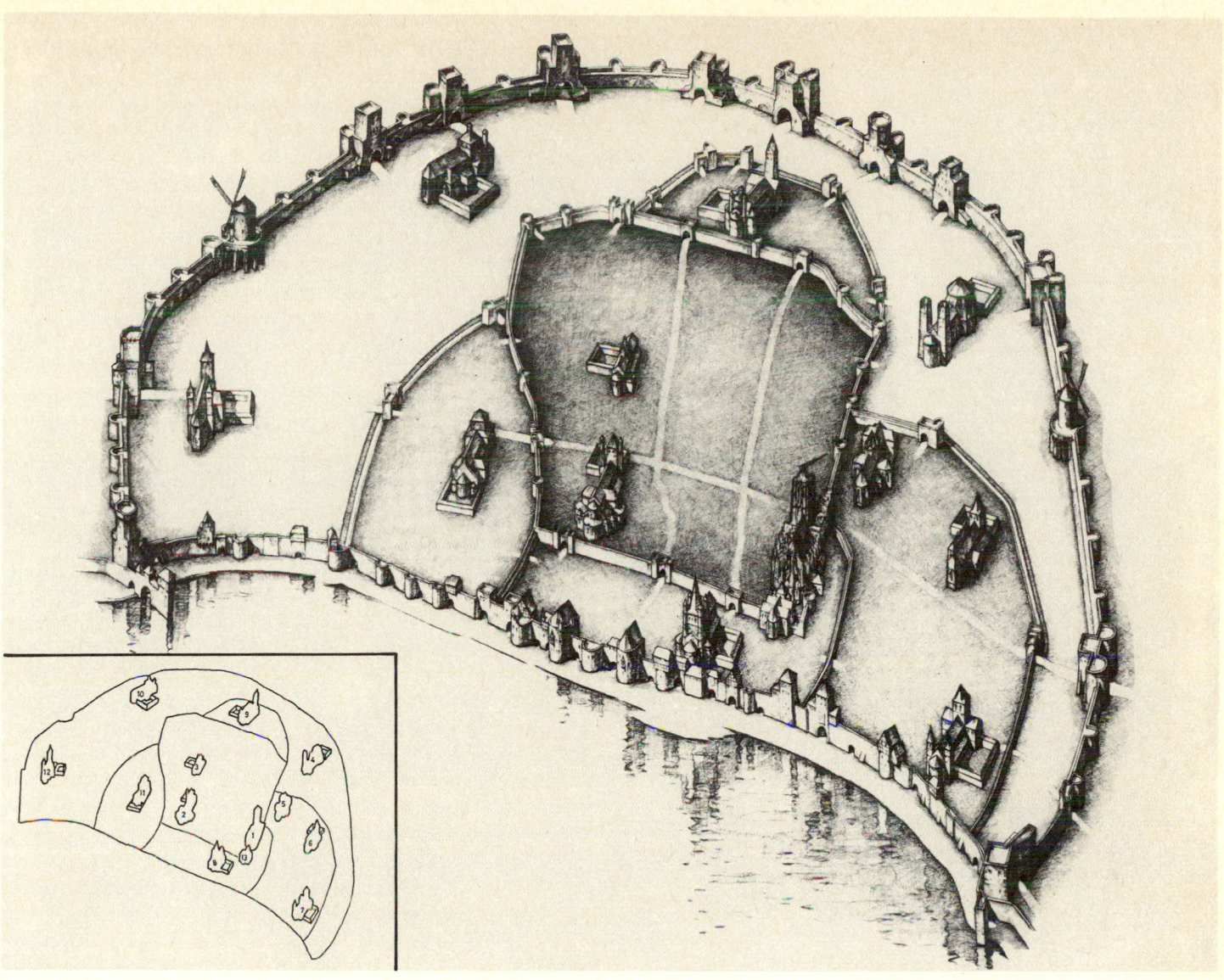

by the number of its monastic and other religious foundations and of its parishes. At that time Cologne was supreme in Germany. Furthermore where, as was the case in the Holy Roman Empire, new sees were created from the eighth to the eleventh century, their founders attempted to attract as many religious houses to them as possible. Bamberg, founded by the Emperor Henry II in 1007, is a famous instance of this. We saw similarly how later none of the large trading towns could do without a mendicant friary. The importance of these monastic complexes for the urban architecture of the Middle Ages cannot be too highly stressed. Along with the walls, the market-place and the cathedral precinct, they determined its appearance. When Anton Wonsam sketched his famous prospect of Cologne from the Rhine in 1531 he even aimed at making the old monastic and collegiate churches of the city visible when they would not have been apparent to the eye.[40] Churches were the crown of a city.

What was the political importance of monastic and other foundations in medieval and Renaissance towns? There were three possibilities: the town could control the monastery, monastery and town could exist in a constant state of tension, or the monastery might dominate the town. Each of these is immediately apparent from the town plan.

216 The monastic and collegiate churches of Cologne, redrawn from the sixteenth-century sketch by Anton Wonsam

1 *Cathedral*
2 *Maria im Kapitol*
3 *St Cecilia*
4 *St Gereon*
5 *St Andrew*
6 *St Ursula*
7 *St Kunibert*
8 *Great St Martin*
9 *Holy Apostles*
10 *St Pantaleon*
11 *St George*
12 *St Severin*
13 *St Maria ad gradus*

COLOGNE AS AN EXAMPLE

Let us take Cologne as an example of the first possibility. In 1180, even before knightly or mendicant Orders or the houses of the Carthusians and, centuries later, the Jesuits had further hemmed in the area of the townsfolk, the new town walls held thirteen, or counting St Heribert in Deutz, fourteen monasteries and collegiate foundations. The last to be founded was St Maria ad Gradus in 1075, before the death of St Anno. They were all suppressed by a stroke of the pen on 2 June 1802, some of them after more than a thousand years' existence. It is astonishing that between the eleventh and nineteenth centuries no further institution of the kind was added, nor did one of them dissolve. For the mendicant and knightly Orders created differently constituted ensembles. The fourteen complexes of buildings remained enduring components of the city's appearance. They consisted, apart from the cathedral chapter, of seven houses of canons, three of canonesses, and three Benedictine monasteries. Only four of them lay inside the old Roman walls: the cathedral, the college of St Andrew, and the female houses of Sts Cecilia and Maria im Kapitol. With the first enlargement of the town up to the Rhine in the tenth century, the Benedictine monastery of Great St Martin's was inserted into the densely built commercial quarter as a new religious centre. The Benedictine monastery of St Heribert in Deutz was the next to arise. The town grew by stealthily including the old monasteries and foundations within the compass of its walls, swallowing first of all St George to the south, then the Holy Apostles to the west, and St Ursula and St Kunibert to the north. Not till the final wall were the last three establishments incorporated: St Gereon, St Severin and the Benedictine St Pantaleon. It is well known that this wall of 1180 was never breached by any foe until 1791. The town and its religious houses could feel themselves safe behind its gates and towers. It seemed to have been built for eternity. For six hundred years there were no incursions. But during the whole of this time the city and the foundations had to strive to come to terms with one another.

Let us pick on one example, St Pantaleon, the oldest and largest Benedictine monastery in the city, which dominated the highest of the hills on the perimeter of the town. In addition to the abbey church with its Ottonian west-work and the tomb of the Empress Theophanu, the monastery possessed a second, parish church, a special hospice and one of the earliest cloisters (tenth or early eleventh century), of which bits survive, encased in the conventual buildings. It disposed, as the model shows, of its own gardens and vineyards. The enclosing walls denoted it as a place enjoying certain immunities. It never aspired to princely state; for it was not *reichsunmittelbar*, not immune from any jurisdiction but the Emperor's, like St Emmeram in Regensburg, which we shall discuss shortly. It enjoyed Cologne's rule of law, preserved its independence as an abbey, and attempted to maintain its special liberties against the rights of the city. St Pantaleon had the same obligations and privileges with respect to the city as each of the other thirteen foundations, with which it could vie in a contest as fruitful as that, in another way, of the great merchant-houses of the community. There were only limited possibilities of expansion. The main aim of the monastery was to hold onto what had been attained, and not to try and expand. Its atmosphere was one of well-balanced contentment, based on moderate wealth, moderate asceticism and unspectacular piety.

Ardour did not feature in the art of Cologne. Not one of the monasteries or other foundations felt called upon to replace their haphazard medieval buildings with Baroque show-pieces. They were content with piecemeal renovation. If one were to write the history of the monastic architecture of Cologne in the late and post-medieval era, its emphasis would lie on describing, besides what was built for new establishments, the process that led to the increasing autonomy of the dwellings of the individual canons or religious. In the end every monk of good family had his own set of rooms, and every canon his own residence. The cultural life of the city from the fifteenth to the eighteenth century was largely determined by commissions from these canons and canonesses. It is significant

217 *St Pantaleon, Cologne, the west front (c. 1000)*

that the two great museums of the city grew out of the bequests of two cathedral canons in the nineteenth and twentieth centuries – the Wallraf and the Schnütgen Collections.

The plan of Regensburg reflects a quite different situation. Until the secularization virtually half the land belonged, not only as property but also as territory, to four great ecclesiastical organizations that had succeeded in maintaining their sovereign status: the cathedral chapter, and the monasteries of St Emmeram, Obermünster and Niedermünster. But equally, since the twelfth century the citizens had managed to acquire and preserve the status of a free city of the Empire. It was a powerful commonwealth, whose declining foreign trade was at least to some extent compensated for after the sixteenth century by its choice as the location of the perpetual *Reichstag* (Imperial Diet). There were thus altogether five sovereign bodies co-existing behind a common city wall down the centuries. Each one of them, and the free abbey of St Emmeram above all the rest, had to support the state becoming to princes of the Empire. This called for greater efforts than in Cologne. Yet the balance of power ensured that one part could not challenge the others. This state of affairs gave rise to exceedingly tangled relationships between the monastic republics, the city and the bishop, and sometimes the Bavarian dukes as well. It is not the least of the causes behind Regensburg's being the finest surviving medieval German town, that many of these relationships were expressed as architecture – legal claims and nexuses in stone.

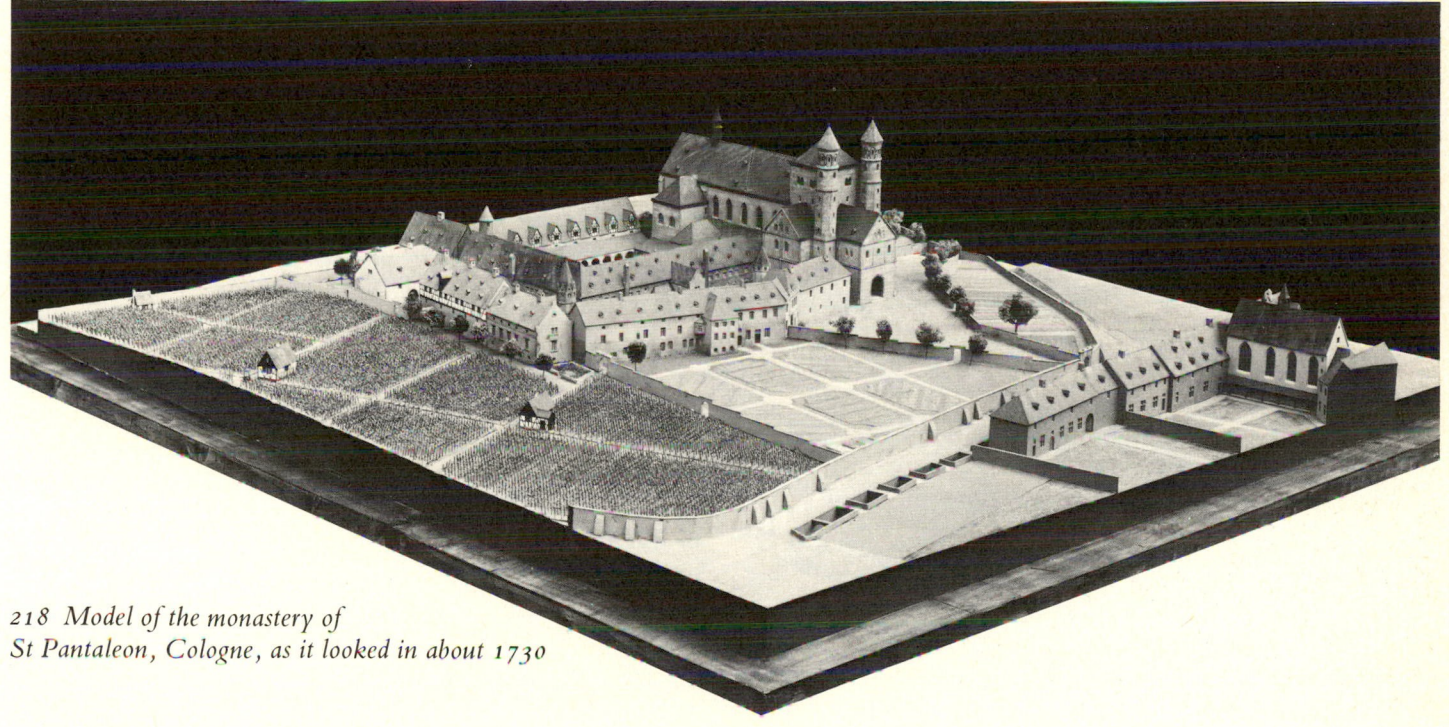

218 Model of the monastery of St Pantaleon, Cologne, as it looked in about 1730

SAINT-PHILIBERT IN TOURNUS

The situation was quite different in cases where a solitary monastery faced the growth of a parasite town that it could neither assert itself over, nor yet do without. There is a very large number of instances of towns developing out of settlements of menials and craftsmen outside a free-standing monastery, which attempted to define rights of their own against those of the monastery. This recurrent situation can be studied with the aid of the plan of the Abbey and town of Saint-Philibert in Tournus, whose layout has remained unchanged since the end of the Middle Ages. The monastery formed a walled zone to the north,

219 Tournus, France. Plan showing the Abbey in relation to the town walls and other public buildings
1 *St Philibert*
2 *Charité*
3 *St Valérien*
4 *St André*
5 *La Madeleine*
6 *Town Hall*
7 *Hospital*

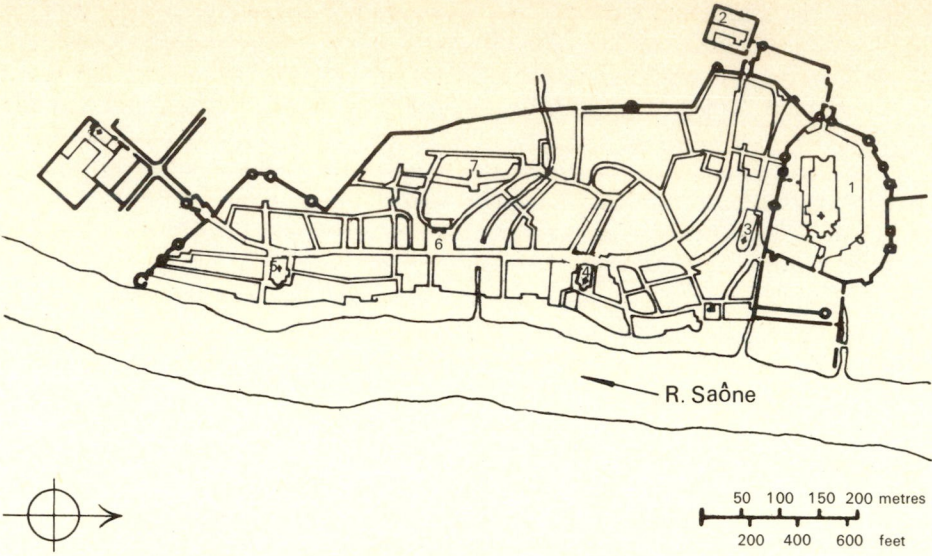

R. Saône

50 100 150 200 metres

200   400   600 feet

220 Tournus, view from the river, looking north-west

heavily fortified with defensive towers. The town evolved into an autonomous community in the south. The massive and lofty defensive works of the abbey, tightly enclosing the early Romanesque church towering above them and the zone of tranquillity round the cloister, made the most of the antithesis between two breeds of architecture. The effect is enhanced through the sweep of the walls against which the monastery nestles being set off by the broad expanse of the Saône. The innate grandeur of the church is accentuated by its insertion into the narrow confines of the fortifications. After the fifteenth century the superior authorities of the state saw to it that no further conflicts could develop. Yet the abbots were still concerned with keeping the fortifications in good repair.

ST GALLEN

An engraving by Merian of the town and abbey of St Gallen affords a more compelling sidelight upon an antagonism that was not to be resolved for centuries. Matthäus Merian relied here on the aerial plan of 1596 by Melchior Frank, whose slight errors he mostly repeated, but occasionally corrected. He must therefore have had more than this one source (Bibl. 53, Vol. II, pp. 47–65). Every chronicle of the town and the abbey can be read as if it were the legend to this engraving. One only needs the additional knowledge that the land round the town belonged to the sovereign territory of the abbot – that town and abbey were held in each other's grip. They had to come to terms with one another.

The picture presented by the monastery to the south-west of the town shows that no more than the rudiments of the Carolingian plan were realized. The abbey precincts were set apart from the town in 1566 by the so-called partition wall, following in essentials the line of the old walls of the abbey. Furthermore, the abbot upheld his right to his own gateway breaching the town walls, the Karlstor to the south. As early as 953, Abbot Anno arranged to protect the *famuli* of the abbey settled around it with defensive works that probably took in the whole area subsequently occupied by the old town. At that time there were no limits to the abbey's authority over the settlers in its service. In the course of the thirteenth century the townsfolk were able to negotiate for themselves a degree of independence. At the end of the fourteenth century they extended their town by a suburb to the north. The rise of the town was fostered by a decline of the abbey at the beginning of the fifteenth century, such that in 1411 it held no more than two monks, one of whom had nominated himself abbot and the other prior. The decision shortly afterward to allow burghers' sons to profess led to the abbey's rapid recovery. In 1489 under the commoner Abbot Ulrich Rösch from Wangen, it was proposed to transfer the monastery out to Rorschach; but this came to nothing through the opposition of the townsfolk. But the latter accepted the Reformation with immoderate haste. Conflicts over the authority of the abbey played their part in this. A passionate bout of iconoclasm, made notorious by a thorough description, destroyed the artistic treasures of the town and the abbey in 1527. Fresh attempts were made thereafter to come to some *modus vivendi*. In the eighteenth century the abbey was once again so powerful that it was enabled to put up one of the finest groups of public buildings in the Baroque within the narrow confines of the old walls, including ranges for the monks, a prelatial palace, and the abbey church. It would be a mistake to single out the genius of the artists, the building mania of the abbots or the princely pretensions of their patronage as the occasion of these cultural endeavours: they were required by the constitutional position of the abbey. It had to declare its status in the parlance of the eighteenth century.

Looking at the sixteenth-century monastic precinct on its own, it is apparent that the church lay to the east of the oval, and the conventual buildings were grouped round the southern cloister. The abbot's palace, the old *palatium*, lay in the centre of the monastic complex. The town itself had appreciated the wisdom of having only one narrow door, mostly kept locked, maintaining the connection between the abbey and the town proper. The Protestant townsfolk lived asunder from the Catholic monks. The town-hall (E), grouped with the civic slaughterhouse (G), and granary (F), formed a deliberate counter-point to the abbey church at the end of the great market. The town boasted two parish churches, the earlier St Lorenz directly outside the abbey gates, and St Mang in the extreme north. There was also the small Beguine convent of St Katharina (I),

221 St Gallen, bird's-eye view of the town and monastery before the eighteenth-century rebuilding

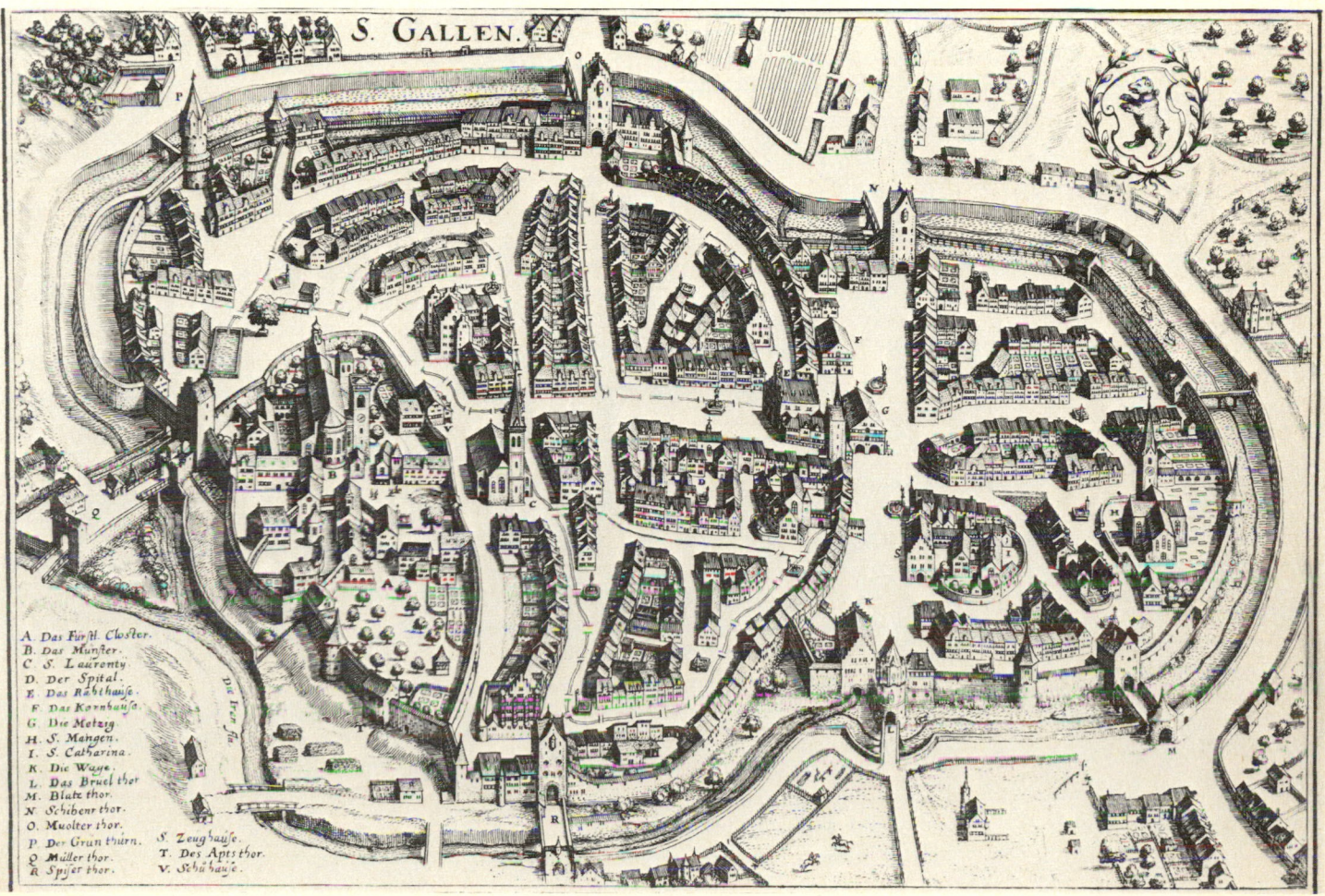

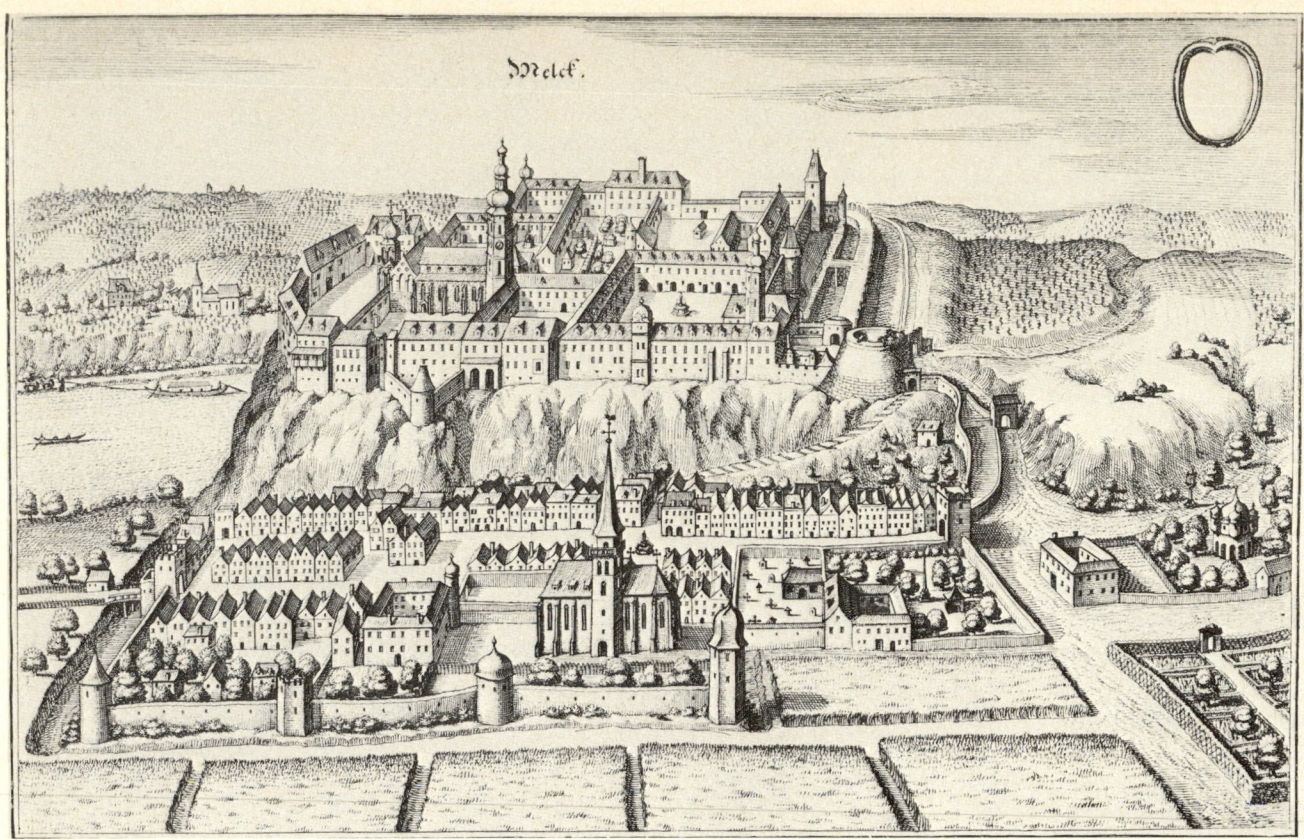

222 *Melk. View from the south of the earlier monastery, at the beginning of the seventeenth century*

whose handful of inmates heroically resisted the suppression of their establishment by the Reformers from 1526 to 1555. Only the local school (V), right up against the abbey walls, seems to embody an older tradition, under which all instruction lay in the hands of the abbey. We have substantial proof that the abbey was constantly enhanced by piecemeal additions within its precincts before it embarked in 1755 on the famous campaign of total reconstruction, fifty years exactly before its dissolution by the decree of the Great Council of 5 May 1805. In 1755, as with the Carolingian plan of 820, circumstances prevented the realization of a self-sufficient monastic community down to the last detail, such as we encounter in Weingarten or Ottobeuren.

MELK

St Gallen is the monument to a conflict which issued in the victory of the younger institution of the town over the older one of the abbey. Things took a quite different course where a monastery had evolved out of a castle on a rocky outcrop. In all such cases so long as the monastery survived as an agent of government, it maintained its sway over the civil settlement.

The case was similar with the episcopal sees of the Holy Roman Empire. If one examines their political fate before secularization, it emerges that wherever the bishop possessed a castle overlooking the town, he was able to assert his suzerainty over the rising commons, whereas where the lie of the land ruled out a stronghold he was beaten off in the short or the long run. Thus, Würzburg, Bamberg, Eichstädt, Passau, Freising, Chur and, surpassing all the others, the incomparable Salzburg, all remained under the bishop's temporal rule. The commons prevailed in Cologne, Worms, Speyer, Strasbourg, Basle and Augsburg. There were also towns, of which we have seen that Regensburg was an example, where circumstances forced bishop and free city into a prickly co-

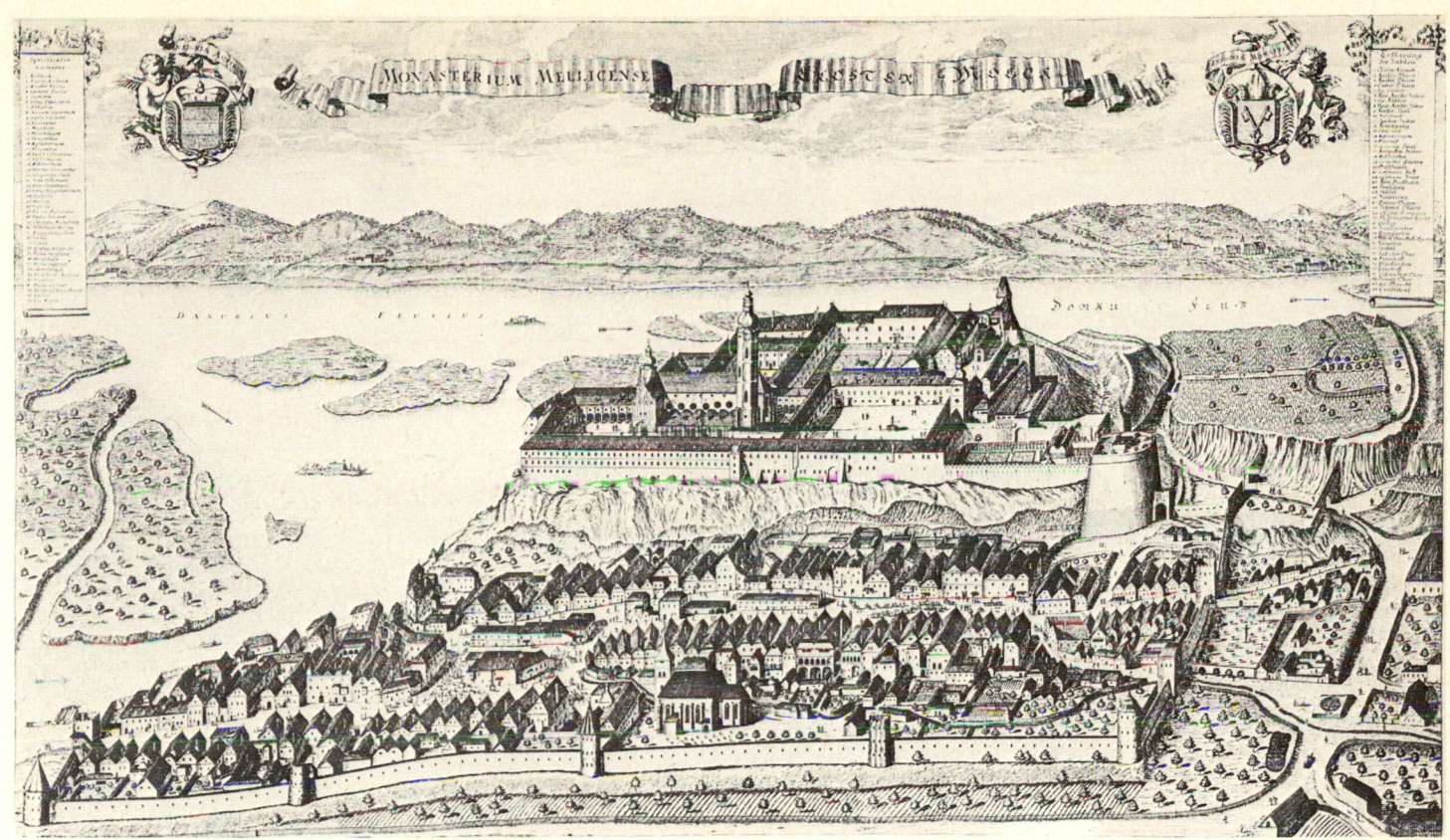

223 Melk. View from the same direction, showing the monastery about a hundred years later

existence. This general rule, that a stronghold was vital for supremacy in or over a town, is also applicable to monastic settlements, though these rarely grew to be good-size towns.

Melk is a case in point. The monastic village, and later town, never really had a chance against the impregnable monastery on its escarpment. This began as the castle appointed by the Babenbergs after the Battle of the Lech, with the sure eye of that age for the advantages of a site. Leopold I is reputed to have planted a house of canons within it. Leopold II found that he could shift his seat further eastwards along the bleak rock. He handed over his old castle to the Benedictines. It had a splendid career, withstanding several sieges, finishing up by beating off the Turks. It is also one of the few monasteries in Europe never to have been secularized. The Melk Reform of 1418 assured it of new life in a time of general decline. From the late sixteenth century onwards numerous energetic abbots did much for its prosperity and buildings, culminating in Abbot Berthold Dietmayr (1700-33), who in 1702 commissioned from Prandtauer the grandiose reconstruction that we admire today, the most important Baroque monastery to be so sited.

Both Merian's engraving from the beginning of the seventeenth century and that of Pfeffel and Engelbrecht from the beginning of the eighteenth disclose that the High Baroque abbey made use of existing elements of the plan in its layout. The rudiments of a solution were at hand (*v.i.* p. 209). The two engravings together show the expansion of town and monastery in the half-century after the Thirty Years' War. The table of the mountain is wholly covered by monastic courts and ranges. The land falls away in sheer cliffs on every side. A powerful round tower protects and envelops the sole entrance. The town was fortified as well, but the people knew that true safety was only to be found inside the abbey walls. They lived in the keeping, in the shadow, and in the refulgence of the abbey. Their dependence is reflected in the shape of their churches, their houses,

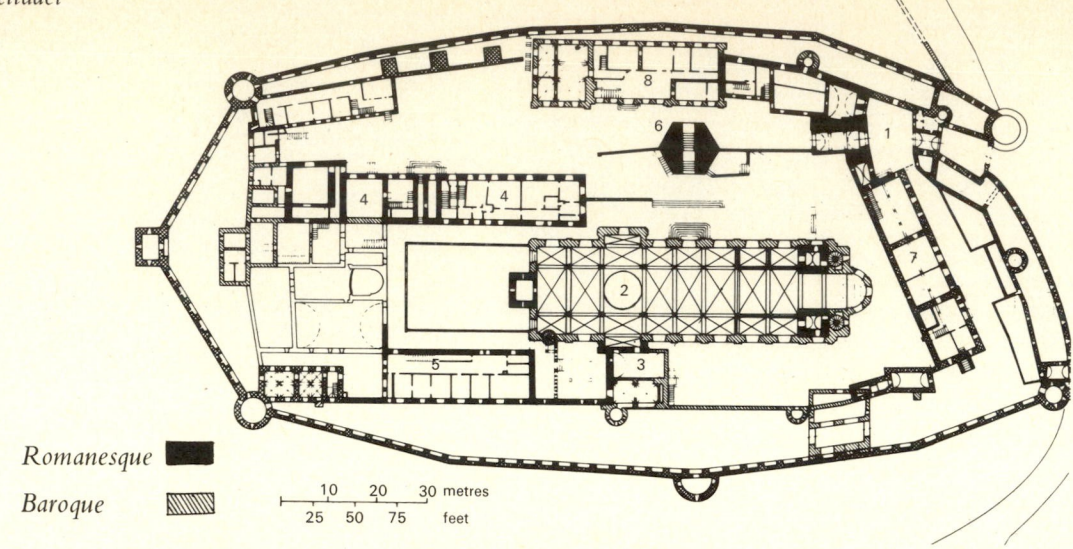

224 Gross-Comburg, a monastic citadel
1 *Gateway*
2 *Church*
3 *Chapter-house*
4 *Dorter*
5 *Refectory*
6 *Mortuary chapel*
7 *Guest-house*
8 *Abbot's palace*

Romanesque

Baroque

and in the course of their streets. Only the abbey might indulge in monumental architecture. The complex must have looked magnificent even in the Middle Ages. The Gothic church, consecrated in 1429, was itself ambitious. The Margraves, and later the Emperors, made important contributions to its decoration. Improvements were made to the existing complex for almost seven hundred years, before the High Baroque transfigured this mixture of the pragmatic and the awe-inspiring in a grand design.

GROSS-COMBURG

One characteristic of such sites from first to last was that the church was set in the centre of the conventual buildings. The monastic ranges were displaced to the edge of the declivity, and the church commanded the open courtyard in the centre. Many medieval sites are similar in this respect. The best surviving example is supplied by Gross-Comburg. Like Melk, it is one of a large number of castles that were endowed by rulers as monastic foundations in the course of the religious revival most fervently promoted by Cluny and Hirsau. The impetus was given by Conrad II's endowment of Limburg on the Hardt in 1025, following his election as Emperor. Lambach followed in 1056, Banz in 1069. The latter was endowed by Countess Alberade of Schweinfurt. Comburg was founded between 1075 and 1081 by Count Burkhard of Rothenburg and Comburg. St Paul im Lavanttal was endowed by Counts Engelbert I and Richard of Spanheim, Neresheim in 1106 by Count Hartmann I of Dillingen and his consort. Bishops also instituted monasteries in several of the castles in their possession. An outstanding example is Siegburg near Cologne, which Anno II made over to the Benedictines in 1064. On none of these hilltops or plateaux could the Benedictine monastic schema come to full fruition. The cloister and conventual buildings had either to be placed to the north of the church, as in Limburg, Melk, or Lambach, or by its eastern apse, as in Lorsch, Kastl, or Heiligenberg, or even, as at Comburg, by its western apse.

The early history of Comburg Abbey casts light upon the problems peculiar to such foundations. The castle belonged to four brothers, one of whom, as a cleric of Würzburg, renounced his inheritance, whilst the eldest got the family seat of Rothenburg, leaving the other two, as partisans of Pope and Emperor respectively, to feud within their common castle. Whilst the Ghibelline Rugger was on a journey to Rome in 1081, the Guelf Burkhard overran the whole castle, endowed a monastery there which he himself entered, allied himself to the powerful Archbishop of Mainz, gave the direction of the monastery to its founding abbot, a monk called Gunter from Hirsau, who regained the trust of the Imperial House, and set about the construction of church and conventual buildings. Rugger had to accept the *fait accompli*. Under Abbot Hartwig (1104-39) the abbey had a halcyon period that left its mark architecturally. Emperors came to like sojourning there, like Conrad III over Christmas 1140 and Henry VI in 1191. One look at the plan shows that the defensive walls were frequently moved outward in the course of its history. In 1488 the monks were replaced by an aristocratic house of canons, and in 1494 the provost, Seyfried vom Holtz, put up a second wall at the east end, and reinforced the first with round towers. The third defensive wall, which survives almost in its entirety, was put up in 1562-75. This is a late Gothic example with an elevated defensive passage without gun emplacements, whose military value was thus slight even at the time it was built. However, it looks imposing.

Comburg too had only one entrance. It lies in the east, and leads through a defensive gate containing a chapel dedicated to St Michael above. On entering one sees the great church to the left, and before one the singular hexagonal Romanesque building used as an ossuary and Chapel of the Dead,[41] and to the right the guesthouse. Domestic buildings and stables link up with the side of the gatehouse. This layout may go back to comparable buildings in the baronial castle. It is only logical that the conventual buildings should be disposed round the cloister on the most sheltered and protected side west of the church, opposite that of the entrance. The chapter-house thus lay directly alongside the southern transept of the church. Dorter, refectory, abbatial buildings and kitchens lay round the court. The foundation stayed poor. On account of its poverty it was even spared by the peasants in the general uprising of 1525. Renovation was always provided for by donations. But even the Baroque hardly laid hands on the disposition of the buildings. As in Banz, their castellar character was not just preserved, but consistently brought out, not without an eye for their romantic beauty. This effect was appreciated just as much in the Middle Ages as in the Baroque.

225 Gross-Comburg, from the south-east, dominating the little town at its foot

226 *St Michael appeared in a dream to St Aubert, Bishop of Avranches, and commanded him to build him a sanctuary on the rock of Mont-Saint-Michel. In order that the bishop might remember, the archangel tapped him on the head, leaving a neat hole in his skull. Illustration from a twelfth-century manuscript*

227 *Mont-Saint-Michel, section through La Merveille, looking east. At ground level is the cellar, above that the Salle des Chevaliers and above that the cloister with the refectory (formerly dorter) behind it. The church is on the right*

MONT-SAINT-MICHEL

This applies even more strongly to the most important architecturally of the medieval castellar monasteries – Mont-Saint-Michel. On the face of it this 250 feet high cone of rock rising sheer out of the sea only invited a hermitage, and not a monastery at all. In 708 St Aubert, Bishop of Avranches, was vouchsafed an apparition of the Archangel Michael on the former Celtic funeral mount which in those days was still clothed in woods. He drew on the cult in San Galgano, begged relics from there, and put up an oratory as a goal for pilgrimages. It was to be served by monks living in single cells scattered round the cone. Almost two hundred years later the Dukes of Normandy saw that it was necessary to tighten up the organization of the cult and the pilgrim traffic. Hence a Benedictine monastery arose in 966, housing at first thirty, then forty, and by the thirteenth century sixty monks. For centuries the Benedictines exerted themselves to encase the cone layerwise with what there was no room for on the level. Progress was constantly endangered by fires, landslips, and the collapse of buildings. A military role in wars with England played its part. Every reverse only led to an improved solution. The idea of combining the monastery with a castle, a sanctuary and the seat of a knightly Order proved viable. Thus emerged a paradigm of medieval architecture, exaltedly conceived of as such by its builders, and tenderly amplified and preserved down the centuries, until the French Revolution abused even this. The abbey became a prison.

In 1966 the French *Monuments Historiques* put on a millenary exhibition round the holy mount. It afforded the opportunity of presenting the work of restoration done in successive campaigns since 1872. It attempted the almost hopeless task of using maps and models to present the visitor with the layers of the abbey analysed on the one hand historically, and on the other hand topographically. Here, it was possible to draw on the plans and sections done by the first restorer E. Corroyer in 1872. Building never ceased on this abbey. Numerous rulers felt bound to support building ventures; numerous abbots succumbed to the temptation of indulging thoughts of the practicability of aggrandisement. Three great campaigns of building stand out from the rest and govern its present-day appearance. Let us call them the abbey of the Norman dukes, the abbey of the English kings, and the abbey of the French kings. The first campaign was responsible for the pre-Romanesque abbey of the tenth century and the early Romanesque one of the eleventh, the second for the Romanesque abbey of the twelfth century, and the third for the Gothic abbey of the thirteenth, admiringly called *La Merveille*.

The tenth-century monks constructed the seven-bayed church of Notre-Dame-sous-Terre over St Aubert's round oratory on the highest point of the conical rock, and laid out the conventual buildings on three floors to the north of it by the entry. The guest-rooms were underneath, and above them the two-aisled *promenoir* in lieu of a cloister, a small library and the refectory, and on top the dorter. We have then a tall building set against the foot of the rock and climbing to its peak. The importance of Mont-Saint-Michel as an abbey and as a fortress steadily increased with the rise of the Norman duchy, its conquest of England in 1066 and the union of Kingdom and duchy. The eleventh century built its great Norman abbey on the summit, over Notre-Dame-sous-Terre, but parts of it upon all-too daring substructures constantly collapsed. The cone must be visualized as entirely encased in monastic buildings by 1100; a stone cloak with the church for hood.

The High Romanesque monastery of the twelfth century is the work of the Abbot Robert de Torigni (1154–86), a friend, counsellor and kinsman of Henry II of England. In a considered attempt to exploit the site more rationally, the entry of the abbey was transferred from the north-west to the south-west in 1180. The old three-storied conventual building was complemented by a new one, containing the guest-house, the infirmary, the abbot's palace, and a court-room. At the same time the church was given a twin-towered façade, in whose portico the abbot found his last resting-place. It was later torn down.

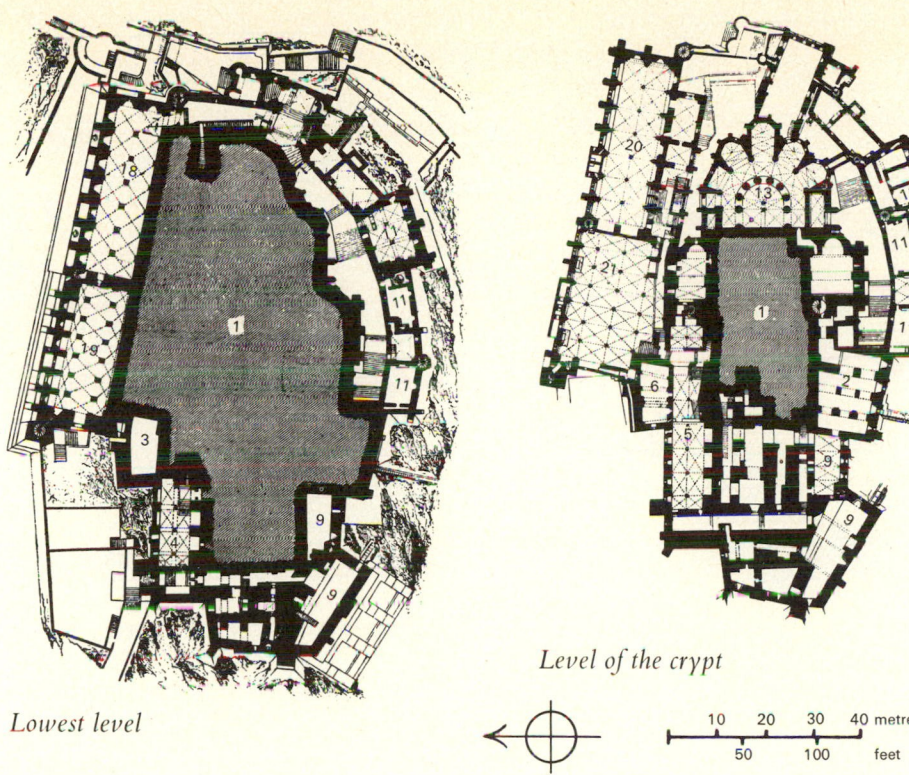
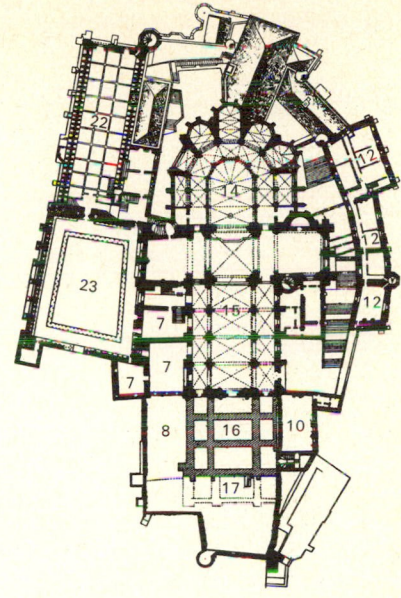

Level of the crypt

Level of the church

Lowest level

10 20 30 40 metres

50 100 feet

228 Mont-Saint-Michel

The overall character of the abbey was altered by the institution of the Brotherhood of Saint-Michel-de-la-Mer in 1210. From Philip Augustus through Saint Louis to Philip the Fair possession of the place was regarded as crucial by the French monarchy. Knightly elements took their place beside monastic ones. Abbot Jourdain began the work of aggrandisement in 1206. Abbot Raoul des Isles (*ob.* 1228) completed *La Merveille*, Abbot Richard Tourstin shifted the entry to its present place in the north-east, and hemmed in the way to the choir and the south side of the church with administrative buildings, palaces for guests and a new seat for the abbot. It was left to the fourteenth and fifteenth centuries to build up the defences. The *Merveille* comprises everything in the great tract to the north-east: the pilgrim hostel and cellar in the ground floor, the refectory and admirable knights' hall in the floor above this, and on top the dorter[42] and the new cloister. By the death of the abbot in 1228 these buildings were finished, characteristic expressions of the new 'Royal Gothic' of the Île de France in their soaring height and in the delicacy of their details. Whilst their precursors had always had three storeys, deliberate play was now made with the artistic possibilities of this sequence. The palace was the scenario for the legendary defence of the mount against the English armies by Louis d'Estouteville and his 119 knights in 1425, a defence that came to rank with Joan of Arc alone as a symbol of resistance.

The architecture had been so contrived that monastic life could go on undisturbed throughout these warlike upheavals. The monks had brought together on the top floor everything requisite for conventual life. Church, cloister and dormitory lay on one level. Only for meals did they have to descend a storey, to where the refectory and kitchens lay in front of the knights' hall, which were in turn supplied from the cellars beneath. There was even a room for the sick on the highest floor. Only the chapter-house was not executed as planned. Thus whereas the entrance was moved about three times, the monastery buildings retained their original place in the north-east, and were ever more adventurously constructed.

1	Solid rock	
2	Notre-Dame-sous-Terre	*Remains of*
3	Site of kitchen	*the first*
4	Crypt de l'Aquilon	*monastic*
5	Promenoir	*buildings*
6	Site of refectory	*(eleventh*
7	Site of claustral buildings	*century)*
8	Site of dorter	
9	Site of administrative offices, abbot's apartments, guests' lodgings, etc.	*South-western range built by Torigni (twelfth century, destroyed)*
10	Site of infirmary	
11	Abbot's apartments	*Thirteenth-century south range built by Tourstin*
12	Guests' lodgings	
13	Crypt des Gros Piliers	
14	Choir	
15	Nave	
16	Site of demolished west end of nave	*The church*
17	Site of old west front	
18	'Almonry', pilgrims' hostel	
19	Cellar	
20	Old refectory ('Salle des hotes')	
21	Knights' Hall ('Salle des chevaliers')	*La Merveille*
22	Old dorter (later refectory)	
23	Cloister	

229 *Mont–Saint–Michel, three parts of La Merveille. Right: the former dorter, later refectory*

230 *The cloister, with on the left the entrance to the dorter*

231 *The Salle des Chevaliers*

*232 Mont-Saint-Michel from the east. The central mass is the church,
that to the right La Merveille*

233 *San Giorgio Maggiore, the island monastery of Venice, by Palladio*

SANTA MARIA POMPOSA

In Italy, where urban life survived or soon recovered after the Fall of the Empire, monasteries had far less chance of turning into sovereign institutions than in the town-free Holy Roman Empire. The right of the flourishing urban communities, such as the maritime cities of Venice, Pisa and Genoa since the eleventh century, the Lombard towns since the twelfth, and Florence, Siena and Lucca in Tuscany since the thirteenth century, to exercise full administrative power over the monasteries within their walls, and mostly over those built on their territory as well, was never in question. The monasteries did possess special immunities, like every ecclesiastical institution in this period. Abbots and popular preachers sometimes managed to acquire worldly as well as spiritual power. Only exceptionally did the monasteries have any political influence. In no case is their prominence in the urban scene expressive of such influence. Never, since the twelfth century, had they owned territories on which men lived as their subjects. They certainly represented sanctuaries which the municipal bailiffs might not penetrate, but no-one was checked by such immunity on crucial occasions. Even a monastery so commandingly isolated as San Giorgio Maggiore, before the entry to San Marco in Venice, was never effectively fortified, and never laid claim to any degree of autonomy. Its extensive buildings were not on this account any the less impressive in their monumentality; but they were the expression of a demanding and deeply serious artistic intent, not of political power. The only exceptions to this in Italy are a few foundations from the early centuries that were singled out as free abbeys by the favour of the German Emperors. Santa Maria Pomposa is the best surviving example of one of these.

The abbey belongs to a string of urban refuges, in which remnants of the Roman population, from Ravenna in the south to Grado in the north, sought rescue from the pursuing Germans. In common with many of these, it has an atmosphere of forlornness amidst uninhabitable wastes, which guaranteed them from molestation. In the sixth century the Benedictines founded a monastery in the Po delta, which was promised a flourishing future by extensive cultivation of land reclaimed from forest. The first certain record of it is actually in a letter of 874 from Pope John VIII to the Emperor Louis II. The abbey won its independence through the favour of the Ottonian Emperors. In 1045 it was overlord of a considerable area between the Po, the Gauro, and the sea. It had other estates beyond this 'island'. This was its apogee. The high campanile that surveyed its whole realm was a token of its power. The church was decorated with exceptional lavishness. Of the conventual buildings, the chapter-house, the refectory, and remains of the dorter survive from round the vanished cloister. They are successors to the original buildings, whilst preserving an arrangement that probably goes back to the tenth or eleventh centuries. It is known that the whole complex was surrounded by a high wall which also had room for numerous buildings for guests and outhouses.

The *grandezza* of the whole is astonishing, but most remarkable is the long, narrow *Palazzo della Ragione* set in front of the monastic buildings to the west. It dates from the thirteenth century, but its original features have been distorted by restorations. The site as a whole is as authentic as it is distinctive. What we have is a large building serving as the administrative seat of the abbot and overlord, which accordingly faces outward from its position in the west of the site, though also opening inward toward the church by means of a loggia. With this building the abbey vied with the communes; it embodies the claim to lordship and suggests the abbot's princely status. It informs strangers that the abbey claimed to be a state in its own right. Its size, and its position and distance with regard to the church betokened the dignity it sought to convey.

An abbey with territorial rights was the exception in Italy. It formed one of the institutions of imperial Italy, and shared the latter's decline. Farfa, the most powerful of them, ought to be mentioned at this point. There were of course country abbeys that for a time possessed great worldly authority; we encountered them in our chapter on Cistercian houses. Others again played important

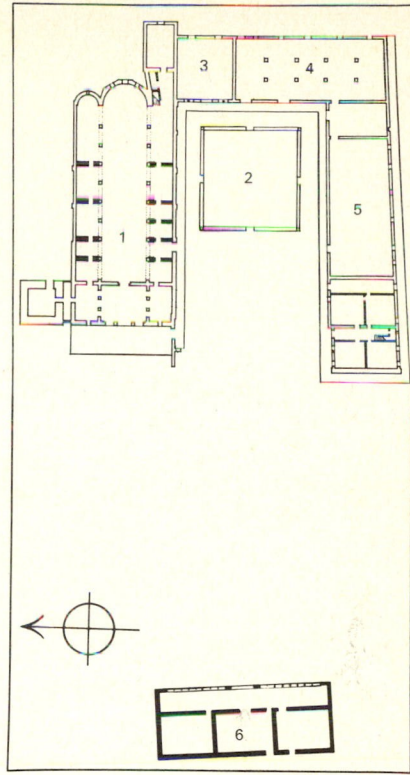

234 *Santa Maria Pomposa, plan*
1 *Church*
2 *Cloister*
3 *Chapter-house*
4 *Dorter (above)*
5 *Refectory*
6 *Palazzo della Ragione*

235 *Santa Maria Pomposa from the air, looking north. The block on the left is the much altered Palazzo della Ragione*

236 *Monreale, Sicily. The fountain and the corner of the cloister. Founded by William II in 1174*

237 *The Superga, on a hill outside Turin. Founded as a mausoleum for the Piedmontese royal family and completed by Juvara in 1731*

roles in the cultural life of their country for short intervals as royal abbeys, that is to say as royal seats or foundations, which found expression in their architecture. They were never very many. But they range from Monreale near Palermo, endowed by the Norman Prince William II in 1174, to the Superga above Turin, completed by Juvara in 1731 as the mausoleum of the royal house of Piedmont and as a memorial to Prince Eugene's victory of 1706 over the French. In both cases the monastic buildings efface themselves beside the church, whilst the incomparable cloister of Palermo is more a piece of princely patronage of the arts, than a gallery for the monks. The unheard-of elaboration of the shafts of the columns and of the capitals, especially of those round the fountain-pavilion, arises from the synthesis of a Western motif with Islamic refinement, using the resources of Norman art. There was a state residence in Monreale too. In a world in which every political organization modelled itself upon the idea of the godly state, a foundation such as Monreale can be described as a government manifesto. The monastic court breaks free and becomes a monument to princely statecraft.

SPANISH MONASTERIES AS ROYAL RESIDENCES

An entirely different picture is presented by surveying a series of major Spanish and Portuguese monasteries. Spain has always been a monarchical country. In no other part of Europe did the monarchy possess such all-pervasive influence. This has to do with the fact that its kings were the supreme champions of the *Reconquista*. Wherever Islam was thrust back, monasteries instantly sprang up for the spiritual, and often the military, security of the conquered areas. Many of these monasteries were also fortresses. The kings built residences in several of them. The conjunction of monasteries and royal palaces did not remain peculiar to the Iberian peninsula, but it became a distinctive feature of it. It is not legitimate to compare this with the imperial apartments, halls, and ranges in the free abbeys of Germany. These were built by the abbeys for the Emperor, and were a sign that an abbey felt it owed allegiance to none but him. They symbolized its liberties. In Spain, kings endowed monasteries with their palaces. And this was symptomatic of a monastery's dependence on the monarchy. The monks subserved the royal power.

OVIEDO

Let us take a few examples out of many. Oviedo, the capital of the Asturias, is dominated by a group of buildings composed of the royal palace, episcopal seat, abbey and other ecclesiastical foundations. Its founder, King Fruela (b. 722, ruled 757-68), adorned his residence with both the Abbey of San Vicente and the Cathedral of San Salvador. As in many early towns, abbot and bishop were one. After the murder of Fruela, his successor Silo (774-83) moved his residence to Santiana de Pravia. Fruela's son, Alfonso the Chaste (791-812), refounded Oviedo. Conscious of the threat from the Arabs, he fortified not only the town but also the area containing the residence and its ecclesiastical ancillaries. Within the narrow confines of the wall stood the rebuilt palace, the enlarged cathedral, a church dedicated to the Virgin, containing the vaults of the kings, the chapels of Santa Leocadia and San Juan, and a royal nunnery. Everything that it was thought desirable should be spared from the upheavals of the time was concentrated in the '*antigua acrópolis religioso-politica*'. This set a precedent that was to provoke imaginative contrivance for centuries.

CISTERCIAN ABBEYS AS RESIDENCES

Oviedo originated as a palace and cathedral. The religious houses were subsequent additions to its spiritual core. They then gained in administrative importance, for the royal chanceries frequently drew on them for secretaries. But in the later Middle Ages the process was to be the other way round. Monastic establishments came first. The kings who had sponsored them then sometimes added a palace. The court went about its business in the lee of a monastery, whose piety

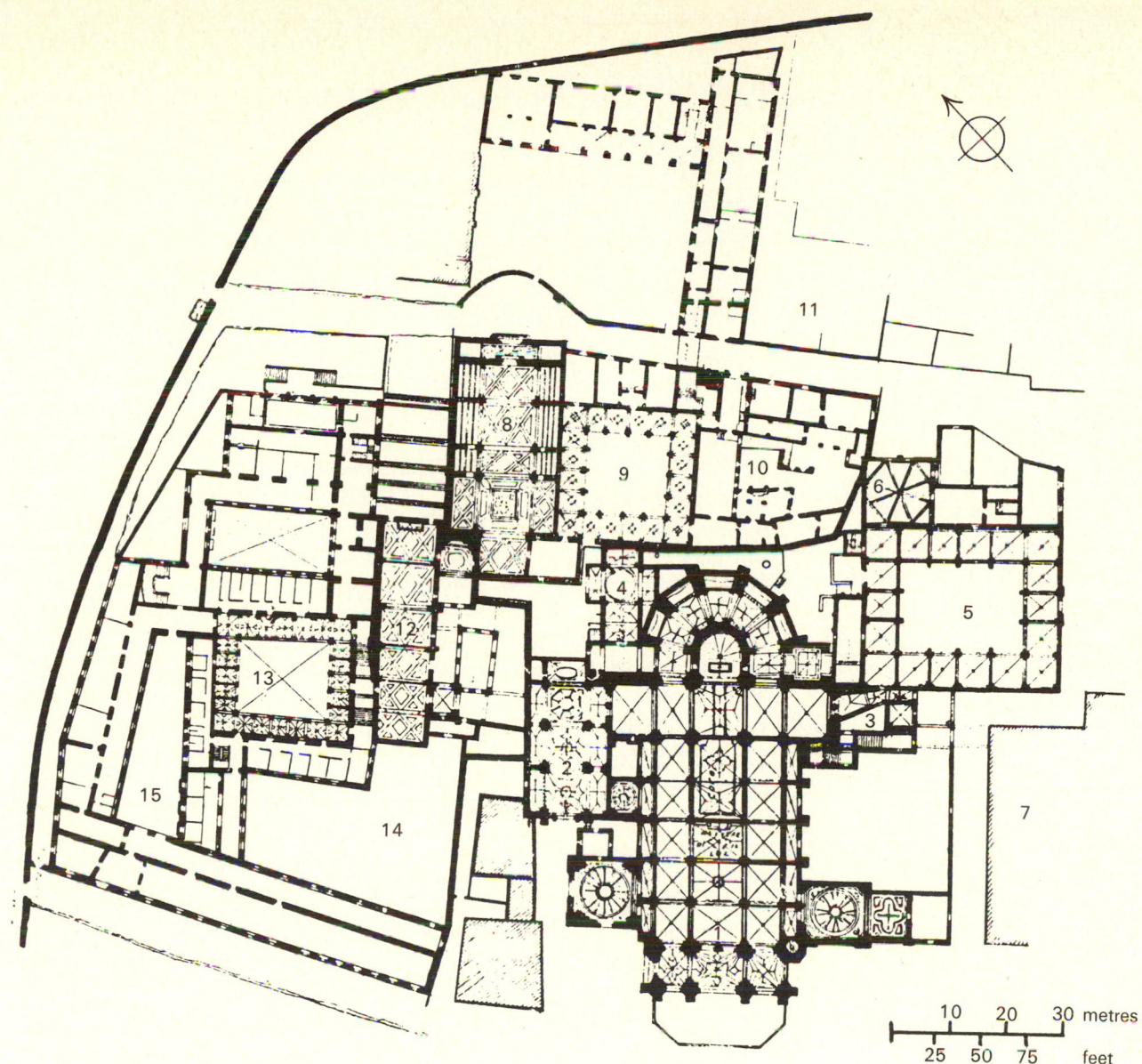

238 Oviedo, Spain. The complex of abbey-cathedral-palace founded by King Fruela in the eighth century

affected its way of life. In spite of his rank, and without forfeiting any of his rights, the king sometimes wanted to feel a monk like other monks. This is embodied in the three Cistercian abbeys that were more successful in achieving political importance than any others. They are the abbeys of Santas Creus and Poblet in Catalonian Aragon, and Las Huelgas in Castile – the only nunnery amongst the royal abbeys, to which, with a degree of centralism which was only conceivable in Spain, all other nunneries in the country were to be subordinate.

Both Santas Creus and Poblet have classic Cistercian layouts. Both occupy an elongated rectangle with their jumble of buildings. In Santas Creus the domestic offices, the hostels and the abbot's palace lie to the west round a long, broad entrance court containing St Bernard's fountain. The church and the chief monastic buildings lie in the centre, and the royal palace round its own cloister to the east. Here it must be remembered that in this third zone destinations changed, and the abbey took over much that had been built for the court. It would distract us from our theme were I to retail here the history of the three royal palaces of Santas Creus, the first of which was built by Pedro III (1276-85),

1 Cathedral
2 Chapel of Our Lady, founded by Alfonso the Chaste
3 Camera santa
4 Sacristy
5 Cathedral cloister
6 Chapter-house
7 Bishop's palace
8 Church of S. Vicente
9 Cloister of S. Vicente
10 Monastery of S. Vicente
11 Garden of S. Vicente
12 Church of S. Pelayo
13 Cloister of S. Pelayo
14 Garden of S. Pelayo
15 Royal palace

the second by Jaime II (1291-1327), and the third by Pedro IV (*ob.* 1387). One project rapidly succeeded and overlaid another. The abbey took over what had been spurned by later rulers, and finished it off with different ends in mind. The eastern palace court returned to being a cloister. Whilst Pedro III and Jaime had regarded the abbey as their chief seat, Pedro IV preferred Poblet. Only the two first-named are buried in the church of Santas Crues, the latter with his wife, Blanche of Anjou. On the other hand only Pedro IV's palace survives, in greater part at least. This 50 feet × 115 feet rectangle uses the foundations of the first palace, and was itself later imitated in Poblet (Bibl. 172, 173). It is enough to note here that because of the Spanish consciousness of rank, it went without saying that the palace should lie in the east, at the conclusion of any progress through the abbey, and not in the west by the entrance. This persists in the Escorial.

The ground-plan of Poblet is exactly the same. The abbey was founded in 1149 by Count Ramón Berenguer IV of Barcelona (1139-62). It was thus from the first a princely foundation. Jaime I (*ob.* 1276) was laid to rest here; his successors Pedro III and Jaime II, as we saw, in Santas Creus; Pedro IV in Poblet once more, the object of his special favour. Pedro IV built the first palace of Poblet, Martin el Humano (1396-1414) began the second around 1397, which in Chuecas's judgment (Bibl. 171) would have been not only the most beautiful medieval palace in a monastery, but also altogether the mightiest Gothic palace in Spain, had it been possible to complete it. Poblet – incidentally the only Cistercian abbey in Spain to have been revived as such – was laid out according to the same principles as Santas Creus. It differs in that its core is enclosed by great defensive works, embracing both the monastic buildings and the royal palace. Extensive domestic and administrative offices lie to the west outside these fortifications. The palace rises over massive ramparts to the east. It covers a large area, with the royal apartments between the two mighty towers. We are confronted by a late fourteenth- and early fifteenth-century residence that bears comparison with the papal Palace of Avignon.

239 Santas Creus. The jumble of buildings contains both a Cistercian abbey on the extreme left, and a royal residence for the kings of Aragon

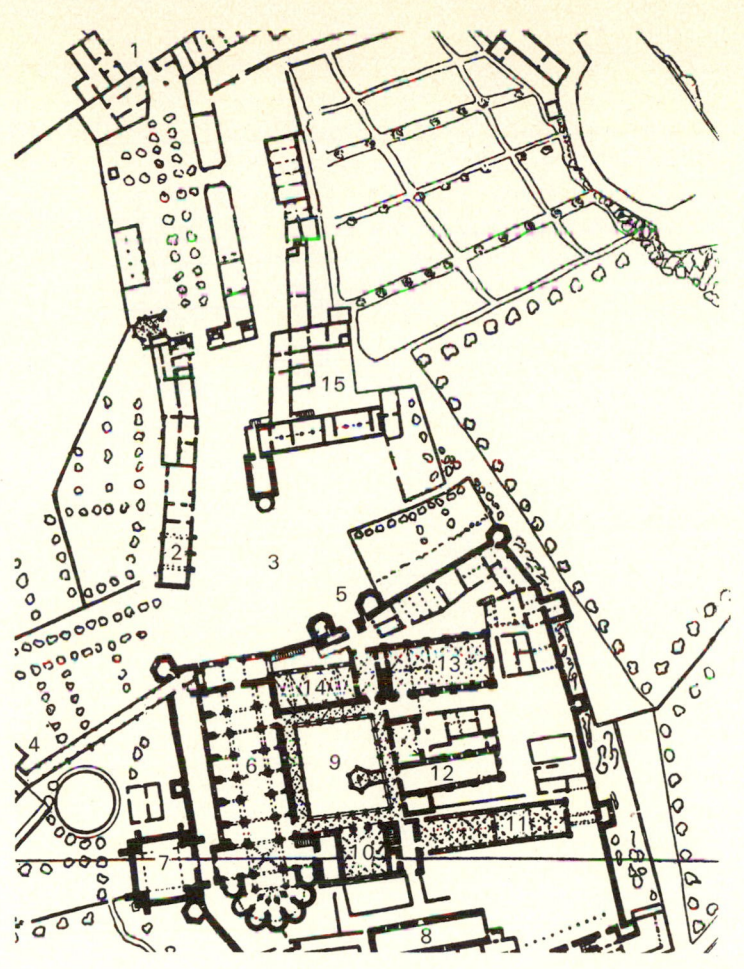

240 Poblet, another combination of Cistercian abbey and palace
1. Entrance
2. Old abbot's palace
3. Plaza mayor
4. New abbot's palace (off plan)
5. Puerta Real (Royal Gate)
6. Church
7. New sacristy
8. Palace of Pedro IV (originally infirmary)
9. Cloister
10. Chapter-house
11. Library (dorter above)
12. Refectory
13. Lay-brothers' refectory
14. Palace of King Martin (originally lay-brothers' dorter)
15. Guests' lodgings, stables, etc.

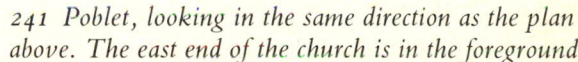

241 Poblet, looking in the same direction as the plan above. The east end of the church is in the foreground

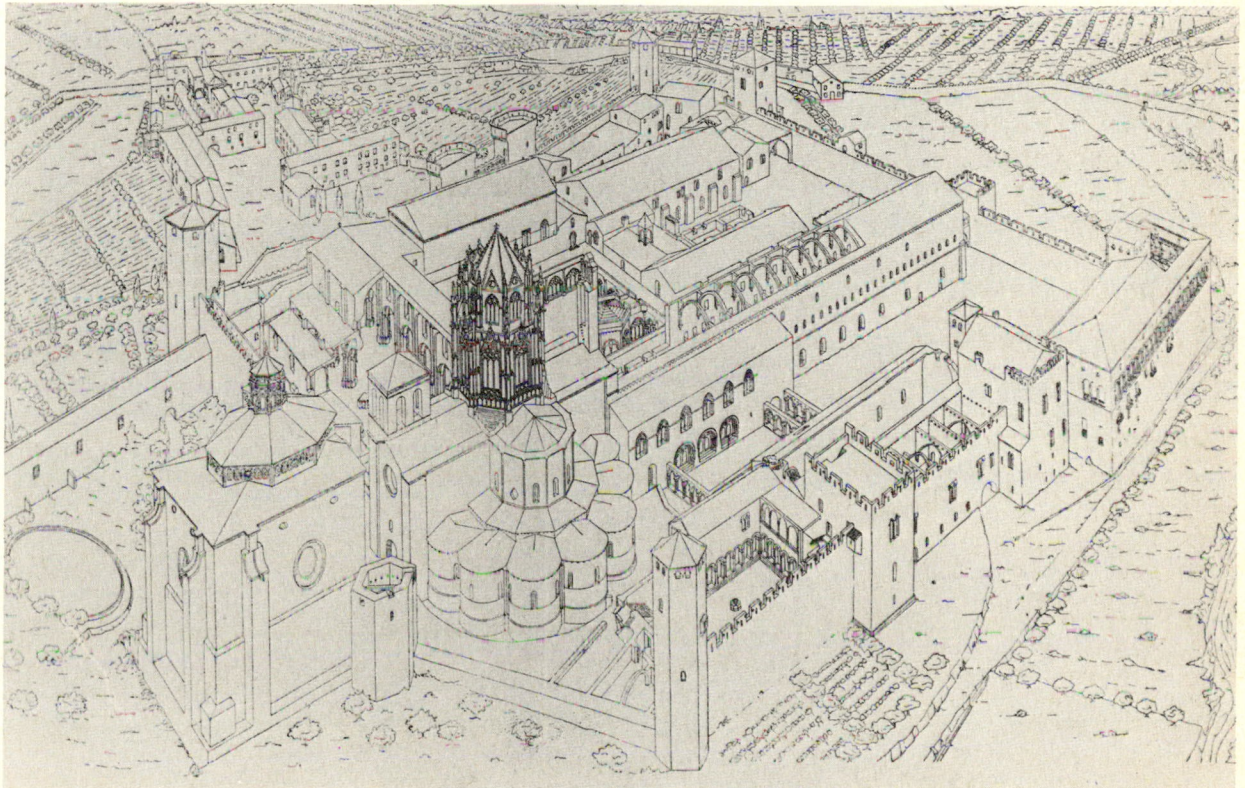

THE ESCORIAL

The classic embodiment of the conception of a conjoined monastery and royal palace occurred in the Escorial. This originated in a vow of Philip II's to build St Lawrence a monastery, after he had ordered one in St Quentin dedicated to that saint to be razed to the ground on the occasion of a battle against France in 1554, and was reinforced by the desire to institutionalize his father's sanctuary in the last years of his life. Charles V had lived in a villa directly adjacent to the church of the Hieronymite monastery of San Yuste. Philip II himself had long had his own cell in the Hieronymite monastery of Guisando. After Charles V's death in 1558, Philip further saw it as his mission to create a burial-place for his dynasty commensurate with the stature of the new Spanish monarchy. His plans for a monastery serving as the seat of government, not far from the village of El Escorial, were meant to realize these overlapping aims.

For us to comprehend it, we need to be familiar with the special association of the Hieronymites with the Spanish Crown. They form an Order that in this guise exists only in Spain. It grew out of an idea related to that inspiring the Carthusians. Alfonso of Castile (1312–50) brought together hermits from retreats scattered all over the kingdom, round the church of St Bartholomew's, Lupiana, in the province of Toledo. Not long afterward the Lord High Chamberlain, Pietro Fernandas Peche of Guadalajara, his brother Alfonso, Bishop of Jéan, the Portuguese Basco, and other friends from the great nobility entered this Congregation. His negotiations with Pope Gregory XI issued in the confirmation of a Rule, in its essentials that of St Augustine, with certain additions from St Jerome's admonitions to monks. The original intention of living as Franciscan Terti-

242 *The Escorial, culmination of the peculiarly Spanish union of monastery and royal residence. An engraving of 1587, looking east. Compare with the plan on p. 198*

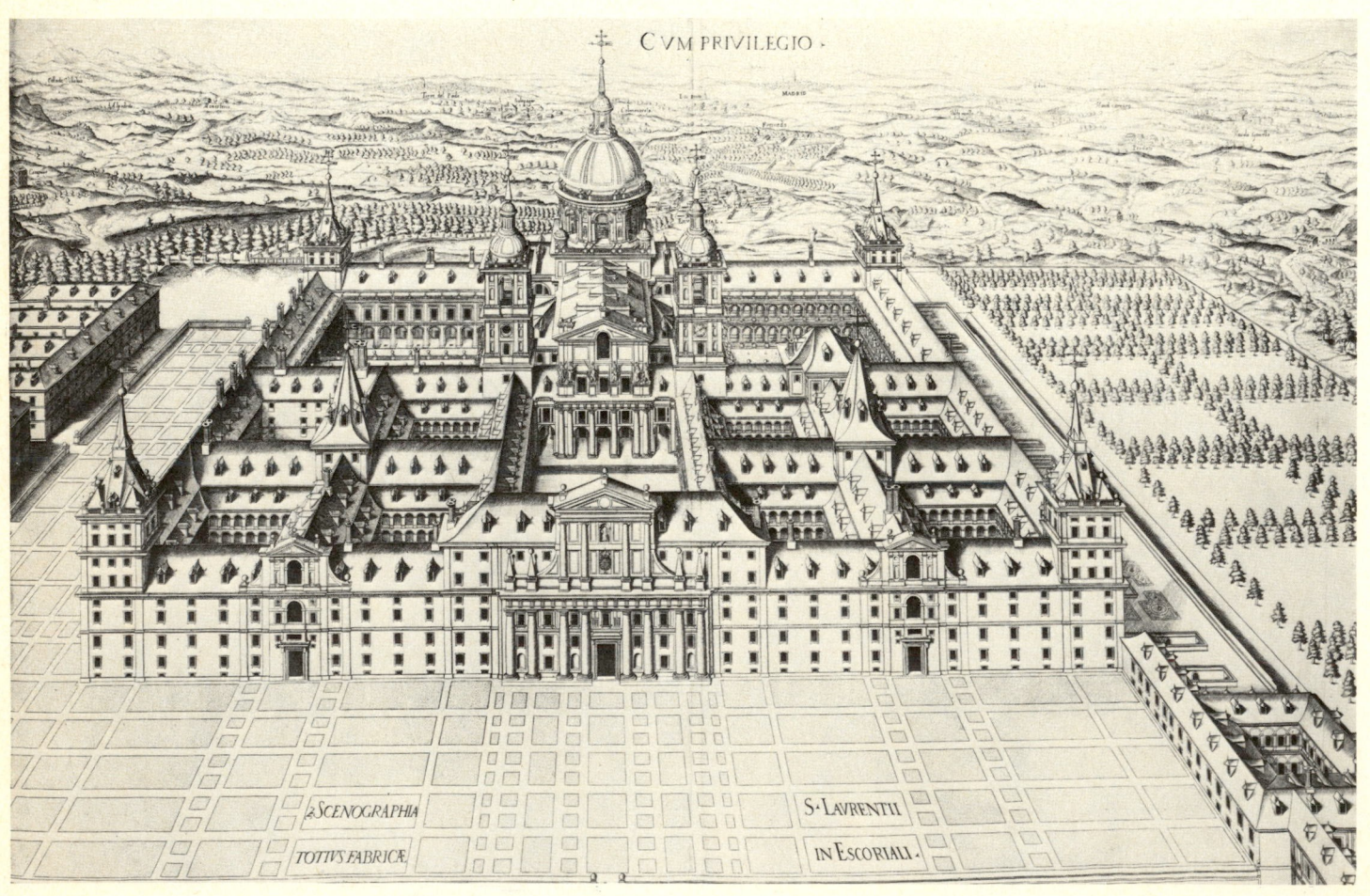

243 *The Escorial, the southern façade. The whole of this range was occupied by the monks*

aries (as laymen that is) amidst the monks was surrendered. But it remained a feature of the Order that it kept open house for laymen from the higher ranks of society to share, some for short periods and some for ever, the monks' rigorous life of asceticism and study. Here even kings could live the monk's life. By 1415 there were already twenty-five establishments. The most important was Our Lady of Guadalupe in the Estremadura, founded in 1389. The royal house had a palace there too. The Hieronymite Fray José de Siguenza (1544-1606) in his description of the *Fundacion del Monasterio de el Escorial* reveals that one of the building regulations of the Hieronymites required several monastic courts, in order to accommodate the brethren's cells and to prolong the processional ways. In addition to the *claustrum mayor* Guadalupe contained two smaller courts. A certain architectural grandeur was characteristic of Hieronymite monasteries from the first. Like Philip II in Guisando, each monk disposed of several rooms. Large libraries became a tradition. Accommodation was good, but fasts were severe.

The basic design of the Escorial derived from palace architecture. The Alcazar of Toledo supplied the pattern for its large rectangular shape. The architect was the royal builder, Juan de Toledo, alongside whom the Hieronymites appointed a monk, Antonio de Villacastin, as his master of works. It must have been preceded

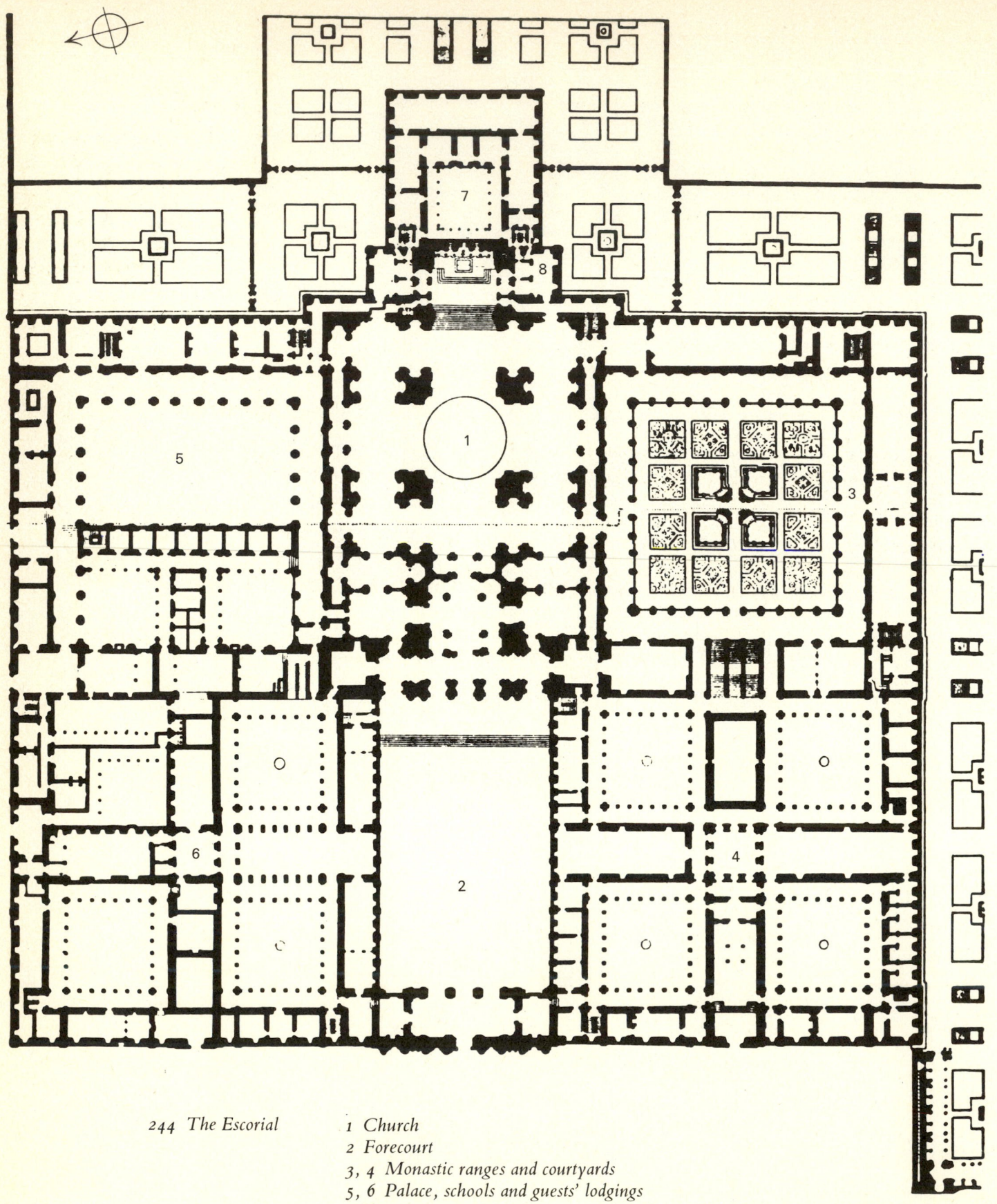

244   *The Escorial*

1 *Church*
2 *Forecourt*
3, 4 *Monastic ranges and courtyards*
5, 6 *Palace, schools and guests' lodgings*
7 *Royal apartments*
8 *King Philip's bedroom*

by careful studies of proportions, for the whole complex was built using measurements conforming to the Golden Rule. It was aesthetically ambitious from the start.

In 1561, four years after his vow, Philip had told the General Chapter of the Order in St Bartholomew's in Lupiana of his plan to build a monastery for fifty monks. Only in the following year was a site chosen at the foot of the Guadamarra mountains. The foundation-stone was laid in 1563. Philip had already referred to the project as El Escorial in 1562. We are faced by an institution that is totally coherent. We need not concern ourselves here with its place in the context of Mannerist architecture. It is the first rigorous axially symmetric layout in Western monastic architecture. It was reputed to be of the King's invention, elaborated by Juan Baptista de Toledo. And indeed the overall design fits Philip II's character exactly. It reflects his conception of the king's position vis-à-vis Church and State. Hence Juan de Herrera (1530-97), who took over control of the project after Juan de Toledo's death in 1567, had little discretion to make any major alteration. He refined the proportions, provided the mathematical calculations, curtailed the ranges and enlarged the courtyards. Even instructions to provide rooms for two hundred instead of for fifty monks made no difference. Monks stood like soldiers at the King's disposal. The lessons of the plan are comparable to those of a tract on the Spanish political system.

At the centre is the church (1), through which and through whose forecourt (2) the main axis runs. This grandiose structure served at one and the same time as the royal family's oratory, as church to the abbey, and as national cathedral. Its crypt was the burial-place of the Spanish kings. As was customary the ranges and courts of the monastery (3, 4) lay to the south, whilst the palace, together with schools and lodgings for court functionaries, lay to the north (5, 6), as in the St Gall plan. The private apartments of the king and his family had the choicest situation (7). They lay like the church on the central axis, to the east of the choir, the *capilla mayor*, which they embraced. They were the culmination and climax, only reached after traversing several forecourts and suites of rooms.

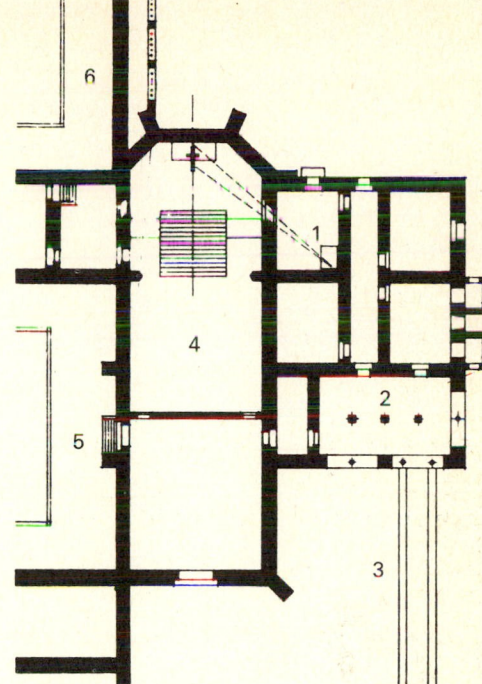

245 At San Yuste, the monastery to which Charles V retired, the old emperor occupied a room next to the church so that he could see the high altar from his bed
1 King's bedroom
2 Titian's Trinity ('La Gloria')
3 Rampa
4 Church
5 Old cloister
6 New cloister

246 King Philip II's bedroom in the Escorial (No. 8 in the plan on p. 198) copied the arrangements made by his father at San Yuste

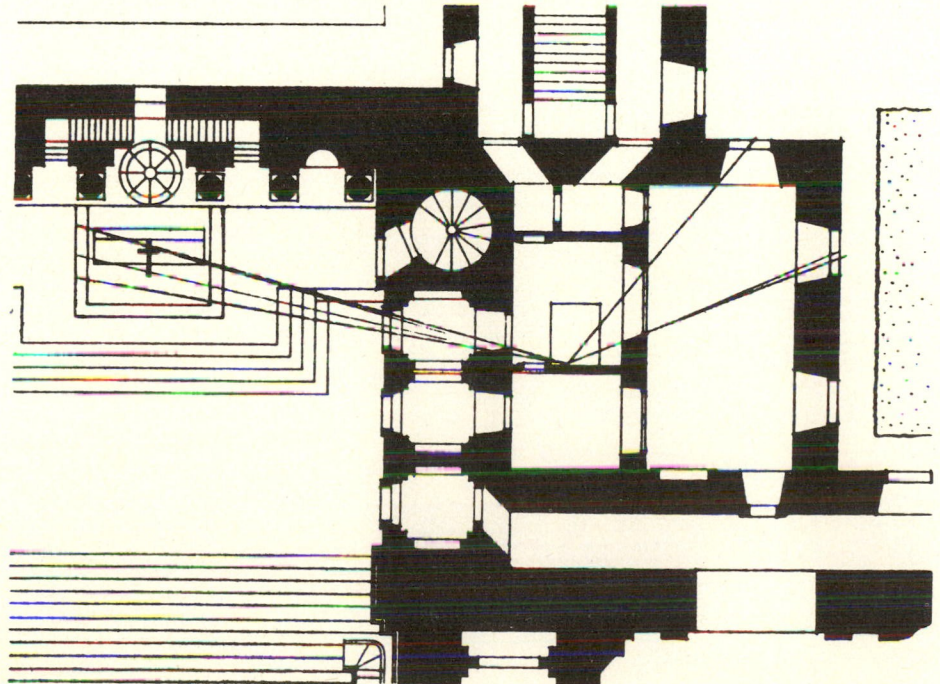

Their proximity to the sanctuary set the seal on their status in this world and the next. Individual details were kept modest. But their very modesty was a mark of distinction. The power of the king was beyond the power of pomp to convey. The Escorial should be compared with Versailles in order to realize the differences between the propaganda of the Spanish and French monarchies in their heyday. The centre of Versailles was exclusively occupied by the bed-chamber, in which the king rose and retired like the sun. The chapel was pushed to one side. In the Escorial the apartments of the royal family are set round the chancel. This is as if to say that power, to be legitimate, requires piety and orthodoxy. The king's rooms were furthermore on the same side as the monastery. His bed-chamber aligned itself with the monks' cells. The queen was allocated the palace side – which was also the Epistle side of the church – communicating with the women's quarters, which were distinct from those of the men. The infantas lived round the palace court (3). In arranging things so that he could see the High Altar from his bed, Philip was copying in his own chamber and its relationship to the church, that of San Yuste, in which his father died.[43] There the eye of the dying Emperor had been able to rest on Titian's representation of the Trinity, the *Gloria*. This imitation of San Yuste must have been intended right from the outset. Immediately behind Philip's apartment a staircase led to the royal crypt housing his dead – his father, his wives, and the infantas snatched away in childhood.

The same hierarchic logic governs the subdivision of the monastic ranges on the south side. It is a variation of the Benedictine schema, in which the position of the abbot and the prior is strikingly set off from the monks. The whole of the great court of the abbey is reserved to them (II). The prior's apartments lay on the ground floor, whilst on the upper floor the abbot's apartments lay to the east and the monks' cells to the south. The intermediate range to the west held the audience chamber and the Lady Chapel underneath, and the wardrobe and the novices' dorter above. Of the four small monastic courts, the two easterly ones served the monks, and the westerly ones the sick and the convalescent. The ground floor of the transverse range running from east to west was filled by the lavatorium, a staircase, and the kitchens; that running from north to south by a workshop, the stairs, and the refectory. On the upper floor of the latter were the library and a further dorter. All the lesser rooms were so cunningly slotted into place, that the conventual framework complemented that of court ceremonial. Nothing had been neglected. This monastic palace is a symbol of the government of Spain and of the world. It owed more to Philip II than to his architects. It was not sycophancy but the truth when contemporaries spoke of an idea of Philip's, carried out by his builders.

One should not overestimate the influence of the Escorial on the princely abbeys of the Baroque. The palatial German monasteries sprang from far-flung roots. Nonetheless, it must have made a considerable impression on ecclesiastical rulers that the first and noblest of the royal palaces of the West, hovering as an ideal before the eyes of every monarch at the end of the sixteenth century, was no less an abbey.

Princely Abbeys of the Baroque

There is one last large self-contained group of foundations in which the monastic idea gave rise to bold new architecture. This is that of the Baroque abbeys of Southern Central Europe – the seventeenth- and eighteenth-century monasteries of Austria, Bavaria, Swabia and Switzerland, and a few in Franconia and on the Rhine that had preserved their political and ecclesiastical independence. All were huge institutions. Many of them were subject only to the Emperor, but even those subject to lesser princes enjoyed the special liberties that in the period under consideration were essential to the flowering of monastic and artistic life.

I have spoken of these as a self-contained group, despite the occasional great Baroque abbeys that were built in Italy, Spain, Portugal, and even, in a certain sense, in France. Joan Evans has compiled a large volume on the monuments of French monastic architecture from the Renaissance to the Revolution (Bibl. 185), but the findings are unimpressive. It is true that there were a number of noble church façades and a series of huge palatial tracts and stately interiors, but none gives any sense of indigenous, organic architectural development. They were the product of architects' offices in Paris. This poses the question of what difference in circumstances accounts for the picture being so much richer in the German-speaking countries alone.

It would be possible to maintain that the monastic idea as such was outworn, that the Protestant lands were timely in turning their backs on it, and that Henry VIII had chosen the right moment when, between 1534-39, he ordered the dissolution of all the English monasteries and expelled the monks. There is a certain logic in the fact that monasteries in the Catholic lands of France, Spain and Italy subsequently flourished less than those in faith-torn Germany, where the exertions of the Counter-Reformation also reinvigorated monastic life. Yet it was neither the Jesuits, the driving force behind the Counter-Reformation, nor the Capuchins, who set their stamp on the devotional life of the age, who inspired the new fecundity of monastic architecture. Jesuit churches are not relevant here, for all their undeniable art-historical significance. Even their colleges resemble great civic institutions, and possess but slight importance for the history of palace architecture, and none at all for that of monastic building. All, or virtually all, large Baroque abbeys are in the countryside, and though they contributed to the Counter-Reformation, they flourished because of a different set of social, economic, political and religious causes.

The occasion for the decline of monastic life in the Catholic countries of Italy, Spain, Portugal and France was the system of appointments *in commendam*. An accord of 1519 between Pope Leo X and François I vested the right of appointment to almost all French abbacies in the king. Clairvaux was among the few exceptions. The usage was an old one – the Carolingians, and thereafter many of the German Emperors, regarded it as their just right to appoint abbots as they pleased. The church had always fought against this disposal of benefices, but now it was sanctioned. The French monarchy liberally bestowed abbatial titles and incomes upon its favourites and those who had served it. These royal appointees included laymen, Protestants, numerous scions of the royal house, and above all the great prelates – archbishops and cardinals – and leading statesmen. Richelieu was abbot or prior of twenty monasteries in his time, including Cluny, Cîteaux, Saint-Riquier near Abbeville, St Arnulf near Metz and Saint-Benoît-sur-Loire. Mazarin is supposed to have held twenty-seven abbacies. Even artists were requited with monasteries instead of payment. Primaticcio was titular Abbot of Saint-Martin-des-Aires, Philibert de l'Orme of Saint-Éloi-les-Noyon and Yvry-la-Bataille, whilst the poet Ronsard was made Prior of Saint-Comé-les-Tours and of Croixval. Even Huguenot leaders were bought off with abbeys, like Coligny with Saint-Benoît-sur-Loire. The Comte de Vexin, Louis XIV's son by Madame de Montespan, held the two richest monasteries in the Île de France, Saint-Denis and Saint-Germain-des-Prés. With the surrender of the incomes of a monastery to an absentee abbot its conventual and spiritual life frequently suffered, and its artistic life always did. A rich magnate might occasionally do something for his monastery, but this munificence always involved the imposition of something alien from without, and not the spontaneous generation of something indigenous from within. Nothing took root.

The monks themselves tried to counteract all this by linking up in congregations. The most successful of these was the Benedictine one of Saint-Maur. Most French establishments placed themselves under this head Parisian house, whose importance in the intellectual life of the Order cannot be overrated. But they could not reinvigorate the distinctive life of each abbey; quite the contrary – they brought about in the religious sphere what government *in commendam* had done in the financial one. The tasks of the individual abbeys were dictated to them by a Benedictine bureaucracy. Whether they were to grow or be run down was centrally contrived, on grounds that were reasonable and in keeping with the times, but which deprived them of an opportunity of spontaneous expansion. These officials negotiated, for instance, with Robert de Cotte and other architects in the eighteenth century over the list of the most pressing renovations needed in the various monasteries. In many places medieval buildings were replaced by markedly plain, classicizing architecture which was regarded as decent and rational, but which sometimes lent the monastery the character of a *château*, or more frequently of some official institution. Individual buildings were degraded and perverted from their true purpose with astonishing unconcern. A notorious example was the large refectory of the old Abbey of Saint-Bénigne in Dijon, which was especially admired even at the time, but was turned nonetheless into a coach-house. This was a use often recommended by the Congregation of Saint-Maur for refectories. It was due to the collaboration of the Maurists and the *abbés commendataires* that it was thought attentive and becoming to provide each individual monk in Clairvaux with rococo apartments, comprising at least one salon besides the bedchamber.

The system of appointments *in commendam*, just like, in its own way, the Reformation, only made headway because most monasteries in the fifteenth and sixteenth centuries were in a state of increasing collapse. The larger institutions were depleted. In smaller communities there was not a proper quorum. Wherever increasing numbers of the aristocracy and bourgeoisie sent their offspring into monasteries merely to provide for them, a moral rot set in. And buildings decayed with morals. No decade was wanting in desperate attempts to reinvigorate the monastic idea. Monasteries were like a fleet becalmed; their timbers rotted. Occasionally someone might occupy his idle time in the most sumptuous internal decoration of his ship. The fifteenth century was the heyday for improvements in the living arrangements of the monasteries. Occasionally a single skiff, fully rigged, and assisted by oars, might successfully be brought in motion again. But it was vain to wait for a great wind from afar to carry the whole fleet before it. There was no new kind of organization in these centuries capable of setting the builders a new task. The poetic peace of the monasteries could not cover up for the want of discipline within. Everything was set for an age-long slumber,

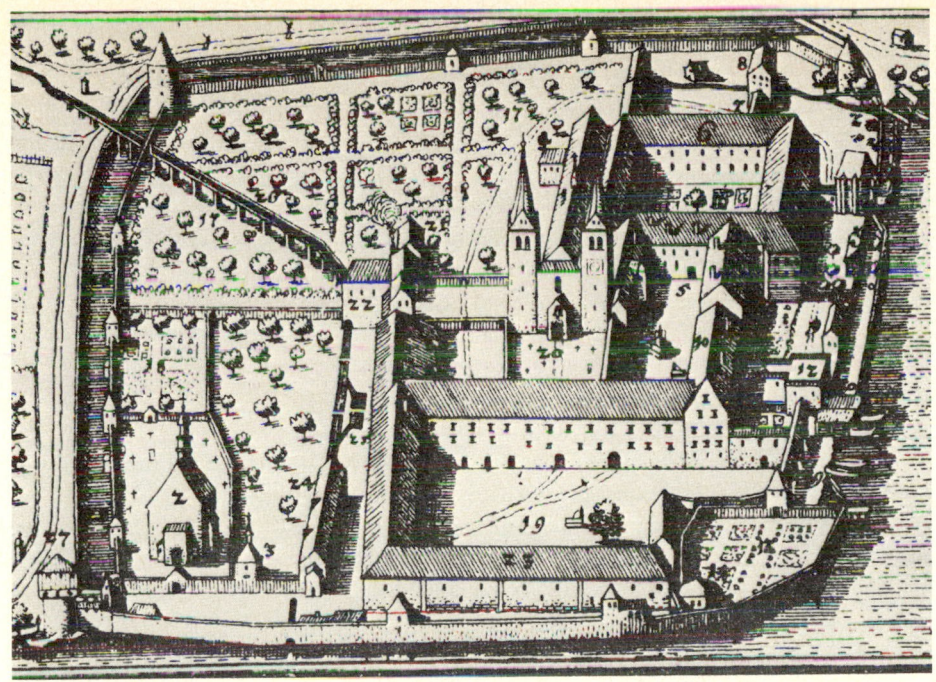

247 *The monastery of Tegernsee, in Bavaria. Engraving by Matthäus Merian, 1644*

though the irruptions of wars and the Reformation were to provide several rude awakenings.

In this period the monastery was reconstituted, but without this being inspired by any novel architectural idea. The Benedictines gave up sleeping in a common chamber (*v.s.* p. 136). Monasteries were made more comfortable, details were improved on – here a new range was added, or a larger room, there an oriel, crenellation, farm buildings and all kinds of extensions; one thing or many, but never a whole. By the end of the process, and this is the crucial point, the monks ended up with everything under one roof, frequently in a building with three wings, inside of which was the cloister. Chapter-house, refectory, kitchens and cells were now all contained inside this large quadrangle. It was preceded by the farmyard, and possibly by an abbot's palace, an infirmary and a hostel. We have given specific, mostly Italian, examples where, as in San Marco in Florence, a more gifted architect has succeeded in creating a lucid embodiment of the tendency. With the aid of innumerable engraved representations from the sixteenth and seventeenth centuries we can follow this uniform progression from the irregular monastic groupings of the Middle Ages to the homogeneous ensembles of the Baroque in several places. It was bound to happen in all the countries of Europe. Though the first large monastery to be all subsumed in one structure, into which the church also fitted, was that of the Escorial, one should not thence conclude that this was the great inspiration of Baroque abbeys. Its role as a royal palace was not imitable. The emphases had to be differently placed. The architects of the great free abbeys of the Holy Roman Empire and of Switzerland were confronted with the task of finding some new and original solution.

Let us examine the position of a monastery at the beginning of the seventeenth century with the aid of the relatively modest example of Tegernsee, in Bavaria. This was not one of the mighty free abbeys of Swabia or one of the great imperial abbeys of Austria. Tegernsee lived from farming, and to a lesser extent from skilled crafts, and its position was a relatively protected one at the foot of the mountains.

Around 1640 – that is to say in the middle of the Thirty Years' War – Matthäus Merian published a bird's eye view engraving of Tegernsee, which shows us first of all the whole *See* (lake) as the territory of the abbey, and then four views of the abbey itself in the corners, of which our sketch reproduces that from the lake, or western, side. The abbey was protected on two sides by the lake, and on the other two by a watercourse and, after 1740, by a wall. It was supplied with spring water from the mountains by a special aqueduct. In accordance with the Rule, the extensive gardens and the graveyard and its chapel were within the defensible area. Three large courts are to be distinguished beside and in front of the church – the conventual court of the monks, already under one roof; preceding this the prelatial court, with the abbot's house, administrative building and church, grouped round a well; and further to the west, immediately on the lakefront, the great domestic court, with its stalls, barns, and workshops. The jumble of buildings current in the Middle Ages was reduced to three blocks, set round three courts – conventual, prelatial, and domestic. But these three courts themselves were only casually related. This was the ineluctable task facing the Baroque architect: how was he to unite the three courts in an artistically pleasing and comprehensible whole? Whereas the transformation of the manifold buildings round the cloister had followed inevitably upon the renunciation of a common dormitory, the attempt to combine the three great courts posed dilemmas soluble only by creative genius. They were by no means always satisfactorily solved. The task was rendered no easier by the desire of most communities to alter the existing layout as little as possible. The church was almost invariably rebuilt where it was – when it was not just incorporated. The monks were also mostly reluctant to move the conventual court from its old set of buildings. It was natural that the path of entry should no longer be dominated, as it had been from the plan of St Gallen right up to Merian's illustration of Tegernsee, by the domestic courtyard, but instead by the prelatial court or the church. At Tegernsee itself the whole area between the lake and the church was made into a prelatial, or state, court

248 Ochsenhausen, air view. No distinction is yet made between the monastic buildings proper and those belonging to the abbot in his role as temporal ruler

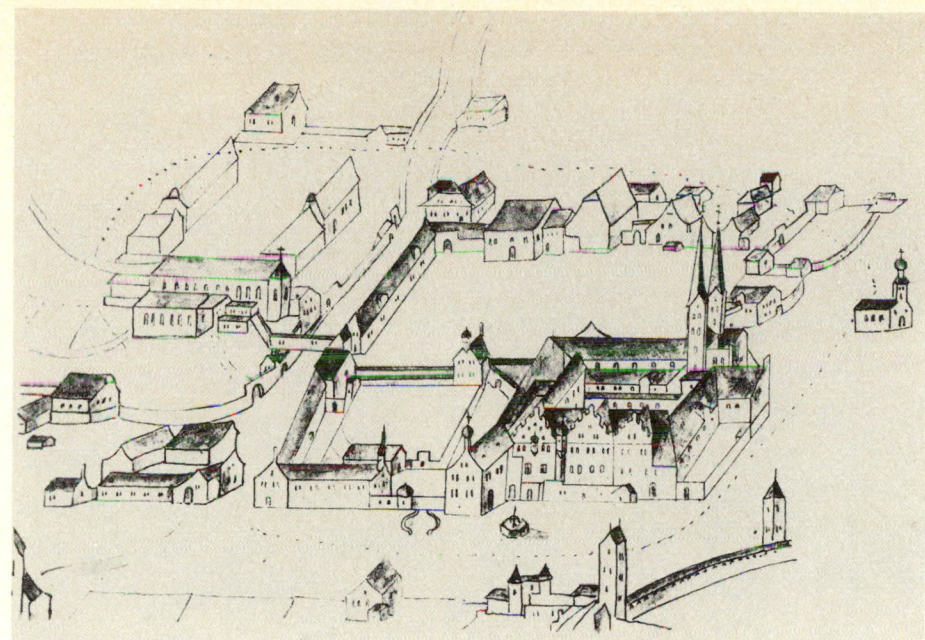

249 *The old abbey at Kempten, before 1632: a patchwork of buildings without demarcation of function*

at the beginning of the eighteenth century – a great quadrangle with two fountains in the middle – whilst the domestic court was pushed so far northwards to the left that what we see on the plan as its left arm now closed it to the right. But this is nothing compared with the examples afforded by Austria, Switzerland and the sovereign monastic states of Swabia.

The question of the origins of the Baroque abbeys of Southern Central Europe cannot be treated chronologically (Bibl. 178, 179 and 180). It is not the beginnings, when the problem posed was not yet recognized as such, that are interesting, but the solutions which were ultimately arrived at – in Weingarten, Ottobeuren, Melk, Göttweig, Wiblingen and St Blasien. Around 1600 there was a general desire to give the prelate's wing in a monastery the dimensions and aspect of a *Schloss*. Many monasteries in the Middle Ages had had a governmental role alongside their conventual one, but only now was there a desire to give it a predominating architectural expression. The sovereign abbots who sat with counts and princes in the *Reichstag* at Regensburg, and those of mesne institutions who encountered figures from the great nobility at provincial diets, felt it incumbent on them to adopt the same outward display and the same manner of life. At first there was no thought to make a sharp division between this palace and the conventual zone. In Ochsenhausen the palatial block put up in the early seventeenth century (1612-32) clasps the church and commands the landscape from its high point of vantage. It was simply a Swabian *Schloss*. The questions of the separation of the prelatial range from the convent proper, and of how these should be related to the domestic court, did not yet seem important.

The architectural history of the princely abbey of Kempten is more illuminating about the situation around the middle of the seventeenth century. This abbey was by far the largest and richest in Swabia, a monastic state whose inmates were all of noble birth. There was constant strife with the Protestant-inclined townsfolk. Before its destruction by the Swedes, eagerly abetted by the townsfolk, in 1632, this influential abbey put up with a jumble of buildings that had lost their medieval coherence, and had not found a modern substitute. The result was a patchwork. Facing the town, it displayed a trio of gabled houses that could have belonged to merchants.

Immediately after the Peace of Westphalia in 1648, the prince-abbot, Giel von Gielsberg, planned an immense new monastery. Though during his incumbency

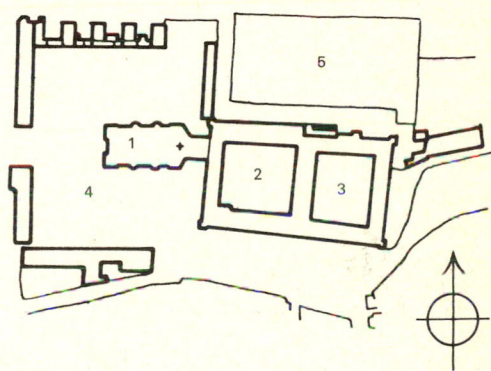

250 *The rebuilt abbey of Kempten, the distinction between monastery and administrative centre now expressed in the planning*
1 *Abbey church*
2 *Monastic cloister*
3 *Abbot's palace*
4 *Conventual court*
5 *Garden*

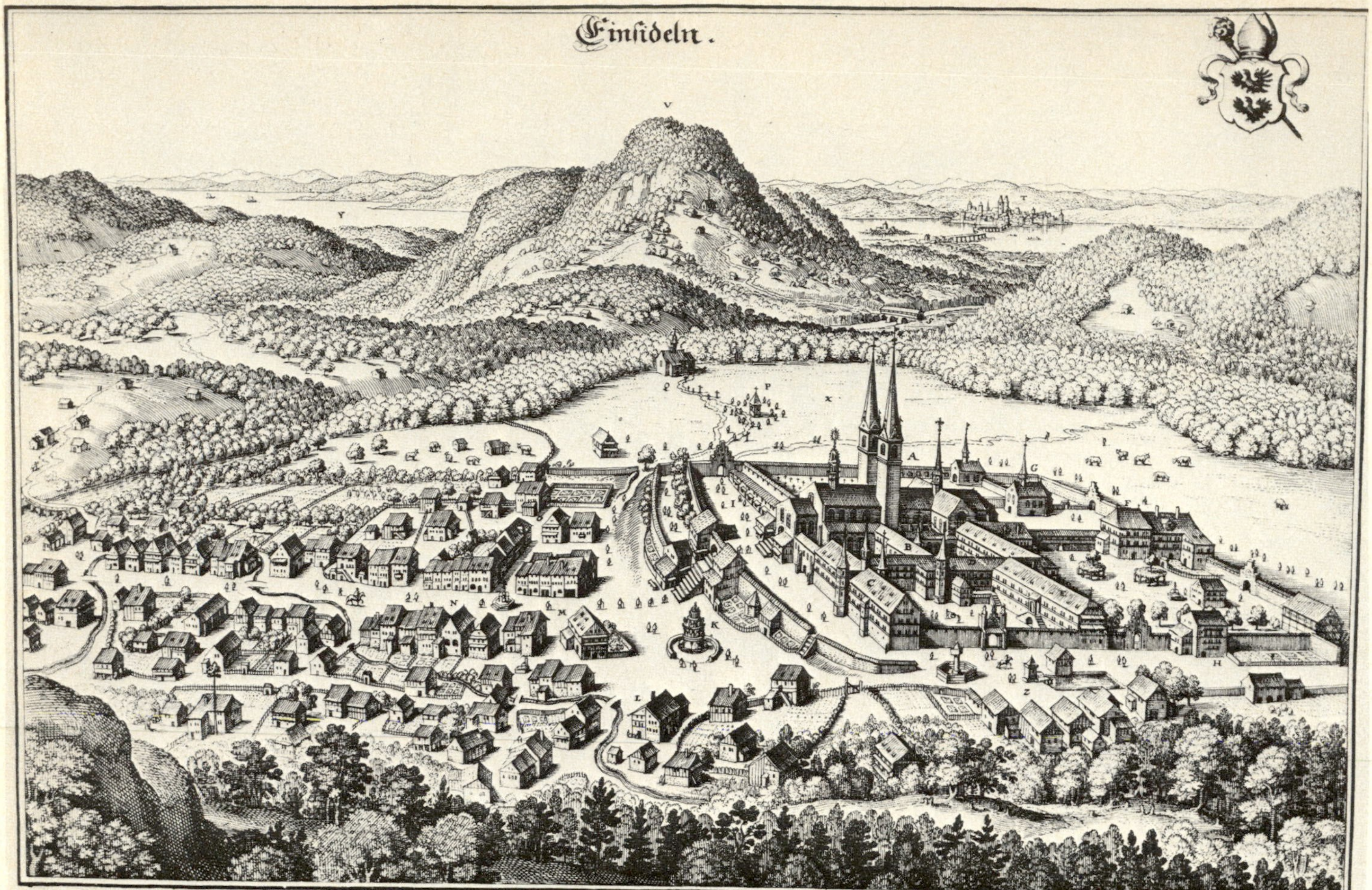

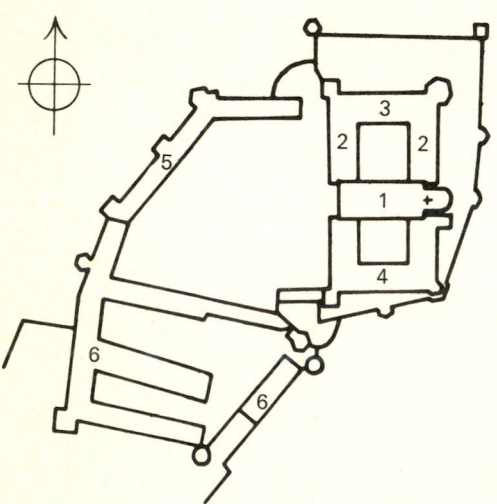

Einfidelu.

A. *Vnfer Frawen Münfter*   D. *Das gemein Gafthaufe*   G. *S. Maria Magdalena*   K. *S. Meinrads Brunne*   N. *Zum Schlüßel*   Q. *S. Gangolff*   T. *Statt Rapperswed*   Y. *Zürich See*
B. *S. Iohan capell*   E. *Das ander Gafthaufe*   H. *Marftall*   L. *Wirtshaus zum Schwert*   O. *zum Adler*   R. *Die Sust*   V. *Der Ekel berg*   Z. *Die Moteig*
C. *Des Hoch Prelaten Wohnung*   F. *Bibliothec*   I. *Krämergaßen*   M. *Rabthaufe*   P. *Das Kreutz*   S. *Teuffel bruck*   X. *Der Brüel*

251 Einsiedeln. Bird's-eye view of the old abbey by Merian, 1644

252 Vorau. Secular and monastic precincts are separated by the church, as at the Escorial

1 Abbey church
2 State apartments and abbot's chapel
3 Library
4 Monastic buildings
5 Outbuildings
6 Farm buildings

the abbey only housed about eight religious, since the Swabian nobility prevented the admission of non-nobles, a large new abbey church and an imposing official residence went up – the very first to be built after the Thirty Years' War. A comparison of the plans reveals that the abbey was thoroughly re-orientated, though the two noble courts still lack any organic relationship with the choir of the church, the only object being to display fine palatial frontages towards the town and the formal garden. It was magnificent in parts, but there was no overall design to make it worthy of more than a mention in a history of monastic architecture. By little after 1650, things were not so far advanced.

It was W. Herrmann (Bibl. 178) who pointed out that the house of Augustinian canons at Vorau in Styria was the first monastery since the Escorial to adopt the idea of two symmetrical wings flanking a centrepiece formed by the dominating façade of the church. Between 1619 and 1649 arose the conventual block to the south (4), and to the north the almost identical block of the 'abbey', with its library (3), state apartments (2) and prelate's chapel. The large forecourt was bounded by coach-houses and stables, whilst the farm-buildings lay outside this symmetrical grouping (6).

It was not until the turn of the century that Caspar Moosbrugger saw how to give this symmetrical layout an air of true monumentality in his inspired designs for Einsiedeln in Switzerland. We turn once again to Merian for the state of things before rebuilding. One only needs to see how the abbey stands, on terraced ramparts above the village, with a backdrop of mountains, to realize that it cried

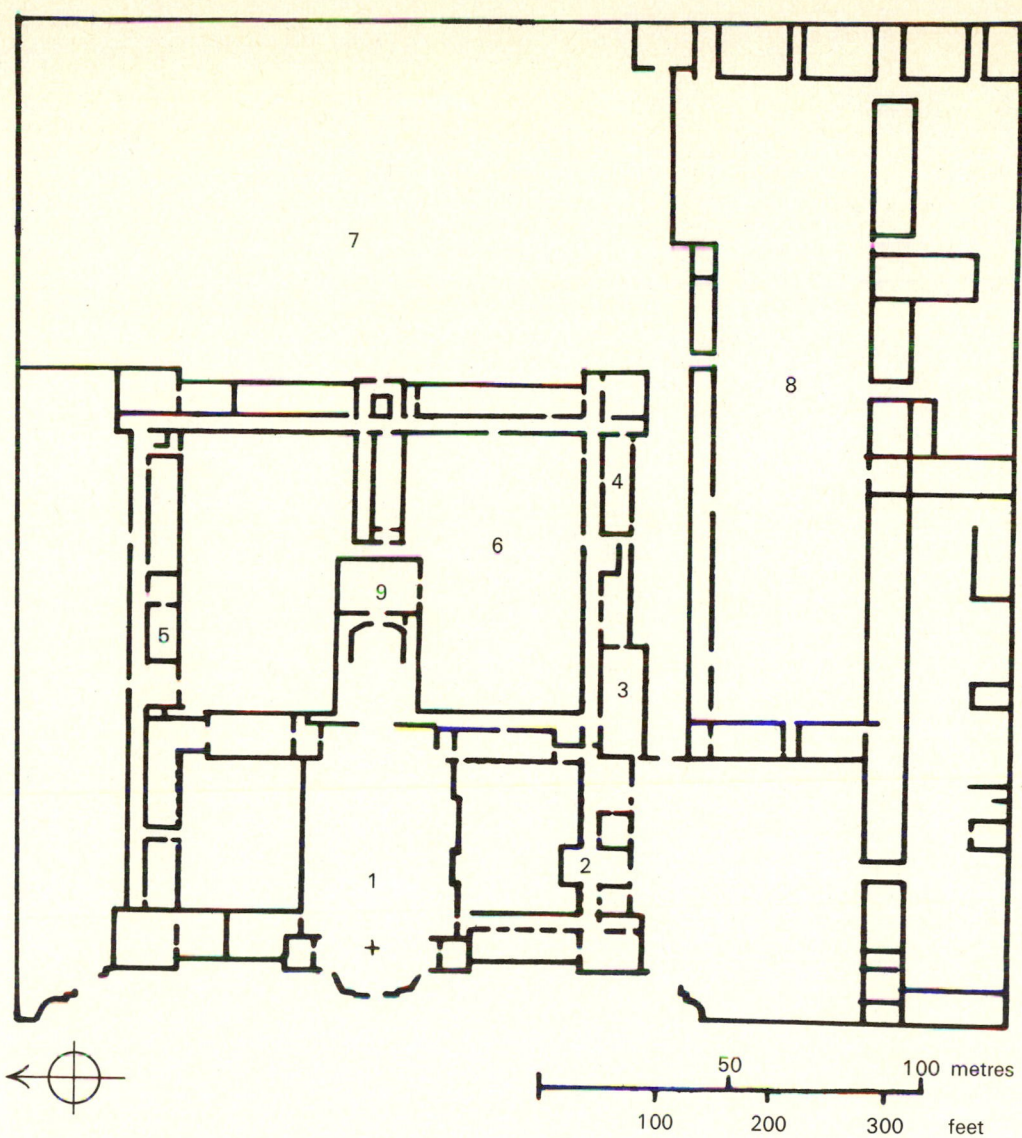

253 *Einsiedeln. The new*
monastery, begun in the early
eighteenth century
1 *Abbey church*
2 *Staircase*
3 *Refectory*
4 *Chapter-house*
5 *Library*
6 *Monastic garden*
7 *Palace garden*
8 *Farm buildings*
9 *Sacristy*

out for Baroque treatment. All the ingredients were there. Plans for rebuilding
had been mulled over since 1633, but a start was only made on the monastery in
1704. Work began on the church in 1720, and it was consecrated in 1735. Work
continued on the area of the forecourt and its steps, on the range of workshops,
and lastly on the stables, until 1770. It became the epitome of Baroque monastic
planning, distinguished by its elevated position upon an open square, dominated
by the twin-towered façade of the centrally sited church, which bows vigorously outwards, and by the identical appearance of the palatial ranges enclosing
inner courts, with the domestic buildings behind, and in part to one side, but in
any case withdrawn from view. Einsiedeln was only to be surpassed by Weingarten, whose original design goes back to Caspar's brother, Andreas Moosbrugger, and on whose construction not only the Vorarlbergers worked but also
Enrico Zuccalli and, more especially, D. G. Frisoni. Here the façade of the church
is richer but the palatial ranges are plainer than in Einsiedeln. The ideal design,
which probably only dates from around 1750, thirty-five years after building
was begun, shows the measure of its aspirations. It places the plan of the abbey
like a hallowed object on an altar, and turns the prospect into an altarpiece. The
abbey has come to symbolize perfection. Its courts, ranges, and galleries proclaimed the church to be the queen of a celestial city. Here too the conventual
court was planned to the south and right of the church, and the prelatial court
left of it to the north, whilst the domestic court was again placed behind it.
According to the ideal design the latter was both to be made a part of and sub-

ordinated to the main ensemble. This layout was imitated by several monasteries, but never surpassed. Behind such unheard-of magnificence was always the noble ideal of creating in a monastery the embodiment of the *Civitas Dei* on earth. Monastic, civic and divine government were to be proclaimed as founded on the same principles.

To understand these buildings one must see that they clamoured to be understood as a sign of the optimism which, after the decades of the Thirty Years' War, wars against the French and the Turks, and the Wars of the Spanish and Austrian Successions, sought to introduce a new order in the world. Measured against the political aims of Potsdam, Versailles or St Petersburg, these endeavours may appear anachronistic. The middle-class devotees of the Enlightenment could never forgive the great abbots their allegedly inadequate stewardship. Modern economics have been able to demonstrate that these monastic feudatories of the Holy Roman Empire mostly did the right thing. One has only to look at the country churches and the village halls of these monastic states to see that they were better administered than those of secular princes. Such manifestations of the concentrated artistic activity of a region in its countryside are themselves something *sui generis*.

As economic units the monasteries of the second half of the seventeenth and of the eighteenth century were superior to any other institution. Not only did they dispose of the cheapest labour in the shape of the monks and lay-brothers, but each one of these could devote all his efforts to the common good. There was no private sector. The monasteries were the swiftest to recover from the horrors of wars. Their ability to arrive at the model running of their estates often enabled them to organize new building campaigns long before towns and secular princes. On these occasions, as in the Middle Ages – but not always – first the monastery would be rebuilt, and then it would be crowned by the new church. Many abbeys and priories again became centres for research, even, indeed especially, in the natural sciences, as in Ochsenhausen, Weingarten, St Blasien, Tegernsee, Kremsmünster, St Florian and Melk. In almost every monastery members of the middle class predominated over those from the aristocracy. Most of the great connoisseurs and builders amongst the Baroque abbots were of middle-class origin; some distinguished examples were the sons of artisans. There were even brewers' sons amongst the prelates. The career of one of these prelates is amazing when viewed against the background of the rigid hierarchical organization of society in that age. To have the chance of building a Weingarten, an Ottobeuren, a Banz, Melk or St Florian was the most life-enhancing thing which could happen to the once humble novice-sons of coppersmiths, farmers and masons. Small tradesmen's sons from Wangen or Biberach on the Riss rose through the monasteries, and through the monasteries alone, to the position of peers of the Empire.

The demands of a site, attachment to an existing conventual church, and frequently also the desire to displace the prelatial range to the back or toward the south, so that it might look out over terraces onto a formal garden, account for the fact that large monasteries did not actually often employ the classic schema of Weingarten and Einsiedeln. The desire for such modifications and complications presented architects with a challenge that resulted in remarkable architecture. No other century was so fertile in such diversely individual creations as this, the last century of Western monastic architecture. Totting up the free abbeys represented at Regensburg, with those held in chief of a mesne lord in Bavaria or Franconia that claimed almost the same status – amongst which were Waldsassen, Banz, Tegernsee, Wessobrunn, Benediktbeuren and Fürstenfeldbruck, as well as smaller houses like Rott am Inn, Diessen and Schäftlarn – and adding to the list the occasionally yet huger institutions in Austria and the main ones in Switzerland, one reaches a figure of over sixty Baroque abbeys, for the most part superbly intact, and which defy classification. To these should be added a few in Bohemia and Silesia, though those in the latter initiated nothing after Frederick the Great had introduced a new administration there; and in the same way monastic lordships in Alsace had no opportunity for self-expression after its cession to France.

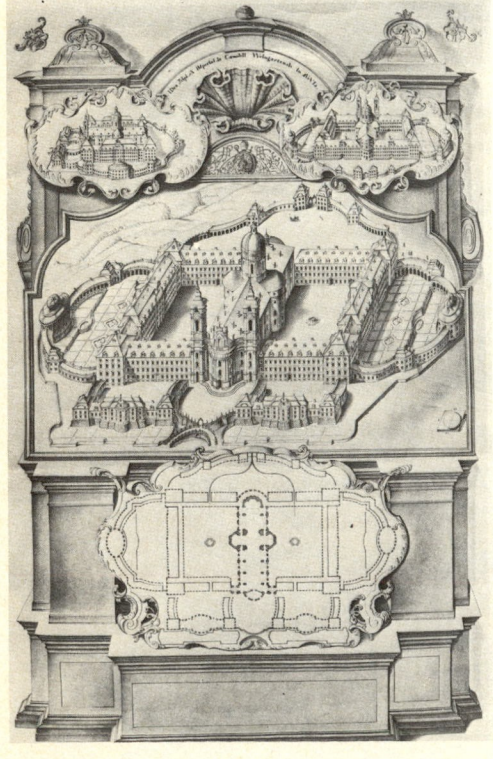

254 *Weingarten, the ideal Baroque monastery as it was conceived by its architects*

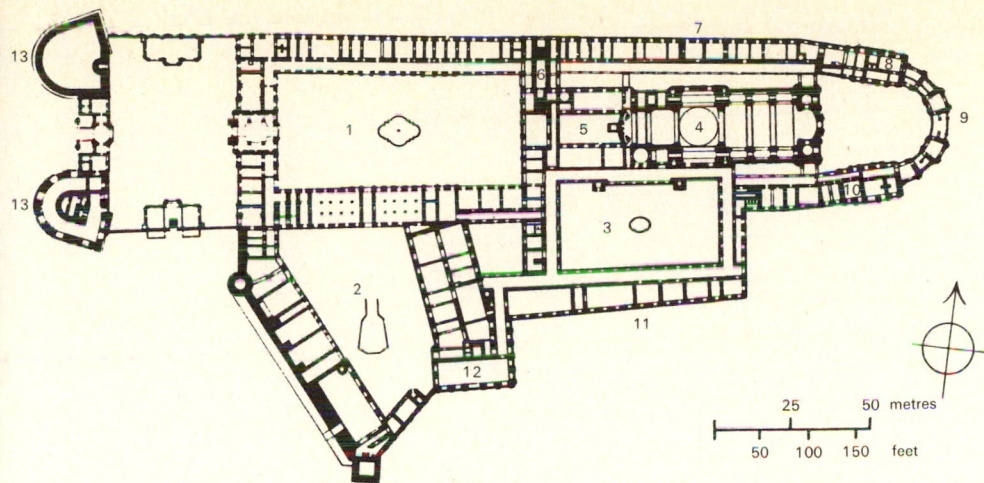

255 *Melk, the masterpiece of Jacob Prandtauer, begun 1701. For views of the earlier monastery see pls 222 and 223*

Many of these monasteries are enthroned in a dominant position on a hill-top or a plateau of rock. They all exploit the antithesis between the interminable horizontals of the ranges, whose uniformity is relieved by breaking them forward at intervals, and the soaring verticals of the church, with its towers and domes. Most of them contrived to use the domestic buildings to intensify the monumental quality of the whole ensemble. Many employed the inexhaustible motifs of Baroque formal gardens to articulate the surrounds of their monasteries. In all of them the appearance of the ranges round the three historic courts was carefully graduated according to their destination. There was meanwhile full awareness of the need to eke out the features that had called for grandiose architecture in the first place, in order to break up the monotony of sheer lines of buildings. These features were: the imperial hall (*Kaisersaal*) and imperial apartments, the ceremonial staircase, the library, and, less conspicuously, the dining-hall, which was often complemented by a summer refectory on the garden front. The potent elaboration of Baroque libraries reflects the importance now attributed to learning by the monasteries, whilst the resplendent imperial halls reflect their political claim to recognize no superior but the Emperor.

The rock-set abbeys of Austria have a special claim to attention, the most important being Melk, Klosterneuburg, Göttweig and Kremsmünster. St Florian, though not actually on a rock, belongs in this context.

We have already noticed that in Melk the medieval and Renaissance abbey had supplied the makings of the ensemble produced for Abbot Berthold Dietmayr by the great specialist in monastic architecture, Jacob Prandtauer (from 1701 onwards). There was no need for him to alter the respective situations of the prelatial court in front of the church, the domestic court tucked to the right, and the conventual court to the south of the church. The real problem was presented by the church's alignment, since its eastern end, the choir, was toward the entrance. His inspiration was to make the climax of his composition the famous façade toward the Danube, which takes up the curve of the cliff and transposes it into majestic architecture. In order to justify the grandeur of this, he drew the two key features of the library and the imperial hall out to the ends of their respective ranges and made them flank the forecourt thus formed; the library, as was appropriate, to the south on the side of the monks, and the *Kaisersaal* accordingly to the north, on the side of the staircase and guest-rooms. The three most exalted components of the abbey are thus seen as a group. The entrance to the abbey in the east did not forfeit its dignity, but it renounced any special claim to attention. Here Prandtauer exercised restraint. What was on the other hand the rear for the visitor could not avoid becoming the main frontage, dominated

256 *Melk from the west, the façade of the church rising behind the open terrace*

257 Melk: the church, looking east

258 Melk: the library (No. 10 on the plan)

259 (Below). Melk: air-view from the north-west

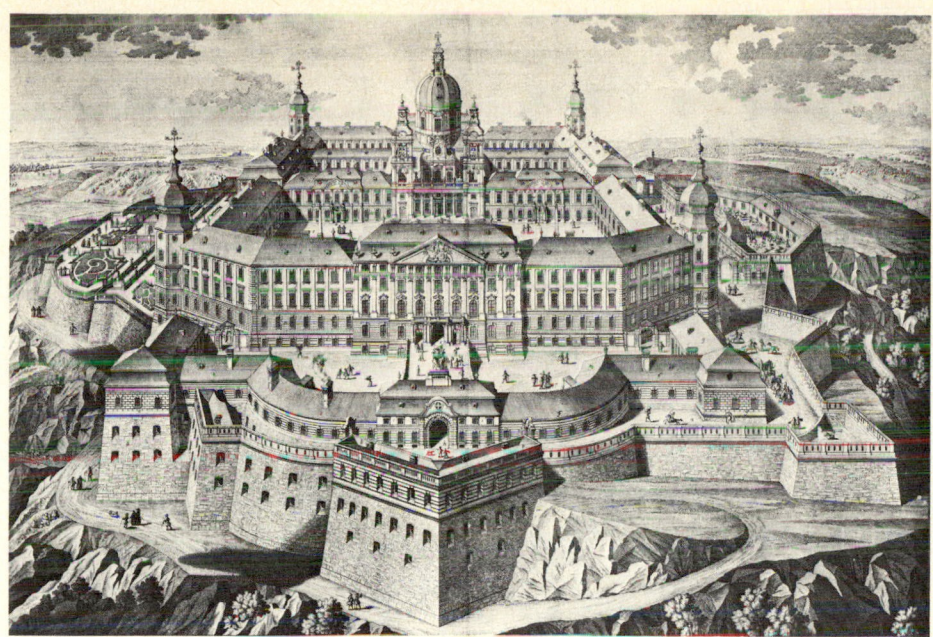

260 Göttweig: the abbey as planned by Lucas von Hildebrandt but never built

by the church façade and towers. The factors governing the appearance of the abbey were accentuated for greater effect; the side over the town was made longer than necessary, whilst the end over the river was packed still more tightly and steeply together.

Melk had already been designed, and substantial parts of it carried out, when in 1719 a fire prompted Gottfried Bessel, the Abbot of Göttweig, to negotiate the building of a complete monastery with the Vice-Chancellor of the Empire, Friedrich Carl von Schönborn, and his architect, Lucas von Hildebrandt. There can be no doubt whatsoever that Melk must have acted as a spur to the utmost endeavours on the part of every other abbey in the Danube valley. Vienna wanted to outbid such perfection. This is how Friedrich Carl writes to his uncle Lothar Franz, the Archbishop of Mainz and Bamberg: '*In simili* the *totum praelaticum* Göttweig, whereon we diligently exercised our compasses on Thursday, and the good Jean Lucca (Hildebrandt), *crudelem situ* just as he was in the Austrian Chancery, verily dashed off a masterpiece *nostri temporis, ratione situs* on this devilish bit of rock; whereas now this *opus* would have been *summe perfectum* both *in architectico et symetrico, quod tandem ipsius sfera* he would on the other hand have thus saved the prelate a good 1,000 paces with a passage cutting through the High Altar, which went awry on account of (its being) squalid *circa vitam et commercium humanum*, so that now hopefully *saltem ad 3°4 gastos primores aut ordinarios* he is indeed to set it decently to rights, whereby the *opus totum* will come *in summa perfectione, amen*.'[44] The count seems to have pointed out to the architect that his splendid design would have disrupted the internal running of the abbey, because the prelate's short-cut into the church would have meant emerging abruptly in the sanctuary from parts filled with the bustle and dirt of human activity. He found fault with the overlong means of access, calling them '*bestial- isch*', and contrary to '*commercium humanum*'. Lothar Franz had already written, not without a trace of wry amusement, 'What is now going to be brewed up by the Lord Prelate of Kottweig (*sic*) under H.E. the Vice-Chancellor's direction and with the participation of Jean Luca will probably not savour so very much of the monks'. The Schönborns regarded the design as their very own project. Hildebrandt took advantage of the rocky site to give proof of his experience as a trained expert in fortifications. We see a wholly symmetrical monastery within

261 *St Florian: the grand staircase (No. 4 on plan opposite)*

a pattern-like plan similar on each of its sides, and with a domed church in the centre. It is well known that only a fraction of it was completed.

The planned accommodation far exceeded the needs of the abbey. Unlike Melk, Einsiedeln or Weingarten, its details depart from monastic requirements. The process of evolution had reached a watershed. The whole was to suggest a crown weighing on the landscape, rather as Hildebrandt's other masterpiece, Prince Eugene's Belvedere, suggested a huge campaigning-tent. This was truly a celestial city. It must have been this design that prompted the Emperor Charles VI in 1730 to stand forth in his turn as the builder of a monastery – one that, comparable to the Escorial, was equally to serve as the summer residence of the court. Interestingly enough in view of the date, the commission for Klosterneuburg was given to an Italian, Donato Allio, who produced his first bombastic design in 1730. The plan envisaged a wholly symmetrical layout, a great rectangle on a terraced plateau overlooking the Danube, with four courts, and nine domes, that were all overshadowed by the one on the church and its two towers. Especially noteworthy is the huge formal garden that was to merge into the countryside behind. By the Emperor's death in 1740 scarcely a quarter of it had been realized.

Like Melk, and in contradistinction to the other pair of palatial abbeys dominating the valley of the Danube, Klosterneuburg and Göttweig, the Baroque monastery of St Florian evolved piecemeal from its medieval predecessor. The south arm of the cloister, which still stands, and which was subsequently to set the scale for the great court, dates back to 1630. In 1676 the monastery embarked on its first large building since the Thirty Years' War, the domestic or dairy court, forming an enclosed quadrangle before the main façade, which ranks amongst the finest examples of farm-buildings. Then in 1686 Carlo Carlone began to build the Baroque church as a memorial to the relief of Vienna from the Turks in 1683, on the same foundations as its Gothic predecessor, and then made a start on the adjoining 650-foot long façade, which was carried on by Prandtauer and his successors. Despite a strict injunction against building by the Emperor, the most enterprising prior, the brewer's son Johann B. Födermayr, erected the marble saloon and the elegant summer refectory projecting into the

262 *St Florian, air-view*

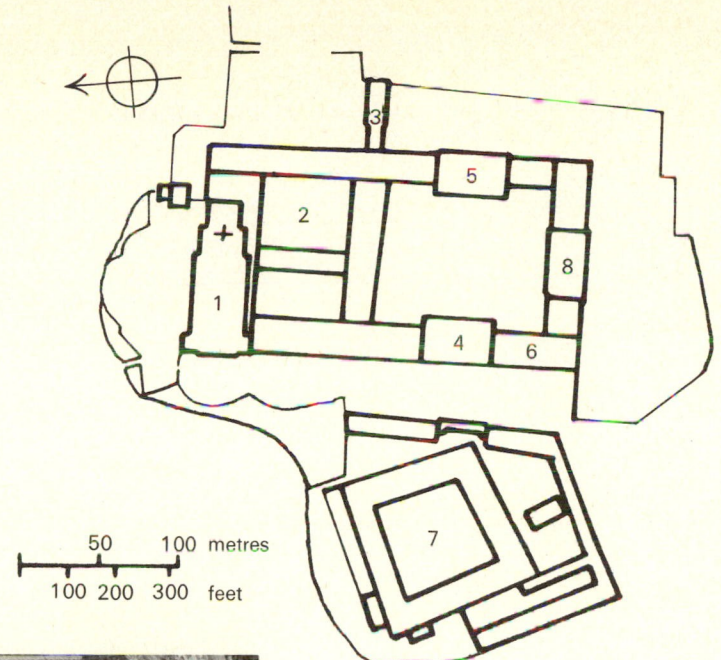

263 *St Florian, plan*
1 *Abbey church*
2 *Monastic buildings*
3 *Summer refectory*
4 *Grand staircase*
5 *Library*
6 *Imperial apartments*
7 *Farm buildings*
8 *Marble saloon (Kaisersaal)*

264–66 *St Florian. Left: Kaisersaal (No. 8 on plan). Below left: library (No. 5). Below: façade of the grand staircase (No. 4) from the interior court*

garden. He also put up Schloss Hohenbrunn on the site of his old home. We owe the great staircase to his predecessor, and the library to his successor. Marble saloon, library and staircase provided the quadrangle of the prelatial court with all the highlights provided for in the project. Everything else was left to the detailing.

Let us turn from Austria to the monasteries of the German Empire.

The Lords Spiritual of Swabia alone included no less than twenty-five representatives of free abbeys. Whether one ranks them by the size of their incomes, their territory, or in population, as these stood in 1792, the first seven in every case are all establishments that undertook great schemes of building in the Baroque. They are as follows:

		guilders	*square miles*	*inhabitants*
1.	Kempten	150,000	*ca.* 335	*ca.* 50,000
2.	Weingarten	97,000	125	14,000
3.	Ochsenhausen	95,000	75	6,000
4.	Obermarchtal	80,000	65	7,000
5.	Salem	78,000	130	6,000
6.	Zwiefalten	74,000	70	8,000
7.	Ottobeuren	68,000	70	10,000

Ottobeuren was actually not always recognized as *reichsunmittelbar*. Many of the remaining free abbeys also undertook important building projects; one could cite Schussenried, Buchau, Neresheim, Weissenau, Rot an der Rot, and the already-mentioned Charterhouse of Buxheim. There was another group of

267 Ottobeuren, the theatre

268 Ottobeuren, the Kaisersaal (Imperial hall)

abbeys of comparable rank which, though ruling over *reichsunmittelbar* territories within the Empire, preferred not to be represented in Regensburg. These
include the Swiss St Gallen, the Upper Austrian St Blasien in the Black Forest,
and Wiblingen, whose lands near Ulm formed a part of Austria. There were
also a number of *reichsunmittelbar* institutions outside the confines of Swabia,
whose representatives in Regensburg could also show one another their projects.
Such were Amorbach and Fulda, in northernmost Franconia and in Hesse, and
the Cistercian monastery of Burtscheid near Aachen, or the remote but still
imposing Corvey. There were also colleges of canons and other foundations that
were not monasteries in the strict sense of the word, but which fell under their
influence as architecture. One might mention the attractive house of Augustinian
canons in Ellwangen, or the one set amidst the wooded highlands of Berchtes-
gaden, of which it was said that its territory was higher than it was wide. Then
there were establishments that sought to make good their claim to independence
through the very scale of their architecture; this was the mainspring of the Baroque rebuilding of the Cistercian monastery of Schöntal on the Jagst. It was
inevitable that these monastic states should include the field of art and architecture in their rivalry, where the political cunning, economic ability or breadth of
interests of the ruling abbot could be decisive. But the facts bear out the state-
ment that the only monasteries that succeeded in initiating viable architectural
undertakings were those where monastic discipline had been restored.

At the outset stood Kempten, Ochsenhausen and Weingarten. They also
topped the list in resources. Ottobeuren was responsible for the masterpiece of
the heyday of building in the middle years of the century. Wiblingen and St
Blasien merit special attention as the last epigones of the movement.

The monastery and church of Ottobeuren are in the last analysis the work of
the abbot, Rupert (II) Ness (1710–40), the son of a coppersmith in Wangen,

who kept a diary which gives us precise information about the progress of the work and of the attitudes inspiring it. He coined the motto of the three 'P''s requisite for building – Patience, Prudence and a well-filled Purse (Document XV). He first set about creating the economic and political preconditions for building, by liquidating the debts of the abbey and subtracting it from the jurisdiction of the Bishop of Augsburg. He then procured numerous designs from Franz Beer, J. J. Herkomer, and Christian Thumb, but ended up by entrusting the work to the indigenous Father Christoph Vogt, and thus himself holding the reins. The monastery was built from 1711 to 1725. Twelve years then passed before he laid the foundation-stone of the church in 1737. Unexpected obstacles were put in the way of building both by the nature of the sub-soil and by the water-table. Though once again numerous designs were proffered and commissioned – from C. A. Maini, K. Radmiller, Dominikus Zimmermann and Joseph Schmutzer – the execution of the church lay once more in the hands of the unassuming Vogt. The entry in Ness's diary for 1 March 1736 reads: 'Spoke just now with Mr Simpert Kramer about the new church, and because (I) already had a heap of designs (I) have taken a little from each and mean to pick the best, to which end (I) granted his request to make a sketch and submit it to me for approval.' In the Baroque as earlier in the Middle Ages the client's word was mostly decisive. He alone saw to the effective employment of the horde of craftsmen and artists who flocked to Ottobeuren. He alone considered the project in

269 Ottobeuren, air view

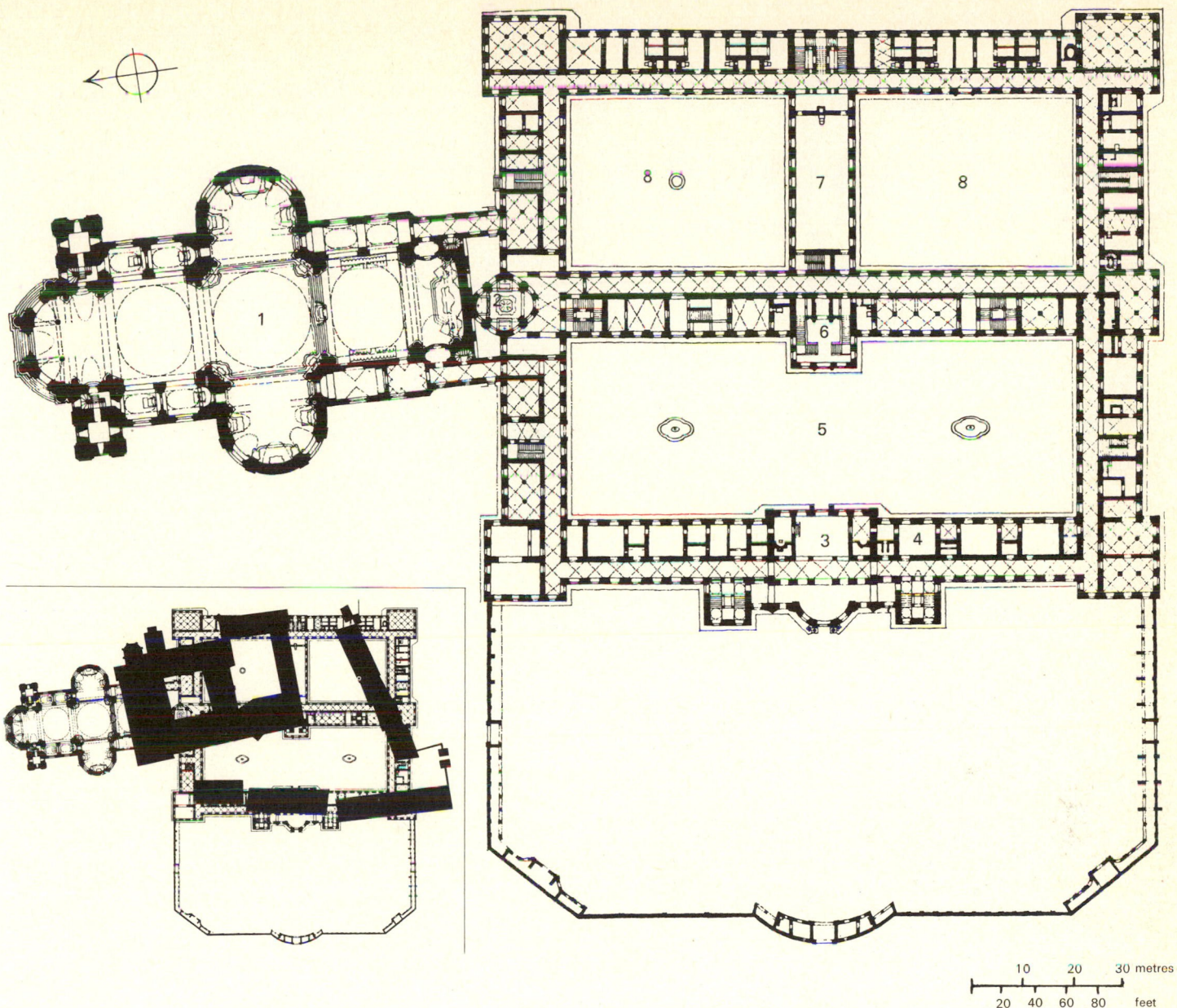

10   20   30 metres

20   40   60   80   feet

its entirety. That in 1747, ten years after it was initiated, his successor then entrusted the modification and completion of the church to Johann Michael Fischer – and thus to a real genius – belongs to another story.

Rupert Ness took no account of the realities of the existing abbey whatsoever. He even renounced the eastward orientation of the Gothic church. The huge square of the new monastery began by only leaving the old church standing, but aligned itself on none of the former axes or lines of building. The whole thing was contained between the formal garden to the west and the abbot's garden to the south. The *Kaisersaal* and princely apartments – parts which were expressly excluded from the sealed-off zone of the monks – faced westwards. The centre tract was filled by the abbot's apartments – the so-called 'Red' or Winter Abbey, containing his fine reception-room, drawing-room and bed-chamber, in which stood that singular piece of quasi-architectural furniture that the abbot had had made as his writing-desk. It is the vastest and the most drawer-filled writing-desk that I know. A description of the desks of the sovereign prelates would fill a chapter on its own. They were what thrones were to princes – symbols of government. The conventual court lay to the east, and was split into two courts by a range containing the refectory, a heated room for study, and the great

270 Ottobeuren, plan
1 *Abbey church*
2 *Abbot's chapel*
3 *Staircase to the Kaisersaal*
4 *Princely apartments*
5 *Abbot's court*
6 *Staircase to abbot's apartments*
7 *Refectory*
8 *Conventual court*

271 *(Inset) Plan of the old abbey of Ottobeuren superimposed upon the new. Note how the earlier church, the block on the far left, was normally orientated, whereas the later has its altar at the south*

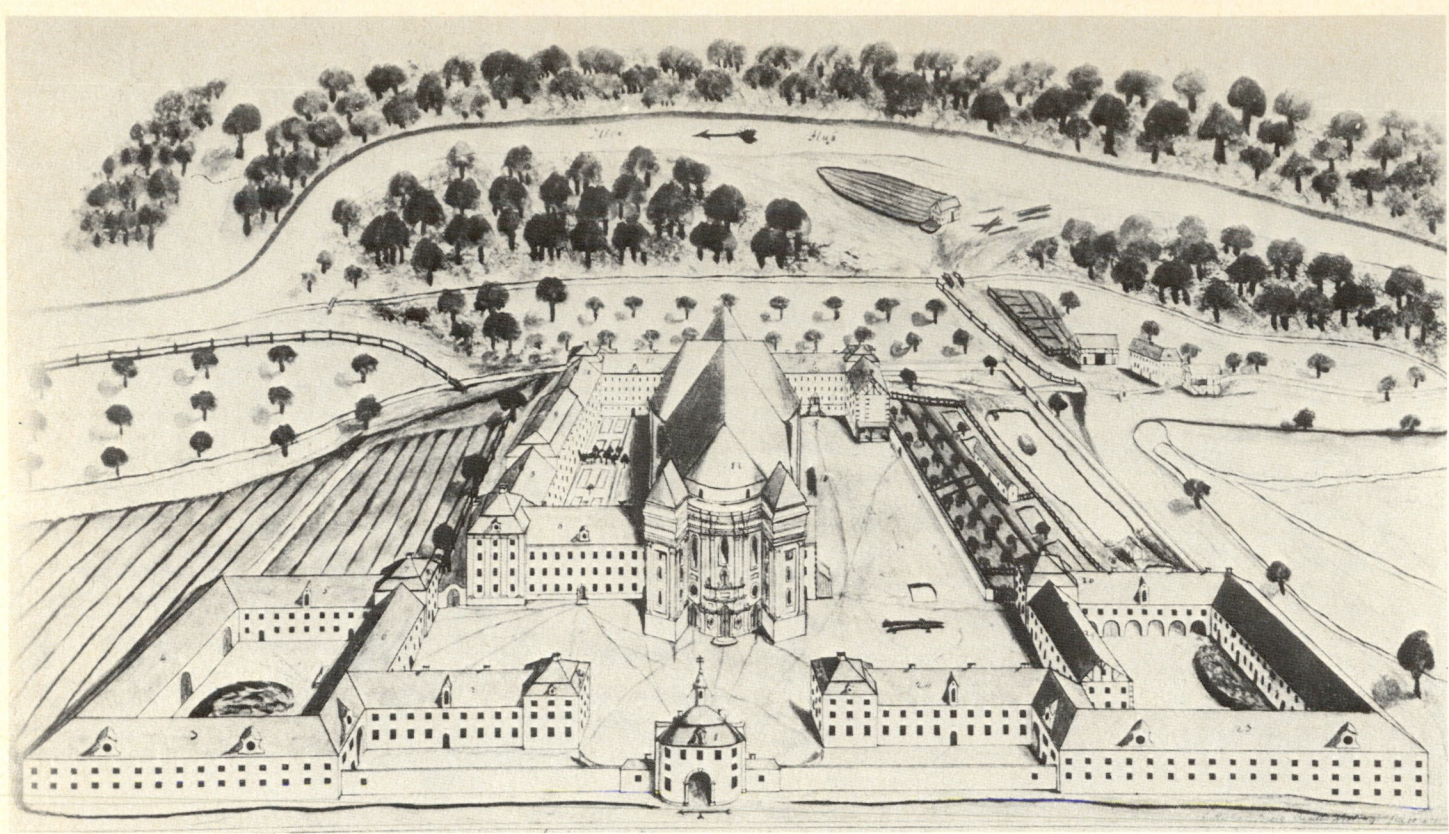

272 *Wiblingen as it looked, only partially completed, at the beginning of the nineteenth century*

273 *Wiblingen, the library*

library. The interiors were decorated with fine Italian and Wessobrunn stucco, whilst the exterior has a rustic simplicity that is consciously inferior to the Austrian abbeys in its very choice of ornament.

The abbot's chapel makes a transition to the abbey church, which projects into the open on the model of Kempten, standing askew in front of the square block almost like a horse in front of its carriage. There is much that is traditionally Swabian in this complex, with its plethora of roofs. This is in keeping with the meadows surrounding it. The solemn symphony of Johann Michael Fischer's majestic interior comes as the absolute peak of Baroque ecclesiastical architecture. Here at last is a treasury of everything time had accumulated in the way of ideas, iconographic programmes, and formal experience; a last epiphany of the celestial city, paradise on this earth.

In Wiblingen too the eighteenth century embarked on a Baroque reconstruction that admitted no constraint by its predecessors. The abbey had suffered terribly from the Wars. Immediately after the end of the War of Spanish Succession in 1714, Abbot Modestus made a start with the domestic offices, which were largely complete by 1729. He retained the domestic court in the old site to the west, but lent it the air of a seigneurial forecourt by means of symmetry, and by punctuating it with pavilions repeating the motif of the gatehouse. The harmonious composition formed by these offices at the point of entry was the chief inspiration in Wiblingen. It owed a lot to Schloss layouts, which employed stables and coach-houses toward similar ends. This forecourt played its part in determining the appearance of the much later designs for the church façade. Abbot Meinrad (1730-62) then began work on the body of the monastery, according to yet more substantial plans, which were in great part only realized by restorers in the twentieth century, after it had become part of Ulm University. The western ranges to right and left of the church were intended to house the prelate's apartments and the guest-rooms, and the eastern ranges to house the convent. The church was only fitted into this composition after 1772, by the master-mason, Johann Georg Specht. After 1778 the painter Januarius Zick also had a say in its architectural appearance within. The result was a perfectly modulated building. Architecturally, it almost stands on a par with Ottobeuren, and its frescoes, considered in isolation, surpass those of the latter. But the unifying principle was no longer the same. Didacticism takes the place of symbolism. Whereas in the latter we were joint actors in the great *theatrum sacrum* of the Church Triumphant, here we are back in Sunday school, though the instruction has indeed a noble ring to it. The uncompleted façade of the church takes account of the inspired composition formed by the domestic offices round the seigneurial forecourt. It lacks dramatic effect, and does not address itself to our emotions, by comparison with Weingarten or Ottobeuren. Wiblingen is an extensive complex that appears both rural and noble.

This last phase is marked by a certain ambiguity in the destination and combination of the various ranges. This emerges even more clearly in the plans for St Blasien, with which we end this survey.

St Blasien in the Black Forest was the last monastery in the eighteenth century to undertake a great building campaign. The ground for it was the acquisition of the county of Bonndorf, thanks to which the abbot, whose actual abbey formed part of the Emperor's Austrian dominions, was declared a prince of the Empire in 1746. Under Abbot Gerbert (1764-93), who was an excellent scholar, the abbey experienced both a scholastic and an artistic heyday. A fire in 1768 occasioned plans for rebuilding. Pierre Michel d'Ixnard, who was mostly based in Strasbourg, made designs which survive in the fair copy done by his Vorarlberg assistant, Salzmann. It only later emerged that more of the old convent could be salvaged than had been thought. The monastic buildings were completed in 1777, and the church, whose domed rotunda imitated the Pantheon, in 1783. This, the last great monastery of the Old Order, is the embodiment of Neo-Classicism and the Enlightenment.

The plan, from which the executed version differed in several particulars, reveals that the sure sense of the Baroque for ornamental arrangement was lost. One need only compare this design with the ideal visions of Weingarten and

274 Wiblingen, ceiling frescoes of the abbey church

275 Wiblingen, as completed in the twentieth century, with symmetrical north and south ranges

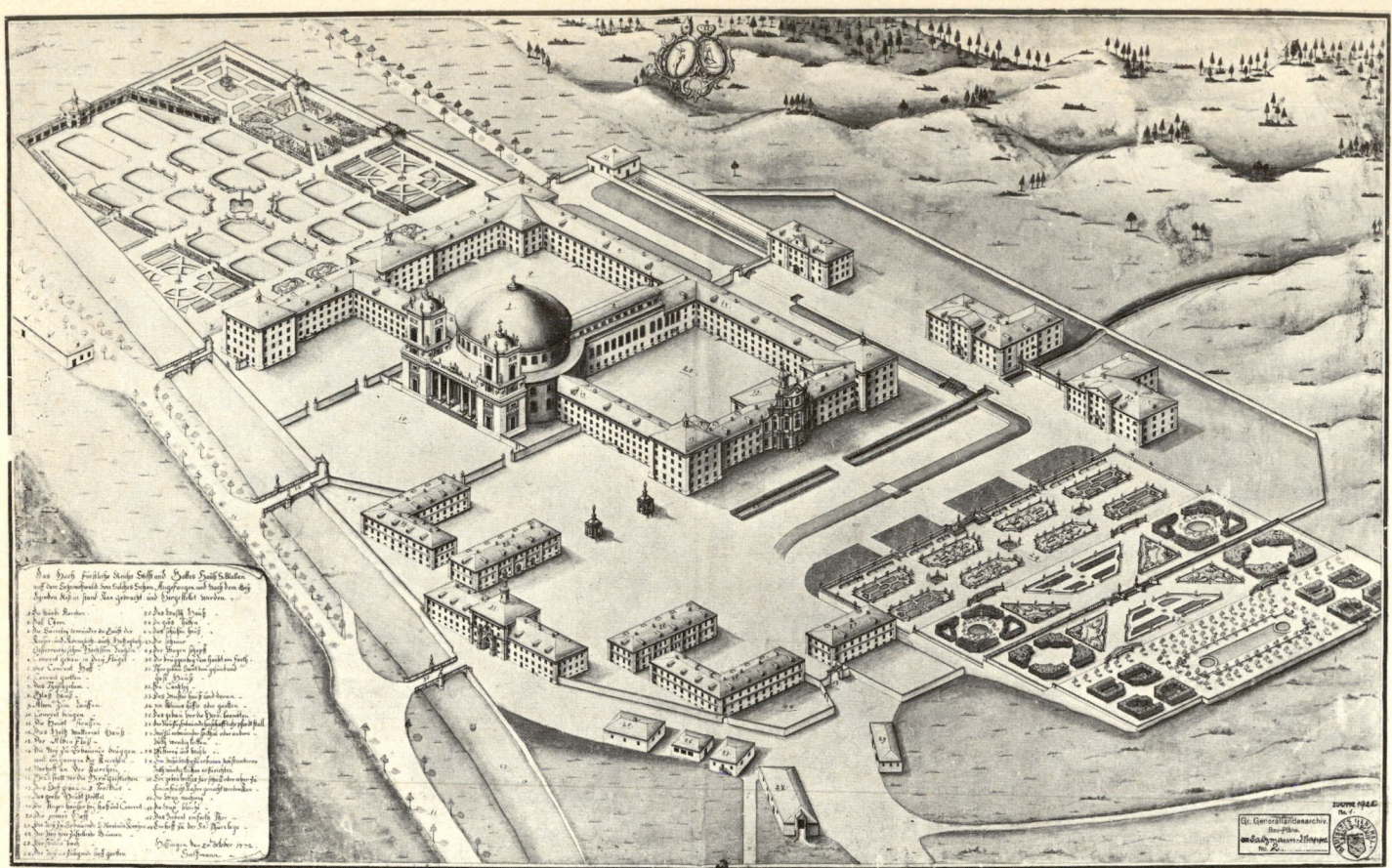

276 St Blasien. The design, made by d'Ixnard in 1768 but not fully carried out, is analysed in the text below

Göttweig, or with the ensembles of Einsiedeln or Melk, to see the implications of this observation. The schema itself survives. There is the church in the middle, with the conventual court to its left and the prelatial court to its right; the climax of the former is the refectory, with the conventual garden stretching before it, and of the latter the great block with the triumphal staircase surviving from the Baroque abbey. In front of it is the main formal garden (No. 24). Strangely, this garden is separated from the entrance by the drive, which goes over the bridge (30), through the gatehouse (31), past two fountains (21, 22) to the main door. The gatehouse is flanked by two buildings containing the chancery (32) and offices (35), which appear like unsecured blocks placed on the ground. There are a number of other buildings like those in the background whose exact purpose the draughtsman was unable to specify (40, 38, 39). Here is an attempt at enlightened and rational order, which is quite illusory. Everything has been neatly measured out as if for Prussian Grenadiers, and not in the service of a higher ideal. The abbey is now a princely residence, a learned republic, the seat of government, an agricultural concern, and a pastoral mission; but it no longer aspires to be the *Civitas Dei* on earth. It must be admitted that St Blasien was associated with the French Enlightenment no less through the efforts of the architect's clients than through his own. Around 1770 it could hardly have been otherwise. In these same years a team of scholars compiled some of the most important historical works of the age, first and foremost a history of the monasteries, colleges and sees of the Holy Roman Empire, those nine volumes of the *Germania Sacra* which they managed to publish before the secularization. It is significant that history prospers when symbolism loses its hold. Monastic architecture has always given precise information about spiritual conditions. It is an outstanding thing that so few decades before being dissolved, the abbeys and priories of Southern Germany could produce such magnificent syntheses of the Christian outlook. Doom struck several institutions that were still in their prime.

II

Secularization and Fresh Beginnings

An account of monastic architecture would not be complete without touching on the great onslaught on the monasteries, prepared by the Enlightenment and released by the French Revolution, which made a virtually clean sweep of them. There was hardly a monastery in France or Germany which was not secularized, and attempts were subsequently made in Spain, Portugal and Italy to spread this to what had at first been spared. One must turn to Austria or Switzerland to find such few – admittedly some of the finest – as never ceased to celebrate the *Opus Dei* in their churches. But we must also point to the attempts that were made in several places to revive the monastic idea which began soon after the Congress of Vienna. Statistics of existing institutions present an impressive picture. It is astonishing how great the number of houses of the various Orders is, and how many of the old Orders go on, whilst new communities constantly spring up. It must of course be admitted that in most cases the monks and nuns simply went back to their old, evacuated convents. New architectural ventures like Ludwig I's romantic monastery of St Bonifaz in Munich (*v.i.* p. 225), or Le Corbusier's bold project for the Dominicans in La Tourette near Lyons (*v.i.* p. 226), are rare.

Justice demands that one should speak here of the historic crime by which the idealism of the monks was impugned, their treasures were barbarously scattered and destroyed, their monasteries sold, their churches deconsecrated, and many of the finest of them torn down. Cluny was sold in 1798, its church blown up in 1811, the ruins used as a quarry up to 1823, till finally they were accorded protection in 1826. Precious codices were flung down from the ox-carts taking treasures from Bavarian and Swabian monasteries to the national libraries in Munich and Stuttgart, in order to fill the ruts in the muddied roads. There are moving accounts of the distress of the expelled monks and nuns and of their despair over the destruction of the life's work of generations. In Germany, Catholic and Protestant princely houses were indistinguishable in the enthusiasm with which they took part in the acquisition of vacant abbeys promised to them as compensation for slight losses on the far side of the Rhine, presented in recognition of their services, or just sold to them for a pittance. Many families sit on their plunder to this day. In France numerous factories and families prospered on the proceeds of monastic acquisitions. Monastic booty played a large part in the capital formation generating the Industrial Revolution. History has accepted the fact without counting the cost. Hardly a voice was raised to defend the monasteries. Scarcely anyone joined the young Tieck in regretting the removal of a centuries-old imperial legacy from a cathedral chapter like Bamberg. Men believed themselves justified as long as they saved the most important works from destruction in new collections. Many of the most important artistic centres of France, Spain and the Holy Roman Empire were deprived of everything of worth that was movable in favour of national collections. Such was the case with Regensburg, Weingarten or Tegernsee. People were nervously on the lookout for suitable uses to which the buildings could be put. Monasteries were turned into borstals, like Brauweiler or Ebrach; lunatic asylums, like Schussenried, Zwiefalten or Weissenau; actual prisons, like Clairvaux, Fontevrault, Mont-Saint-Michel or Aniane – to cite some of the more famous instances in France alone; in towns usually into barracks, like Santa Maria Novella and Santo Spirito in Florence; and ultimately into schools as well. Most Parisian monasteries began by being prisons, whilst the Dominican friary, as their clubhouse, gave the Jacobins their name, and the house of the Augustinians was first of all a *depôt* for works of art, and since 1820 the École des Beaux-Arts. With grim tenacity the government's commissars unearthed the remotest and humblest houses, and where they managed to escape through good political connections or through their situation, later decades repaired the omission. Montalembert reports that he saw fine columns and capitals from famous churches and cloisters used as paving for the local roads. Every museum of medieval art, every library holding medieval manuscripts owes the bulk of its treasures to ownerless monastic property; indeed this formed the very basis of the existence of such museums as the Musée de Cluny in Paris, the Germanisches Nationalmuseum in Nürnberg, the Bayerisches Nationalmuseum in Munich or the Wallraf-Richartz-Museum in Cologne. One type of institution took over from the other. Many of the most attractive museums were themselves installed in monasteries – as in Nuremberg, Regensburg, and Pisa. Sometimes a monastery was so profusely decorated that, like San Marco in Florence, it was left as a museum.

The onslaught on monasteries was organized like a campaign. Catholic countries were especially determined to show their progressiveness. In Munich, at 3 o'clock in the morning of 3 November 1802, forty commissioners were dispatched in every direction with instructions to use the monasteries' own horses to remove everything from them, with the exception of a monstrance, a ciborium and no more than six cheap chalices. In France bans on and expropriations of monasteries occurred sporadically up to the threshold of our own era. Those who had returned saw themselves expelled for a second and even a third time. Monasteries remained unpalatable to both anti-clerical France and national-liberal Germany, save where – as in the case of Wilhelm II's predilection for the Benedictines – a romantic sense of history protected them. As late as 1862 the last monastery in the Canton of Zurich, the beautiful Rheinau, was suppressed after stormy sessions in the city council. All the attempts of its noble and able abbot, Leodegar Ineichen (1810-76) were in vain. One ought to read the statements made before him by the three leading Protestants: Jakob Brunner the moderator of the Zurich church, Johann Jakob Rutlimann the leading lawyer of the city, and Sulzer the Chairman of Winterthur Council. 'Only one crime is laid to the charge of the monks of Rheinau – that their estates are worth two millions', exclaimed Sulzer. Most of the Catholics on the Zurich Council subsequently also voted for secularization.[45]

The will to secularization was deep-rooted. It combined three currents, fed from old and distant sources. It gathered strength to sweep everything away from the fact that it was so long held back that a changed world held the monasteries to be obsolete as political institutions, and their works of art and architecture to be worthless. The arts that they had helped to shape stood in the service of the then ruling powers. Artists, who have so willingly joined the ranks of the opposition since the beginning of the nineteenth century, condemned them, as did literary and philosophical figures.

The first of the three currents had its source in Protestantism. The Reformation, like all earlier sects, repudiated monasticism. There are only a dwindling number of attempts to rethink it in terms of the new faith. Husum, whose abbot is currently the Protestant bishop of one of the German Länder, is one such attempt. Attempts to found religious communities outside the Catholic church have never found an echo. This is no place to investigate the psychological and religious roots of this remarkable phenomenon. Voluntary submission to a self-appointed authority held no appeal for people whose aim was the transformation of existing institutions whose deformities they could observe. Almost wherever

Protestantism took hold it dissolved monasteries and made sees of them, whilst obstructing new foundations. Where there was no alternative use for the buildings, they were demolished. Henry VIII was most ruthless of all. He ended by prohibiting all monasteries in 1539, and most of them were senselessly destroyed. Seven ships brought the colossal artistic plunder to Rouen, where it was put up for auction. The monastic history of this island was cut off at this point. Many of the ruins just mouldered until their present conservation. Splendid country houses were often ensconced in the walls of old abbeys. Even where they survive almost in their entirety and have assumed new functions, they have wanted the vigour to thrive architecturally. They became dead. The best-preserved Benedictine monastery in England, Canterbury Cathedral Church and Priory, illustrates this. Often this very lifelessness has been their salvation. They have been used to house schools and estate offices, which adjusted themselves to their surroundings. We owe to this the best-preserved Cistercian monasteries in Germany, Maulbronn and Eberbach.

The second and third currents flowed from differing attitudes and spiritual climates. Let us call them the destructive urge of unreason, and the reforming zeal of reason. One derived from the groundswell of popular emotion, which took objection to any form of authority. Throughout the wars of history, men have rooted about in the monasteries in their path like boys in an ant-heap. It was deeply satisfying to destroy them. Furthermore, ever since the seventeenth century many of the most intelligent men of their time had clashed with monasteries as the enemies of all progress. 'A monk', Voltaire asked, 'what kind of profession is that? It is to have none at all, to bind oneself by an irrevocable oath to oppose reason and be a slave, whilst living at others' expense.'[46] These forces from above and below conspired together after 1766 in France and 1781 in Austria and did not slacken until every last monastery in France, Germany and Italy was suppressed. The wealth of the monasteries itself added fuel to the process. But men also hoped to emancipate themselves from the weight of history holding the future to ransom.

Let us first take an example of the forces from below – just one of countless hundreds. A visitor moved by the sight of one of the more imposing sets of ruins of a Cistercian abbey is often tempted to re-read the story of its destruction, as the author did in Orval in Belgium.

In 1637 a French contingent from the army of the Maréchal de Chatillon, whom Richelieu had ordered to support the Swedish cause in Germany, arrived at the monastery. 'On 2 August two bands of assorted Swedes and Frenchmen broke their way into the monastery and looted it thoroughly. They erupted first into the domestic court, and then penetrated the other buildings, taking the cloister, the sacristy and the church . . . they destroyed the tabernacle with blows from an axe, and dragged off the bells and chalices, and all the decorations and movables from the church, the library and everywhere else. They first desecrated the altar and then hacked it to pieces, knocked down the statues, and broke off their hands, feet and heads. The church and the domestic court were burnt down the same evening. The ruins of the church, whose vaults held, were used by the monks as a lavatory and as a stable for the horses. Many report that the High Altar was used as a manger. On 11 August the monastery was set fire to on all four corners and razed to the ground. Since the flames did not succeed in reaching the vaults of the church, on 13 August forty French knights plotted together, took burning bundles of straw in their hands and cried, "Let's burn it all to the ground!". They set fire to the church and the conventual buildings simultaneously. The conflagration lasted four whole days, and did not spare even the choir-stalls. The whole abbey burnt down with the exception of the small chapel of Notre Dame de Montaigue, which is set high up some distance away.'[47]

The abbey managed to recover in the late seventeenth and eighteenth century. The old buildings were painstakingly restored. Revenues from their estates brought about a new heyday. It was also to the fore in learning. In 1757 over a million francs lay in its treasury, and were employed on a colossal rebuilding out of fear of a fresh seizure. L. B. Dewez (1731-1812) incorporated large parts of the restored medieval monastery in his design, but added an imposing Baroque ensemble. As rebuilt it was held to be the most magnificent Baroque *château* in the country. As in Clairvaux each monk now had his own elegant apartments. The architect was to live to see General Laisson's troops, led by the village parson and abetted by the local populace, plunder the abbey yet again on 23 June 1793. The conflagration was not allowed to die out for six weeks, until the last room of the abbey had collapsed. The tenacity with which not only the foreign soldiers, but also the local people engaged in its destruction suggests that old hatreds were also at work here. 'See that the estates of the Church are sold, for we can never be freed from these wild beasts until their lairs are destroyed and they are smoked out', wrote Madame Roland in 1790.[48] Orval is just one example of the thousands that then perished. There are contrasting instances, where the local population defended and rescued their churches and monasteries. Nowhere did they prevent the expulsion of the monks and nuns. For where primitive urges spared them, an enlightened administration repaired the omission.

As early as 1666 Colbert wrote that famous letter to Louis XIV about the damage done to the state by monasticism. Similar voices are heard throughout the Middle Ages. Even Charlemagne had refused to countenance considerable evasions from military service on the pretext of taking the vows. 'Nuns and other sisters', wrote Colbert, 'not only avoid working for the common good, but also deprive the state of all the children that they might have borne. It would then perhaps be wise to make profession somewhat more difficult, and to limit the custom of giving nuns dowries and pensions.' Louis XIV answered with deliberate sense and moderation: 'One should limit the numbers in this profession to those applying themselves to the education of the people and to the care of the Sacrament, or to those that set a shining example by their asceticism.'[49] He further added that there were to be no new foundations without the express permission of the king. For more than a century there was to be no respite from the chorus of those intent on limiting the freedom of action of the monasteries by only tolerating those engaged in education, care of the sick, or pastoral duties. Contemplation was not thought to have any value. In 1766, exactly a hundred years after Colbert's letter, a commission was set up which attempted to limit the number of religious establishments by the suppression of numerous houses. Nonetheless in 1770, France still held 412 Benedictine monasteries, 251 Cistercian abbeys, 66 Charterhouses, 92 Premonstratensian houses, 568 friaries belonging to the Franciscans, 179 to the Dominicans, and 157 to the Augustinians, 429 Capuchin establishments, and 191 that were Carmelite, as well as, in 1788, about 1,500 nunneries containing 37,000 nuns. Whereas voices never ceased to be raised about the moral depravity of the male houses, even Revolutionary France had to admit to the inspiring conduct of the nuns, and their importance in popular education. In 1769 special edicts began to limit the activities of the friars in Bavaria. In 1778 the Franciscans were restricted to 400 brethren, and the Capuchins to 450. In 1781 Joseph II of Austria issued the famous decree forbidding all monasteries whose inmates 'lead only a contemplative life, and contribute nothing to the good of their neighbour or civil society'. This closed about 700 monasteries, including every Carthusian priory. Nonetheless this law had the simultaneous effect of favouring the great establishments by entrusting extensive areas to their pastoral care. Austria is one of the few countries in Europe in which rich and important monasteries were never secularized. A total ban on monasteries was first pronounced in Paris in 1790. It was one of the principles of Napoleonic administration to extend this to all countries in which he or his generals attained to mastery; from Belgium in 1796 to the Kingdom of Italy in 1806, the Grand Duchy of Tuscany in 1808, and the Papal States in 1809. Joseph Bonaparte hastened to dissolve the monasteries in the Kingdom of Naples, and what escaped him was finished off by his successor Marat in 1809. In Spain Napoleonic rule was too shaky to make more than a successful start, but this was made good after 1821. Of the 1,700 houses then still in existence, 800 were then shut. In 1835 the government insisted on the dissolution of all monasteries with less than twelve monks or nuns. In Madrid on 18 January 1836 the last thirty-seven male houses were banned. This had been preceded by a decree in Portugal shutting all monasteries. The tendency even caught on in Central and North America. Enlightened administrations everywhere turned against monasteries. In 1874 the Swiss constitution forbade 'the erection of new, or the restoration of suppressed, monasteries or religious Orders'. No-one was any longer to be allowed refuge from the century.

Yet the monastic idea could not be stamped out. Resistance promoted a new idealism. Reports of abuses cease, and those of new foundations increase, throughout the nineteenth century. It is remarkable how quickly the last members of the old Orders got together again after 1820 or 1830. With the backing of Rome it was possible to reconstitute them. New Orders and new Congregations were founded. There was seldom a lack of vocations. Educational and missionary activity presented great challenges. Various rulers, and even private individuals, founded and encouraged monasteries. Even the most exacting contemplative Orders found adherents. The monastic situation in the late nineteenth and twentieth centuries presents a panoramic prospect to the eye. An indigenous style was even found for the construction and decoration of monastery churches – here Beuron springs to mind.

The conventual buildings were, it is true, less noteworthy. When an Order did not go back to the model of its medieval precursors, as we saw with the Carthusians (*v.s.* p. 124) their buildings mostly looked as if they could have served, without any great modifications, as orphanages or old people's homes. It is furthermore impossible to distinguish between the Orders on the basis of the motifs or layouts that they employed. Monastic establishments ceased to be a mirror of their Rules; general, superimposed ideas governed their overall plan. One example will again suffice.

In 1826 Ludwig I of Bavaria commissioned Georg Friedrich Ziebland to build a basilica in honour of St Boniface, which, as a monument of Christianity, was to make an exact foil to the monument of Hellenism represented by the Glyptothek opposite. The plan had been decided on by 1822 (details in Bibl. 234). Ziebland was sent to Italy on a journey lasting from 1826 to 1829 in order to make studies that would profit his designs. 'It is my intention', the king addressed the twenty-six-year-old architect on his first audience, 'to build a church in Munich to St Boniface, the Apostle of the German and Bavarian people, and it is to be a basilica. I have chosen you to build it; but since I want it to be a faithful example of a basilica both in form and in spirit, I am sending you to Italy for a number of years. You are to study sedulously the basilicas to be found there, and to submit plans of them to me. The foundation-stone will however only be laid in 1835, on my silver wedding-day. But I lay down certain specifications here and now: the basilica must form a companion-piece to the Glyptothek opposite and adhere to the Corinthian Greek style; it is to have five aisles, and be roughly the size of the three-aisled basilica outside Ravenna, St Apollinaris in Classe.' One is amazed how exactly the king knew what he wanted. The architect had three years in which to make his Italian studies, and a further six till the foundation-stone was to be laid. In the meantime the plan grew in scope. An exhibition gallery was to be put opposite the Glyptothek, with a Benedictine monastery attached to it, at whose other end was to be the great basilica, which was to serve both as monastery- and parish-church. At the ceremonial laying of the foundation-stone the ruling idea was repeatedly mentioned. The king had only laid one foundation-stone for all three buildings, betokening that art, learning and religion were to go hand in hand. The monastery's chief pursuit was to be research. There was to be a separate chaplaincy to serve the parish. By 1847 the buildings were complete. In 1850 the church was consecrated.

1 *Basilica of St Boniface*
2 *Combined monastery and art gallery*
3 *Glyptothek (sculpture gallery)*
4 *Propylaeum*
5 *Königsplatz*

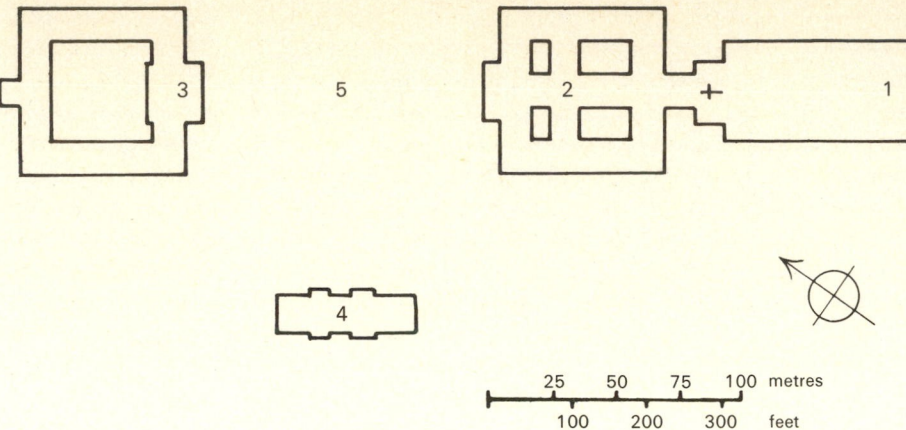

277 The complex of museum, monument and monastery commissioned by Ludwig I in Munich in 1826

278 St Boniface, Munich. A capital from the façade

The monastery is a three-storeyed building with two internal courts. It is linked structurally to the exhibition gallery, which today houses minor classical art. The sides do not betray any caesura between the monastery and this Temple of the Muses. The allocation of space inside the monastery has only slight correspondencies with the Benedictine schema. The refectory lies (or rather lay, since it was destroyed in the Second World War) on the ground floor, and was decorated with a Last Supper by Heinrich Hess, who took Leonardo's as his model. It is noteworthy that pictures were everywhere accompanied or replaced by inscriptions alluding to the higher significance of the rooms – quotations from the psalms, the Gospels, or the Rule. On the first floor lay the abbot's apartments, a recreation-room as it was called, a reading-room for the day's quota of literature, and fifteen single rooms for the monks or for guests. The great chapter-house was displaced to the second floor, alongside further single rooms, whilst the whole of the north side adjacent to the exhibition-gallery was occupied by the library. The monks were comfortably installed, but their organic connection with the church had gone, as had the cloister, whilst the chapter-house and refectory were two floors apart. The monastery's underlying significance was intended to be brought out by pictures and inscriptions rather than by its layout. The literacy and intellectual premises of the royal concept were thus apparent in every detail. Contrary to the original intention, the abbey also assumed parochial responsibility after the project was completed. After his deposition in 1848 Ludwig I assured its future by donations. He had already acquired the pilgrimage church of Andechs, with all its appertaining buildings, estates and rights, as an outpost for the new monastery in 1846. His desire was to associate the new foundation with the traditions of an older place that had lost its *raison d'être* through secularization.

We have only taken one building to represent the nineteenth century, and we shall take only one for the twentieth – La Tourette. I am aware that this will not do full justice to the attempts of modern monasticism to create novel and indigenous contexts for itself. Only the direction that these imaginative efforts take will emerge. Le Corbusier's work is anyway unique in its logicality. In this complex the innate rationalism, lucidity and intellectual rigour of the Dominican Order and its French beginnings enter the present.

On a journey through Italy in 1907 Le Corbusier was struck by the Carthusian priory of Galluzzo outside Florence.[50] He went back to his travel notes in evolving the principles behind the Immeubles Villas in the early twenties and the *Unité d'Habitation* of Marseilles in 1953. He became aware of the advantages deriving from solitary life in a community. In his researches into the *Modulor* he draws expressly on this interplay between the cells and the communal rooms in the Charterhouse of Ema (as it was called by guides of the period, after the stream flowing through Galluzzo). Here was a prototype using a principle that seemed to him ideal for structuring the life of the masses. This architect, like the founder of an Order, felt the urge to draw up rules and plans for living. The inhabitant of the *Ville Radieuse,* like the Carthusian in his cellular abode, finds an apartment equipped with everything that the architect foresees he will want or need. In 1953, in the same year as he was busy on plans for the 'House of the City', Father Couturier commissioned him to build a Dominican friary. Le Corbusier spent three years on the plans. At the suggestion of the friars he also studied the Cistercian abbey of Le Thoronet in southern France, which represented their

279 St Boniface, Munich. The façade of the church

280-82 La Tourette, by Le Corbusier: plan of the three floors

1 Church
2 Reception rooms
3 Porter's lodge
4 Lay-brothers' common room
5 Lay-brothers' study
6 Oratory
7 Library
8 Lecture-rooms
9 Study
10 Common-room
11 Corridors or 'cloister'
12 'Atrium'
13 W.C.
14 Pantry
15 Refectory
16 Chapter-house
17 Lower church, with chapels
18 High altar
19 Sacristy
20 Spiral staircase connecting all three floors
21 Sick-rooms
22 Treatment room
23 Guests' rooms
24 Monks' cells
25 Director of studies' cell
26 Novices' cells
27 Lay-brothers' cells

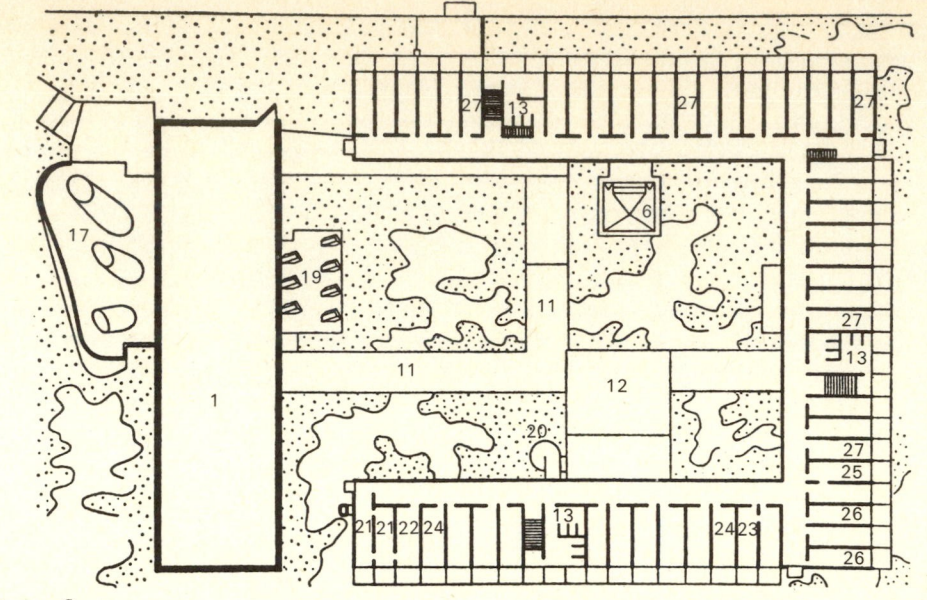

Upper floor

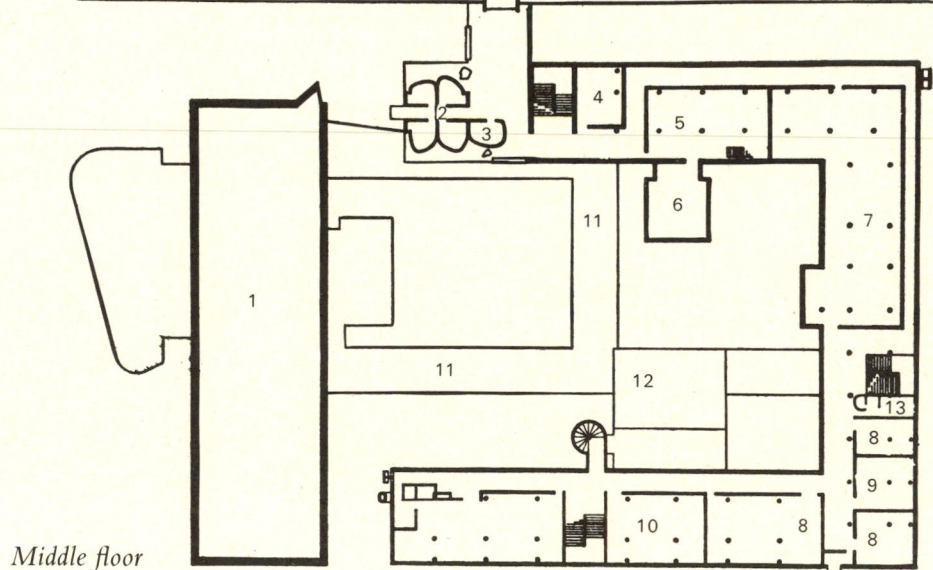

Middle floor

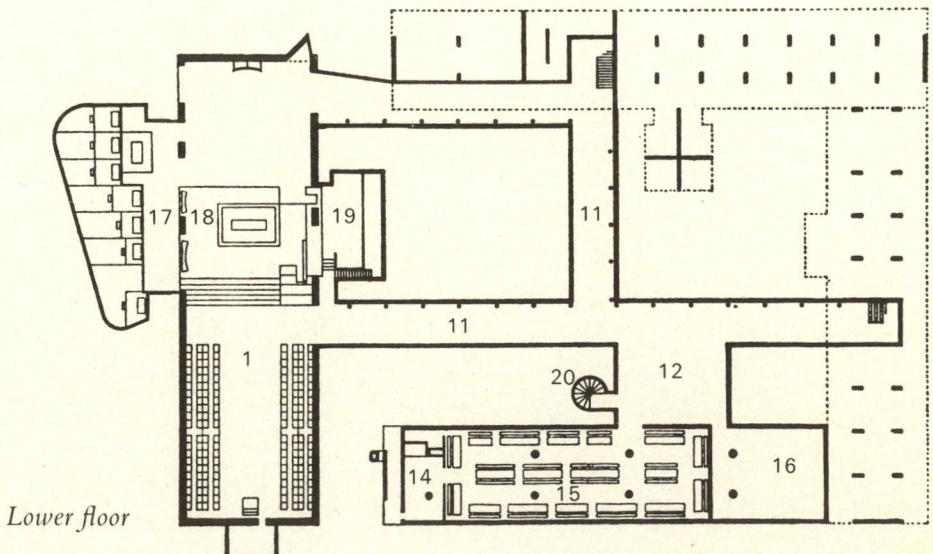

Lower floor

ideal. Never, he is reported to have said, did a client make so little opposition to his designs. Never, we should like to add, did a client approach him with such a lucid conception of what he wanted. Here is the old schema of a Benedictine monastery, enhanced by the Dominican desire – which had been achieved in the most important of their medieval houses – that a friary should also be a seminary for members of the Order and a centre of theological research. In 1960 the building was finally completed.

The sloping ground of La Tourette's hill-top site above the village of Evreux-sur-l'Abresle, south of Lyons, encouraged its deployment on three levels. There are parts all on ground level, and others of one or two storeys. It was an inspiration to situate the scholastic floor between the ground-floor containing the church, cloister, refectory and chapter-house, and that above with cells planned as study-bedrooms. It was then natural for the entrance-way to be led up to this middle floor, which was the only one accessible to the public. The plan shows the porter's lodge and four other little reception-rooms where Le Corbusier gives rein to his pleasure in minute circularly-contained rooms. As in the old Benedictine monasteries therefore, church, cloister, refectory, and chapter-house to the south, are all situated at ground level, whilst the bedrooms are put up above. In conformity with the Rule these are divided into cells for the sick, for guests, lay-brothers, and priests. They all issue onto an inner corridor, and all have the same long, narrow shape, but in contrast with the past they also give onto bright balconies, from which one is meant to see far and wide. The central scholastic floor is divided into classrooms, lecture-rooms, and common-rooms for lay-brethren and for the friars. The largest room houses the library. There is

283 La Tourette, view from the south-west. The two top storeys, with their small openings, contain the monks' cells

284 La Tourette, air view also from the south-west. The church occupies the far side, the north. The small building with pyramid roof inside the square is the oratory

also a small oratory, which stands like a fountain pavilion in a place apart off the inner court, and whose shape – its conical roof – marks it out as a sacred structure. Here we see the immediate influence of Le Thoronet. Everything is constructed of bare concrete. The building looks as if it came straight out of a mould, and this is intentional. There is a sense of intellectual energy, informing a plan that determines everything by reference to the Rule. Nothing is left to chance, or to the vagaries of the individual. Form is under the clear, sharp and lucid control of the intellect.

It was a Carthusian priory that supplied the model for the young Corbusier's idea of a modern housing-estate. Its celled houses associated with communal rooms struck him as a pattern for the organization of mass-dwellings. In the Dominican friary that he was entrusted with, the old *maître* could amplify on this idea. This seems like a beginning that opens up wide prospects ahead.

285 La Tourette, the refectory

Selections from Documentary
Sources

Notes

Bibliography

List of Illustrations

Index

Selections from Documentary Sources

1   From St Benedict's Rule

S. Benedicti Regula Monasteriorum, ed. Cuthbert Butler, 2nd edn Freiburg 1927.
The Rule was composed at Monte Cassino in several stages from 534 onwards. The original manuscript was carried to Rome for safety after the Lombard invasions, returned to Monte Cassino in 742, was whisked off from a Saracen raid to Teano in 883, where it was lost in a fire in 896. Charlemagne had a transcript made, from which two monks from Reichenau prepared an exact copy around 820, which survives as Codex 914 of the abbey library of St Gallen. The best critical editions of the text are: B. Linderbauer, *S. Benedicti Regula Monasteriorum*, Bonn 1928, and Butler's edition cited here.

The translation used is, with minor adjustments, that of Cardinal Gasquet, in *The Rule of Saint Benedict*, London 1936 (first published in 1909).

Caput III: Quotiens aliqua praecipua agenda sunt in monasterio, convocet abbas omnem congregationem, et dicat ipse unde agitur. Et audiens consilium fratrum tractet apud se, et quod utilius iudicaverit faciat. Ideo autem omnes ad consilium vocari diximus, quia saepe iuniori Dominus revelat quod melius est. . . .

Caput IV: . . . Actus vitae suae omni hora custodire. – In omni loco Deum se respicere pro certo scire. – Cogitationes malas cordi suo advenientes mox ad Christum allidere, et seniori spirituali patefacere. – Os suum a malo vel pravo eloquio custodire. – Multum loqui non amare. – Verba vana aut risui apta non loqui. – Risum multum aut excussum non amare. . . .

Praecepta Dei factis cotidie adimplere. – Castitatem amare. – Nullum odire. – Zelum non habere. – Invidiam non exercere. – Contentionem non amare. – Elationem fugere. – Et seniores venerare. – Iuniores diligere. –

. . . Officina vero, ubi haec omnia diligenter operemur, claustra sunt monasterii et stabilitas in congregatione. . . .

Caput XVI: Ut ait Propheta: Septies in die laudem dixi tibi. Qui septenarius sacratus numerus a nobis sic implebitur, si Matutino, Primae, Tertiae, Sextae, Nonae, Vesperae, Completoriique tempore nostrae servitutis officia persolvamus; quia de his diurnis Horis dixit: Septies in die laudem dixi tibi. Nam de nocturnis Vigiliis idem ipse Propheta ait: Media nocte surgebam ad confitendum tibi. Ergo his temporibus referamus laudes creatori nostro super iudicia iustitiae suae, id est, Matutinis, Prima, Tertia, Sexta, Nona, Vespera, Completorio; et nocte surgamus ad confitendum ei. . . .

Caput XXII: Singuli per singula lecta dormiant. Lectisternia pro modo conversationis, secundum dispensationem abbatis sui, accipiant. Si potest fieri, omnes in uno loco dormiant: sin autem multitudo non sinit, deni aut viceni cum senioribus, qui super eos solliciti sint, pausent. Candela iugiter in eadem cella ardeat usque mane. Vestiti dormiant, et cincti cingulis aut

Ch. 3: Whenever any weighty matters have to be transacted in the monastery let the abbot call together all the community and himself propose the matter for discussion. After hearing the advice of the brethren let him consider it in his own mind, and then do what he shall judge most expedient. We ordain that all must be called to council, because the Lord often reveals to a younger member what is best. . . .

Ch. 4 (the Instruments of Good Works): To watch over the actions of one's life every hour of the day. – To know for certain that God sees one everywhere. – To dash at once against Christ evil thoughts which rise up in the mind, and to reveal all such to one's spiritual father. – To guard one's lips against uttering evil or wicked words. – Not to be fond of much talking. – Not to speak idle words or such as move to laughter. – Not to love much or boisterous laughter . . . Daily in one's acts to keep God's commandments. – To love chastity. – To hate no man. – Not to be jealous or envious. – Not to love wrangling. – To show no arrogant spirit. – To reverence the old. – To love the young. – . . . Steadfastly abiding in the community, the workshop where all these instruments are made use of is the cloister of the monastery.

Ch. 16 (How the day's Divine Office is to be said): The prophet says, 'Seven times a day have I sung Thy praises'. This sacred number of seven will be kept by us if we perform the duties of our service in the Hours of Lauds, Prime, Tierce, Sext, None, Evensong and Compline. It was of these day Hours that the prophet said, 'Seven times a day have I sung Thy praises', for of the night watches the same prophet says, 'At midnight I arose to confess to Thee'. At these times therefore let us give praise to our Creator for His just judgments, that is, at Lauds, Prime, Tierce, Sext, None, Evensong, and Compline, and at night let us rise to confess to Him.

Ch. 22 (How the monks are to sleep): All shall sleep in separate beds and each shall receive, according to the appointment of his abbot, bedclothes, fitted to the condition of his life. If it be possible let them sleep in a common dormitory, but if their great number will not allow this they may sleep in tens or twenties, with seniors to have charge of them. Let a

funibus, ut cultellos suos ad latus suum non adhibeant dum dormiunt, ne forte per somnum vulnerent dormientem; et ut parati sint monachi semper, et facto signo absque mora surgentes, festinent invicem se praevenire ad Opus Dei. . . .

Caput XXXI: Cellerarius monasterii eligatur de congregatione sapiens, maturus moribus, sobrius, non multum edax, non elatus, non turbulentus, non iniuriosus, non tardus, non prodigus, sed timens Deum, qui omni congregationi sit sicut pater. . . .

Omnia vasa monasterii cunctamque substantiam ac si altaris vasa sacrata conspiciat. Nihil ducat negligendum. . . .

Caput XXXVI: . . . Quibus fratribus infirmis sit cella super se deputata, et servitor timens Deum et diligens ac sollicitus. Balnearum usus infirmis quotiens expedit offeratur: sanis autem, et maxime iuvenibus, tardius concedatur. . . .

Caput XLV: Si quis, dum pronuntiat psalmum, antiphonam vel lectionem, fallitus fuerit, nisi satisfactione ibi coram omnibus humiliatus fuerit, maiori vindictae subiaceat; quippe qui noluit humilitate corrigere quod neglegentia deliquit. . . .

Caput XLVIII: Otiositas inimica est animae; et ideo certis temporibus occupari debent fratres in labore manuum, certis iterum horis in lectione divina. . . . In Quadragesimae vero diebus, a mane usque tertiam plenam vacent lectionibus suis, et usque decimam horam plenam operentur quod eis iniungiter. In quibus diebus Quadragesimae accipiant omnes singulos codices de bibliotheca, quos per ordinem ex integro legant: qui codices in caput Quadragesimae dandi sunt. Ante omnia sane deputentur unus aut duo seniores, qui circumeant monasterium horis quibus vacant fratres lectioni, et videant ne forte inveniatur frater acediosus, qui vacat otio aut fabulis, et non est intentus lectioni. . . .

Caput LIII: Omnes supervenientes hospites tamquam Christus suscipiantur, quia ipse dicturus est: Hospes fui, et suscepistis me. . . . Suscepti autem hospites ducantur ad orationem, et postea sedeat cum eis prior, aut cui iusserit ipse. Legatur coram hospite lex divina ut aedificetur, et post haec omnis ei exhibeatur humanitas. . . . Aquam in manibus abbas hospitibus det; pedes hospitibus omnibus tam abbas quam cuncta congregatio lavet. . . . Coquina abbatis et hospitum super se sit, ut incertis horis supervenientes hospites, qui numquam desunt monasterio, non inquietentur fratres. . . .

Caput LVII: Artifices si sunt in monasterio, cum omni humilitate faci- Quotiens tamen minus sunt hospites, quos vult de fratribus vocare in ipsius sit potestate. . . .

Caput LVII: Artifices si sunt in monaterio, cum omni humilitate faciant ipsas artes, si permiserit abbas. Quod si aliquis ex eis extollitur pro scientia artis suae, eo quod videatur aliquid conferre monasterio, hic talis erigatur ab ipsa arte et denuo per eam non transeat, nisi forte humiliatio ei iterum abbas iubeat. . . .

Caput LXVI: Qui portarius cellam debebit habere iuxta portam, ut venientes semper praesentem inveniant a quo responsum accipiant. Et mox ut aliquis pulsaverit aut pauper clamaverit: Deo gratias, respondeat aut: Benedic; . . . Monasterium autem, si possit fieri, ita debet constitui, ut omnia necessaria, id est, aqua, molendinum, hortus, vel artes diversae intra monasterium exerceantur. . . .

candle be constantly burning in the room until morning, and let the monks sleep clothed and girt with girdles or cords; but they are not to have knives by their sides in their beds, lest perchance they be injured whilst sleeping. In this way the monks shall always be ready to rise quickly when the signal is given, and hasten each one to come before his brother to the Divine Office. . . .

Ch. 31 (What manner of man the cellarer of the monastery ought to be): Let one of the community be chosen as cellarer of the monastery, who is wise, mature in character, temperate, not a great eater, not arrogant nor quarrelsome, nor insolent, and not a dawdler, nor wasteful, but one who fears God and is as a father to the community . . . Let him look upon all the vessels and goods of the monastery as if they were the consecrated chalices of the altar. He must not think anything can be neglected. . . .

Ch. 36 (Of the sick brethren): . . . For the sick brethren let a separate cell be set apart with an attendant who is God-fearing, diligent and painstaking. Let the use of baths be granted to the sick as often as it shall be expedient, but to those in health, and especially to the young, they shall be more reluctantly conceded. . . .

Ch. 45 (Of those who blunder in the oratory): If anyone, whilst reciting a psalm, responsory, antiphon or lesson, make any mistake, and do not at once make humble satisfaction for it before all, let him be subjected to greater punishment, as being one who is unwilling to correct by humility what he has done amiss through negligence. . . . .

Ch. 48 (Of daily manual labour): Idleness is an enemy of the soul. Because this is so the brethren ought to be occupied at specified times in manual labour, and at other fixed hours in holy reading . . . On the days of Lent, from the morning till the end of the third hour, the brethren are to have time for reading, after which let them work at what is set them to do till the close of the tenth hour. During these Lenten days let each one have some book from the library which he shall read through carefully. These books are to be given out at the beginning of Lent. It is of much import that one or two seniors be appointed to go about the monastery at such times as the brethren are free to read, in order to see that no one is slothful, given to idleness or foolish talking instead of reading. . . .

Ch. 53 (On the reception of guests): Let all guests who come be received as Christ would be, because He will say, 'I was a stranger, and ye took me in'. . . . Let guests, after their reception, be conducted to prayer, and then the prior, or anyone he may order, shall sit with them. Let the Divine Law be read in the presence of the guest for his edification, and after this let all courtesy be shown to him. . . . Let the abbot pour water on the hands of the guests, and let him and all the community wash their feet. . . . Let the kitchen of the abbot and the guests be apart, so that strangers, who are never absent from the monastery, coming in at irregular hours, may not disturb the community. . . .

Ch. 56 (The abbot's table): The abbot shall always take his meals with the guests and strangers. But when there are few guests, he may invite any of the brethren he may choose. . . .

Ch. 57 (Of the artificers of the monastery): Let such craftsmen as be in the monastery ply their trade in all lowliness of mind, if the abbot allow it. But if any be puffed up by his skill in his craft, and think the monastery indebted to him for it, such a one shall be shifted from his handicraft, and not attempt it again till such time as, having learnt a low opinion of himself, the abbot shall bid him resume. . . .

Ch. 66 (The porter of the monastery): . . . This porter should have his cell near the door, that those who arrive may always find him there to give an answer. As soon as anyone shall knock, or some poor man shall call for help, let him reply 'Thanks be to God' or invoke a blessing . . . The monastery however itself ought, if possible, to be so constructed as to contain within it all necessities, that is, water, mill, garden and (places for) the various crafts which are exercised within a monastery. . . .

II　From the Life of St Philibert, Abbot of Jumièges

This extract is from the *Vita S. Filiberti Abbatis Gemeticensis, auctore gemeticensi monacho anonymo*, ed. Lucas d'Achery et Joh. Mabillon, in: *Acta SS. Ord. S. Benedicti*, Saec. II, Paris, 1969, pp. 819ff.

In contrast to Schlosser (Bibl. 27, pp. 11ff.), we also print here the introductory passages concerning preparations for building the abbey, which shed light on the forethought involved.

The quotation is from Psalm 119, verse 165.

5. Sed quia perfecti viri semper perfectiora sectantur, coepit Sacerdos Domini Sanctorum coenobia circuire, ut aliquid emolumenti ex susceptione sanctitatis valeret accipere. Lustrans Luxovium et Bobium vel reliqua coenobia, sub norma sancti Columbani degentia, atque omnia monasteria, quae in intra suum gremium Francia et Italia ac tota concludit Burgundia, astuta intentione providens, ut prudentissima apis, quidquid melioribus florere vidit studiis, hoc suis traxit exemplis. . . .

6. Sed cum divina virtus lumen illius super candelabrum vellet constituere, ut lampas sanctitatis illius longe lateque fulgurante virtutum radio deberet splendere, posuit in corde Viri sanctissimi, ut ex proprio labore deberet monasterium fabricare. Tunc a rege Francorum Chlodoveo nomine, atque eius regina, vocabulo Baldechilde, locum in pago Rotomagensi, quem vetusto vocabulo Gemeticum antiquitas consueverat nuncupare, obtinens suggestione supplici, nobile ibidem coenobium visus est construxisse. . . .

7. Ubi eius (sc. Spiritus Sancti) providentia construxit per quadrum moenia turrita mole surgentia, claustra receptionis mira, adventantibus opportuna. Introrsus domus alma fulget habitantibus digna: ab Euro surgens ecclesia crucis instar erecta, cuius apicem obtinet alma Virgo Maria. . . . Vergit a Meridie cellula ipsius Sancti Dei, petreo margine florescente. Operosa saxis claustra comitantur arcus, variumque decus oblectans animum, cinctum triumphantibus lymphis. Duplex vergens ad Austrum ducentorum nonaginta pedum longitudine, quinquaginta in latitudine, eminet domus quiescendi obtentu. Singula per lecta lux radiat per fenestras, vitrum penetrans lychnus fovet adspectus legentis. Subter aedes geminae duobus officiis opportunae. Hinc falerna servanda conduntur, hinc prandia clara parantur; ibique conveniunt qui digne Christo deserviunt, nihil habentes proprium, nullo egentes compendio, quia sperantes in Domino non deficient omni bono, ut vere in eis impleatur scriptum: Pax multa diligentibus legem tuam, Domine, et non est illis scandalum. Caritas ibidem fulget mira, abstinentia magna, humilitas summa, castitas per omnia.

5. But because perfect men always strive after greater perfection, the Priest of the Lord began to tour the monasteries of His Saints, in order to be in a position to pick up anything that might be of profit to holiness. He visited Luxeuil and Bobbio, and other monasteries living after the Rule of St Columba, and indeed all monasteries in the bosom of France and Italy, and all of Burgundy and, with sage forethought like the most sapient bee, whatever he saw to flourish through greater zeal, that he took for his example. . . .

6. But since divine excellence desired to set its light upon a candelabrum, through which the lamp of holiness should cast far and wide the refulgent beam of its righteousness, it put into the heart of this most holy Man, that of his own efforts he should build a monastery. Then, obtaining by humble supplication from Clovis, King of the Franks, and his queen, Baldechilde, a site in the district of Rouen, called *Gemeticum* by the ancients, he was seen to construct there a noble monastery. . . .

7. There, Divine Providence built battlemented ramparts rising up in a massive square (or rectangle), an enclosure of remarkable capacity, appropriate for those who came to it. Within shines the life-giving house, worthy of its inmates: beginning at the east, the church rose up by the Euro in the shape of a cross, and Mary the bountiful Virgin claims the head of it. . . . The cell of God's Saint himself looks out from the south, adorned with an edging of stone. Arcades accompany the laboriously stone-built cloister; the soul is delighted by varied decoration and girt about with bubbling waters. The two-storeyed dormitory, two hundred and ninety feet long and fifty wide, points southwards. Light shines through windows above each bed, penetrating like a lamp through the glass to assist the eyesight of those reading. Underneath are twin rooms suitable for two different purposes: one is a buttery for wines to be served from, the other is for preparing wholesome food; there gather those who worthily serve Christ, calling no thing their own, needing to store up nothing, because, trusting in God, they want nothing for their welfare, so that through them the saying is truly fulfilled: 'Great peace have they which love thy law, O Lord, and nothing shall offend them.' Here shines wondrous love, great abstinence, the highest humility, chastity in all.

III　From the Edicts of Aachen (816–817)

Synodi Primae Aquisgranensis Decreta and *Synodi Secundae Aquisgranensis Decreta*

At the behest of Louis the Pious two monkish synods, presided over by Benedict of Aniane, took place in August 816 and July 817, and issued supplementary ordinances for the observation of St Benedict's Rule. They aimed at the standardization of monastic life in all Frankish monasteries. Comparison of their respective decrees reveals that the more rigorous regulations pushed through in 816 by Benedict of Aniane were mitigated in 817 by an opposition party to which Haito, the Abbot of Reichenau, seems to have belonged. These more lenient regulations played a part in the formulation of the St Gallen plan. As Walter Horn has shown, they chiefly concerned the special status of the abbot, with his own living-quarters and dining-room. But amongst these brief extracts I have included a few regulations that re-assert the importance of the Rule.

The text of the *Decreta* is that found in Semmler's new edition in the *Corpus consuetudinem Monasticarum* (ed. K. Hallinger) I, Siegburg 1963, pp. 451ff. and 469ff.

Synodi Primae Aquisgranensis Decreta

Anno incarnationis domini nostri Jesu Christi DCCCXVI imperii vero gloriosissimi principis Hluduvici tertio anno X. kalendas septembris cum in domo Aquis palatii quae ad Lateranis dicitur abbates cum quam pluribus

Edicts of the First Synod of Aachen, 816

In the year of the incarnation of our lord Jesus Christ 816, and in the third year of the rule of the indeed most glorious prince Louis, on the 23rd of August, it was decided by the abbots sitting conjointly with several of

una cum suis resedissent monachis haec quae subsecuntur capitula communi consilio ac pari voluntate inviolabiliter a regularibus conservari decreverunt.

I. capitulum, ut abbates mox ut ad monasteria sua remeaverint regulam per singula verba discutientes pleniter legant et intellegentes domino oppitulante efficaciter cum monachis suis implere studeant.

II. capitulum, ut monachi omnes qui possunt memoriter discant regulam.

III. capitulum, ut officium iuxta quod in regula sancti Benedicti continetur celebrent.

IV. capitulum, ut in coquina, in pistrino et in ceteris officinis propriis operentur manibus et vestimenta sua lavent oportuno tempore.

VII. capitulum, ut balneis generaliter tantum in Nativitate et in Pascha Domini veruntamen separatim utantur.

XXV. capitulum, ut abbas vel quispiam fratrum ad portam monasterii cum hospitibus non reficiat, in refectorio autem eis humanitatem manducandi ac bibendi exibeat. Ipse tamen ea cibi potusque mensura contentus sit quam reliqui fratres accipiunt. Si vero propter hospitem voluerit ad solitam mensuram fratribus sibique aliquid augere in sua maneat potestate.

XXVI. capitulum, ut servitores non ad unam mensam sed in propriis locis post refectionem fratrum reficiant quibus eadem lectio quae fratribus recitata est recitatur.

Synodi Secundae Aquisgranensis Decreta
Anno incarnationis domini nostri Jesu Christi DCCCXVIImo imperii vero gloriosissimi principis Hluduvici quarto anno VI. idus iulii cum in domo Aquis palatii quae Lateranis dicitur abbates cum quam pluribus resideret monachis haec subsequuntur capitula communi consilio ac pari voluntate inviolabiliter observari decreverunt.

IV. capitulum, ut abbatibus liceat cellas habere in quibus monachi sint aut canonici et abbas praevideat ne minus de monachis ibi habitare permittat quam sex.

V. capitulum, ut scola in monasterio non habeatur nisi eorum qui oblati sunt.

XIV. capitulum, ut laici in refectorium causa manducandi vel bibendi non ducantur.

XXIV. capitulum, ut dormitorium iuxta oratorium constituatur ubi supervenientes monachi dormiant.

XXIX. capitulum, ut docti fratres eligantur qui cum hospitibus loquantur.

---

their monks in the building called 'Lateran' in the palace of Aachen, by common counsel and with joint accord, that the following chapters should inviolably be observed by all monks.

Chapter I: As soon as the abbots return to their monasteries, they shall read the Rule through word by word, and having understood it, shall with the aid of the Lord seek with their monks truly to fulfil it.

Chapter II: Every monk who can is to learn the Rule by heart.

Chapter III: Divine office shall be celebrated as it is laid down in the Rule of St Benedict.

Chapter IV: That monks shall work with their own hands in the kitchens, in the bakery, and in other workshops, and shall wash their robes on due occasion.

Chapter VII: They shall as a rule only take (warm) baths at Christmas and at Easter, though separately.

Chapter XXV: Neither an abbot nor any of the monks shall eat with guests at the door of the monastery, but he may offer them all the courtesies of food and drink in the refectory. He himself shall rest content with the portions of food and drink received by the other brethren. If at the instance of his guest he wishes to add to the wonted portion of the brethren and himself, he is empowered to do so.

Chapter XXVI: The menials shall not eat at the common table, but in a place of their own after the meal of the brethren, but the same lesson shall be read to them as to the brethren.

Edicts of the Second Synod of Aachen, 817
In the year of the incarnation of our Lord Jesus Christ 817, and in the fourth year of the rule of the indeed most glorious prince Louis, on the 10th of July, it was decided by the abbots sitting with several of their monks in the building called 'Lateran' in the palace of Aachen, by common counsel and with joint accord, that the following chapters should be inviolably observed.

Chapter IV: That abbots shall be allowed to have cells in which monks or canons live (together) and that the abbot shall see to it that he does not allow less than six monks to live there.

Chapter V: That there shall be no school in the monastery save for oblates.

Chapter XIV: That laymen shall not be led into the refectory to eat or drink.

Chapter XXIV: That the dormitory for visiting monks shall be situated next to the oratory.

Chapter XXIX: That learned brethren shall be selected to make conversation with the guests.

IV   From the History of the Abbots of Fontenelle

This extract from the *Gesta abbatum Fontanellensium*, composed by an unknown monk from this monastery in the last years of the reign of Louis I, is taken from the *Mon. Germ. Hist., Scriptores*, Vol. II, ed. Georg Heinrich Pertz, Hanover 1829 (Cap. 17: *Gesta Ansgisi abbatis Fontanellensis coenobii*, pp. 296ff.).

Schlosser's text (Bibl. 27) purges this of its numerous orthographic errors. Those passages that in the view of the editor were later insertions were also denoted by brackets. It should also be remarked that the editor, contrary to the usual art-historical interpretation, took *cum diversis pogiis* (see below) to mean *cum diversis gradibus*.

Aedificia autem publica ac privata ab ipso coepta et consummata haec sunt.

Inprimis Dormitorium fratrum nobilissimum construi fecit longitudinis pedum CCVIII, latitudinis vero XXVII; porro omnis eius fabrica porrigitur in altitudine pedum LXIV; cuius muri de calce fortissima ac viscosa arenaque rufa et fossili lapideque tofoso ac probato constructi sunt. Habet quoque solarium in medio sui, pavimento optimo decoratum, cui desuper est laquear nobilissimis picturis ornatum; continentur in ipsa domo desuper fenestrae vitreae, cunctaque eius fabrica, excepta maceria, de materia quercuum durabilium condita est, tegulaeque ipsius universae clavis ferreis desuper affixae; habet sursum trabes et deorsum.

Post quod aedificavit aliam domum, quae vocatur refectorium, quam ita per medium maceria ad hoc constructa dividere fecit, ut una pars refectorii, altera foret cellarii, de eadem videlicet materia similique mensura sicut et dormitorium; quam variis picturis decorari in maceria et in laqueari fecit de Madalulfo, egregio pictore Cameracensis ecclesiae.

Tertiam nempe fecit domum egregiam construi quam maiorem vocant, quae ad orientem versa, ab una fronte contingit dormitorium, ab altera adhaeret refectorio; ubi cameram et caminatum necnon et alia plurima aedificari mandavit; sed adveniente morte eiusdem, hoc opus ex parte imperfectum remansit.

Haec tria egregia tecta ita constituta sunt; dormitorium videlicet ab una fronte versum est plagae septentrionali, ab altera australi, et adhaeret ab ea basilicae S. Petri; refectorium similiter versum est eisdem plagis, et est fere contiguum a parte meridiana absidae basilicae S. Petri; porro illa maior domus, sicut supra diximus, constituta est.

Ecclesia autem S. Petri a parte meridiana sita est, versa tamen ad orientem; ipsa etiam a parte occidentali 30 pedum in longitudine ac totidem in latitudine accrevit, constructo desuper coenaculo; quam in honore Domini Dei Salvatoris nostri Jesu Christi dedicandam fore praeoptabat; sed et ipsum opus propter mortem eius tam citam imperfectum remansit. In eadem autem Basilica S. Petri pyramidem quadrangulam altitudinis XXXV pedum de ligno tornatili compositam, in culmine turris eiusdem ecclesiae collocari iussit; quam plumbo stanno ac cupro deaurato cooperiri iussit, triaque ibidem signa posuit; nam antea nimis humile hoc opus erat. Ipsam nanque turrim simulque absidam tegulis plumbeis a novo cooperiri iussit. Iussit praeterea aliam condere domum iuxta absidam basilicae S. Petri ad plagam septentrionalem, quam conventus sive curiae quae graece Beleuterion dicitur, appellari placuit, propter quod consilium in ea de qualibet re perquirentes convenire fratres soliti sint; ibi nanque in pulpito lectio quotidie recitatur; ibi quicquid regularis auctoritas agendum suadet, deliberatur; in qua etiam monumentum nominis sui collocare iussit, ut dum vitae praesentis terminum daret, illic a suis deponeretur.

[Item ante dormitorium, refectorium et domum illam, quam maiorem nominavimus, porticus honestas cum diversis pogiis aedificari iussit, quibus trabes imposuit ac iuxta mensuram eorundem tectorum in longum extendit; in medio autem porticus, quae ante dormitorium sita videtur, domum cartarum constituit;] domum vero, qua librorum copia conservaretur, quae graece pyrgiscos dicitur, ante refectorium collocavit, cuius tegulas clavis ferreis configi fecit.

These are the buildings both public and private that he (Ansegis) began and completed.

In the first place he had the most noble monks' dorter built 208 feet long and 27 feet wide; furthermore, the structure that it is in is raised to a height of 64 feet throughout; the walls of this are constructed of solid tufa and a strong, binding mortar made of lime, reddish river-sand, and pebbles. There is also a chamber in the middle of it, laid with an exquisite pavement, and with a panelled ceiling adorned with the finest paintings above. This same building also has upper windows of glass, and apart from the walls, everything is constructed of the most lasting oak, whilst the roof-tiles are all held in place with iron nails; it has cressets above and below.

Then he built another building, called the refectory, which he had divided down the middle by a wall, so constructed that one part served as a refectory and the other for stores. This building is of the same measurements and materials as the dorter, and he had the walls and the panelled ceiling decorated with paintings by Madalulfo, the famous painter of the church of Cambrai.

Then indeed he had a third superb building built, called the *Domus Maior*, which points eastwards and joins up with the dorter at one end, and with the refectory at the other. There he commanded a chamber and a warming-room (?) and several other rooms to be built, but being overtaken by death, this work remained partially incomplete.

Here is how these three noble buildings are disposed: one end of the dorter points northwards, and the other end southwards, from which there is access to the basilica of St Peter; the refectory likewise faces the same directions, and at its southern end is almost contiguous with the apse of St Peter's; finally comes the *Domus Maior* as we have described it.

The church of St Peter lies to the south, but is orientated toward the east. Its western end was enlarged (by Ansegis) by 30 feet in length and the same in breadth, and a small chamber was constructed above this which he intended to be dedicated in honour of our Lord God and Saviour, Jesus Christ, but which was also left unfinished on account of his sudden death. He further ordered that a 35 foot high spire made of finely wrought wood be placed on top of the church tower and that it should be sheathed in an alloy of lead and tin with copper gilding, and placed three symbols on it; for before that it was altogether too modest. Indeed he ordered both this tower and the apse to be re-covered with lead tiles. Besides all this he also ordered another building to be put up on the north side of St Peter's by the apse, which it is proper to call the assembly- or court-house – *Bouleterion* in Greek – because the brethren are wont to gather there to take counsel over anything whatsoever. There is also a daily reading from a pulpit there, and deliberation over what the authority of the Rule advises should be done. He also ordained that a memorial should be put up there to his name, so that when (God) set an end to his life on this earth, he might be laid to rest there by his fellows.

[He also commanded that in front of the dorter, the refectory, and what we have called the domus maior, should be built graceful porticoes with varied arches, on top of which he placed beams that he extended as far as the length of their roofs. In the middle of the portico that is seen in front of the dorter he created a cartulary.] The building for the conservation of books – called *Pyrgiskos* in Greek – he situated in front of the refectory, and had its tiles held fast by iron nails.

V   From Hildemar's Commentary on St Benedict's Rule (*c.* 850)

Expositio regulae ab Hildemaro tradita

Hildemar, a monk from Corbie, was summoned by Archbishop Angilbert II of Milan, also a Frank, to the Lombard monastery of Civate where, following on from the earliest commentary on the Rule by Paul the Deacon, he expounded a commentary to his pupils, which is preserved by several transcriptions. Our extracts are taken from Mittermüller's edition, *Vita et regula SS. P. Benedicti una cum expositio regulae*, Regensburg 1880, vol. III. Glosses by pupils and copyists have crept into the text, and were wrongly attributed to Hildemar by Mittermüller.

The first of the following texts is an attempted exposition of the knotty sentence in the Rule: '*Officina vero, ubi haec omnia diligenter operemur, claustra sunt monasterii et stabilitas in congregatione.*' To unravel it one has to know that sometimes the whole monastery was described as an *officina* – the workshop of God – and that Hildemar, whom a lucid translation escaped on account of his inadequate Latin, sometimes took *claustra* to mean the whole conventual area, and sometimes only the cloister. The translation takes account of this inconsistent usage.

P. 182 sqq.: Sunt enim officina domus in quibus diversae artes operantur, i.e. ubi alii consuunt vestimenta, alii calciamenta, alii fabricant spatham et gladios, alii claves et caetera alia diversa. Et bene dixit, claustram monasterii esse officina, quia sicut in officinis diversae artes a diversis magistris, ut diximus, aguntur, ita et in monasterio diversae operationes in singulis locis fiunt, i.e. cum alii legunt, alii cantant, alii operantur aliquid manibus, alii laborant in coquina, et caetera his similia. . . . Officinum vero est, ubi aliquod opus Dei agitur vel artificia aliqua operantur. Et bene dixit 'stabilitas in congregatione', quia haec omnia artificia non possunt agere, nisi fuerint in congregatione. Forte dicit aliquis: Volo haec agere aliqua foris. Respondendum est illi: Non. Quare? Quia S. Benedictus dicit: ubi haec omnia diligenter operemur, claustra sunt monasterii et stabilitas in congregatione; et ideo talia debent fieri claustra monasterii, ubi ista, quae diximus, sine occasione peccati fieri possunt. Nam sunt multi minus intelligentes occasionem peccati, aut arctam claustram faciunt minus, quam debent, aut certe maiorem, quam oportet: sed talem debet abbas constituere claustram et sic grandem, ubi ea, quae monachus debet agere, in claustra monasterii operetur, ubi debet consuere vel lavare pannos aut lectioni vacare, aut domus esse infirmorum, et caetera his similia; quia si maior fuerit, quam oportet, cum vadit frater, invenit laicum aut extraneum, cum quo loquitur, aut aliquid dat aut accipit sine licentia abbatis, et invenitur occasio peccandi. Similiter si arcta fuerit, i.e. parva pro necessitate aliquid agendi, tunc facit transgressionem exiendo; nam hortus non est in claustra, in quam nullus debet intrare, nisi ille, cui commissum est. Nam ille abbas debet constituere claustram ita aptam, in qua possit esse stabilitas in congregatione et vagationis nulla esse occasio. Dicunt enim multi, quia claustra monasterii centum pedes debet habere in omni parte, minus non, qui parva est; si autem velis plus, potest fieri. Claustra enim dixit de illa curtina, ubi monachi sunt, i.e. quae est inter porticum et porticum. Et hoc notandum est, quia multa sunt, quae dixi, quae quantum ad exteriorem hominem attinent, in claustra non possunt fieri, veluti est, mortuum sepelire aut infirmum visitare.

p. 406 sq.: 'Cella', quam dicit, non dicit de una mansione, sed de claustra dicit. Quomodo enim possunt esse simul in una mansione quatuor fratres, cum unus moritur ex illis, alter vero vomit, tertius vult manducare, quartus etiam sedet ad exitum? Absque dubio, cum ita sint, non sufficit unum cubiculum omnibus, quia non sibi convenit ille, qui manducat, cum illo, qui in sua praesentia vomit, et cum illo, qui sedet ad exitum aut etiam cum illo, qui moritur. Ergo cum ita sint, necessariae sunt diversae mansiones pro diversis et variis infirmitatibus. . . . Quae domus infirmorum oratorium debet prope habere, in quo infirmi missam saltem iacendo possint audire et communionem accipere . . . Quam cellam debet abbas facere, talem, ubi et ipse in infirmitate sua iaceat, quatenus et

Conventual enclosure. Officina means the buildings in which various crafts are practised, i.e. where some sew clothes and others shoes, where broadswords and longswords are made by some, and keys and all sorts of other things by others. And [Benedict] does well to call the conventual enclosure the *officina*, because just as we have said, various artificers ply their several trades in these, so in a monastery various activities are performed in divers places, some singing, others reading, and others again doing something with their hands or working in the kitchen, and suchlike. . . . The true workshop is where some part of God's Work is being performed, or where some craft is practised. '*Stabilitas in congregatione*' is equally well said, because none of these activities could be carried on save in a community. Someone perhaps says, 'I want to do this in another place'. The reply must be no. Why? Because St Benedict says, 'Steadfastly abiding in the community, the monastic enclosures are where we are to perform all these things diligently'. For this reason the conventual enclosures of monasteries must be so constructed that the things that we have mentioned can be performed without affording sin a chance. For many are not aware enough of the likelihood of sin, so that they make the confines of the enclosure smaller than they should, or even, larger than is fitting. An abbot should however make the convent of such a size, that the things which a monk must do can be done in the monastery close – there he should be able to sew, wash clothes, or spend time in reading, and there should be found the infirmary building and suchlike. For if it is made larger than it should be, when a brother traverses it he will find some layman or stranger with whom to talk or exchange something without the abbot's permission, and he will be exposed to temptation. Likewise, if it is confined, i.e. [too] small for performing something necessary within it, then [a monk] transgresses by going outside it; for the garden does not form part of the conventual area, which no-one may enter unless he is entitled to. And so an abbot must construct his convent so justly that fixity in the community can be achieved there, and so that there is no pretext for roaming. Many indeed say that the cloister of monasteries should be a hundred feet square; not less, which would be [too] small. For what he [St Benedict] meant by *claustra* was the curtained-off parts where the monks are, i.e. between one portico and another. This must be understood because many of the things that I have mentioned pertain to the outer man, such as the burial of the dead or visitation of the sick, and cannot be performed in the 'cloister' [in this sense].

Infirmaries. When he [St Benedict] said 'cell', he did not mean one building, but a [distinct] cloister. How indeed should forty brethren, of whom one is dying, another is vomiting, a third desires to eat, and a fourth again is sitting on the close-stool, all exist under one roof. For there is no doubt that if things are so, one chamber is insufficient for everyone, because it is not suitable for someone who is eating to have in his presence another who is being sick, or who is on the close-stool, or who indeed is dying. Since things are like this, different buildings are necessary for sundry and manifold diseases. . . . This infirmary should have a chapel nearby in which the sick can at least hear the Mass lying down and can take communion. . . . The abbot must also make a cell for himself such

hospitibus et ad se venientibus possit loqui, si tanta necessitas fuerit, sine impedimento infirmorum, et cum ipsis infirmis, qui iam de lecto possunt surgere, manducare valeat.

p. 611 sq.: Verum quia dicit regula de hospitibus suscipiendis: 'et domus Dei sapienter a sapientibus administretur', intelligunt, quia dormitorium, ubi monachi suscipi debent, habetur separatum a laicorum cubiculo, i.e. ubi laici iacent, eo quod laici possunt stare usque mediam noctem et loqui et iocari, et monachi non debent, sed magis silentium habere et orare. Ideo iuxta oratorium illorum monachorum hospitum est dormitorium, ubi ipsi iaceant soli reverenter, et possint nocte surgere, qua hora velint, et ire in ecclesiam. Vasalli autem sui sint in alio loco, ubi laici sunt. Et tunc ille frater monasterii, qui tarde venit, in istorum dormitorio recipitur et ibi etiam manducat et dormit, qui unum sunt monachi. Quod si dormitorium monachorum hospitum non est iuxta oratorium propter orationem faciendam, sed cum laicis, tunc domus Dei non sapienter a sapientibus ministratur.

that, lying there in his own illness, guests and visitors can talk with him, if need be, without disturbance of the sick, and which is suitable for eating in with those of the sick capable of being up again.

Accommodation for visiting monks. It is a true thing which the Rule says of the reception of guests, 'and the House of the Lord shall be administered wisely by the wise', for they comprehend that the dorter where the monks are to be received must be kept separate from the chamber of the laity, i.e. where laymen lie, so that the latter can stay up talking and amusing themselves into the middle of the night, which monks ought not to do, but rather be silent and pray. Hence the oratory of monkish guests is next to their dorter, where they lie singly and reverently, and can rise in the night at whatever hour they like and go into the church. Their retinue however are to be elsewhere, with the laity. So also, any brother of the monastery [any monk?] who arrives late is to be accommodated in this same dorter, and thus eat and sleep [with those] who are all monks together. But if the dorter for monkish guests is not next to an oratory to facilitate prayer, but with laymen, then the House of the Lord is not being administered wisely by the wise.

VI   A description of the monastery of Farfa (Cluny II, *c.* 1042–1049)

Descriptio Farvensis Monasterii
Consuetudines monasticae, I Consuetudines Farvenses, ed. Bruno Albers, Freiburg 1900, lib. II, cap. I, pp. 137-39.
It is generally accepted that this description is actually of Odilo's Cluny, not least because it does not fit in with the topography of Farfa.

Ecclesia longitudinis CXL pedes habeat, altitudinis XL et tres; fenestrae vitreae CLX.

Capitulum vero XL et V pedes longitudinis, latitudinis XXX et quatuor. Ad orientem fenestrae IV, contra septentrionem tres. Contra occidentem XII balcones, et per unumquemque duae columnae affixae in eis.

Auditorium XXX pedes longitudinis; camera vero nonaginta pedes longitudinis.

Dormitorium longitudinis CLX pedes, latitudinis XXX et IV; omnes vero fenestrae vitreae quae in eo sunt XC et septem, et omnes habent in altitudine staturam hominis, quantum se potest extendere usque ad summitatem digiti, latitudinis vero pedes II et semissem unum; altitudinis murorum XX et tres pedes.

Latrina LXX pedes longitudinis, latitudinis XX et tres; sellae XL et quinque in ipsa domo ordinatae sunt, et per unamquamque sellam aptata est fenestrula in muro altitudinis pedes II, latitudinis semissem unum, et super ipsas sellulas compositas struem lignorum, et super ipsam constructionem lignorum factae sunt fenestrae X et VII, altitudinis tres pedes, latitudinis pedem et semissem.

Calefactorium XX et V pedes latitudinis eademque mensura longitudinis; a ianua ecclesiae usque ad ostium calefactorii pedes LXXV.

Refectorium longitudinis pedes LXXXX, latitudinis XXV; altitudinis murorum XXIII; fenestrae vitreae, quae in eo sunt, ex utraque parte octo, et omnes habent altitudinis pedes V, latitudinis tres.

Coquina regularis XXX pedes longitudine, et latitudine XX et V; coquina laicorum eademque mensura.

Cellarii vero longitudo LXX, latitudo LX pedes.

Elemosynarum quippe cella pedes latitudinis X, longitudinis LX, ad similitudinem latitudinis cellarii.

Galilaea longitudinis LX et quinque pedes, et duae turres sint in ipsius galilaeae fronte constitutae; et subter ipsas atrium est ubi laici stant, ut non impediant processionem.

A porta meridiana usque ad portam aquilonariam pedes CCLXXX.

The *church* is to be 140 feet long and 43 feet high, with 160 glass windows.

The *chapter-house* is 45 feet long and 34 feet wide. It has four windows to the east and three to the north. To the west it has a twelve-bayed arcade [?], and double columns [?] are fixed between each bay.

The *parlour* is 30 feet long, and the *camera* 90 feet long.

The *dorter* is 160 feet long and 34 feet wide; it has 97 windows, all of glass, and they are all the height of a man stretched out to the tip of his fingers, with a width of 2½ feet; the walls are 23 feet high.

The *latrine* is 70 feet long, and 23 feet wide. 45 seats are arranged there, and for each seat there is a little window in the wall two feet high and half a foot wide; above the arrangement of the seats [one sees] a layer [?] of timbers, and 17 windows, three feet high and one and a half feet wide, have been made above this timber construction.

The *warming-house* is 25 feet wide and the same amount long; there are 75 feet from the church door to the warming-house entrance.

The *refectory* is 90 feet long and 25 feet wide, with 23-foot high walls. There are eight glazed windows to each of the two sides, all five feet high and three wide.

The *monks' kitchen* is 30 feet long and 25 feet wide; the *lay kitchen* is the same size.

The *cellar* is 70 feet long and 60 feet wide.

The *almonry* is however 10 feet long and 60 feet wide, in keeping with the width of the cellar.

The *galilee* is 65 feet long, with two towers built into its façade; underneath them is the *narthex*, where the laity stand so as not to get in the way of the processions.

There are 280 feet from the south gate to the north gate.

Sacristia pedes longitudinis L et VIII cum turre, quae in capite eius constituta est.

Oratorium Sanctae Mariae longitudinis XL et quinque pedes, latitudinis XX; murorum altitudinis XX et III.

Infirmis sex cellulae deputatae sunto. Prima cellula infirmorum latitudinem XX et VII pedes, longitudinem XXIII habet cum lectis octo et cellulis totidem, in porticu iuxta murum ipsius cellulae deforis et claustura praedictae cellulae habet latitudinis pedes XII. Secunda cellula similiter per omnia est coaptata. Tertia eodemque modo. Similiter etiam et quarta. Quinta sit minor, ubi conveniant infirmi ad lavandum pedes diebus sabbatorum, vel illi fratres qui exuti sunt ad mutandum. Sexta cellula praeparata sit ubi famuli servientes illis lavent scutellulas et omnia utensilia.

Iuxta galilaeam constructum debet esse palatium longitudinis CXXX et V pedum, ad recipiendum omnes supervenientes homines, qui cum equitibus adventaverint monasterio. Ex una parte ipsius domus sint praeparati XL lecti et totidem pulvilli ex pallio ubi requiescant viri tantum, cum latrinis XL. Ex alia namque parte ordinati sint lectuli XXX ubi comitissae vel aliae honestae mulieres pausent, cum latrinis XXX, ubi solae ipsae suas indigerias procurent. In medio autem ipsius palatii affixae sint mensae, sicuti refectorii tabulae, ubi edant tam viri quam mulieres. In festivitatibus magnis sit ipsa domus adornata cum cortinis et palliis et bancalibus in sedilibus ipsorum.

In fronte ipsius sit alia domus longitudinis ped. XLV, latitudinis XXX. Nam ipsius longitudo pertingat usque ad sacristiam, et ibi sedeant omnes sartores atque sutores ad suendum quod camerarius eis praecipit; et ut praeparatam habeant ibi tabulam longitudinis XXX ped., et alia tabula affixa sit cum ea, quarum latitudo ambarum tabularum habeat VII pedes. Nam inter istam mansionem et sacristiam, atque ecclesiam nec non et galilaeam sit cimiterium, ubi laici sepeliantur.

A porta meridiana usque ad portam septentrionalem contra occidentem sit constructa domus longitudinis CCLXXX ped., latitudinis XXV; et ibi construantur stabulae equorum per mansiunculas partitas, et desuper sit solarium ubi famuli edant atque dormiant, et mensas habeant ibi ordinatas longitudinis LXXX ped., latitudinis vero IV. Et quotquot ex adventantibus non possunt reficere ad illam mansionem quam superius diximus, reficiant ad istam.

Et in capite ipsius mansionis sit locus aptitatus ubi conveniant omnes illi homines qui absque equitibus deveniunt, et caritatem ex cibo et potu, in quantum convenientia fuerit, ibi recipiant ab eleemosynario fratre.

Extra refectorium namque fratrum, LX pedum in capite latrinae sint cryptae duodecim, et totidem dolii praeparati ubi temporibus constitutis balnea fratribus praeparentur.

Et post istam positionem construatur cella novitiorum, et sit angulata in quadrimodis, videlicet in prima ut meditentur, in secunda reficiant, in tertia dormiant, in quarta latrina ex latere.

Iuxta istam sit disposita alia cella, ubi aurifices vel inclusores seu vitrei magistri conveniant ad faciendam ipsam artem.

Inter cryptas et cellas novitiorum atque aurificum habeant domum longitudinis CXXV ped., latitudinis vero XXV, et eius longitudo perveniat usque ad pistrinum. Ipsum namque in longitudine, cum turre quae in capite eius constructa est, LXX ped., latitudinis XX.

Including the *tower* built at the head of it, the *sacristy* measures 58 feet in length.

The *Lady Chapel* is 45 feet long and 20 wide, with walls 23 feet high.

Six small cells are set apart for the *sick*. The first is 27 feet wide and 32 feet long, and has eight beds and as many tiny cells in the portico against its outside wall, and the cloister of the said cells is twelve feet across. The second small cell is in every respect like the first. Likewise the third and the fourth. The fifth, where the sick come for foot-washing on the Sabbath or those brothers who are undressed so as to change (into sick-clothes?), is to be smaller. The sixth small cell is to be organized for the menials attending them [the sick] to wash the dishes and all the [medical ?] utensils.

Next to the galilee is to be constructed the *palatium*, 135 feet in length, to accommodate all visitors arriving at the monastery with their mounted retinues. Forty beds are to be prepared on one side of the said building, and as many cushions of rich material, for men alone to repose on, and with 40 latrines. On the other side are to be disposed 30 little beds where countesses and other gentlewomen may rest, with 30 latrines for them alone to relieve themselves. Tables are to be set in the middle of this palace, like those in the refectory, at which both men and women may eat. At high festivals this building may be adorned with hangings and rich stuffs and with coverings on the seats.

Opposite it there is to be *another building* 45 feet long and 30 wide. For it is to extend lengthwise as far as the sacristy, and there are to sit the tailors and cobblers making whatever the chamberlain prescribes. They are to have a work-bench placed there, 30 feet long, and another table attached to it, so that the width of the two tables together is to be 7 feet. Furthermore, in the area between this workshop, the sacristy and the church as far as the galilee, is to be the *cemetery* where the laity are to be buried.

A *building* 280 feet long and 25 feet wide stretching from the north to the south gate, is to be constructed to the west; there *stables* are to be installed, split up into loose-boxes, and with a loft above for the menials to eat and sleep in, and they are to have tables set there, 80 feet long and 4 wide. And any of the visitors who cannot eat in the building we described earlier may eat here.

And at the end of this building a place shall be prepared where all such men as arrive not in a retinue may foregather and receive charity in the form of food and drink, as much as shall seem fit, from the brother almoner.

Outside the monks' refectory and 60 feet from the end of the latrines, twelve sunken chambers with as many tubs are to be organized, where *baths* may be prepared for the brethren at the appointed times.

And at the back of this is to be constructed the *noviciate* in the form of a square, that is, so that they may meditate in the first (side), eat in the second, and sleep in the third, whilst the latrines (may project) from one side in the fourth.

Other *cells* are to be placed nearby, in which *goldsmiths* or *enamellists* [?] or *master stainers* may gather to practise their craft.

They (the craftsmen?) are to have a *building* 25 feet wide and 125 feet long, extending between the bathhouses and the cells of the novices and the goldsmiths as far as the *bakery*, which together with the tower erected at one end of it measures 70 feet in length and 20 in width.

VII   From the Life of Abbot Odilo of Cluny (994–1049)

Vita Sancti Odilonis, auctore Jotsaldo Sylviniacensis monacho. Migne, *P.L.* CXLII, col. 908.

C. XI. 38: . . . Et praeter haec interiora, fuerunt in eo [Odilone] extrinsecus gloriosa studia in aedificiis locorum sanctorum construendis, renovandis, et ornamentis undecumque adquirendis. Demonstrat hoc Cluniacus, suus principalis locus, in cunctis suis aedificiis interius et exterius, praeter parietes ecclesiae, ab ipso studiose renovatus et ornamentis multipliciter adornatus; ubi etiam in novissimis suis claustrum construxit columnis marmoreis, ex ultimis partibus illius provinciae, ac per rapidissimos Durentiae Rhodanique cursus non sine magno labore advectis, mirabiliter decoratum. De quo solitus erat gloriari ut iocundi erat habitus, 'invenisse se ligneum et relinquere marmoreum', ad exemplum Octaviani Caesaris, quem describunt historiae Romam invenisse latericiam et reliquisse marmoream.

Incepit etiam ciborium super altare sancti Petri, cuius columnas vestivit argento cum nigello pulchro opere decoratas.

. . . and besides these interior (virtues), there was in him (Odilo) externally a glorious ardour in constructing, renovating and acquiring adornments from wheresoever it might be for buildings in holy places. Cluny, his chief seat, shows this, the interiors and exteriors of all its buildings – save only the walls of the church – having been eagerly renovated by him and variously adorned with ornament; there also in his last (years) he made a cloister, admirably decorated with marble columns from the furthest parts of that province, transported not without great labour by the headlong currents of the Durande and the Rhône. In which he was wont to glory and to remark in jest, that he 'had found it wood and left it marble', in imitation of Augustus Caesar, of whom chronicles say that he found Rome made of brick, and left it made of marble. He also began work on the ciborium above the altar of St Peter, whose columns he sheathed in silver and decorated with fine niello-work.

VIII   Concerning the French journey of Peter Damian and his transalpine itinerary

De Gallica Patri Damiani Profectione et eius ultramontano Itinere. Unknown travelling-companion, around 1063. *Monumenta Germaniae Historica, Scriptores,* vol. XXX, ii, p. 1043.

p. 1043: . . . Quomodo cunctae lapideae officinae monastico dispositae sunt ordine; quomodo ecclesia maxima et arcuata plurimis munita altaribus, sanctorum reliquiis non modice condita, thesauro plurimo et diverso ditissima; quomodo claustrum ingens et ipsa sui pulchritudine ad inhabitandum se quasi monachos invitare videtur; quomodo sufficiens est dormitorium et pre continuo trium lucernarum lumine aliquid umquam nocivum in eo peragi quasi ab eo prohibetur; quomodo refectorium nulla superstitione depictum, sed sancta extremitate constructum largum reficiendis fratribus prebet consessum; quomodo per cunctas officinas ubicumque aqua necessaria quaeritur, per occultos meatus statim mirabiliter sponte diffluit: haec et alia de predicto monasterio dicerem, . . .

[Cluny] . . . How all the stone-built workshops are disposed in monastic order; how the great and vaulted church is furnished with numerous altars, endowed with no ordinary number of relics, and inordinately wealthy with the most huge and varied treasure; how the cloister is vast and by its very beauty appears as if it invites the monks to dwell there; how ample the dorter is, and how through the constant light from three lamps it virtually precludes any noxious thing being ever done there; how the refectory, painted not with any superstitions, but with the Last Judgment [?], is built so large that it makes it possible for all the brethren to eat at one sitting; how in all the workshops and wheresoever necessary water is sought, it marvellously flows out at once and of its own accord from hidden channels: these and other things might I relate of the said monastery, . . .

IX   How St Hugh, admonished by divine revelation, improved the construction of the church of Cluny both in extent and quality

Qualiter beatus Hugo divina revelatione admonitus Cluniacensis basilicae structuram in qualitate et quantitate melioraverit. Bibliotheca Cluniacensis, ed. Martinus Marrier et Andreas Quercetanus, 1614, reprint 1915, cols. 457 ff., *Cap. de alicuius miraculorum quorundam S. Hugonis Abbatis relationis manuscriptae collectore monacho quodam, ut videtur, Cluniacensi.*

. . . Nam quidam Abbas Monasterii cui Balma vocabulum est, Gunzo nomine, vir magnae simplicitatis et honestatis, de Abbate factus claustralis, dum aliquando gravi langore paralysis Cluniaci deficeret, itaût ad extrema iam se devenisse crederet, quadam nocte vidit sibi assistere ipsos Apostolos Petrum et Paulum, cum protomartyre Stephano, quorum primus atque princeps, beatus videlicet Petrus, postquam ab ipso, qui essent requisitus, et suum nomen atque sociorum edidisset, sic est exorsus: Surge frater ocius, et Hugoni Abbati huius Ecclesiae haec nostra defer mandata. Angustias basilicae nostrae fratrum multitudo ferre vix potest, et volumus, ut ampliorem Abbas ipse aedificet, nec de sumptibus diffidat, nostrum erit providere de omnibus quae huic operi necessaria fuerint. Cui ille, Legationem, inquit, istam suscipere non audeo, quia neque fides

. . . Now when a certain abbot of the monastery called Baume, a man by the name of Gunzo of great simplicity and nobleness of character, whom the Abbot [Hugh] had admitted into the monastery [Cluny], was wasting away at Cluny in some kind of grave prostration from a stroke, such that he already believed himself to be at death's door, he saw one night by his bedside the actual Apostles Peter and Paul, with Stephen the first martyr. The first and chief of these – that is to say, the blessed Peter – after he had been asked who they were, pronounced his own and his companions' names, and then spoke as follows: 'Brother, arise swiftly and convey this injunction of ours to Hugh, the Abbot of this church. The throng of brethren can scarcely tolerate for much longer the crampedness of our church, and we want the abbot to build it larger without being afraid of

verbis adhiberetur. Et Apostolus Petrus: Huic legationi tu prae caeteris es electus, ut ex collata tibi sanitate fides verbis accedat. Adiecit etiam addendos ei septem annos si fideliter impositam sibi perageret obedientiam, beatum vero Hugonem si parere differret, incommodum quod relator evaserat, subiturum. His dictis ipse funiculos tendere visus est, ipse longitudinis atque latitudinis metiri quantitatem. Ostendit ei etiam basilicae qualitatem fabricandae, menti eius et dimensionis et schematis memoriam tenacius haerere praecipiens.

Expergefactus frater pro quo tabulae funereae sonus expectabatur, Abbati se sospes obtulit. Referuntur ex ordine quaecumque monacho dicta fuerant, vel ostensa. Qui cum videret fratrem sospitem factum post visionem, cui morbus interitum minabatur, et audisset in se revoluendum langorem si retardaret operis inchoationem, nec coelestem opem defuturam si inciperet, credidit, adquievit, incepit, et Deo iuvante habitationi gloriae Dei tantam ac talem basilicam intra XX. annos construxit, ut capacitorne sit magnitudine, an arte mirabilior, difficile iudicetur. Haec eius decoris et gloriae eius, quam, si liceat credi coelestibus incolis in huiusmodi usus humana placere domicilia, quoddam deambulatorium dicas Angelorum. In hac velut eductos de carcere Monachos refovet libera quaedam planicies, ita se monasticis accommodans institutis, ut angustia chori necesse non sit permisceri ordines, non stationes confundi, vel foras quemlibet evagari. Verum omni die quasi Pascha celebrant, quia transire meruerunt in quandam Galilaeam, et libertatis novae gaudio laetari, non murmurantes depressura, sed gratulantes ex latitudinis copia, qua possunt vacare contemplationi divinae absque tristitia. Supersunt plurima quibus dicendis occuparemur, nisi loca divinis adscripta obsequiis plus laudis ex habitantium merito, quam ex manu artificum sortirentur. Quod profecto huic de qua loquimur structurae accessit, quae cum splendidissima sit ingenio opificis, multo est ex suo habitatore splendidior. Utriusque autem gloriae, gregis scilicet et loci, beatus Hugo sollicitus institit procurator coram Deo et eius Angelis, pura dicturus conscientia, Domine dilexi decorem domus tuae, et locum habitationis gloriae tuae. . . .

the expense, for it will be our affair to make provision for everything necessary to this project.' To which [Gunzo] replied: 'I do not dare to take this message, because trust will not be placed in my words.' The Apostle Peter then said: 'You have been chosen in preference to all others for this message, in order that your words may gain credence from your recovered health.' He added that seven years would be added to Gunzo's life if he faithfully carried out the task entrusted to him, but that the blessed Hugh would undergo the misfortune that the messenger had escaped if he dallied in his obedience. Having said this, he was seen by Gunzo to draw out measuring-ropes and measure off the length and breadth (of the church). He also showed him in what manner the church was to be built, instructing him to commit both its dimensions and its design securely to memory.

Thus aroused, the brother for whom the sound of funeral tolling was momently expected, showed himself in perfect health to the abbot. Everything that had been said or shown to him was now told in the order it happened by the monk. When Hugh saw this brother, whom sickness had threatened to remove, fully recovered following the vision, and heard that the malady would turn on him if he delayed in making a start on the work, and that heavenly aid would not be wanting if he began, he believed, gave his assent, and began the work, and with God's help erected for the dwelling of the glory of God [Ps. 26, v. 8] in the space of twenty years such a church, that it is difficult to judge whether it is more marvellous in its magnitude or in its artistry. Its decoration and magnificence are such that, if it be permissible to imagine a human habitation of this kind affording pleasure to heavenly inhabitants, you would call this the walk of the angels. Its uncluttered spaces revive the monks as if they have been released from prison, and so adapt themselves to the monastic offices that a cramped choir no longer means that different grades of monk have to be mixed together, or that positions get confused, or that anyone is made to hover outside. Every day the monks worship as if it were Easter, because they have earned the right to pass over into a kind of Galilee and to rejoice with joy in their new freedom, not grumbling because of want of space, but rejoicing because of the ample room in which they can wander in contemplation of God without melancholy. There remains much more that we could busy ourselves in saying, did not places set apart for divine worship earn more praise from the merit of their inhabitants than from the hands of artists. Which applies indeed to the building of which we speak which, exceedingly splendid as it is through the skill of the architect, is much more so through its indweller. Furthermore, the blessed Hugh concerned with the glory of both – his monastery and his flock – might plead as proctor before God and his angels, saying with a pure heart, 'Lord, I have loved the habitation of thy house, and the place where thine honour dwelleth'.

X   From St Bernard's polemic against grandiose architecture (*c.* 1124)

S. Bernardi Abbatis – Apologia ad Guillelmum – Sancti Theoderici Abbatem
In his famous Apologia Bernard takes up a position opposed to the extravagance of Romanesque churches and cloisters. His piece is aimed at the Cluniacs and Abbot Suger of Saint-Denis alike. In it, the prevailing Romanesque style is repudiated, and the way made clear for the Gothic which was to come. There is no English translation, though there is a French one in the *Oeuvres Complètes de Saint Bernard*, Paris 1873, Vol. II. pp. 304ff. Its cultural context emerges best from Erwin Panofsky's *Abbot Suger*, Princeton 1946; and Otto von Simson's *The Gothic Cathedral*, New York 1955, pp. 43ff.
The text used is from Migne, *Patrologia Latina* CLXXXII, 914-16.

Omitto oratoriorum immensas altitudines, immoderatas longitudines, supervacuas latitudines, sumptuosas depolitiones, curiosas depictiones, quae dum orantium in se retorquent aspectum, impediunt et affectum, et mihi quodammodo repraesentant antiquum ritum Judaeorum. Sed esto, fiant haec ad honorem Dei. Illud autem interrogo monachus monachos, quod in gentilibus gentilis arguebat: »*Dicite* (ait ille), *pontifices, in sancto quid facit aurum?*« Ergo autem dico: Dicite, pauperes; non enim attendo

I do not speak of the immense height of [Cluniac] churches, or of their immoderate length, their excessive width, sumptuous decoration and finely executed pictures, which divert the attention of those who are praying to themselves and impede devotion, recalling to some extent for me the ancient rite of the Jews. Let them be, it may be that they are after all to God's honour. I however, as a monk, put to you monks the same question with which a gentile chid the gentiles: 'Tell me, you priests,' he

verbum, sed sensum; dicite, inquam, pauperes, si tamen pauperes, in sancto quid facit aurum? Et quidem alia causa est episcoporum, alia monachorum. Scimus namque quod illi, sapientibus et insipientibus debitores cum sint, carnalis populi devotionem, quia spiritualibus non possunt corporalibus excitant ornamentis. Nos vero qui jam de populo exivimus: qui mundi quaeque pretiosa ac speciosa pro Christo reliquimus, qui omnia pulcre lucentia, canore mulcentia, suave olentia, dulce sapientia, tactu placentia, cuncta denique oblectamenta corporea arbitrari sumus ut stercora, ut Christum lucrifaciamus: quorum, quaeso, in his devotionem excitare intendimus? Quem, inquam, ex his fructum requirimus, stultorum admirationem an simplicium oblationem? An quoniam commixti sumus inter gentes, forte didicimus opera eorum et servimus adhuc sculptibilibus eorum?

Et ut aperte loquar, an hoc totum facit avaritia, quae est idolorum servitus? Et non requirimus fructum, sed datum. Si quaeris quo modo: miro, inquam, modo. Tali quadam arte spargitur aes ut multiplicetur; expenditur ut augeatur, et effusio copiam parit. Ipso quippe visu sumptuosarum, sed mirandarum vanitatum, accenduntur homines magis ad offerendum, quam ad orandum. Sic opes opibus hauriuntur, sic pecunia pecuniam trahit: quia nescio quo pacto, ubi amplius divitiarum cernitur, ibi offertur libentius. Auro tectis reliquiis saginantur oculi et loculi aperiuntur. Ostenditur pulcherrima forma sancti vel sanctae alicujus et eo creditur sanctior, quo coloratior. Currunt homines ad osculandum, invitantur ad donandum; et magis mirantur pulchra quam venerantur sacra. Ponuntur dehinc in ecclesia gemmatae non coronae, sed rotae circumseptae lampadibus, sed non minus fulgentes insertis lapidibus. Cernimus et pro candelabris arbores quasdam erectas, multo aeris pondere miro artificis opere fabricatas, nec magis coruscantes superpositis lucernis quam suis gemmis. Quid, putas, in his omnibus quaeritur, poenitentium compunctio an intuentium admiratio? O vanitas vanitatum, sed non vanior quam insanior! Fulget ecclesia in parietibus, et in pauperibus eget! Suos lapides induit auro, et suos filios nudos deserit! De sumptibus egenorum servitur oculis divitum. Inveniunt curiosi quo delectentur, et non inveniunt miseri quo sustententur; ut quid saltem sanctorum imagines non reveremur, quibus utique ipsum, quod pedibus conculcatur, scatet pavimentum? Saepe spuitur in ore angeli, saepe alicujus sanctorum facies calcibus tunditur transeuntium. Et si non sacris his imaginibus, cur vel non parcitur pulcris coloribus? Cur decoras quod mox foedandum est? Cur depingis quod necesse est conculari? Quid ibi valent venustae formae, ubi pulvere maculantur assiduo? Denique, quid haec ad pauperes, ad monachos, ad spirituales viros? . . .

Caeterum in claustris coram legentibus fratribus quid facit ridicula monstruositas, mira quaedam deformis formositas ac formosa deformitas? Quid ibi immundae simiae? quid feri leones? quid monstruosi centauri? quid semihomines? quid maculosae tigrides? quid milites pugnantes? quid venatores tubicinantes? Videas sub uno capite multa corpora, et rursus in uno corpore capita multa. Cernitur hinc in quadrupede cauda serpentis, illinc in pisce caput quadrupedis. Ibi bestia praefert equum, capram trahens retro dimidiam; hic cornutum animal equum gestat posterius. Tam multa denique, tamque mira diversarum formarum ubique varietas apparet, ut magis legere libeat in marmoribus quam in codicibus, totumque diem occupare singula ista mirando quam in lege Dei meditando. Proh Deo! si non pudet ineptiarum, cur vel non piget expensarum?

said, 'what business has gold in the sanctuary?' (Persius, Satire II). And so I say to you: 'Tell me you paupers,' (I alter a word, not the meaning), 'Tell me, if paupers you are, what business has gold in the sanctuary?' It is of course another matter with bishops rather than monks. For we know that the former, answerable for the wise and the ignorant alike, stir up the devotion of the carnal populace with material adornments, spiritual ones being of no avail. We however, we who have cut ourselves off from the populace, who have renounced anything precious or attractive for the sake of Christ, we who account as filth everything of shining beauty, soothing harmony, everything sweet-smelling, delicious tasting and pleasing to the touch, everything, in short, that the body takes delight in, in order that we may attain Christ – whose devotion, I ask, do we expect to arouse by these means? What fruits do we seek from them – the wonder of the stupid and the offerings of the simple? Wherefore are we set amongst the people – is it perhaps to learn their ways to the extent that we serve their idols?

But to speak quite openly, avarice, which is nothing but idolatry, is the source of all this. We are not seeking any good from this, but gifts. If you ask me how, I reply – in a remarkable way. There is a certain art of laying out money so that it multiplies; one spends it so that it increases, and largesse produces plenty. For through the sight of extravagant but marvellous vanities, men are more moved to contribute offerings than to pray. I do not know the secret of it, but where they discern greater riches, they give more freely. Eyes feast on gold-mounted reliquaries, and purses gape. A beautiful statue of a male or female saint is exposed to view, and the gaudier it is the holier it is believed to be. Men rush up and kiss it – and are asked for an offering; and it is more admired for its beauty than venerated for its sanctity. Whereupon they are not just gem-studded crown-lights that are placed in churches, but wheels bedight with lamps no less sparkling than the stones they are set with. We also see great tree-like things installed as candelabra, made with wonderful craftsmanship out of a mass of bronze, coruscating no less with the lights placed upon them than with their precious stones. What, do you imagine, is (the effect) sought in all these things – the contrition of the penitent or the gasps of the gapers? Oh, vanity of vanities! – but more senseless than vain. The walls of the church are resplendent, but its poor go in want. Its stones are adorned with gold, and its children are forsaken and want for clothes. The tithes of the poor go to charm the eyes of the rich. Connoisseurs find things to delight in, but the poor find nothing to sustain them. Should we not at least reverence the images of the saints, with which the very paving that is trodden underfoot abounds? Often the face of an angel is spat upon, or the visage of some saint is scuffed by the feet of passers-by. If there is no respect for the sanctity of these images, then why not at least avoid wasting the exquisite colours? Why decorate what is soon bound to be dirtied? Why paint what is inevitably trodden underfoot? What is the use of lovely figures where they will be soiled by constant dust? Last of all, what good are they to *paupers*, to monks, to men who live by the spirit? . . .

What is more, what is the point of ridiculous monstrosities in the cloister where there are brethren reading – I mean those extraordinary deformed beauties and beautiful deformities? What are those lascivious apes doing, those fierce lions, monstrous centaurs, half-men, and spotted pards, what is the meaning of fighting soldiers and horn-blowing hunters? You can see several bodies attached to one head or, the other way round, many heads joined to one body. Here a serpent's tail is to be seen on a four-footed beast; there a fish with an animal's head. There is a creature starting out as a horse, whilst the rear half of a goat brings up the rear; here a horned beast generates the rear of a horse. Indeed there are so many things, and everywhere such an extraordinary variety of hybrid forms, that it is more diverting to decipher marble than the text before you, and to spend the whole day in gazing at such singularities in preference to meditating upon God's laws. Good God! If one is not ashamed of such impropriety, why not at least rue the expense?

XI   A selection of regulations concerning art and architecture made by the Cistercians' General Chapter (1134 and after)

Instituta generalis capituli apud Cistercium
The annual assemblies of the abbots of Cistercian monasteries in Cîteaux issued decrees binding on the whole Order. The earliest written record of such regulations dates from 1134, and hence from the crucial creative decade, in terms of the history of Cistercian monastic architecture. Individually, most of the regulations are certainly earlier than this.

The extracts come from: *Analecta Divionensia: les monuments primitifs de la Règle Cistercienne, publ. d'après les manuscrits de l'abbaye de Cîteaux*, par Ph. Guignard, Dijon 1878. Cf. Mortet-Dechamps, *Recueil de Textes relatifs à l'histoire de l'Architecture. . . .* Paris 1929, pp. 30ff.

C. 1.: In civitatibus, castellis, villis, nulla nostra construenda sunt cenobia, sed in locis a conversatione hominum semotis.

Ch. 1: None of our monasteries is to be constructed in towns, castles or villages, but in places remote from human intercourse.

C. 12.: Duodecim monachi cum abbate tercio decimo ad cenobia nova transmittantur: nec tamen illuc destinentur donec locus . . . domibus . . . aptetur, oratorio, refectorio, dormitorio, cella hospitum et portarii . . .

Ch. 12: Twelve monks, thirteen including the abbot, are to be sent out to (found) new monasteries; but they are not to be picked for this until the site is appointed with buildings – that is to say with a chapel, refectory, dorter, and cells for the porter and for guests. . . .

C. 20.: Sculpture vel picture in ecclesiis nostris seu in officinis aliquibus monasterii ne fiant, interdicimus, quia dum talibus intenditur, utilitas bone meditationis vel disciplina religiose gravitatis sepe negligitur. Cruces tamen pictas, que sunt lignee, habemus.

Ch. 20: We forbid there to be any statues or pictures in our churches or in any other rooms of a monastery of ours, because, when attention is paid to such things, the advantages of sound meditation and training in religious gravity are often neglected. But we have painted wooden crosses.

C. 21.: Non est congruum ut extra portam monasterii domus aliqua ad habitandum construatur, nisi animalium, quia periculum animarum inde potest nasci.

Ch. 21: It is not suitable that any building for living in be constructed outside the gate of a monastery, save for animals, because this could put souls in jeopardy.

C. 31.: . . . Quod si quis contra statuta capituli . . . edificare presumpserit, remota omni dispensatione edificia cadant, expense et opera pereant.

Ch. 31: But if anyone shall presume to build in contempt of the statutes of the Chapter, these buildings shall come down, without any pardon, and the expense and labour shall be in vain.

C. 80.: Vitree albe fiant et sine crucibus et picturis.

Ch. 80: Let windows be of clear glass, without crosses and pictures.

(1157) C. 16.: Turres lapideae ad campanas non fiant. Domus extra portam cadant.

(1157) Ch. 16: There shall be no bell-towers of stone. Buildings outside the gates must come down.

(1182) C. 11.: Vitreae picturae infra terminum duorum annorum emendentur; alioquin ex nunc abbas et prior et cellerarius omni sexta feria jejunent in pane et aqua, donec sint emendatae.

(1182) Ch. 11: Stained-glass windows are to be replaced within the space of two years; otherwise the abbot, prior and cellarer are henceforward all to fast on bread and water every sixth day until they are replaced.

(1213) C. 1.: Auctoritate capituli generalis inhibetur ne de cetero fiant in ordine picturae, sculturae, praeterquam imaginem Salvatoris Christi, neque varietates pavimentorum, nec superfluitates aedificiorum et victualium; et a nullo abbate portentur scrinia quae vulgo cofria appellantur.

(1213) Ch. 1: It is hereby forbidden by authority of the General Chapter that there be from henceforth in the Order any pictures, sculpture – save for the image of Christ our Saviour – or any variegated floors, or anything unnecessary in the way of buildings or victuals. Nor is any abbot to allow writing-chests, vulgarly known as 'coffers'.

XII   From the Life of St Bernard. The building of the second monastery of Clairvaux

S. Bernardi, Clarevallensis Abbatis, vita prima, lib. II, auct. Ernaldo
The incidents were probably noted down as they happened, and assembled shortly after the death of the saint. Nonetheless, it should be remarked that they only regain their full freshness in their context. The Cistercian interest in the water-supply of their institutions makes its first appearance here.

Mabillon, *S. Bernardi opera*, vol. II, 1690, cols. 1103-04; Migne, *Patrologia Latina* CLXXXV, cols. 284-88: Mortet-Deschamps, 1929, pp. 25ff. There is a very fine English translation by Geoffrey Webb and Adrian Walker, in *St Bernard of Clairvaux*, London 1960, pp. 87-8.

Aderant ci in consilio venerabilis fratres sui; aderat Godefridus, prior eiusdem loci, propinquus eius in carne et spiritu, vir sapiens et constans, . . . postea in ecclesia Lingonensi factus episcopus . . .

He could call on the advice of his venerable brethren; there was Godfrey, the prior there, close to him in body and in spirit and a wise and steadfast man . . . afterward made bishop of Langres . . . (Prior of Clairvaux from 1130, Bishop of Langres from 1139).

Hic ergo atque alii plures viri providi, et de communi utilitate solliciti, virum Dei, cuius conversatione in caelis erat, aliquando descendere compellebant, et indicabant ei quae domus necessitas exigebat. Insinuant itaque ei locum angustum et incommodum, in quo consederant nec capacem tantae multitudinis: et cum quotidie catervatim adventantium numerus augeretur, non posse eos intra constructas recipi officinas, et vix oratorium solis sufficere monachis. Addunt etiam se considerasse inferius aptam planitiem, et opportunitatem fluminis, quod infra illabitur, ibique locum esse spatiosum ad omnes monasterii necessitates, ad prata, ad colonias, ad virgulta et vineas et si silvae videatur dessse clausura, facile hoc parietibus lapideis, quorum ingens ibi copia est, posse suppleri. In primis vir Dei non acquievit consilio: »Videtis, inquit, quia multis expensis et sudoribus iam domus lapidae consummatae sunt, aquaeductus cum maximis sumptibus per singulas officinas traducti. Si haec omnia confregerimus, poterunt homines saeculi male de nobis sentire, quod aut leves sumus et mutabiles, aut nimiae, quas tamen non habemus, divitiae nos faciunt insanire. Cumque certissimum vobis sit, penes nos esse pecunias, verbo evangelico vobis dico, quia aedificaturo turrim futuri operis necesse est supputare expensas: alioquin cum coeperit, et defecerit, dicetur: *Hic homo fatuus coepit aedificare, et non consummare.*«

Ad haec fratres respondent: »Si consummatis iis quae ad monasterium pertinent, habitatores cessasset mittere Deus, stare posset sententia, et cessandum ab operibus rationabilis esset censura. Nunc vero cum quotidie gregem suum Deus multiplicet, aut repellendi sunt quos mittit, aut providenda mansio, in qua suscipiantur. Nec dubium est, qui parat mansores, quin praeparet mansiones. Absit autem, ut pro diffidentia sumptuum confusionis hujus incurramus discrimina.« Audiens haec abbas, fide et caritate eorum delectus est, et aliquando tandem consiliis acquievit. . . .

Audivit hoc sanctae memoriae nobilissimus princeps Theobaldus, et multa in sumptus dedit, et ampliora spopondit subsidia. Audierunt episcopi regionum, et viri inclyti, et negotiatores terrae, et hilari animo sine exactore ultro ad opus Dei copiosa contulere suffragia. Abundantibus sumptibus, conductis festinanter operariis, ipsi fratres per omnia incumbebant operibus. Alii caedebant ligna (alii lapides conquadrabant, alii muros struebant), alii diffusis limitibus partiebantur fluvium, et extollebant saltus aquarum ad molas. Sed et fullones, et pistores, et coriarii, et fabri, aliique artifices, congruas aptabant suis operibus machinas ut scaturiret et prodiret, ubicumque opportunum esset, in omni domo subterraneis canalibus deductus rivus ultro ebuliens; et demum, congruis ministeriis per omnes officinas expletis, purgata domo, ad cardinalem alveum reverterentur quae diffusae fuerant aquae, et flumini propriam redderent quantitatem. Inopinata celeritate consummati sunt muri, totum monasterii ambitum spatiosissime complectentes. Surrexit domus, et quasi viventem atque motabilem haberet nuper nata ecclesia, in brevi profecit et crevit.

He and many other far-sighted men who were concerned for the good of the community once forced the man of God, whose head was in the heavens, to come down to earth, and they pointed out to him the effect that the buildings were having. They informed him that the site that they had settled in was constricted and inconvenient, and could not hold such numbers; moreover, since the horde of arrivals was swollen each day, it was no longer possible to accommodate them in the buildings constructed, and the chapel was scarcely adequate for the monks alone. They added that they considered the plain lower down and the advantages of the river which flowed down there to be suitable, whilst the situation there was extensive enough for all the needs of the monastery – for its meadows, fields, orchards and vineyards –; and if the enclosure afforded by trees appeared to be lacking, it was easy to make up for this with walls of stone, of which there was a vast quantity there. At first the man of God did not fall in with this advice. 'See,' he said, 'how the buildings have already been built in stone with great sweat and at great expense, and how the water-conduits have at great cost been led to the various rooms. If we throw away all this, people in the world will think badly of us, that we are either frivolous and mutable, or that excessive wealth – though we have no such thing – has turned our heads. Since you are quite certain that we do have funds to hand, I recall to you the saying of the Gospel, that in building a tower it is essential to compute the expenses of work to come, lest it be said of one who makes a start and then leaves off: "This foolish fellow began to build, and (could) not finish."' (Luke Ch. 14, v. 30).

To which the brethren replied: 'If God had ceased to send inmates once everything pertaining to the monastery was complete, your opinion would be valid, and the decision to call an end to building-works would be reasonable. But now that each day God multiplies his flock, either those whom he sends are to be turned away, or a mansion must be provided in which to accommodate them. How can there be any doubt that He who supplies inmates will provide accommodation (for them)? God forbid moreover, that out of want of confidence in our resources we should run the risk of this confusion.' Hearing this, the abbot took pleasure in their faith and charity, and at last consented to the plans. . . .

The most noble Count Thibault [of Champagne] of sacred memory heard of this, and donated greatly to the costs and pledged himself to further assistance. The local bishops, distinguished men, and merchants of the country also heard, and of their own free will brought plenteous aid to God's work with a joyous heart. Resources flowed, workmen were swiftly assembled, and the brethren too threw themselves into the work in every way. Some felled trees, some dressed stone, others built walls, and others again parted the river from its scattered channels and diverted the flow of its waters to a mill. But fullers too, and bakers, tanners, smiths and other craftsmen all organized their respective machinery for their work so that the babbling brook, carried hither and yon by buried conduits to every building, gushed and welled up wherever there was occasion for it; then, having fulfilled their appointed tasks through all the workshops, and the monastery having been cleansed, the waters, which were split up, returned to the main river bed, and restored to the river its own true volume. The walls were completed with unlooked-for rapidity, embracing in a great sweep the whole extent of the monastery. The convent arose, and the new-born church made progress and grew as if it had life and motion.

XIII   A description of Clairvaux (from the beginning of the thirteenth century)

Descriptio positionis seu situationis Monasterii Clarae-Velensis
Migne, *Patrologia Latina*, CLXXXV, 569-71; cf. also the French translation of the whole text in: M. H. d'Arbois de Jubainville, *Études sur l'état intérieur des abbayes cisterciennes et principalement de Clairvaux au XIIᵉ et XIIIᵉ siècle*, Paris 1858, pp. 329-34.
The author uses the literary device of following the course of the river in order to take us through the monastery. But in doing so he also testifies to the special importance of the water-supply in Cistercian monasteries. I pare the text down to its characteristic passages.

Si situm Clarae Vallis nosse desideras, haec tibi scripta sint pro speculo. Duo montes non longe ab abbatia habent initium, qui primo angustae vallis interiectione distincti, quo magis ad abbatiam appropiant, maiore hiatu fauces dilatant: quorum alter alterum abbatiae latus dimidium, alter totum occupat. . . .

Porro abbatiae pars posterior in latam desinit planitiem, cuius partem non modicam murus occupat, qui abbatiam diffuso cingit ambitu. Intra huius septa multae et variae arbores variis fecundae fructibus instar nemoris pomarium faciunt: quod infirmorum cellae contiguum, infirmitates fratrum non mediocri levat solatio, dum spatiosum spatiantibus praebet deambulatorium, arstuantibus quoque suave reclinatorium. . . .

Ubi pomarium desinit, incipit hortus intercisis distinctus areolis, vel potius divisus rivulis intercurrentibus. . . . Aqua haec piscibus alendis et rigandis oleribus duplici ministerio servit: cui Alba, famosi nominis fluvius, indefesso meatu fomenta ministrat. Hic per multas abbatiae officinas transitum faciens ubique pro fideli obsequio post se benedictionem relinquit. . . . Ipse quidem mediam vallem flexuosum intersecans per alveum quem non natura, sed fratrum industria fecit, dimidium sui mittit in abbatiam . . .

Et si forte amnis ipse inundas, impetuoso excursu proruit, obiectu muri retroactus, subtus quo eum necesse est fluere, in se ipsum recurrit, et refluum denuo defluus amplexatur. Intromissus vero quantum murus, portarii vice, permisit, primum in molendinum impetum facit, ubi multum sollicitus est, et tubatur erga plurima, tum molarum mole far comminuendo, tum farinam cribro subtili segregando a furfure.

Hic iam vicina, domo caldariam implet . . . Sed nec sic se absolvit. Eum enim ad se fullones invitant, qui sunt molendino sollicitus est, quo fratres vescantur, ita apud eos paret, quo et vestiantur. Ille autem non contradicit . . . sed graves illos, sive pistillos, sive malleos dicere mavis, vel certe pedes ligneos – nam hoc nomen saltuoso fullonum negotio magis videtur congruere – alternatim elevans atque deponens, gravi labore fullones absolvit: . . . Tot ergo volubiles rotas rotatu rapido circumducens, sic spumeus exit, ut ipse quasi moli et mollior fieri videatur.

Excipitur dehinc a domo coriari, ubi conficiendis his quae ad fratrum calceamenta sunt necessaria, operosam exhibet sedulitatem. Deinde, minutatim se et per membra multa disturbuens, singulas officinas officioso discursu perscrutatur, ubique diligenter inquirens quid et quo ipsius ministerio opus habeat, coquendis, cribrandis, vertendis, terendis, rigandis, lavandis, molendis, molliendis, suum sine contradictione praestans obsequium. Postremo . . . asportans immunditias, omnia post se munda relinquit; et iam peracto strenue propter quod venerat, rapida celeritate festinat ad fluvium, . . . redeamus ad rivulos, quos post nos reliquimus, qui derivati a fluvio, passivis per prata vagantur excursibus . . . Hi rivuli vel potius sulci post peractum officium fluvio qui eos evomuerat absorbentur, et iam totus simul Alba collectus prono decursu per devexa festinat. . . .

If you want to become familiar with the site of Clairvaux, let these words be as a mirror for you. Two mountains begin to rise not far from the abbey and are at first separated by the incision of a narrow valley, through the widening aperture of which they are cloven into a gorge as they get nearer the abbey. One of them occupies half of one side which the abbey is on, the other occupies the whole (of the other side). . . .

Further on, the rear of the abbey protrudes into a broad plain, no small part of which is enclosed by the wall that surrounds the abbey with its extensive circuit. Inside the confines of this, many and varied trees profuse in divers fruits make an orchard like a grove. Being contiguous to the infirmary, it affords no slight consolation to the sick brethren, since it offers a spacious walk to the up and about, and a pleasant resting-place for those who are hot. . . .

Where the orchard ends, a garden divided up into small patches by streams flowing between them begins. . . . This water serves a dual function, in nurturing fish and irrigating vegetables. It is fed from the inexhaustible flow of the renowned Aube. Making its way through the many offices of the abbey, it everywhere leaves a blessing behind it by virtue of its faithful service. . . . It cuts through the middle of the valley, winding through a channel made not by nature, but by the labour of the monks, and dispatches half its volume into the abbey. . . .

And if on occasion its swollen current impetuously overflows it is driven back by the wall of the sluice under which it has to flow and flows back into itself, and the downward flow once more embraces what has flooded back. But insofar as the sluice, acting as a porter, lets it in, it makes a first assault upon the mill, where it is greatly churned up and thrown in several directions, now pulverizing the grain in the mill-stones, and now separating the flour from the bran with a fine sieve.

Now it fills the cauldron in the building nearby. . . . But it has not yet finished, for the fullers invite it to them. Just as it is busy (for those) who are in the mill by which the brethren are fed, it now appears at the place by which they are clothed. It does not say nay . . . but instead, alternately raising and lowering the heavy pestles, or as you might prefer to say, hammers – though wooden feet might seem a more appropriate name for this leaping work of the fullers – it relieves the fullers of heavy labour. . . . As it turns so many chattering wheels round in swift rotation, it makes a foamy exit, and seems as if it was itself ground and made softer.

It is then intercepted by the building of the tanners, where it shows industrious application in making the things necessary for the brethren's shoes. Thereupon, apportioning itself piecemeal among a number of arms, it seeks out individual buildings in its obliging rounds, diligently enquiring everywhere what work has (need) of it and for what task – whether for cooking, sieving, turning, grinding, watering, washing, milling or softening, lending its compliance without gainsaying. Finally . . . bearing away the refuse, it leaves everything spick and span behind it. Having vigorously carried out everything for which it came, it hurries back to the river with great speed. . . . Here let us return to the streams we left behind us and which, diverted from the river, wandered through the meadows in idle loops . . . these streams, or rather ditches, once their task is done, are absorbed by the river which spewed them forth; now the Aube, all together once more, rushes down the slope in headlong descent. . . .

XIV   From the Statutes of the Franciscans (1260)

Even the Friars Minor issued statutes against extravagance in building, which in many details follow on from the regulations of the Cistercians. The first written record of customs, that are themselves earlier, dates from 1260. In 1310 they were renewed in a stricter form at the General Chapter in Padua. They only have a bearing on church architecture, not on that of the friaries.

Fr. Ehrle, *Die ältesten Redactionen der Generalconstitution des Franziskanerordens*, in: *Archiv für Literatur und Kirchengeschichte des Mittelalters*, VI 1892, pp. 69 & 87 ff. – V. Mortet et P. Deschamps, *Recueil de Textes*, Paris 1929, pp. 285-87.

Incipiunt constitutiones generales ordinis fratrum Minorum, editae et confirmatae in Capitulo generali apud Narbonam, anno Domini 1260, decima iunii, tempore reverendi patris fratris Bonaventurae, octavi ministri generalis; et postea fuit cardinalis Sanctae Romanae Ecclesiae et nunc canonizatus . . .

. . . Cum autem curiositas et superfluitas directe obviet paupertati, ordinamus quod aedificiorum curiositas in picturis, celaturis, fenestris, columnis et huiusmodi, aut superfluitas in longitudine, latitudine et altitudine secundum loci conditionem arctius evitetur. Qui autem transgressores huius constitutionis fuerint, graviter puniantur, et principales de locis irrevocabiliter expellantur, nisi per ministrum generalem fuerint restituti. Et ad hoc firmiter teneantur visitatores, si ministri fuerint negligentes.

Ecclesiae autem nullo modo fiant testudinatae excepta maiori capella. Campanile ecclesiae ad modum turris de cetero nusquam fiat; item fenestrae vitreae istoriatae vel picturatae de cetero nusquam fiant, excepto quod in principali vitrea, post maius altare chori, haberi possint imagines Crucifixi, beatae Virginis, beati Johannis, beati Francisci et beati Antonii tantum; et si de cetero factae fuerint, per visitatores amoveantur.

Here begin the general constitutions of the Order of the Friars Minor, edited and confirmed in the General Chapter at Narbonne, on 10 June in the year of our Lord 1260, in the time of the reverend father, brother Bonaventura, eighth minister-general, who afterward became cardinal of the Holy Roman Church and is now canonized. . . .

. . . Since exquisite craftsmanship and superfluity are directly contrary to poverty, we order that such exquisite craftsmanship, whether in pictures, sculpture, windows, columns and suchlike, and any superfluity in length, width or height above what is fitting to the requirements of the place, be more strictly avoided. Any who transgress against this constitution are to be severely punished, and the chief officials are to be irrevocably expelled from their establishments, unless they are re-installed by the minister-general. And let the visitors be quite firm on this if the ministers have been negligent over it.

Churches shall in no wise be vaulted, save for the presbytery. Nor shall their campanile be anywhere made like a tower. Similarly, no figural stained glass windows shall be made, save that in the main window in the choir behind the high altar, images of the Crucifix, and of the blessed Virgin, St John, St Francis and St Anthony alone may be permitted. If any others are made they are to be removed by the visitors.

XV   From the monastic diary of Abbot Rupert II of Ottobeuren

From 1710 to 1740 that great Baroque builder, Abbot Rupert II, the son of a smith called Ness from the free city of Wangen, entered in the fourteen huge volumes of his official diary everything that seemed noteworthy during his period of office. It is wholly Baroque in its scope and organization, being subdivided into 'Politica, Ecclesiastica and Oeconomica', into which is inserted everything, from newspaper extracts, round-robins, honours and decrees, to extracts from letters, records of payments and wholly personal comments. These bundles reflect the abbot's own nature – vigorously uninhibited and without literary pretensions; his utterly straightforward firmness and piety is only surpassed by the simple love of art and the passion for building that governed his whole approach.

We assemble here a few remarks from this diary, taken from the extracts found in Norbert Lieb (Bibl. 204, pp. 10-14; Bibl. 202, pp. 284-321).

»Euer Hochwürden lassen sich doch in ihren jungen Jahren (sit venia verbo!) den Geiz nit überbünden, im Alter kommt solcher von selbsten, sondern eine memoria (sagt allzeit mein Herkhomer, der sich untertänig empfiehlt) der Nachwelt erlassen. Was Euer Hochwürden Schönes und Herrliches bauen, darf jederman sehen, aber die Fuchsen in der Truhen lasset man nit gehen unter die Augen. Um viel Geld ist man uns neidig, niemand Gescheiter um eine schöne Wohnung.

Approval and criticism
A letter of 9 November 1713 from Gerhard Oberleitner, the Abbot of St Mang in Füssen.

'Let your Reverence not give yourself over to meanness whilst you are still young (*sit venia verbo*!) – that comes of itself in old age – but leaves a *memoria* (as my Herkhomer, who sends you his respects, is always saying) to the world to come. Everyone may see something beautiful and splendid that your Reverence builds, whereas there is no pleasure to the sight to be had from coffers of hard cash. People are jealous of us if we have a lot of money, but no-one else can be any the better off from a fine building.' (cf. p. 304 for a similar motivation at Orval.)

On 23 May 1724 Abbot Rupert reacted as follows to the accusation of the Prelate of Neresheim that the construction of the monastery of

»Scandalum acceptum, non datum. Meine Intention geht nit dahin, sondern ad honorem SS. Trinitatis, cui unice consecravi, talem domum Dei zu bauen, S. Ordini et Abbatiae convenientiem.... Ich habe vermeint, ich mache mir coram Deo et hominibus ein meritum . . ., muß aber den Lohn von Menschen entschlagen und noch von dem lieben Gott allein erwarten. . . . Es ist eben schon meistens – Gott Lob! – gebaut! Kanns nit mehr abbrechen und muß ad honorem Dei continuiren, solang Gott will. Wann mir Gott die Gnade gibt, auch die Kirche zu bauen, so werde ich wohl alle Kräfte anwenden, einen raren Tempel SS. Trinitati zu bauen, wogegen das Klostergebäu nichts sein soll!«

»Pecunia, patientia et prudentia seind die drei Elementa, mit welchen man bauen muß.«

»Es hat mich bedunkhen wollen, es hätte ein mehrers geschehen sollen; allein kann man bei dem Bauen nit alles nach Wunsch haben. Und braucht das Bauen nit nur Geld, sondern auch Geduld, und damit es nit schlecht herauskomme, presupponiert es Verstand und iudicia architectonica mit guter Invention, ohne welches weder Geld noch Geduld appliziert ist . . .«

»Diese Zeit habe mit Mr Sympert Kramer, bisheriger Maurermeister, wegen einer neuen Klosterkirche geredt, und weilen schon viele Kirchenriß in Händen hatte, so habe aus allen etwas gezogen und vermeint das Beste zu erwählen, zu welchem Ende ihm auf sein Ersuchen erlaubt, einen Aufriß zu machen und mir zur Approbation vorzulegen, welches er dann auch getan. Nachdem nun solches geschehen und ein so anderes dabei advertiert, also habe zu besserer Einsicht des ganzen Werkes auch verlangt, daß er ein förmliches Modell über den Abriß mache, damit alle besser sehen und erkennen mögen, wie die Kirche sich in allen Stücken in- und auswendig praesentiere.«

»Mr Sympert Kramer Maurermeister hat diesen verstrichenen Winter ein Modell von Holz elaborirt. Das Modell ist teils mit einer offenen cupula und teils mit einer vertruckhten cupula unter Dach gestellt worden, damit man davon den Unterschied sehe und von beiden das Ratsamere erwählen könne, wie dann die Fundamente schon darauf angelegt werden. Es finden sich eben rationes pro und contra eine offene cupula. Eine offene cupula macht auswendig einer Kirche großes Ansehen und Majestät, wie man an mehreren Orten sieht, braucht aber große und kostbare Unterhaltung. Eine vertruckhte cupula aber hat auswendig kein sonderliches Aussehen, ist aber leichter zu unterhalten und macht inwendig eine Kirche allerdings annehmlicher, als wann die cupula zu hoch aufsteigt; wie denn die hohe cupula von der Grundebene bis 225 Schuh aufsteigt samt der Laterne, herentwegen bei der vertruckhten cupula samt der Laterne sich bis 175 Schuh extendirt, so auch eine schöne Höhe.«

»Es haben sich dubio ereignen wollen, ob man nicht einen architectum bestellen und dem Maurermeister adjungieren solle. Weilen aber solchen dermalen für unnötig erachtet, also wird Mr Simpert Kramer mit angefangenen Fundamenten in nomine Domini continuiren. Gemelte dubia sind von einigen architectis in vicinia movirt worden, mehrenteils ex aemulatione et studio proprii commodi, als welche gerne die Ehre und Nutzen gehabt hätten, die Kirche zu bauen, ohngeachtet dieselben im ganzen Riß und angelegten Fundamenten nichts auszustellen gewußt, sondern approbirt haben.«

»H. Dominicus Zimmermann Architectus von Landtsperg hat 2 Kirchenriß proiectirt, welche mir wohlgefallen, sonderbar der eine mit dem Ovalgewölb, welcher per gratiam dei suo tempore könnte gebraucht und aufgeführt werden. Der andere in einer völligen Rundung ist zwar schön, aber zu hoch und lang auf unseren Platz, mithin pretioser auszuführen als der erste und vielleicht nit so annehmlich und commod. Es zeigt sich zwar in diesem anderen Riß eine große Magnificenz und

Ottobeuren 'goes grossly and inadmissibly beyond the bounds of *modestiam religiosam*':

'Offence has been taken, not given. You have mistaken my intention, which is to build such a house of God in honour of the Holy Trinity, to whom alone I have dedicated it, and for the use of the Holy Order and this Abbey. . . . I should have thought that I had acquired for myself a merit in the eyes of God and men . . . , but I must renounce the thought of human gratitude, and expect it from the Good Lord alone. . . . In any case it is – thank God! – to a large extent already built. I can't break off now, and must go on for the honour of God, God willing. If God of his grace also lets me build the church, then I shall exert myself to the utmost to build a rare temple to the Holy Trinity, beside which the conventual buildings shall be nothing!'

Planning and intentions

Diary entry for 20 October 1727:
'Patience, prudence and a well-filled purse are the three *Elementa* with which one must build.'

Diary entry for 31 October 1726:
'It happened to occur to me that much more should have been done; save that in building one can never have everything as one wants it. Building needs not only money, but patience, and, if it is not to turn out badly, it presupposes good judgement and *iudicia architectonica*, together with good ideas, without which neither money nor patience is of any use . . .'

Diary entry for 1 March 1736:
'I have lately been speaking with Mr Sympert Kramer, up till now the master-mason, about a new monastery church; and since I already had many designs to hand, I have taken something from each of them and intend to select the best, to which end I granted his request to make a design and submit it to me for approval, which he then did. When this had been done, and a quite different (design) had emerged in the process, in order to have a better grasp of the thing as a whole I also asked him to make a scale model from the design so that everyone can get a better idea of how the church will appear in every detail inside and out.'

Diary entry for 31 March 1739:
'This last winter the master-mason, Mr Sympert Kramer, made a wooden model. The model shows the two alternatives of a full dome on a drum, and a shallow semi-dome under a roof, so that one can see the difference and choose the better of the two, and proceed to lay the foundations accordingly. There are arguments for and against a full dome. A full dome makes the outside of a church very majestic and imposing, as one sees in many places, but it requires massive and expensive support. A semi-dome makes no great impression from without, but is easier to support, and creates a more agreeable impression from within than when a dome is too lofty – in this case the tall dome taken with the lantern would rise 225 feet above the ground, whilst the semi-dome taken with the lantern would rise 175 feet, itself no mean height.'

Diary entry for 6 July 1739:
'Doubts have arisen as to whether one should not employ an architect to work in concert with the mason. Since this is regarded as unnecessary for the present, Mr Simpert Kramer will proceed upon the existing foundations in the name of the Lord. The said doubts have been sown by certain architects nearby, mostly out of rivalry and the pursuit of their own advantage, as they would gladly have had the honour and profit from building the church. Paying no attention to these I found nothing to alter in the already-laid foundations or in the design as a whole, but expressed my approval.'

Diary entry for 6 December 1732:
'Herr Dominicus Zimmermann, the Landtsperg architect, has proposed 2 designs for the church which I like, one of them is a singular design with an oval vault, which, *per gratiam dei suo tempore*, might be used and executed. The other, which is wholly circular, is indeed beautiful but too high and long for our site, besides being more expensive to execute than the other, and perhaps not even as agreeable and suitable. This second design indeed displays great majesty and magnificence, but when

Maiestät, wenn man aber considerrit die unsrige Landsart, so vielen Winden, Witterungen, sowohl Sommers als Winters Zeiten unterworfen, so ist nit ratsam dergleichen zu bauen, weilen die Conservation ein ewiges Kapital wäre. Wäre also der Meinung, der erstere meritirte vor anderen in Consideration gezogen zu werden, maßen die Länge auf den Platz proportionirt, so bestehen kann in 260 Schuh, wie der Riß anzeigt, ohne daß man in die Tiefe des Spitalgartens käme; die Breite wäre wieder a proportione sowohl des Klostergebäus als des äußeren Platzes, so die Kirche occupiren sollte. Gäbe gleichwohlen Ansehen, Magnificenz und Maiestät, so viele als in hoc loco gebührt templo domini sancto und die vires monasterii ertragen möchten. Es würde auch dieses Proiect alle anderen Gebäu im Kloster übertreffen und sich zeigen, daß man verlange, Gott allein die größte Ehre in domo sua zu erweisen und nach allen Kräften zu promoviren.«

»Wenigst habe pro moderno stylo et aevo getracht, allmögliches zu observiren ex gratia Dei, wie es dann die Approbation von diesiger Welt hat.«

»Meine Intention ist, daß der Kreuzgang lauter gute Gedanken ex obiectis pictis verursachen möge.«

»Man solle in nomine Domini pro maiori gloria Jesu auch den Anfang zu der neuen Kirche machen.«
»Meinerseits werde ich nicht ermangeln lassen alle Kräfte anzuwenden, ut etiam domus Dei aedificetur.«

»Dahero inskünftig mit ihnen leidelicher zu tractiren; allein wie es geht bei der Welt: Ein Bauherr steht unter der Gewalt dieser Leute und wenn man an einem Ort menagiren will, so wissen sie an einem anderen Ort zu helfen.«

»Weil Herr B(ergmiller) unter den Künstlern jetziger Zeit gerechnet wird, so habe auch von seiner Hand etwas machen lassen.«

». . . ein schönes und andächtiges Stück, so alle admiriren.«

». . . eine schöne Gelegenheit tam pro Conventu quam Abbati dem Gottesdienst und Devotion abzuwarten.«

»Die Bilder sind schon wohlgemacht, doch ossequiren die Leut meine Gedanken in diesem nicht, daß sie die Stellungen mir nicht also einrichten, ut magis reluceat aliqua similitudo inter figuram et figuratum, wie ich das Concept angegeben und anfangs geführt; wenn ich schon befehle, daß sie mir vorher die Stellungen nur mit Reißblei projectiren und zur Approbation oder Correction übergeben, so haben doch die Künstler ihre Eigensinnigkeit.«
»Die Malerei ist gut; doch aber assequirt er meine Intention in der Stellung figurae et figurati, so eine Parallele und similitudinem geben und haben soll, niemals recht, wenn ich schon alles vorsage.«

»Nos qui vivimus können uns kaum noch einbilden die Situation des alten Klosters – was wird denjenigen ebendavon einige Ideen machen können, welche es niemals gesehen?«

weather, both in summer and winter – it is not advisable to build like this; one considers our local conditions – subject to so much windy and bad its upkeep would be a never-ending saga. (I) am inclined to think that the first one most deserves to be taken into consideration; measuring its length against the site, this could be 260 feet, as the plan shows, without intruding upon the infirmary garden; the width in turn would be in proportion both with the conventual buildings, and with the open space that the church would have to occupy. It would also be as imposing, magnificent and majestic as is meet for a hallowed temple of the Lord in this spot, and as the brethren would tolerate. At the same time this project would surpass all the other buildings in the monastery and declare that one desired to reserve for God alone the greatest honour in his house, and to serve him to the utmost.'

Diary entry for 31 October 1726:
'At least I have striven in accordance with the modern style and times to see that everything is done in keeping with God's grace, just as it has the approval of this world.'

Diary entry for 28 May 1722:
'My intention is that the cloister will occasion nothing but good thoughts by virtue of the things painted there.'

Decision of the Chapter of 13 October 1736
'In the name of the Lord and to the greater glory of Christ let a start now be made on the new church.'
To which the abbot: 'For myself, I shall spare no pains to exert every effort, so that thus the house of the Lord may be built.'

Praise and criticism of particular artists

Diary entry of 20 October 1727:
Concerning the extravagant demands of the Italian stuccadors at the autumnal settlement of accounts: 'In the future then to bargain with them more patiently; for that is the way of it – a client is under the thumb of these people, and when someone in one place wants to assert control, then they know of another place to make themselves useful.'

Diary entry for 3 December 1726:
'Since Herr B(ergmüller) is accounted one of the modern artists, I have also commissioned something from his hand.'

Diary entry for 1 June 1724:
On Amigoni's altarpiece: 'A beautiful and reverent piece, admired by all.'
On the whole structure together with its pictures: 'A fine place for both the Community and the Abbot to linger before Divine Service and Prayers.'

Diary entries of 15 February 1722 and 20 April 1723:
On the work of the painter Hieronymus Hau: 'The pictures are well executed, but the figures do not agree with my ideas in this respect, that they are not disposed according to my conception and as I originally directed, so that there should be a greater reflection of some kinship between the image and the thing figured; this, though I instruct artists to sketch out their compositions in pencil beforehand and to submit them for approval or correction – but they are an obstinate lot.'
'The painting is good, nonetheless however much I specify everything beforehand, it never really complies with my intention that the disposition of the figures and the subject should be congruous and analogous.'

Joy over completion of the work

Diary entry for 15 January 1729:
'We who are alive now can scarcely form a picture of the appearance of the old monastery; what idea of it will those people be able to have who have never seen it?'

Notes

1 Mann, A., *Grossbauten vorkarlischer Zeit und aus der Epoche von Karl dem Grossen bis zu Lothar I*, in: *Karl der Grosse, Lebenswerk und Nachleben*, ed. by Wolfgang Braunfels, Vol. III: *Karolingische Kunst*, Düsseldorf 1965, p. 320.

2 Hubert, J., *L'Europe des Invasions*, Paris 1967, p. 64.

3 Document No. III, Ch. II.

4 Gerstenberg, K., *Die deutschen Baumeisterbildnisse des Mittelalters*, Berlin 1966, p. 5.

5 Effmann, W., *Centula – St Riquier, Eine Untersuchung zur Geschichte der kirchlichen Baukunst in der Karolingerzeit*, Münster 1912, p. 56.

6 Levillain, L., *Les statuts de l'abbaye de Corbie promulgués par Adlard en 822*, in: *Le Moyen Age* XIII, 1900, pp. 352ff.

7 Cipolla, C., *Una 'Abbrevatio' inedita dei beni dell'abbazia di Bobbio*, in: *Rivista Storica Benedictina* I, 1906, pp. 3ff.

8 Dopsch, A., in: *Vierteljahresschrift für Sozial- und Wirtschaftsgeschichte XIII*, 1916, pp. 41-70.
I owe many thanks to Walter Horn, of the University of Berkeley, California, for allowing me to inspect his manuscript on the St Gallen plan just before it went to press.

9 Mittermüller, R., *Vita et Regula SS. P. Benedicti una cum expositione Regula a Hildemaro tradita*, Ratisbonae 1880.
Hildemar was called by Angilbert II (824-60) from Corbie to the monastery of Civate near Lake Como as a teacher, and his pupils recorded his instructions around 850.

10 Marrier, Dom M. and Duchesne, A., *Bibliotheca Cluniacensis*, Paris 1614, reprinted, Protat frères, Macon 1915:
Col. 1666 (for the year 1245): *Et sciendum est quod infra ambitum monasterii Cluniacensis, habuit hospitum domnus Papa cum Capellanis suis, et cum omni privata familia. Et Eps. Silvanectensis cum familia. Domnus Rex Franciae cum matre sua, et fratre suo, et sorore sua, et cum tota ipsorum familia privata. Et domnus Imperator Constantinopolitanus cum tota familia, et multi alii milites Clerici, Religiosi, de quibus non fit mentio. Et tamen nunquam propter hoc Monachi amiserunt dormitorium, neque refectorium, neque Monasterium, neque Capitulum, neque Infirmariam, neque Cellariam, neque Coquinam, neque aliquam de Officinis deputatis Conventui.*

11 Wilmart, Dom A., *Le couvent et la bibliothèque de Cluny vers le milieu du XIe siècle*, in: *Revue Mabillon* 11 (1922). 89-124.

12 Probably rightly, but in contrast to his earlier views, Conant now situates the fountain on the western corner of the southern arm of the cloister, instead of in the middle of it.

13 Quoted from: Otto, Bishop of Freising, *Chronik oder die Geschichte der zwei Staaten*, translated into German by Adolf Schmidt and edited by Walter Lammers, Darmstadt 1960, pp. 560ff.

14 Simson, O. von, *The Gothic Cathedral*, 1958, pp. 93ff.

15 Meglinger, J., *Descriptio Itineris Cisterciensis*, in: *Migne PL*, CLXXXV, 2, cols. 1566-1622.

16 Esser, K. H., *Über den Kirchenbau des Hl. Bernhard von Clairvaux*, in: *Archiv für mittelrheinische Kirchengeschichte* 5, 1953, pp. 195-221. In this article Esser presents the plans from his excavations, with the proof of Bernard's presence and the planning activity of Achard.

17 Pourbus made mistakes in the identification of certain buildings and ranges; the designations of the eastern and southern arms of the cloister are, for instance, certainly the wrong way round.

18 Leistikow, D., *Hospitalbauten in Europa aus zehn Jahrhunderten. Ein Beitrag zur Geschichte des Krankenhausbaus*, Ingelheim 1967 pp. 29ff.

19 in: *La Chartreuse de Champmol, Catalogue de l'Exposition au Musée de Dijon en 1960.*

20 St Francis was at first buried in the small cemetery near S. Giorgio, where Sta Chiara now stands. I am inclined to doubt Hertlein's theory that the reported desire to be buried in a refuse tip by the gallows outside the town was a subsequent pious invention. It ties in perfectly with the poetic literalness of his imitation of Christ; but it is also the only real reason for the eccentric choice of site for the sepulchral church.

21 The small and late Hohenstaufen *palatium* and town of Hagenau, for instance, with a population that never rose above 3,000, and that was mostly under 2,000, contained 11 establishments of the following Orders: Premonstratensian 1189-1789; Franciscan 1222-1789; Poor Clares 1280-99; Austin friars 1282-1789; Dominicans 1293-1789; Penitents 1310-?; Williamites 1311-1614; Hospitallers 1354-1535; Beguines 1390-1789; Jesuits 1604-1765; Capuchins 1628-1789: six of which, therefore, lasted until the French Revolution.

22 Hauck, A., *Kirchengeschichte Deutschlands*, Berlin 1958 (9th edition), Vol. IV, p. 409.

23 Davidsohn, R., *Forschungen zur Geschichte* von Florenz IV, Berlin 1908, p. 483. The author relates the vision of a monk called Bartolus from Pisa in 1385, according to which one of the builders of Santa Croce, the Prior Giovenale degli Agli, appeared to him in his sleep in order to tell him that in Hell he was struck eternally on the temples by the very masons' chisels that had created the admired and virtuoso, but reprehensible, work. Centuries later we can still sympathize with the spleen of the brother whose meditation was upset by the endless hammering.

24 Richa, G., *Notizie istoriche delle chiese fiorentine divisi nei suoi quartieri*, Firenze 1754/62.

25 Unless I am mistaken, the chapter-house of Brauweiler is the only one from before the beginning of the fourteenth century whose painting survives. The early dating to the incumbency of its builder Amilius (1135-49) was proposed by Beseler, H., *Zu den Monumentmalereien im Kapitelsaal von Brauweiler*, in: *Jahrbuch der Rheinischen Denkmalpflege*, XIII, 1960, pp. 98-124. Neither the source of the varied iconographic programme, nor its relevance to a chapter-house is known. Cf. Clemen, P., *Die romanische Monumentalmalerei in den Rheinlanden*, Düsseldorf 1916, pp. 358-404.

26 Marrier, Dom M. and Duchesne, A., *Bibliotheca Cluniacensis*, Paris 1614, reprinted by Protat freres, Macon 1915.
Col. 1640 (on the abbacy of Hugh of Semur, 1049-1109): *Ista domus Refectorii habetur gloriosa in picturis tam novi quam veteris Testamenti, principium fundatorem et benefactorem Coenobii Cluniacensis cum immensa imagine Christi, et*

repraesentatione magni ipsius iudicii. . . .

27 Cf. Vertova, L., *I cenacoli fiorentini*, Turin, 1965.

28 Cohn, W., in: Offner, R., *A critical and historical corpus of Florentine painting*, New York 1956, Vol. VI, Section III, pp. 122-35.

29 The number of bishoprics in England before the introduction of Henry VIII's reforms is normally given as 17, but sometimes as 19. This is because Bath and Wells, and Coventry and Lichfield sometimes count as one bishopric, sometimes as two. The latter mode of reckoning gives alongside the ten monastery-cathedrals, nine secular cathedrals of the 'old foundation': Chester, Exeter, Hereford, Lichfield, Lincoln, London, Salisbury, Wells and York.

30 H. M. Taylor, 'The Anglo-Saxon Cathedral Church at Canterbury', *The Archaeological Journal*, CXXVI (1969), 101-330.

31 David Knowles and J. K. S. St Joseph, *Monastic Sites from the Air*, Cambridge 1952.

32 Nikolaus Pevsner, *The Buildings of England, County Durham*, London 1953, p. 17.

33 C. E. Woodruff and W. Danks, *Memorials of the Cathedral and Priory of Christ Church*, London 1912, pp. 52ff. R. Willis, *The Conventual Buildings of the Monastery of Christ Church*, London 1868, p. 175; cf. also *The Canterbury Psalter*, ed. Mortimer R. James, London 1935, Text pp. 52ff. and Pls 284/85.

34 L. H. Heydenreich, *Ein Jerusalem-Plan aus der Zeit der Kreuzfahrer*, in *Miscellanea pro Arte*, Düsseldorf 1965, pp. 83ff.

35 I take the plan from A. W. Clapham, *The Archaeological Journal* LXXXVI, 1929, p. 239. The plan uses colours to distinguish the building periods.

36 According to J. Bilson, *On the Discovery of Some Remains of the Chapter-House of Beverley Minster*, in *Archaeologica* LV 1895, pp. 425ff., circa 1120; according to Bibl. 21, p. 62 and Pl. 58a, 'first half of 12th century'. The dating in Bibl. 19, 1950, 'circa 1160' is certainly too late.

37 Bibl. 20 & 21.

38 Wolfgang Goetz, *Zentralbau und Zentralbautendenz in der gotischen Architektur*, Berlin 1968, p. 312ff.

39 F. Nordström 1955, pp. 265ff.

40 Braunfels, W., *Anton Wonsams Kölnprospekt von 1531 in der Geschichte des Sehens*, in: *Wallraf-Richartz-Jahrbuch* XXII.

41 Mont-Saint-Michel had a similar ossuary; cf. Schmitt, O., *Zur Deutung des spätromanischen Zentralbaus auf der Komburg*, in: *Die Klosterbaukunst*, 1951.

42 I rely on the old designations due to E. Corroyer in 1872. More recent research regards the place as a refectory, which it probably was used as once the monks had given up having a common dorter in the fifteenth century. For one thing the 56 slit-like windows pronounce it as a dorter, with one for each bed. A wealth of windows also distinguishes the dorter in Cluny. They were mandatory for a dorter, never for a refectory, and were for each monk to read by during the siesta.

43 I could find no general plan that correctly reproduced the royal apartments as shown on the detailed plans.

44 Grimschitz, B., *Johann Lukas von Hildebrandt*, Vienna and Munich 1959, p. 99.

45 Boesch, G., *Vom Untergang der Abtei Rheinau*, Zurich 1956.

46 This quotation was already used by Montalembert, in *Les Moines d'occident*, Paris 1860-77.

47 Goffient, H. J. F., *Documents pour l'histoire de l'abbaye d'Orval: Annales de l'institut archéologique du Luxembourg V*, 1867, p. 165; *III. Pillage et incendie de l'abbaye d'Orval en 1637*.

48 See note 46.

49 Hautecoeur, L., *Histoire de l'architecture classique en France*, Part II, Paris 1948.

50 Cf. Serenyi, P., *Le Corbusier, Fourier, and the monastery of Ema*, in: *The Art Bulletin* XLIX, 1967, pp. 227-86, including citations from: Le Corbusier, *The Marseilles Block*, London 1953, p. 45 and Le Corbusier, *Modulor*, Cambridge, Mass. 1954, pp. 27ff. There is a good analysis of monastic functionalism in: Rowe, C., *The Dominican monastery of La Tourette*, in: *Architectural Review*, 1961, pp. 400-10.

Bibliography

My purpose in making this selection from the vast mass of material on Western monasticism has been twofold. On the one hand I have listed the literature on which I have drawn in the text; on the other, I have tried to give the reader an idea of the extent of the field from which I have chosen some of the most important examples. For easier reference, the titles have been arranged in chapter order. Within each chapter, the order is that of the year of publication. The titles have also been numbered to facilitate brief reference in the text. This selection covers only a fraction of the material available on Western monasticism. A complete bibliography has never been attempted, and would probably prove an impossible task.

1 History of monasticism and monastic architecture

a basic descriptions and sources.

1 Hallinger, K., *Corpus Consuetudinum Monasticarum*, Siegburg 1963.

2 Hélyot, P., *Dictionnaire des Ordres religieux*, ed. M. L. Badiche, in: Migne, J. P., *Encyclopédie Théologique*, vols. XX–XXIII, 1847–1859.

3 Lenoir, A., *Architecture monastique*. Collection de documents inédits sur l'histoire de France, 3e série, Archéologie VII, Paris 1852.

4 Migne, J. P., *Dictionnaire des Abbayes*, 1856

5 *The Cambridge Medieval History*, ed. H. M. Gwatkin, Cambridge 1911–36.

6 *Sancti Benedicti Regula Monasteriorum*, ed. Lutzbertus Butler, Freiburg 1927.

7 Hilpisch, St., *Geschichte des Benediktinischen Mönchtums*, Freiburg 1927.

8 Heimbucher, M., *Die Orden und Kongregationen der katholischen Kirche*, Munich-Paderborn-Vienna 1933/34; reprinted 1965.

9 Heussi, K., *Ursprung des Mönchtums*, Tübingen 1936.

10 Dom Cottineau, *Répertoire topobibliographique des abbayes et des prieurs*, 2 vols., Macon 1939.

11 Schmitz, Ph., *Geschichte des Benediktinerordens*, Zurich-Einsiedeln 1947–60, 4 vols.

12 Balthasar, H.-U. von, *Die großen Ordensregeln*, Einsiedeln-Zurich-Cologne 1948.

13 *Die Klosterbaukunst*, Working report of the Franco-German art historians' meeting, Mainz 1951.

14 Eschapasse, M., *L'Architecture Bénédictine en Europe*, Paris 1963.

b according to countries

15 *Monasticon Anglicanum*, 6 vols., Sir William Dugdale, London 1817–30.

16 Knowles, D. and Hadcock, *Medieval Religious Houses in England and Wales*, London 1946–53.

17 —, *The Monastic Order in England*, Cambridge 1950.

18 —, *The Religious Orders in England*, 3 vols., 1956–61.

19 Cook, G. H., *English Monasteries in the Middle Ages*, London 1961.

20 Sanderius, A., *Chorographia sacrae Brabantiae*, Brussels 1659.

21 Germain, M., *Monasticon Gallicanum*, reprint ed. Peigné-Delacourt, 1882.

22 Grossi, P., *Le abbazie benedictine*, Florence 1957.

23 Puig I Caldafalch. *L'arcitectura romànica a Catalunya*, Barcelona 1909.

24 Lamperez y Romea, V., *Historia de la arquitectura cristiana española en el edad media*, 3 vols., Madrid 1930.

25 Azcarate, J. M. de, *Monumentos españoles*, 3 vols., Madrid 1953.

2 Beginnings of the Benedictine monastic schema

a general works

26 Vogüe, M., *Syrie Centrale, Architecture civile et religieuse du 1er au 7e siècle*, 4 vols., Paris 1865–97.

27 Schlosser, J. von, *Abendländische Klosteranlagen des frühen Mittelalters*, Vienna 1889.

28 Hager, G., *Zur Geschichte der abendländischen Klosteranlage*, in: *Zeitschrift für christliche Kunst* 14, 1901.

29 Frendel, J., *Ursprung und Entwicklung der christlichen Klosteranlage*, thesis, Bonn 1927.

30 Butler, H. C., *Early Churches in Syria*, Princeton 1929.

31 Dehlinger, A., *Die Ordensgesetzgebung der Benediktiner und ihre Auswirkung auf die Grundrißgestaltung des benediktinischen Klosterbaus in Deutschland*, Borna-Leipzig 1936.

32 Aubert, M., *Origines du plan bénédictin*, in: *Bulletin Monumental* 1937.

33 Prinz, F., *Frühes Mönchtum in Frankreich*, Munich, Vienna 1965.

b on individual monasteries

34 Hélyot, P., *L'Abbaye de Corbie*, Louvain 1957.

35 Hugot, L., *Kornelimünster, Untersuchung über die baugeschichtliche Entwicklung der ehemaligen Benediktinerklosterkirche*, thesis, Aachen 1965.

36 Effmann, W., *Die Kirche der Abtei Corvey*, Ed. A. Fuchs, Paderborn 1929

37 Groszmann, D., *Die Abteikirche zu Hersfeld*, Kassel 1955.

38 Raumant, E., *The Cloister of Jumièges*, in: *British Archaeological Association*, 3rd series XX–XXI 1957-58.

39 Maris, H., *L'abbaye de Lérins*, 1909.

40 Cristiani, L., *Lérins et ses fondateurs*, Paris 1946.

41 Selzer, W., *Das karolingische Reichskloster Lorsch*, Kassel 1955.

42 Christ, H., *Die sechs Münster der Abtei Reichenau von der Gründung bis zum Ausgang des 12. Jahrhunderts*, Reichenau 1956.

43 Lot, F., *Hariulf, Chronique de l'abbaye de Saint-Riquier,* Paris 1894.

44 —, *Nouvelles recherches sur le texte de la chronique de l'abbaye de Saint Riquier par Hariulf,* in: *Bibliothèque de l'école de Chartres,* LXXII 1941

45 Hubert, J., *Saint Riquier et le monachisme bénédictin en Gaule à l'époque carolingienne,* in: *Settimane di Studio del Centro Italiano di studi sull'alto medioevo,* IV, Spoleto 1957.

46 Bernard, H., *Premières Fouilles à Saint-Riquier,* in: *Karl der Große* Bd. 3, ed. by W. Braunfels and H. Schnitzler, Düsseldorf 1965.

3   The plan of St Gallen

47 Keller, F., *Bauriß des Klosters St Gallen vom Jahre 820,* Zurich 1844.

48 Boeckelmann, W., *Die Wurzel der St Galler Plankirche,* in: *Zeitschrift für Kunstwissenschaft* Vol. VI, 1952.

49 Reinhardt, H., *Der Klosterplan von St Gallen,* St Gallen 1952.

50 Boeckelmann, W., *Der Widerspruch im St Galler Klosterplan,* in: *Zeitschrift für Schweizerische Archäologie und Kunstgeschichte,* Vol. XIX, 1956.

51 Schöne, W., *Das Verhältnis von Zeichnungen und Maßangaben im Kirchengrundriß des St Galler Klosterplans,* in: *Zeitschrift für Kunstwissenschaft,* Vol. XIV, 1960.

52 Weckwerth, A., *Die frühchristliche Basilika und der St Galler Klosterplan,* in: *Zeitschrift für Schweizerische Archäologie und Kunstgeschichte,* Vol. XXI, 1961.

53 Poeschel, E., *Kunstdenkmäler des Kantons St Gallen,* Vol. III, Basle 1961.

54 Duft, J., *Studien zum St Galler Klosterplan,* in: *Mitteilungen zur Vaterländischen Geschichte,* ed. by the Historischer Verein des Kantons St Gallen, St Gallen 1962 (with contributions by B. Bischoff, W. Horn, etc.).

55 Reinle, A., *Neue Gedanken zum St Galler Klosterplan,* in: *Zeitschrift für Schweizerische Archäologie und Kunstgeschichte,* Vol. XXIII, 1963/64.

56 Horn, W., *Das Modell eines karolingischen Idealklosters nach dem Plan von St Gallen,* in: *Ausstellungskatalog Karl der Große,* Aachen 1965.

57 —, *The 'Dimensional Inconsistencies' of the Plan of Saint Gall and the Problem of the Scale of the Plan,* in: *The Art Bulletin,* XLVIII, 1966, p. 285.

4   Cluny and the Cluniacs

a sources and general works

58 Duckett, G. F., *Visitations and Chapters General of the Order of Cluni, in respect of Alsace and Lorraine, etc. 1269-1529,* London 1893.

59 Valous, G. de, *Le Monachisme clunisien des origines au 15e siècle. Vie intérieure des monastères et l'organisation de l'ordre,* Paris 1935.

60 Lamma, P., *Momenti di storiografia cluniacense,* Rome 1961.

61 *Status, chapitres généraux et visites de l'Ordre de Cluny,* Paris 1965.

62 Virey, J., *Un ancien plan de l'Abbaye de Cluny,* Macon 1910.

63 Mettler, A., *Kloster Hirsau,* Augsburg 1928.

64 Greiner, K., *Kloster Hirsaus Geschichte durch 11 Jahrhunderte,* Calw 1929.

65 Smith, J. M., *Cluny in the XI-XII Centuries,* London 1930.

66 Schapiro, M., *The Romanesque Sculpture of Moissac,* in: *Art Bulletin* XIII 1931.

67 Stockhausen, H. von, *Romanische Kreuzgänge in der Provence,* in: *Marburger Jahrbuch für Kunstwissenschaft* 1933.

68 Evans, J., *The romanesque architecture of the order of Cluny,* Cambridge 1938.

69 Deshalieres, F., *Abbaye de Cluny,* in: *Bulletin Monumental,* Vol. CV, 1947.

70 *Travaux du Congrès à Cluny* 1949, Dijon 1950.

71 Evans, J., *Cluniac Art of the Romanesque Period,* Cambridge 1950.

72 Virey, J., *L'Abbaye de Cluny,* Paris 1950.

73 Linck, O., *Mönchtum und Klosterbauten Württembergs im Mittelalter,* Stuttgart 1953.

74 Rey, R., *L'art des cloîtres romans,* Paris 1955.

75 —, *Les cloîtres historiés du Midi dans l'art roman,* in: *Mémoires de la Société Archéologique du Midi de la France* 23, 1955.

76 Tellenbach, G. (ed.), *Neue Forschungen über Cluny und die Cluniazenser* (authors: Wollasch, Mager, Diener), Freiburg 1959.

b K. J. Conant

77 —, *Medieval Excavations at Cluny, the season of 1928,* in: *Speculum* 1929.

78 —, *The third Church at Cluny,* in: *Medieval Studies in Memory of Kingsley Porter* II, Cambridge 1937.

79 —, *A Cluny, congrès scientifique en l'honneur des Saintes Abbés Odon et Odilon,* Dijon 1950.

80 —, *Cluny I and Cluny II,* in: *Bulletin Monumental* 1951.

81 —, *Medieval Excavations at Cluny, Final Station of the Project,* in: *Speculum* 1954.

82 —, *New Results in the Study of Cluny Monastery,* in: *Journal of the Society of Architectural Historians,* October 1957

83 —, *Études nouvelles sur l'abbaye de Cluny,* in: *Bulletin de la société nationale des antiquités de France* 1957.

84 —, *Dernières découvertes à Cluny,* in: *Bulletin de la société nationale des antiquités de France* 1959.

85 —, *Systematic Dimensions in the Buildings of Cluny,* in: *Speculum* 1963.

86 —, *Cluny II and St Bénigne at Dijon,* in: *Archeologia* No. 99, 1965.

5   Cîteaux and the Cistercians

a sources and general works

87 Jogelinus, G., *Notitia abbatiarum ordinis Cisterciensis per orbem universum libros X complerea,* Cologne 1640.

88 —, *Gallia christiana in provincis ecclesiasticas distributa,* Paris 1715.

89 Martène et Durand, *Dialogus inter cluniacensem monachum et cisterciensem, Thesaurus novus anecdotum,* Paris 1717.

90 Jubainville-Guignard, *Les monuments primitifs de la règle cistercienne,* Dijon 1878.

91 Canivez, J. M., *Statuta capitulorum generalium Ordinis Cisterciensis ab anno 1116 ad annum 1786,* Louvain 1933.

92 Aubert, M., *L'architecture cistercienne en France,* Paris 1947.

93 Dimier, M. A., *Recueil de plans d'églises cisterciennes,* Paris 1949.

94 *Mélanges St Bernard, XXIV Congrès de l'Association Bourguignonne des Sociétés Savantes 1953,* Dijon 1954.

95 Paris, J., *Du premier esprit de l'ordre de Cîteaux,* Paris 1954.

96 Bouyer, L., *La spiritualité des Cisterciens,* Paris 1954.

97 Leclercq, J. and others, *S. Bernardi Opera,* 3 vols., Rome 1957-63.

98 Lekai, L. and Schneider, A., *Geschichte und Wirken der Weißen Mönche,* Kempten 1958.

99 Griesser, B., *Exordium magnum cisterciense,* Rome 1961.

100 Zakar, P., *Die Anfänge des Zisterzienserordens,* in: *Analecta Sacri Ordinis Cisterciensis* 10, 1964.

101 Meer, F. Van Der, *Atlas de l'Ordre Cistercien,* Haarlem 1965.

102 Rüttimann, H., *Der Bau- und Kunstbetrieb der Cistercienser unter dem Einfluß der Ordensgesetzgebung im 12. und 13. Jahrhundert,* Bregenz 1911.

103 Rose, H., *Die Baukunst der Zisterzienser,* Munich 1916.

104 Kingsley-Porter, A., *Romanesque Sculpture of the Pilgrimage Roads,* Boston 1923.

105 Aubert, M., *L'architecture cistercienne au XIIe et au XIIIe siècle,* in: *Revue de l'Art* 1937.

106 Mahn, J. B., *L'ordre cistercien et son gouvernement des origines au milieu du XIIIe siècle (1098-1265),* 1945/51.

107 Esser, K. H., *Über die Bedeutung der Zisterzienserkirchen,* in: *Arbeitsbericht, Klosterbaukunst* 1951.

108 Lefevre, J. A., *Le vrai récit primitif des origines de Cîteaux et l'Exordium Parvum? Le Moyen Age* 61, 1955.

109 Hahn, H., *Der frühe Kirchenbau der Zisterzienser, Untersuchungen zur Baugeschichte von Eberbach und ihren europäischen Analogien im 12. Jahrhundert,* Berlin 1957.

110 Winandy, J., *Les origines de Citeaux et les travaux de M. Lefevre,* in: *Revue Bénédictine* 57, 1957.

111 Dimier, M. A., *L'art cistercien,* 1962.

b according to countries

Belgium

112 Clemen, P., *Die Klosterbauten der Cisterzienser in Belgien,* Berlin 1916.

Germany

113 Sauer, J., *Der Cistercienser-Orden und die deutsche Kunst des Mittelalters,* Salzburg 1913.

114 Mettler, A., *Mittelalterliche Klosterkirchen und Klöster der Hirsauer und Zisterzienser in Württemberg*, Stuttgart 1927.

115 Krausen, E., *Die Klöster des Zisterzienserordens in Bayern*, in: *Bayerische Heimatforschung* No. 7, Munich 1953.

116 Eydoux, H. B., *Die Zisterzienserabtei Bebenhausen*, Tübingen 1950.

117 Dörrenberg, J., *Das Zisterzienserkloster Maulbronn*, Würzburg 1938.

118 Clasen, W., *Die Zisterzienserabtei Maulbronn im 12. Jahrhundert und der bernhardinische Klosterplan*, Kiel 1956.

England

119 Hope, J., *Fountains Abbey*, 1900.

120 Bilson, J., *The Architecture of the Cistercians in England*, in: *Archaeological Journal* 1901.

France

121 Chavanne, J. de, *Les débuts des abbayes cisterciennes dans les anciens pays bourguignonnes*, 1953.

122 Horn, W. and Born, E., *The Barns of the Abbey of Beaulieu and its Granges of Great Cuxwell and Beaulieu-St Leonards*, Berkeley and Los Angeles 1965.

123 Ranjard, M., *L'abbaye de Noirlac*, in: *Monuments historiques de la France* 1957.

124 Fontaine, C., *Pontigny, abbaye cistercienne*, 1928.

Italy

125 Serafini, A., *L'Abbazia di Fossanova e le origini dell' architettura gotica nel Lazio*, Rome 1924.

6   Architecture of the Carthusians

a general descriptions

126 Le Masson, *Annales ordinis Cartusiensis*, Part I, Correriae 1687, Meudon 1898.

127 *Maisons de l'ordre des Chartreux*, Montreuil sur Mer 1913.

128 Völckers, O., *Die Klosteranlage der Kartäuser in Deutschland*, in: *Zeitschrift für Bauwesen* 71, 1921.

129 Baumann, E., *Die Kartäuser*, Munster 1930.

130 Mühlberg, S. D., *Die Klosteranlage des Kartäuserordens*, unpublished thesis, Cologne 1949.

131 Meyer, A. de et Smet, J. M. de, *Guigo's 'Consuetudines' van de eerste kartuizers*, Brussels 1951.

b on individual monasteries

132 Le Febvre, I. A., *La Chartreuse de Notre-Dame-des-Prés*, Neuville sous Montreuil-sur-Mer, 1881.

133 Monget, C., *La Chartreuse de Dijon*, 3 vols., Montreuil-sur-Mer 1898.

134 Bauer, J., *Die chemalige freie Reichskartause Buxheim*, Munich 1936.

135 Bligny, B., *Recueil de plus anciens actes de la Grande-Chartreuse (1086-1196)*, Grenoble 1958.

136 Arens, F., *Bau und Ausstattung der Mainzer Kartause*, *Beiträge zur Geschichte der Stadt Mainz* 17, Mainz 1959.

7   Architecture of the mendicant orders

a general descriptions

137 Meyer, J., *Chronica brevis Ordinis Praedicatorum*, Vechta 1927.

138 Sessevalle, F. de, *Histoire générale de l'ordre de Saint Francois*, Paris 1935.

139 Bennett, R. F., *The early Dominicans. Studies in 13th-century Dominican history*, Cambridge 1937.

140 Walz, P. A. M., *Compendium historiae ordinis praedicatorum. Edito altera recognita et aucta*, Rome 1948.

141 Wagner, E., *Historia constitutionum generalium Ordinis Fratrum Minorum*, Rome 1954.

142 Grundmann, H., *Religiöse Bewegungen des Mittelalters*, Darmstadt 1961.

b according to countries

143 Krautheimer, R., *Die Kirchen der Bettelorden in Deutschland*, Cologne 1925.

144 Konow, H., *Die Baukunst der Bettelorden am Oberrhein*, thesis, Freiburg 1938.

145 Fait, I., *Die Bettelordenskirchen zwischen Elbe und Oder*, thesis, Greifswald 1953.

146 Thode, H., *Franz von Assisi und die Anfänge der Kunst der Renaissance in Italien*, 1885, Vienna 1934.

147 Kleinschmidt, B., *Die Basilika San Francesco in Assisi*, Berlin 1915-26.

148 Donin, R. K., *Die Bettelordenskirchen in Österreich*, Baden/Vienna 1935.

149 Frankl, P., review of Donin: *Die Bettelordenskirchen in Österreich*, in: *Kritische Berichte* No. 1, 1937.

150 Bürgler, F., *Die Franziskanerorden in der Schweiz*, 1926.

151 Oberst, J., *Die mittelalterliche Architektur der Dominikaner und Franziskaner in der Schweiz*, Zurich-Leipzig 1927.

8   English cathedral monasteries

152 Gilyard Beer, R., *Abbeys*, London 1958.

153 Knowles, David, *The Religious Orders in England*, 3 vols, London 1948, 1955, 1959.

9   Architectural history of monasteries individually mentioned in the text

El Escorial

154 Rotondo, *Historia descriptiva, artistica y pintoresca del monasterio del Lorenzo, communamente llamado el Escorial*, Madrid 1856-61.

155 Siguenza, F. J. de, *Fundacion del Monasterio de El Escorial*, new ed. Madrid (1963).

156 *Centenario de la Fundacion del Monasterio de San Lorenzo el Real el Escorial 1563-1963*, Vol. II.

Fleury à Saint-Bénoit-sur-Loire

157 Chenesseau, G., *L'abbaye de Fleury à Saint-Bénoit-sur-Loire. Son histoire, ses institutions, ses édifices*, Tours 1931.

Gross-Comburg

158 Gradmann, E., *Die Kunst und Altertumsdenkmale im Königreich Württemberg*, Inventar 1907.

159 Mettler, A., *Die ursprüngliche Bauanlage des Klosters Komburg*, in: *Württembergische Vierteljahrshefte für Landesgeschichte*, New Series 20, 1911.

160 Linck, O., *Vom mittelalterlichen Mönchtum und seinen Bauten in Württemberg*, Stuttgart 1953.

Mont-Saint-Michel

161 Corroyer, E., *Description de l'abbaye du Mont Saint Michel et de ses abords*, Paris 1877.

162 Gout, P., *Mont Saint Michel*, 2 vols., Paris 1910.

163 Besnard, Ch.-H., *Le Mont Saint Michel*, Paris 1912.

164 Mauclair, C., *Le Mont Saint Michel*, Grenoble 1931.

165 Bazin, G., *Le Mont Saint Michel*, 1938.

166 *Millénaire du Mont Saint Michel*, Catalogue de l'exposition, Paris 1966.

Monreale

167 Scheppard, C., *The iconography of the cloister of Monreale*, in: *The Art Bulletin* 31, 1949.

168 Salvini, R., *Il chiostro di Monreale*, Palermo 1962.

Oviedo

169 Selgas, F. de, *El origin de Oviedo*, in: *Boletin de la Sociedad Española de Excursiones* XVI (1908), p. 102-125.

170 Manzanares, R. J., *Fragmentos romanicos del monasterio de San Vicente de Oviedo*, Oviedo 1952.

171 Chueca, G. F., *Casas Reales en monasterios y conventos españoles*, Madrid 1966.

Poblet

172 Amador de Los Rios, R., *Burgos. Barcelona (Molina)* 1888. XXVI (España, sus monumentos y artes . . . 1884-91).

173 Torres Balbas, L., *Arte Almohade, arte nazari, arte mudejar*, Madrid 1949 (Ars Hispana).

Santa Maria Pomposa

174 Salmi, M., *L'Abbazia di Pomposa*, Rome 1950.

St Pantaleon

175 Beseler, H., *Fragen zum ottonischen Kreuzgang des Pantaleonklosters in Köln*, in: *Forschungen zur Kunstgeschichte und christlichen Archäologie*, Vol. III, Wiesbaden 1957.

Tournus

176 Gaudillière, A., in: *Bourgogne Romane*, Paris 1955, pp. 27-66.

10   Princely abbeys of the Baroque

a general

177 Hartig, M., *Bayerns Klöster und ihre Kunstschätze*, Vol. I, Munich 1913.

178 Herrmann, W., *Der hochbarocke Klostertypus*, thesis, Leipzig 1928.

179   Lemperle, H., *Oberschwäbische Kloster-anlagen der Barockzeit und ihre Beziehung zur Landschaft*, thesis, Frankfurt 1936.

180   Kräusel, I., *Die deutschen Klosteranlagen des 17. Jh.*, thesis, Frankfurt 1953.

181   Kohlbach, R., *Die Stifte Steiermarks*, Graz 1953.

182   Bourke, J., *Baroque Churches of Central Europe*, London 1958.

183   Powell, N., *From Baroque to Rococo*, London 1959.

184   *Barock in Oberschwaben*, Katalog der Ausstellung, Weingarten 1963.

185   Evans, J., *Monastic Architecture in France from the Renaissance to the Revolution*, Cambridge 1964.

186   Burrough, T. H. B., *South German Baroque*, London 1965.

187   Hempel, E., *Baroque Art and Architecture in Central Europe*, Harmondsworth 1965.

188   Röhrig, F., *Alte Stifte in Österreich*, Vol. I, Vienna-Munich 1966.

189   Hitchcock, H. R., *Rococo Architecture in Southern Germany*, London 1968.

b on individual monasteries

Einsiedeln
190   Kuhn, A., *Der jetzige Stiftsbau Maria-Einsiedeln*, Einsiedeln 1913.

191   Birchler, L., *Einsiedeln und sein Architekt Br. C. Moosbrugger*, Au 1924.

192   —, *Die Kunstdenkmäler der Schweiz*, Vol. I.

Kempten
193   Rottenkolber, J., *Geschichte des hochfürstlichen Stiftes Kempten*, Munich 1933.

194   Roediger, M., *Die Stiftskirche St Lorenz in Kempten*, Burg bei Magdeburg 1938.

195   Schnell, H., *Die fürstäbtliche Residenz in Kempten*, Munich 1947.

196   Petzet, M., *Stadt und Landkreis Kempten*, Munich 1959.

Klosterneuburg
197   Scicola, G., *Jacob Prandtauer, Entwurf für das Kloster Klosterneuburg*, in: *Jahrbuch des Stiftes Klosterneuburg*, Nf Vol I.

198   Röhrig, F., *Stift Klosterneuburg, Augustiner-Chorberrenstift*, Munich/Zurich 1958.

Melk
199   Kummer, E., *Stift Melk und seine Geschichte*, in: *Katalog der Barockausstellung 'J. Prandtauer und sein Kreis'*, Vienna 1960.

Ochsenhausen
200   Schefold, M., *Reichsabtei Ochsenhausen*, Augsburg 1927.

201   Schnell, H., *Reichsabtei Ochsenhausen*, Kleiner Kunstführer 304/305, Munich 1950.

Ottobeuren
202   Lieb, N., *Ottobeuren und die Barockarchitektur Ostschwabens*, thesis, Munich 1931.

203   Schnell, H., *Ottobeuren, Kloster und Kirche*, Munich 1936.

204   Lieb, N., *Abt Rupert Ness von Ottobeuren*, in: *Lebensbilder aus dem bayerischen Schwaben*, ed. by Freiherr von Pölnitz, vol. I Munich 1952.

205   —, *Benediktinerabtei Ottobeuren*, Munich 1954.

206   Kolb, Ä. and Tüchle, H. (Eds.), *Ottobeuren, Festschrift zur 1200 Jahrfeier*, Augsburg 1964.

207   —, *Benediktinerabtei Ottobeuren*, Ottobeuren 1966.

St Blasien
208   Schmieder, L., *Das Benediktinerkloster St Blasien*, Augsburg 1929.

St Florian
209   Hollnsteiner, J., *Das Chorherrenstift St Florian*, Augsburg-Cologne-Vienna 1928.

210   Kirchner-Doberer, E., *Stift St Florian*, Vienna 1948.

Tegernsee
211   Hartig, M., *Die Benediktinerabtei Tegernsee*.

Vorau
212   Meeraus, R., *Das Chorherrenstift Vorau*, Vienna-Augsburg-Cologne 1928.

213   Fank, P., *Das Chorherrenstift Vorau*, Vorau 1959.

Weingarten
214   Herrmann, W., *Zur Bau- und Künstlergeschichte von Kloster Weingarten*, in: *Münchner Jahrbuch der Bildenden Kunst* NF 3 1926.

215   Drissen, J. H., *Die Barockarchitektur der Abtei Weingarten*, thesis, Frankfurt 1928.

216   Schnell, H., *Weingarten*, Großer Kunstführer 5, Munich 1950.

217   Raichle, A., and Schneider, P., *Weingarten*, Munich 1953.

218   *Weingarten, Festschrift zur 900 Jahrfeier des Klosters 1056-1956*, Weingarten 1956.

Wessobrunn
219   Hager, G., *Die Bautätigkeit im Kloster Wessobrunn und die Wessobrunner Stukkatoren*, in: *Oberbayerisches Archiv für vaterländische Geschichte* vol. XLVIII, 1891.

Wiblingen
220   Feulner, A., *Kloster Wiblingen*, Augsburg 1925.

221   Schwenger, H., *Abtei Wiblingen*, Munich 1930.

Zwiefalten
222   Fiechter, E., *Zwiefalten*, Augsburg 1927

11   Secularization and fresh beginnings

a general descriptions

223   Wolf, A., *Aufhebung der Klöster in Innerösterreich 1782-90*, 1871.

224   Erzberger, M., *Die Säkularisation in Württemberg*, 1902.

225   Scheglmann, A. M., *Geschichte der Säkularisation im rechtsrheinischen Bayern*, 3 Vols., Regensburg 1903-08.

226   Lesne, E., *Histoire de la propriété ecclésiastique en France*, Lille 1910.

227   Buholzer, J., *Die Säkularisation katholischer Kirchengüter während des 18. und 19. Jh.*, Lucerne 1921.

228   Kastner, K., *Die große Säkularisation in Deutschland*, 1926.

229   Hughes, P., *The Reformation in England*, 3 Vols., London 1951-54.

b on individual monasteries

La Tourette
230   Henze, A., *La Tourette, Le Corbusier's erster Klosterbau*, Starnberg 1963.

Orval
231   Tilliere, N., *Histoire de l'abbaye d'Orval*, Gembloux 1897, Hauptwerk; gek. 1927.

Rheinau
232   Erb, A., *Das Kloster Rheinau und die helvetische Revolution*, Zurich 1895.

233   Boesch, G., *Vom Untergang der Abtei Rheinau*, Zurich 1956.

St Boniface in Munich
234   Stubenvoll, B., OSB, *Die Basilika und das Benediktinerstift St Bonifaz in München*, Festschrift zum 25jährigen Jubiläum, Munich 1957.

List of Illustrations

Index